Communities, Livelihoods and Natural Resources

Communities, Livelihoods and Natural Resources

Action Research and Policy Change in Asia

Edited by
Stephen R. Tyler

**Practical
ACTION
PUBLISHING**

International Development Research Centre
Ottawa • Cairo • Dakar • Montevideo • Nairobi • New Delhi • Singapore

Practical Action Publishing Ltd
25 Albert Street, Rugby, CV21 2SD, Warwickshire, UK
www.practicalactionpublishing.com

and the International Development Research Centre
P.O. Box 8500, Ottawa, ON, Canada K1G 3H9
www.idrc.ca/info@idrc.ca

© Intermediate Technology Publications 2006

First published 2006

ISBN 10: 1 85339 638 9
ISBN 13 Paperback: 9781853396380
ISBN Library Ebook: 9781780440101
Book DOI: https://doi.org/10.3362/9781780440101

Since 1974, Practical Action Publishing has published and disseminated books and information in
support of international development work throughout the world. Practical Action Publishing is a
trading name of Practical Action Publishing Ltd (Company Reg. No. 01159018), the wholly owned
publishing company of Practical Action. Practical Action Publishing trades only in support of its
parent charity objectives and any profits are covenanted back to Practical Action (Charity Reg. No.
247257, Group VAT Registration No. 880 9924 76).

Reasonable efforts have been made to publish reliable data and information, but the author and
publisher cannot assume responsibility for the validity of all materials or for the consequences of
their use.

Cover photograph by kind permission of
Renewable Natural Resources Research Centre, Bajo, Bhutan
Index preparation: Indexing Specialists (UK) Ltd
Typeset in Trade Gothic and Stone Serif
by S.J.I. Services

The manufacturer's authorised representative in the EU for product safety is
Lightning Source France, 1 Av. Johannes Gutenberg, 78310 Maurepas, France.
compliance@lightningsource.fr

Contents

Part II: Community-based natural resource management in action

Part III: From local action to policy impact

Foreword

Despite what you see on MTV, there is more to Asia than shopping malls, cell phones and Kentucky Fried Chicken. If you are willing to scratch the surface and follow dirt roads into the hills and forests, it is quickly apparent that many people still cannot enjoy the region's famous prosperity.

These are women who wake up in the morning to fetch water and fuelwood; children who help their parents in the fields and forests; grandparents who wait for their relatives to send money from town. These are people who fish and farm, hunt and harvest, sell a bit, sew a bit, get sick too often and talk to make the day go by. You can list all their belongings on a single page. Often the only real productive assets they have are their knowledge, creativity and willingness to work, a small parcel of borrowed or rented land, and access to places where they can fish and collect wild products – and even much of that is being lost, exhausted or eroded.

No high-yielding crop variety, mosquito net or new well is going to solve all these people's problems. The situations in the various remote and inhospitable places they live in are so diverse that no shoe fits all. The families typically need to do small amounts of many different things to get by; so just improving one of them usually won't help them that much. Although some people may be able to earn more money by moving to town or growing vegetables, for many others those are not real options.

A more promising approach is to provide these people with skills and information, and help them get organized. That can build their self-confidence and give them tools to solve their various problems. Much of this needs to centre on their natural resources, since that is one of the few things they have. Government agencies and NGOs also have to change their policies and the way they do business to support villagers' efforts, instead of making life harder for them. That is particularly true when it comes to policies and practices that affect peoples' access to land, forests, grasslands and fish.

Research can play a very important role in making those things happen, but it cannot be just any old research. It has to be research that is deliberately designed to help local people, government officials, NGOs and other groups think through issues, reflect on their own experiences, support positions that favour poorer and less powerful people, and provide relevant information about markets and technologies. The researchers themselves must be committed to achieving real change and seeing things through. They must also be savvy enough to understand all the different interests that exist in local communities and avoid being hijacked by the agendas of the rich and the powerful. Otherwise, their work may end up leaving out women, tribal peoples and others that usually get forgotten.

For some time now Canada's International Development Research Centre (IDRC) has been working to support precisely that type of research. This book was designed to share some of the more interesting lessons coming out of their research projects on community-based natural resource management in Asia. In particular, it focuses on 11 research projects carried out by national researchers from Bhutan, Cambodia, China, Laos, Mongolia, the Philippines and Vietnam between 1997 and 2004, and shares some of the more general insights coming from all that work.

The stories here are just that: real stories about real lives. By reading them you can get a sense of what the researchers did and why, how they interacted with the different groups, what worked, what didn't and what they took away from it all. You will also get a sense of how the researchers tried to spread the messages about one group's successes and failures to other groups, so that the work could have a larger impact.

There is a lot of wisdom in these pages, as well as common sense. You will find some answers, but no road maps or magic bullets. Each new country or new group of researchers will have to work through their specific situation and find measures that fit for them. This book can inform and inspire the process for doing exactly that. It certainly inspired me.

David Kaimowitz
Director General
Center for International Forestry Research

Acknowledgements

Any editorial effort of this magnitude necessarily involves a lot of support. But this volume is noteworthy for the number of people involved. My task would have been inconceivable without the efforts they contributed. First among these are the men and women, farmers and fishers from all across Asia, whose stories of creativity and persistence are represented here. These are the people who took the biggest risks, were the most generous in sharing their time and wisdom and usually provided the most insightful criticism of the research we report. They may never read these stories, but they have already incorporated their most important lessons. Our shared debt to these people is reiterated by many of the authors in this volume, but I would like to emphasize it at the outset.

The research teams whose work is reported by the case study authors also deserve my heartfelt appreciation. They laboured long and hard with new ideas and challenging methods, struggling to translate these between languages and between very different cultures. Their commitment to learning and to action, in spite of adversities that would have overcome most researchers in developed countries, has earned my deepest admiration and respect.

The authors charged with reporting the teams' work faced the burden of writing in an unfamiliar language, on top of their many other responsibilities. For their patience and persistence in a task made more difficult by long rounds of editorial comments, questions and revisions, I am very grateful.

Special thanks are due to Silke Reichrath, whose organizational skills, attention to detail and sharp editing made a huge difference in tracking and revising early versions of the case manuscripts. I would have been lost (as would much of the text) without her.

This book owes a huge debt to my programme colleagues at IDRC. The research framework and programme cases reported here took shape through their commitment, enthusiasm, criticism and practical field experience. I only hope that I have done justice to the integrity of their vision in assembling the resulting manuscript. My warmest appreciation to John Graham, Ronnie Vernooy, Liz Fajber, Brian Davy, Guy Bessette, Hein Mallee and Wendy Manchur. Thanks also to Stephen McGurk for his encouragement and support. May each of you recognize in these pages a testament to your professionalism and collaboration.

Eric and Katherine Fletcher provided excellent editorial support, giving a consistent format and style to all the myriad details of manuscripts from two dozen different authors.

I also wish to express my appreciation to my wife Barbara, whose tolerance and encouragement enabled me to devote extra time to this project when I was not able to squeeze everything into the confines of a regular working day.

List of figures

List of tables

List of boxes

Acronyms and abbreviations

Acronym	Definition
ADMP	Ancestral Domain Management Plan (Philippines)
ADSDPP	Ancestral Domain Sustainable Development and Protection Plan (Philippines)
AFSC	American Friends Service Committee (Quakers)
CADC	Certificate of Ancestral Domain Claim (Philippines)
CARD	Centre for Agricultural Research and Development (Bhutan)
CARERE	Cambodian Area Regeneration and Rehabilitation project
CBCRM	Community-Based Coastal Resource Management
CBFM	Community-Based Forest Management
CBFMP	Community-Based Forest Management Programme
CBNRM	Community-Based Natural Resource Management
CCs	Commune Councils
CF	Community Forestry
CFRP	Community Forestry Research Project (Cambodia)
CFUG	Community Forest User Group (Bhutan)
CFUGC	CFUG Committee (Bhutan)
CHARMP	Cordillera Highland Agricultural Resources Management Program (Philippines)
CIDA	Canadian International Development Agency
CIDSE	Coopération Internationale pour le Développement et la Solidarité
CIFOR	Centre for International Forestry Research
CONCORED	Consortium of Cordillera Organizations for Resource Equitability and Development (Philippines)
CoRRB	Council of RNR Research of Bhutan
CPRs	Common-pool Resource/s
CRF	Community Revolving Funds
CSC	Cordillera Studies Center (Philippines)
DA	Department of Agriculture (Philippines)
DAFO	District Agriculture and Forestry Office (Laos)
DANIDA	Danish International Development Agency
DAO	Department Administrative Order (Philippines)
DAR	Department of Agrarian Reform (Philippines)

DARD	Department of Agriculture and Rural Development (Vietnam)
DENR	Department of Environment and Natural Resources (Philippines)
DFID	Department for International Development (United Kingdom)
DFW	Department of Forestry and Wildlife (Cambodia)
DoF	Provincial Department of Fisheries (Vietnam)
DoF	Department of Forestry (Bhutan)
DRDS	Department of Research and Development Services (Bhutan)
FA	Forestry Administration
FAO	UN Food and Agriculture Organization
GAAS	Guizhou Academy of Agricultural Sciences
GDI	Gender-related Development Index
GFJCR	Government Fisher Joint Committee on Research (Vietnam)
GIS	Geographical Information System
GPS	Global Positioning System
HDI	Human Development Index
HYV	High-Yielding Varieties
IDRC	International Development Research Centre of Canada
IFAD	International Fund for Agricultural Development
IFDMP	Indigenous Fisheries Development and Management Project (Laos)
IIRR	International Institute of Rural Reconstruction (Philippines)
IPM	Integrated Pest Management (Bhutan)
IPRA	Indigenous Peoples Rights Act (Philippines)
IRRI	International Rice Research Institute (Bhutan)
ISLP	Integrated Sustainable Livelihoods Program (Cambodia)
IUCN	Originally the International Union for the Conservation of Nature, now known as the World Conservation Union, but recognized universally by its acronym
KAFDOC	Khmer Association for Development of Countryside (Cambodia)
LeaRN	Learning and Research Network for CBNRM (Cambodia)
LFAP	Land and Forest Allocation Programme (Laos)
MAFF	Ministry of Agriculture, Forestry. and Fisheries (Cambodia)
MDGs	Millennium Development Goals
MNE	Ministry of Nature and the Environment [Mongolia]
MoA	Ministry of Agriculture (Bhutan)
MoE	Ministry of Environment (Cambodia)
NCIP	National Commission on Indigenous Peoples (Philippines)
NFE	Non-Formal Education
NGO	Non-Governmental Organization
NIA	National Irrigation Administration (Philippines)
NRM	Natural Resource Management
NRMCs	Natural Resource Management Committees

NRMP 2	Ancestral Domain and Natural Resource Management in Sagada, Mountain Province, Northern Philippines
NRMR	Natural Resource Management Research
NTFP	Non-Timber Forest Product
PAR	Participatory Action Research
PCI	Principles, Criteria and Indicators
PDC	Participatory Development Communication
PDR	Peoples' Democratic Republic (Laos)
PKWS	Peam Krasaop Wildlife Sanctuary
PLA	Participatory Learning And Action
PLFO	Provincial Livestock and Fisheries Office (Laos)
PLG	Partnerships for Local Government
PLUP	Participatory Land Use Planning
PM&E	Participatory Monitoring and Evaluation
PMMR	Participatory Management of Mangrove Resources
PNP	Philippine National Police
PRA	Participatory Rural Appraisal
PRDC	Provincial Rural Development Committee (Cambodia)
PRSPs	Poverty Reduction Strategy Plans
RECOFTC	The Regional Community Forestry Training Center for Asia & the Pacific
RNR	Renewable Natural Resources
RNRRC	Renewable Natural Resource Research Centre (Bhutan)
RUA	Royal University of Agriculture (Cambodia)
RUP	Resource Utilization Permit
SDC	Swiss Agency for Development Cooperation
SIDA	Swedish International Development Agency
SUMCNR	Sustainable Management of Common Natural Resources
SWIM	Small-scale Wetland Indigenous Fisheries Management Project (Laos)
SWOT	Strength, Weakness, Opportunity and Threat analysis
UNDP	United Nations Development Programme
UNTAC	United Nations Transitional Authority in Cambodia
VEEM	Vietnam Economic and Environmental Management programme
VISED	Vietnam Institutional Strengthening and Economic Development project
VMC	Village Management Committee
VND	Vietnamese dong (national ‘currency; 1,000 VND = US $0.0628733, as of 13 January 2006)
WUA	Water-User Association (Bhutan)

Biographies of authors

Chapter 3

Ashish Joshia Ingty John is the research coordinator of the Natural Resource Management Research Project in Ratanakiri, Cambodia, which focuses on Community Based Natural Resource Management for indigenous people. The project is part of the decentralized governance programme of the Royal Government of Cambodia. It deals with farmer-based experimentation, participatory land use planning (PLUP), community forestry, community-based eco-tourism, indigenous land rights, communal land titling, conflict resolution, and the planning and management of rural development – all the different aspects of CBNRM. Ashish's mother is a Mikir/Karbi from northeast India and he has a Master's in Veterinary Surgery. Email: carat@camintel.com or ashishingty@yahoo.com

Chea Phalla is the CBNRM research adviser to the project mentioned above. He is a Cambodian and has a lot of experience working with indigenous people, assisting them to map their traditional land use and advocate for their rights. Phalla has a degree in Statistics and Economics from the College of Statistics and Planning, Phnom Penh. He also has a diploma in rural leadership from the Asian Rural Institute in Japan. Email: carererat@camintel.com

Chapter 4

Truong Van Tuyen's background is in rural development. He got his Master's degree from Khon Kaen University, Thailand, and his PhD from the University of the Philippines at Los Baños. He has been a faculty member of Hue University of Agriculture and Forestry since 1986. Dr Tuyen has engaged in participatory research on community-based coastal resource management since 1995. He has also been involved in other social science and rural development research, including research on farming systems and development, on-farm conservation of agro-biodiversity, and integrated assessments of trade and agricultural policies. Email: tvtuyen@dng.vnn.vn

Chapter 5

Le Van An has been the head of the Department of Sciences and International Relations at Hue University of Agriculture and Forestry since 2000. He completed a BSc in Animal Production at the Agricultural University No. 2 in Ha Bac, Vietnam in 1983, an MSc in Livestock Production Systems (1999) and a PhD in Animal Sciences (2004) at the Swedish University of Agricultural Sciences in Uppsala, Sweden. He has been lecturing on animal production and rural development methodologies at Hue University of Agriculture and Forestry since 1983. He has also been working with the Rural Development Programme in Vietnam since 1993. Since 1995, he has been the research team leader for a research project on CBNRM at Hue University of Agriculture and Forestry, which has been funded by IDRC and the Ford Foundation. He is also involved in research and development activities related to natural resources management, the environment and the livelihoods of the upland poor in Vietnam. Email: Levanan-huaf@dng.vnn.vn

Chapter 6

Hijaba Ykhanbai graduated from the Forest Engineering Academy in the former Soviet Union in 1978, and obtained a PhD from the Academy in 1992. He attended courses at Harvard University on Environmental Economics and Policy Analysis, and Macroeconomic Policy and Management. Dr Ykhanbai has spent about 18 years in the Ministry for Nature and the Environment (MNE), serving as a specialist, vice-director, director and policy adviser to the minister. Currently he is the project leader of the Sustainable Management of Common Natural Resources in Mongolia project and the director of the Forest Policy and Coordination Department. Email: ykhanbai@magicnet.mn

Enkhbat Bulgan has a background in language studies. She holds a Master's degree in linguistics from the University of Humanities in Mongolia. She has been working as the secretary and research assistant for the MNE-IDRC research project on Sustainable Management of Common Natural Resources in Mongolia since 2001. Her research interests include community-based pasture and natural resource management, participatory research, and social and gender research in natural resource management. Email: bugi_n@yahoo.com

Chapter 7

Nattaya Tubtim is based in Chiang Mai, Thailand as Regional Research Programme Officer for the Australian Mekong Resource Centre, Sydney University. She is also Coordinator of the Mekong Learning Initiative, a collaborative learning project involving nine Mekong universities, which links community-based natural resource management to wider regional issues. Since completing her Bachelor's degree in Social Sciences for Development at Silpakorn

University in 1989, she has been engaged in applied research in Thailand and Laos, mainly in the field of community-based natural resource management. In 2001, she completed her Master's in Sustainable Development at Chiang Mai University. She has wide experience of community-level processes throughout the Mekong Region. Email: tubtim@loxinfo.co.th

Chapter 8

Kim Nong is the deputy director of the Environmental Education Department in Cambodia's Ministry of the Environment. He is the team leader of the Participatory Management of Coastal Resources project, a project that began in 1997 and emphasizes local decision-making processes for resource management. His research interests include CBNRM, co-management and decentralization. Email: pmmr@online.com.kh

Melissa Marschke recently completed her PhD at the Natural Resources Institute, University of Manitoba. She has worked as a consultant in Southeast Asia since 1999, collaborating with several project teams on issues surrounding community-based management (with an emphasis on writing and analysis). Her research interests include livelihoods, resilience and decision-making. Email: mjmarschkeca@yahoo.com

Chapter 9

Yuan Juanwen is a senior researcher at the Integrated Rural Development Centre, Guizhou Academy of Agricultural Sciences. She is the coordinator for Guizhou of the Women's Capacity Building and Rural Development in China project, which is implemented by the Winrock International Institute for Agricultural Development. She received her Master's degree in Forestry at the University of the Philippines at Los Baños in January 2002. Now she is involved in several projects related to rural development in China. Her interests are community-based natural resource management, gender, and participatory rural development. Email: juanwenyuan@hotmail.com

Sun Qiu has a Master's in Social Development from Ateneo de Manila University in the Philippines. She is doing her PhD in rural development sociology at Wageningen University in the Netherlands. She is a senior researcher and the director of the Integrated Rural Development Centre at the Guizhou Academy of Agricultural Sciences. She was a core team member of the IDRC-funded Community-based Natural Resource Management in Mountainous Areas of Guizhou Province (1995–2001) project, and she is the project leader of the IDRC and Ford Foundation joint funded Promotion of Sustainable Rural Development by Scaling up CBNRM in Guizhou Province, China project. Sun Qiu has extensive experience in community-based natural resource management and in rural development research. Email: qiu_sun@yahoo.com

Chapter 10

Sangay Duba has been the programme director for the RNR Research Centre at Bajo since 2000. He completed a BSc in Agriculture (1988) and an MSc in Agronomy (1994) at the University of the Philippines in Los Baños (UPLB). He started at the RNR Research Centre, then called the Centre for Agricultural Research, in 1989 as assistant research officer, working on mid-altitude rice-based farming systems research. He was actively involved in regional surveys and field studies and acted as a resource person for various agricultural training programmes. He was promoted to be research officer in 1996 as farming systems agronomist. He is the project manager for the Enhancing Productivity Through Integrated Natural Resources Management (EPINARM) Project, which is a four-year project funded by the Swiss Agency for Development and Cooperation (SDC) and IDRC. He was one of the task force members who developed the 2002 CBNRM Framework for Bhutan. Email: sduba@druknet.bt

Mahesh Ghimiray is currently a programme officer for field crops at RNRRC Bajo. He holds a BSc in Agriculture from GB Pant University, Uttar Pradesh, India, and an MPhil in Plant Biodiversity from the University of Reading and Birmingham University, U.K. In 1985, he was appointed as assistant research officer in the then Department of Agriculture and posted at the Agri Research Station, Bhur, Gelephu, as officer-in-charge. In 1990, he transferred to the Centre for Agricultural Research and Development (CARD), now RNRRC Bajo, as national rice coordinator. He was promoted to research officer and then senior research officer and has acted as a resource person/trainer in various agricultural training programmes. He has planned, coordinated and conducted research on rice and other field crops, as well as being involved in the management of the EPINARM Project. Email: mghimire@druknet.bt

Chapter 11

Sy Ramony is the project team leader of the Community Forestry Research Project, funded by IDRC. In addition, Ramony is deputy chief of the Community Protected Area Development Office at the Department of Nature Conservation and Protection at the Ministry of the Environment of Cambodia. He received an Engineering degree in Agronomy from the Royal University of Agriculture, Phnom Penh, Cambodia, in 1992 and an MSc in Natural Resource Management from the Asian Institute of Technology, Bangkok, Thailand, in 1999. Email: Ramony@online.com.kh

Phan Kamnap is the deputy project leader for the Community Forestry Research Project (CFRP) and Deputy Director of the Forestry and Wildlife Training Centre of the Forestry Administration. Kamnap received a Bachelor's degree in Forestry Science from the Royal University of Agriculture in Phnom Penh and a Master's degree in Natural Resources Management from the Asian

Institute of Technology in Thailand. Kamnap has been working with the Community Forestry Research Project, Non-Timber Forest Project (NTFP) and Asian Development Bank's Sustainable Forest Management Project since 1996. Moreover, he works closely with the Forestry Administration, Ministry of the Environment, NGOs, international organizations and local communities. He has been involved with the community forestry network in Cambodia since 1999. Email: phankamnap@online.com.kh or phankamnap@hotmail.com

Chapter 12

The IDRC-funded project on Ancestral Domain and Natural Resource Management in Sagada, Mountain Province, Northern Luzon (1998–2002) was headed by Lorelei C. Mendoza (Economics). This research project was undertaken through the Cordillera Studies Centre, the research arm of the University of the Philippines Baguio. The social science team of the project included three research fellows and three project leaders for the community studies. The research fellows were June Prill-Brett (Anthropology) for ancestral domain, Bienvenido P. Tapang (Economics) for institutional analysis and Arellano A. Colongon, Jr (Political Science) for policy issues. The project leaders for the community studies were Gladys A. Cruz (Economics) for Demang, Victoria Lourdes C. Diaz (Anthropology) and Ma. Cecilia R. San Luis (Sociology) for Fidelisan. The team was ably assisted by Alicia G. Follosco (university researcher). Email: lcmendoza@upb.edu.ph

Chapter 13

Peter O'Hara, an Irish national, has an undergraduate degree in forestry and a graduate degree in development studies. He is currently undertaking a CBNRM-related PhD at the University of East Anglia, UK. At the International Institute of Rural Reconstruction, he coordinates the community forestry research activities. He also facilitates international professional training courses, including a course on Participatory Action Research for CBNRM. Before joining IIRR in 2001, his work experience included positions as a participatory extension adviser on a community forestry project in Gambia, a co-editor of the *Forest, Trees, and People* Newsletter, and a lecturer in extension at the Swedish University of Agricultural Sciences. His professional interests include action learning and transformative communication processes. Email: Peter.Ohara@iirr.org

Chapter 14

Julian Gonsalves has 30 years of experience in international rural and agricultural development and natural resources management. Currently he is a senior adviser to CIP-UPWARD (the International Potato Center's Users Perspectives With Agricultural Research and Development programme) in Los Baños, Philippines, and a short-term consultant. Prior to this he had senior level responsibility for programme development and management at the International Institute of Rural Reconstruction (IIRR), eight years as the director of the Appropriate Technology Unit (ATU) and seven years as the Vice-President-Program. At IIRR he proposed, field-tested and developed the participatory workshop process for documenting best practices and initiated a sustainable agriculture programme with a smallholder focus. He has a PhD in Extension Education and International Agricultural and Rural Development from Cornell University and a Master's degree in Communication (knowledge utilization) from Michigan State University. Email: juliangonsalves@yahoo.com

Lorelei C. Mendoza has been a member of the faculty of the University of the Philippines (UP) Baguio since 1976, when she graduated with a Bachelor of Arts in Social Sciences from UP Baguio. She obtained a Masters of Arts in Economics from the UP School of Economics in 1981 and a Doctorate in Economics from the Catholic University of Leuven in Belgium in 1997. She has conducted research on the livelihoods of farming households in the Cordillera communities, gender and household economics, local governance and local resource management practices. She led the IDRC-funded project on Ancestral Domain and Natural Resource Management in Sagada, Mountain province, Northern Philippines (1998–2002). She served as director of the Cordillera Studies Centre, UP Baguio, in 1990–91 and in 1998–2003. She is currently the dean of the College of Social Sciences, UP Baguio. Email: lcmendoza@upb.edu.ph

Chapter 15

Tony Beck has worked on livelihoods and resilience in India and Bangladesh for a long time – too long some would say! In the last little while he has also worked on results-based management with the UN Secretariat, on poverty and gender equality with a number of agencies, on recovery from major natural disasters and on the evaluation of humanitarian action. Email: tonybeck@shaw.ca

Liz Fajber is a senior program officer at the International Development Research Centre (IDRC) South Asia Regional Office (SARO) in New Delhi. She is active in programming primarily relating to rural development and natural resource management. Her interests focus on social/gender equity; access and tenure issues; local/indigenous knowledge and technologies; multistakeholder approaches; and enhancing community participation in, and benefits from, applied research activities. She has a Master's in Anthropology from McGill University. Email: efajber@idrc.org.in

Chapter 16

Peter Vandergeest is the Director of the York Centre for Asian Research and Associate Professor of Sociology at York University in Toronto. He received his PhD from Cornell University in 1990, and has been researching and writing on socio-ecological transformations in Southeast Asia for the past 20 years. Email: pvander@yorku.ca

Chapter 17

Stephen R. Tyler worked with IDRC's East and Southeast Asia regional office from 1991 to 2005, establishing new interdisciplinary programmes for the region in urban environment, environmental policy, biodiversity and natural resources management. He holds a BSc in physical geography and biology from Trent University, and a PhD in city and regional planning from the University of California, Berkeley. He has undertaken consulting assignments for the World Bank, the Asian Development Bank and other international organizations, and has published on energy policy and urbanization issues as well as natural resource management. He is president of Adaptive Resource Management Ltd in Victoria, BC and works on resource governance and adaptive management in Canada and Asia. Email: adaptive@telus.ca

Hein Mallee's interest and previous work experience in China led him to a PhD at Leyden University, which focused on circulatory rural–urban labour migration as a rural livelihood strategy in China. He subsequently led a large, Dutch-funded rural poverty alleviation project in Anhui province, and then became a programme officer for the Ford Foundation in Beijing, where he was particularly interested in exploring linkages between micro-level fieldwork and wider processes of institutional change and policy formulation. He joined IDRC in January 2004 as a senior programme specialist with the CBNRM programme and is now working with the Rural Poverty and Environment programme. He is based in IDRC's Singapore office. Email: hmallee@idrc.org.sg

Part I
Introduction

CHAPTER 1

Introduction: poverty and environment in practice

Stephen R. Tyler

Global agendas and local change

At the beginning of the 21st century, it is evident that that the destinies of our planet's diverse peoples are closely intertwined. This realization has driven an unprecedented set of international commitments during the past decade. Nations of all political hues have committed to reforms on a broad range of global issues: trade policy, biodiversity conservation, land mines, greenhouse gas emissions, peacekeeping, security and others. However, if these issues are increasingly recognized, defined and framed as being global, the actions to address and implement them mostly fall to local decisions made by governments, individuals, businesses and other organizations. It is precisely when it comes to local action that so many well-intended global efforts fail. This volume offers examples of how to build successful local innovation and action on difficult global issues of poverty and environment.

The actions described in this book respond specifically to the question of how poor rural people can improve their living conditions and the productivity of their resource base through local interventions in natural resource management. As a compendium of research and learning results, the book describes and analyses processes and outcomes from a set of action research projects in Asia. The research cases reported here have all grappled with the difficult issues of how to implement practical and effective development in marginalized, rural areas of poor countries. They were designed to respond directly to the global issues of poverty reduction, environmental and resource degradation, and governance reform.

Because they define quantitative targets across a limited set of indicators, the UN's Millennium Development Goals (MDGs) focus attention and effort on global poverty reduction outcomes. National Poverty Reduction Strategy Plans (PRSPs), which are required by international financial institutions as prerequisites for concessionary loans, are also aimed at poverty outcomes and used by bilateral donors to guide aid priorities. But these large-scale targets and national policy commitments have little to say about what needs to happen at the level of the village – or between village and state levels – in order to reduce poverty. Nor do they offer advice in practice about how to create and gain from opportunities to increase income, spread benefits, reduce risk and secure rights for the poorest of the poor.

Environmental and resource degradation has been widely recognized as a crucial constraint to reducing poverty among the most disadvantaged and marginalized populations in the world, who remain largely rural (UN Millennium Project, 2005). International commitments to rural development and to addressing environmental and resource degradation increasingly identify the need for innovative approaches. Such approaches must focus holistically on diverse ecological and social contexts, and emphasize the meaningful participation of local people in their planning and implementation (Sayer and Campbell, 2004). However, practitioners find this a challenging task, not least because it inevitably involves the engagement of many actors with divergent interests in a process of learning and adaptation. Particularly when faced with the management of common property resources such as water, forests, pasture or fisheries, market-based incentives generate perverse outcomes. Moreover, special forms of collective action are required (Ostrom, 1990; Knox, Meinzen-Dick and Hazell, 1998; Agrawal, 2001).

Recent global studies have also emphasized the need for governance reforms to improve decision-making in rural development. These focus on decentralization of authority for managing resources and delivering services in rural areas (World Bank, 2003). However, experience with decentralization has been at best mixed: administrative deconcentration has often not been accompanied by devolution of authority; local mechanisms are not responsive to policy objectives; and there are risks of replacing ineffective central administration with inequitable local control (Edmunds and Wollenberg, 2003; Ribot, 2003). Practitioners are caught between the exhortations of well-intentioned policies and the complexity of local change in a dynamic political and institutional environment.

Poverty, environmental degradation and governance issues tend to converge in the so-called least favoured areas: zones of marginal agricultural production which have the weakest natural resource endowments, the least political power, and are the most remote from markets. These are areas at risk of getting stuck in a poverty trap which prevents them taking advantage of emerging opportunities (UN Millennium Project, 2005). Conventional approaches argue for more funding to address these interlocking constraints, yet they provide few practical examples of what kinds of investments will address all these concerns.

Cases of local research and action

This volume of case studies showcases research projects in the poorest parts of Asia. The cases represent areas where researchers and their organizations are rarely found and if present, are under-resourced. Research organizations in these areas have had limited formal connections to the networks or incentives of international academic publishing. These case stories are presented by the local researchers who undertook the work. Some of them may have had little formal training in research. Some lack advanced academic degrees. Yet these cases provide insights on a range of new lessons and show positive impacts on poverty, resource sustainability and governance, from the community up to the national policy level.

The emphasis in these cases is not on the analysis of research results. All of the case authors have written research reports (some published) that cover specific data and results in greater detail. The importance of these cases is that they describe what happened and what changed as a result of research interventions. These lessons are primarily lessons of development practice, instead of theory. They speak to rural development practitioners who seek to strengthen rural livelihoods, improve resource management and reduce poverty. The main reason for presenting them in this narrative format is to help practitioners to use the lessons of these innovative projects to undertake effective local action themselves.

These are case stories about research and about action. What is unusual is that the process of research was deliberately structured to encourage collaborative learning with other social actors. This is research in which many people learn often different lessons. Another unusual feature is that the research or learning directly led to local development actions which were facilitated by innovation and evidence. This was not research for academic purposes, but for changing peoples' lives. Finally, this was research which transformed policy from the experience of local innovation and learning.

Just as with the communities we studied, it is a challenge to describe simply what this modest volume is about. Both the story and its message depend on where you stand. Research, local action, policy change: these are the core elements of the cases in this volume. But they pay particular attention to the messy dynamics around how these different processes intersect in practice. These narratives are about building the confidence of social actors who are far removed from power, introducing evidence from scientific analysis and from shared experience, identifying inequities, and engaging practical and positive measures to address complex problems.

Therefore, the narratives are particularly instructive to rural development practitioners who rely on evidence and experience to analyse problems and take actions which will lead to sustainable local change.

Origins of the cases

The 11 cases in this volume are selected from among over 75 research projects supported by Canada's International Development Research Centre (IDRC) programme on Community-based Natural Resource Management (CBNRM) during the period 1997–2004. In most cases, the work described here is the result of several years of site-based fieldwork by multidisciplinary local research teams whose members frequently came from several different organizations. The research work may have covered several successive phases of multiyear project funding, each phase evolving in focus and emphasis from the previous work.

To a large degree, the characteristics of these research cases reflect the particular nature of IDRC's mandate. The centre was created by the government of Canada to build research capacity and to improve development outcomes through support to applied research in developing countries. The centre responds to the priorities of its developing-country partners and directs its financial support and the advisory capacities of its specialist technical staff towards local researchers, with a strategic emphasis on building local expertise. Therefore, these products reflect research not merely located in the South, but research that is led by Southern researchers and their organizations.

Because it is principally a development organization which adopts knowledge generation as a mechanism for achieving development outcomes (rather than a research donor whose objective is mainly academic excellence), the chief measure of success for the centre's work is the adoption of research lessons in practice. Therefore, the links between learning and application attract significant attention as a key element of the centre's task.[1]

IDRC's CBNRM research programme developed a conceptual framework, criteria for evaluating research proposals and a programming strategy for its work in Asia. But the research work in the field was conducted by local partners, and they were responsible for interpreting, adapting, and making sense of the range of methods and tools available. With time and experience, the research teams took the initiative in elaborating and refining the conceptual framework for their work (see Chapter 2). The key starting point was always that their research should address problems of natural resource degradation and local livelihoods through meaningful participation of local men and women in the research process. The centre's strategy for programming in Asia emphasized support to those countries with the weakest research infrastructure, or the least access to external academic networks. These were typically the poorest countries (or the poorest regions of large countries) and those transitional economies that were only just emerging from decades of ideological and political isolation. Not coincidentally, these were also the ones with the most limited international language skills and least access to Western academic literature.

Therefore, early research efforts focused on building capacity through learning by doing, with limited introduction to the integrated, multidisciplinary and participatory research concepts and tools needed for this work. Long-term site-based research was seen as important not only for gaining insight through practice but also for building and monitoring impacts in complex biological and socio-economic systems, and for building relationships between people and organizations not accustomed to working together. Many researchers were field-oriented natural scientists in applied disciplines such as agronomy or forestry, reflecting the prevailing strengths of local research establishments. Particular emphasis was placed on building practical social science research skills to integrate with these backgrounds.[2]

CBNRM researchers worked under difficult field conditions. The programme targeted the poorest and most marginal areas of Asia, usually remote and sometimes seasonally inaccessible. Even for locally based research teams, the working conditions in the field were challenging. And the nature of the research demanded extended periods of fieldwork. The work was not only physically but intellectually challenging: the research teams were pushing the envelope of conventional research practices. In most cases, they were undertaking work which was so different from what their peers and their institute recognized that at the outset they had difficulty even finding the terminology and language to share it. So the cases in this volume represent more than just one-off academic ventures. They are efforts by their authors to distil and communicate the outcomes of many years of challenges, in the field and in their own institutes, and they are products of determination, commitment and integrity as much as of documentation and analysis.

Why this book?

In recent years, a number of concerted efforts by research groups have drawn attention to CBNRM. Some of this literature is addressed in the next chapter in order to situate the work of the cases which follow. Yet, as successful as this work has been in defining a theoretical framework and providing a much richer understanding of participatory research approaches and of collective action in rural development, much of it reports on analytical conclusions and theoretical implications, rather than guides to practice. In particular, it remains challenging to find good first-hand reports on innovative, participatory local research and resource management interventions which would provide procedural insights to practitioners in the field

We also found that much of the academic literature is relatively inaccessible to practitioners, particularly in rural Asia. This situation is changing as foreign-language capabilities improve among rural research organizations, and as new electronic media provide low-cost access to resource materials. However, there is still a significant digital divide in terms of internet access in these countries, and even when high-quality web access is technically available, internal policies at many local organizations restrict access to the necessary equipment. There is a strong need for local-language content and supporting materials in both electronic and print formats.

So while our local research partners have undertaken a variety of efforts to promote and publish their research results in national languages, they also felt it would be beneficial to present them regionally in an international language, so that they would be more accessible to a broader range of practitioners and peers. The exercise of synthesizing work they had undertaken over a lengthy period also proved valuable for the researchers, who were developing a deeper and more critical appreciation of its strengths and weaknesses. In many cases, the products forming the cases in this volume are also being reproduced by their authors in a variety of local formats and languages for other applications.

As the international scientific community has been forced to direct its efforts more and more to complex problems of resource degradation and poverty reduction, it has also had to focus increasingly on participatory approaches to research (Pound et al., 2003; Sayer and Campbell, 2004). Yet the consensus on what constitutes effective field practice in participatory research is still evolving (Vernooy and McDougall, 2003). Such consensus breaks down even further when it comes to development programme implementation. Despite the commitments of almost all international agencies and rural development programmes to the participation of those most affected in programme implementation, there is a wide range of interpretation of what this actually means in practice (Blackburn et al., 1998). Examples of good practice which emphasize field processes, learning, and outcomes in participatory research and action are, therefore, both timely and provocative.

With good reason, those governments faced with the challenges of decentralizing and implementing participatory natural resource management often claim to need additional resources – both in expertise and funding. Donors may be led to believe that solutions to these complex local poverty and environment issues can be achieved by throwing sufficient money and expertise at them. In fact, in many cases, the solutions are known, they require support for local capacity-building, leadership, initiative and learning. Donors, development agencies and national governments are not adept at facilitating local initiative. It is difficult to balance the patience required for local learning and experience so as to build confidence and initiative, with the real possibilities for sharing lessons and principles. It is challenging to recognize and respect local knowledge while still engaging the benefits of scientific enquiry and accumulated technical expertise.

In these areas, the cases presented in this book showcase helpful experiences in extremely challenging contexts. They suggest ways in which CBNRM processes can respond to these development challenges, providing a coherent approach to rural development practice that is especially well-suited to poor, unproductive and marginalized areas. They illustrate how local learning can have a broader influence on framing and implementing policies to better enable the expansion of local livelihoods and the sustainability of natural resource use. Moreover, they demonstrate the importance of local actors – particularly collective actors such as user groups, committees and local government – in generating change through networks of information and influence that extend far beyond a community's territorial boundaries.

At a time when global agendas require concerted local action, we expect that the experiences in this book will find a wide audience.

Producing this book

There are many reasons why local researchers in this field have not been published much – reasons that extend far beyond difficulties of language. Researchers may have little incentive to publish internationally in an environment where such publications play a limited role in their personal career paths. They may be too busy engaging in challenging fieldwork and practice. In addition, their organizations may have such limited funding that writing has been largely unaffordable and devoted to essential reporting and donor interactions. Despite these very real barriers, there is a slowly growing body of literature written by local scholars. The cases published here represent a special effort to bring these voices to a wider international audience.

The book has come together through both individual and collaborative effort at several levels. At the outset, the task was conceived as a series of syntheses of a large body of research activity. Most of the authors of these case studies synthesized the work of their research teams, often involving several other colleagues in their drafting and revision. This process commenced in early 2004, with invitations to the research teams to explore themes for their own work. Participants agreed on a general approach to their cases which would direct attention to the practice of participatory action research, and their reflections on what happened as a result. The drafts of these cases took shape iteratively, through interaction in the teams and with external reviewers, including IDRC professional staff.

All of the cases were presented by their authors at a regional writeshop, held in Tagaytay City, Philippines, 17–26 May 2004. External reviewers (researchers and practitioners) from the Philippines and from Canada, along with IDRC staff, provided comments and feedback to the authors. The writeshop facilities offered editorial and research support to the authors, who then revised their work, and each case underwent extensive discussion and editorial revision through one-on-one coaching, group presentations and feedback sessions, and technical editing. The final editorial content was the responsibility of chapter authors, but they were expected to respond to a wide range of review comments, and were provided with support to facilitate their work. At the end of the writeshop, a weary group of researchers had learned that writing case stories was very different from writing technical research reports for project donors.

In addition to the external reviewers, the authors of the four thematic chapters in this volume also participated in the writeshop. Their task was to synthesize across the various cases around more general themes relevant to the field of CBNRM. The topics of their synthesis chapters only took shape during the course of the writeshop, and were introduced in outline form at its conclusion.

The concentrated and focused time of the writeshop was essential to getting these products completed. Without a committed period of time away from their regular responsibilities, most authors would have been unable to complete the intense writing required. Likewise, editorial review and feedback were concentrated in a short period of time to greatly increase the quality of the raw materials. After the writeshop, authors were able to devote efforts to further revisions and refinement of their essential arguments, and to respond as the manuscript editor pursued editorial questions and revisions. All of the revised cases were circulated, and the thematic chapter authors used these to craft their own chapters, which were further circulated for comment among all the participants and substantively revised before final editing.

Organization of the cases

The cases in this volume are presented in two groups. The first group of five cases from Cambodia, Vietnam, Laos and Mongolia demonstrate how the application of participatory action research in specific sites led to changes in resource management planning and practices. In some cases, the principal effects were on resource tenure, while in others the main interventions involved new applications for increasing the productivity of common and private resources through community organization. But both productivity enhancement and tenure were important elements in all these cases. Especially in terms of tenure, this led many of the cases to address policy issues from the field. The first group of cases (Chapters 3–7) are all based on long-term, site-based fieldwork which provided a grounding for interventions combining local and scientific knowledge.

The second group of cases are similarly grounded in fieldwork, often stretching over many years in several linked sites. However, these cases particularly reflect on the external linkages of the projects and of community organizations. Specifically, they address the ways that field experience and community organizations have been scaled up to new sites, transferred to government agencies or linked to ongoing processes of formal policy change. In the Bhutan case, the authors are explicit about how the research experience has led to significant changes in the natural resource research system there. Therefore, these cases elaborate a bit more on the external and policy implications of the CBNRM action research experience.

All of the cases are oriented to improving the access of marginalized groups to the resource base and helping them to introduce strategies for increasing productivity while conserving ecological integrity. All of them pay attention to the political and social context of this work. All of them are sensitive to the local dynamics introduced by the research project, and attempt to reflect on how those dynamics have played out for different actors involved. One of the important elements which many of the cases address is how the roles of various actors – farmers, local leaders, government officials, researchers – have changed through the process of shared learning by doing.

Synthesizing project results and exploring gaps

The four thematic chapters which follow the cases synthesize the various case experiences and draw conclusions about key CBNRM issues. These chapters distance themselves from the specific projects and cases, and reflect on the development context and the outcomes reported in light of some important debates in the literature related to CBNRM.

In their chapter on pro-poor research, Gonsalves and Mendoza argue that the cases present a number of important characteristics which will be increasingly essential to ensure that international or national research systems continue to generate public goods for development priorities. In response to criticism of research systems for the lack of impact their work has had on poverty reduction, many of these organizations are adopting pro-poor research strategies.

But what does pro-poor research really mean? What would a pro-poor research agenda look like? And how might one assess its effectiveness? Gonsalves and Mendoza argue that these cases model many of the features of pro-poor research. They say it should be pragmatic, participatory and transformative. An important enabling element is the research's ability to utilize local knowledge while addressing complex interactions with physical landscapes. However, they also point to areas which need strengthening. They draw on good practices as described in these cases, which sustain livelihoods while introducing better conflict management measures and which strengthen social science analysis on multidisciplinary teams. This is especially relevant to gender issues associated with resource management, and in reforming research organizations to better enable and foster these practices.

CBNRM interventions are most commonly defined in relation to external issues: resource appropriation, conflict, and tenure rights of local vis-à-vis external agents. In their chapter Beck and Fajber turn the spotlight on to difficult and persistent issues of intra-community inequity. They point to the challenges of addressing the subtle and complex social, gender, and power relations in any community. They remind us of the experience of well-intentioned rural development interventions, both top-down and bottom-up, which have exacerbated local inequities through interventions which are captured by local elites. They point to illustrations of the problems in these cases, and some examples of how researchers have attempted to deal with them. They note some significant successes in addressing these persistent challenges, but also argue for strengthening the analysis and interventions of action research projects. Rather than attempt to be neutral in their orientation, Beck and Fajber argue that CBNRM interventions should be explicitly structured to favour the most marginalized members of the community.

In his synthesis chapter, Vandergeest argues that these cases demonstrate ways in which external CBNRM interventions build communities or modify the nature of pre-existing ones. The resulting 'CBNRM communities' in these cases are typically translocal, because they are connected to other communities and to policy-makers in networks of influence and information exchange. These cases also describe collective local actors, who possess characteristics that are quite different from other collectivities or individual actors, who are capable of intervening in a variety of ways, all of which build from natural resource management into other realms of development. In contrast to the somewhat stylized depictions of the critical literature, Vandergeest sees the CBNRM communities in these cases as seeking strategic opportunities with, rather than opposing, both the state and market forces. While he emphasizes that the communities constructed through the actions described in these cases are contingent results requiring continued effort by many actors, Vandergeest also sees them as promising examples of new approaches to collective action for development.

One of the more consistent – and perhaps more surprising – conclusions from a comparison of these cases is that most have specifically addressed policy issues. In their synthesis chapter, Tyler and Mallee dissect the ways in which the policy influence of these cases has been aided by the context of ongoing – and contested – decentralization processes in most of these countries. This context provided a window of policy flux and an opportunity for local evidence from field experience to affect policy content and implementation. Researchers have proved strategically adept at reaching for these opportunities, using a variety of methods and approaches, sometimes in partnership with local communities themselves or with external advocates. The effectiveness of the policy and policy implementation interventions appears to be related to the transformative effects of engaging key actors in the participatory action research process. As a result, there are significant implications for both policy and research in CBNRM.

Ultimately, this volume demonstrates that the CBNRM research reported in these case studies has had some significant successes in marginal areas of Asia. The work has been transformative in several important senses: the perceptions of problems, recognition of processes and causal links, exposure of power relations, social roles of key actors and utilization of productive resources have all been fundamentally changed through the learning processes described here. These transformations create new social meaning and enable creative responses to difficult problems. CBNRM requires collective local action, but also enables policy action, facilitative support of government agencies and positive individual responses. Transformative learning helps actors align these different kinds of effective action.

Above all, these cases demonstrate how researchers, men and women who rely on resources for their livelihoods, local governments and policy-makers have expanded the possibilities and practices of resource planning and management through processes of shared learning.

CHAPTER 2

Community-based natural resource management: a research approach to rural poverty and environmental degradation

Stephen R. Tyler

In Asia, hundreds of millions of rural men and women in uplands, semi-arid lands and infertile coastal areas are threatened by poverty and the degradation of the natural resource base on which they depend for their immediate livelihoods. These people are mostly far from urban market centres, far from capital cities and far from the minds and lives of the powerful. The ecological systems on which they depend are being depleted of nutrients, stripped of their biological diversity, and control of the valuable resources that remain is sometimes violently contested.

Yet in order to achieve global development agendas for poverty reduction, it is these people who must be reached. Current practices have failed to either significantly reduce poverty in these marginal areas, or to broadly stem the pace of environmental degradation. The problems are intensified as governments around the region decentralize the management of natural resources (Dupar and Badenoch, 2002). Innovations are needed, but what kind of innovations?

This was the challenge which IDRC faced in 1996, as we prepared a new approach for addressing research on poverty reduction and natural resource sustainability in marginal areas of rural Asia. In consultation with partners from national and international research centres throughout the region, the new research programme, CBNRM, was framed (IDRC, 2000). All the cases in this book arose from work sponsored under this programme.

This chapter reviews the rationale for the research approach adopted in the programme and the conceptual framework which has emerged from our partners applying this approach over the years. While each research project supported through the programme was unique, and there were few explicit links between them, the foundations of the CBNRM programme led to the adoption of a consistent set of tools and approaches. This starting point arose from the experiences of IDRC's professional staff and research partners in Asia, and from reviews of research approaches for rural poverty and environment issues in the mid-1990s. Some of the key intellectual threads of the CBNRM research framework will be introduced here (others are addressed in more depth in the synthesis chapters in Part IV of this volume). But the programme, as conceived by the research donor (IDRC), also evolved through its application by partners in the field into a richer and more complete conceptual framework. This framework for action research in CBNRM underlies most of the case narratives presented. This chapter provides the conceptual background to the cases and helps explain the methodological consistency among them.

Why has research failed to reach the poor?

There are close linkages between problems of rural poverty and natural resource degradation. However, each phenomenon is complex, and linkages are not simple in any causal sense. The ecological and geographic constraints of location are major contributors to the spatial concentration of rural poverty. Indeed, most of the rural poor worldwide are found in those least favoured areas where natural and human factors combine to constrain agricultural production and market access (Pender, Hazell and Garrett, 2001).

Classic approaches to rural development research invested in improved technologies to increase production in various sectors: forestry, agriculture, fisheries, livestock or irrigation. IDRC research support helped to build national scientific capacity in Asia in these fields throughout the 1970s and 1980s. Such research had the advantage of being able to connect readily to professionals, academics and government staff who were organized sectorally and trained in different applied science disciplines. This kind of work remains essential to broaden the range of responses available for farmers and to increase yields of staple grains. But it has not been successful in helping poor, marginal farmers to improve their conditions; nor has it been effective in addressing the fundamental causes of resource degradation (Chambers, 1997; Sayer and Campbell, 2004).

The green revolution packages of improved crop varieties and inputs that led to large increases in grain production in Asia did not reach such marginal areas. High-yielding varieties (HYVs) are designed to respond predictably to commercial inputs which standardize the production environment through irrigation, fertilizer and pesticide application. If managed carefully, these can be very effective in productive agro-ecosystems where conditions are broadly consistent and where access to input and product markets is assured.

However, in less favoured areas ecological conditions are heterogeneous. Soils, slopes, altitude and other microclimatic factors such as water availability, quality and accessibility are subject to wide variation over small areas. Farmers' practices are diverse and spread risk across a wide variety of livelihood strategies that are reliant on multiple resources. Standardized technical solutions do not work (Chambers, Pacey and Thrupp, 1989). Researchers and research donors alike could see that while scientific advances could be made in test plots, these were not benefiting the poorest farmers whose fields were much more diverse – if they had fields at all.

Innovations in integrated agriculture and forestry research and in watershed management provided models for joint investigation and management of agro-ecological systems, which spanned the boundaries of conventional, reductionist science in each of these related fields. Farming systems research, which extended the conventional commodity production approach of agricultural research, was one of these. This research approach recognized that poor smallholder farmers could afford neither the inputs nor the risks of HYV monocropping, and instead explored the productivity potential of linking intensive management of trees, staple crops, cover and conditioning crops, livestock and sometimes aquaculture. These joint systems benefited from careful agro-ecological studies to take advantage of nutrient chains, ecological complementarity and soil-replenishing features to strengthen resource productivity under diverse conditions. Low-input agriculture research helped to improve understanding of pest and soil management to enable farmers to improve resource quality and sustainability by reducing chemical use. Agroforestry research helped to validate and expand the range of livelihood options for farmers in forests and uplands by developing more productive tree crops, as well as fodder and tree-crop intercropping. Integrated watershed management demonstrated the links between land use practices and hydrology in conditioning both surface and groundwater supply and quality. The progress of these research efforts extended the ways that agricultural scientists and foresters viewed their roles in resource management. They required greater interaction between researchers and farmers to understand and test existing or novel management systems. The experiences from such work not only expanded the repertoire of applied science research methods, but provided a range of promising options for improving smallholders' livelihoods. These were helpful precedents for CBNRM researchers.

An even more integrated research focus on production systems, or on biophysical and ecological constraints to production, failed to address the problems of access by the poor to key natural resource assets. This is most obvious in the case of arable land, which has led to numerous efforts at land reform and land reallocation throughout Asia. However, it is also true in the case of access to pasture, forests, fisheries or water. These resources, essential to the livelihoods of poor farmers in less favoured areas, cannot easily be allocated to and managed by private households. Utilization decisions by one set of users affect the quantity or quality of resource available for other users of the same resource. Therefore, collective institutions are needed to manage these resources (Knox, Meinzen-Dick and Hazell, 1998). But this posed problems for resource management research. Little was known about such institutions and how to investigate them. Frequently they did not exist, or if they did exist, they were not recognized by governments as capable of management action and hence were not seen as targets for innovation.

The issue of resource tenure also arose in relation to the commercialization of resources. As private commercial interest in rural resources grew, for instance due to industrial plantation crops, large-scale logging, hydroelectric power development and agricultural colonization, the poor found that they could no longer control their local resource base. Both management by central government and private enclosure, which is mainly concerned with maximizing returns from the resource, neglected the role of common property resources on which the poor frequently depend. Commercialization of these common property resources led to changes in the de facto rights of poor local resource users. This excluded and further impoverished them (Dove, 1993; de Koninck, 1997; Beck and Nesmith, 2001).

More generally, natural scientists focusing on biophysical resources neglected institutional linkages to processes of impoverishment. Yet it is precisely the institutions of resource management which must be addressed if targeted poverty reduction measures are to succeed in resource-dependent communities (Béné, 2003). In the face of these persistent difficulties in how to apply research and innovation to the problems of poverty and environmental degradation, the role of scientific specialists in proposing solutions became increasingly discredited. They were proved to be frequently wrong, or had limited impact on actual practice (Chambers 1997; Sayer and Campbell, 2004).

Another part of the problem is that the sectoral organization of science, extension and policy does not match the perspective of the poor farmers themselves. They are obliged to adopt multiple livelihood and subsistence strategies, relying on agriculture, livestock, fish, forest collection, wage labour and a range of other resource utilization strategies, as well as increasingly off-farm labour and remittances. Therefore, technical improvements in one particular production technology may or may not fit within the diverse practices and adaptation strategies of farmers in marginal areas. An example of this relationship would be the seasonal migration of male members of the household, where the ensuing labour scarcity may constrain potential new farming strategies.

For some time, critical scholars of rural development and agricultural research have pointed to the need for a much greater emphasis on the perspectives of poor local farmers. They need to be considered as development actors themselves, with very different perceptions and motivations from external interveners, but who nonetheless have significant, albeit unrecognized, capacities (Chambers, 1983; Scott, 1985; Biggs and Farrington, 1991; Beck, 1994). There was also increasing recognition of the value of indigenous (or traditional) knowledge for informing scientific understanding of agriculture and natural resources and for guiding effective local interventions in environmental management (Berkes, 1993). There is now plenty of evidence in Asia of indigenous practices adapting to constrained environments to improve their productivity (Cairns, 2005).

These emerging lessons from research in applied sciences and rural development pointed towards the need for a new research approach for poverty reduction and natural resource management (see Figure 2.1). They also coincided with other factors that shaped the programming of many international development agencies in the 1990s. The UN Conference on Environment and Development in 1992 adopted the Agenda 21 action programme, responding to the call for sustainable development contained in the report of the World Commission on Environment and Development (Brundtland, 1987; UN Dept of Economic and Social Development, 1992). This high-profile international

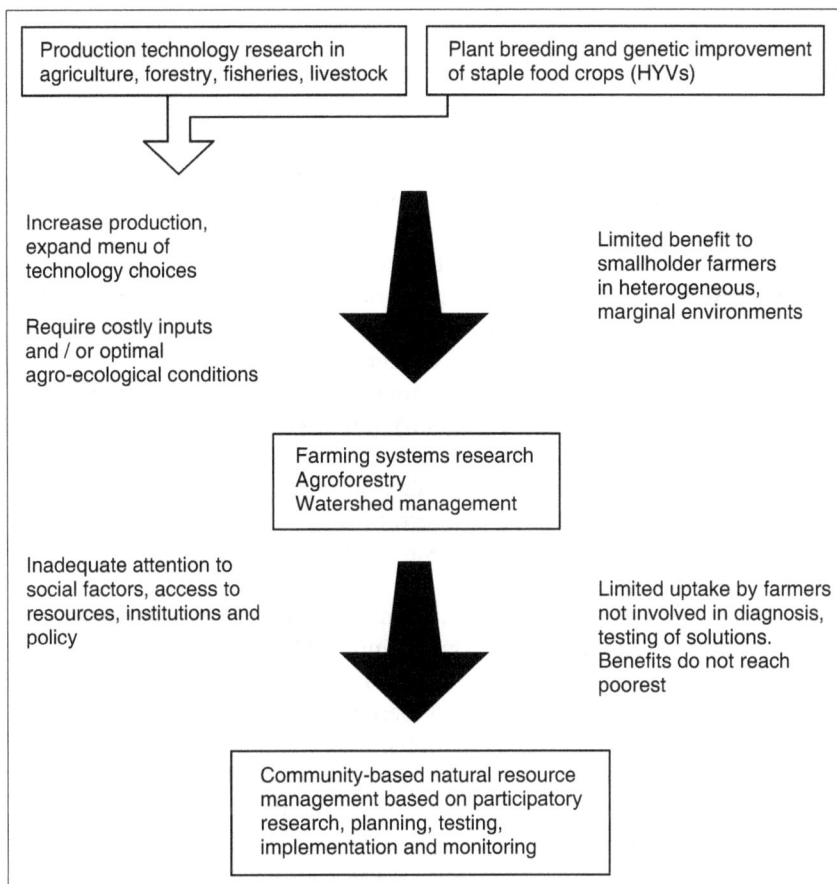

Figure 2.1   Paths to CBNRM research

commitment strongly linked poverty and environment issues, placing them firmly on the development agenda. At the same time, the dominance of the 'Washington consensus' drove development policymaking to reduce the role of the state and emphasize the potential of smallholder farmers to generate economic growth by responding to liberalized markets. Rural development practice came to be strongly influenced by nongovernmental organizations (NGOs), rather than government or international organizations. The rhetoric of participatory development was widely adopted by most organizations engaged in rural development (Ellis and Biggs, 2001), yet rarely tested critically. All of these factors pointed to the need for a programme of applied research which could explore integrated approaches to natural resource management from the perspective of resource users.

Defining CBNRM research

While it is important to have some clarity of basic concepts, the intention from the outset of this programme was that research partners should explore the meaning of CBNRM in practice for themselves. The programme resisted trying to define too specifically what ought to constitute community-based natural resource management. Throughout the 1990s this term came to be popularized in the rhetoric of donors, NGOs and development agencies, and was critically addressed by academics. It was applied to a very broad range of approaches and practices. IDRC's CBNRM research programme started from a set of principles which distinguished its work from that of other researchers and practitioners, and which responded to the particular concerns identified above.

The foundation of the research programme was its focus on poor people and on strengthening their livelihoods. Enquiry was oriented to natural resources, but from the outset the goal of the work was aimed at improving the conditions of poor men and women, where the quality of the resource base was a prime element in their well-being. In this respect, the approach of CBNRM departed from one of the antecedents to this research programme, that of community-based conservation.

In the late 1980s, large international conservation organizations began to work closely with local organizations and communities to support the creation of protected areas and strengthen the conservation of endangered ecosystems. These efforts led to many community-based integrated conservation and development programmes, which attempted to provide local benefits through wildlife and ecosystem protection programmes (Wells and Hannah, 1992). But recent critiques have emphasized the fundamentally co-optive nature of conservation initiatives with indigenous and local communities when goals are defined primarily by governments or external agents (Chapin, 2004). CBNRM took a different starting point, emphasizing that in principle, resource management objectives ought to be locally grounded.

A premise of CBNRM research was that the traditional and local knowledge of resource users deserved to be valued and treated with respect. The conventional professional training of natural and social scientists has led them to dismiss traditional knowledge, especially when it is not formally codified or documented. Yet traditional or local knowledge, in the context of its specific applications and relevant scientific validation, can make important contributions to agriculture and natural resource management (Chambers, Pacey and Thrupp, 1989; DeWalt, 1994). As a point of departure for research, the crucial considerations here were about the meaning of knowledge and the attitudes of researchers more than narrow methodological concerns. We recognized that knowledge has value both for its intrinsic meaning in a particular social context and also for what people can do with it. These different values and meanings of knowledge come from the social context in which knowledge is created and used. Therefore, meanings can be different in local and scientific contexts where knowledge is created and used under different criteria (Berger and Luckman, 1966; Kuhn, 1962). For problem-oriented researchers, it becomes important not just to catalogue and categorize different types of knowledge, but to build understanding and interaction between them. To begin with, this meant that researchers had to find ways to identify and assess knowledge in different forms and from various sources (Grenier, 1998).

In addition to local knowledge, the CBNRM research programme presumed that resource users also had rights to access resources essential to their livelihoods. These rights are typically complex, and can include overlapping customary and legal tenure rights, rights to different kinds of resources at different seasons, and rights which are recognized by different agents under different circumstances. These rights can be held by individuals, family groups or communities defined in various ways. They can be exclusive or shared, sometimes depending on context. Formal or informal rights might only be translated into practical resource access and use under certain conditions. As natural resources in marginal areas come under more pressure from competing users and from degradation, overlapping rights and tenures are increasingly contested (Vandergeest, 1997; Leach, Mearns and Scoones, 1999). Lack of formal rights, conflict over rights, or loss of longstanding resource rights all reduce the incentive for users to invest in managing the resource base and lead to degradation. Understanding these rights and the institutions through which they are contested was taken to be an important prerequisite for effective intervention and change.

The notion of introducing change was fundamental to CBNRM research. The research was intended to yield practical short-term benefits for resource users through improved natural resource management. This was not to be merely an exercise in analysis and theory- or model-building. The learning was to produce concrete, implementable and sustainable innovations to benefit local farmers and fishers. Depending on the problems and context, these were often linked to technical efforts to improve resource productivity, such as through introducing new agricultural, agroforestry, aquaculture, livestock or integrated techniques. But they could also include designing and introducing new institutions which might be required to resolve crucial conflicts or secure collective tenure. The research was premised on the notion that in these marginal agricultural contexts, where common property resources were essential to the livelihoods of the poor, both technological and institutional innovations would ultimately be needed. Hence, the question of where to start was largely a pragmatic one. In order for innovations to be adopted and adapted by resource users themselves, they had to be practical, sensible and understandable. They had to be tested and validated by the users, who were male and female farmers and fishers. In addition, they had to be endorsed by the best available knowledge of the researchers themselves.

CBNRM research was also intended to recognize from the outset that communities are ill-defined and heterogeneous. Interests diverge, wealth and power separate, social relations are complex and dynamic, and history matters. Differences of culture, ethnicity and language can make these characteristics opaque to outsiders, whether from the other side of the river or the other side of the planet. Researchers were encouraged not to romanticize the community and its potential for natural resource management, and to start from where local people were, rather than from any idealized notion of appropriate practices. Local situations are idiosyncratic and easily misinterpreted by outsiders, especially those with a predetermined agenda.

Applying innovations in the field meant recognizing that local change and development requires the agency of local men and women, who are capable of responsible and creative choices to improve their own circumstances. It was also crucial to obtain the support of local government, which can – and often must – endorse innovative resource management practices. For example, many of the research activities dealt with institutional innovations such as tenure and resource access, as well as individual and collective management interventions for resources which were not privately owned. Therefore, any research effort that expected to generate usable innovations had to address the concerns of local people and governments. The best way to do that was to ensure that these actors were fully engaged in the research at its outset, and that their voices were influential in directing the enquiry.

The research approach described above has several important implications, which are significant enough to be considered as underlying design principles for the research programme. First, and most important, the CBNRM research programme was premised on meaningful participation by local men and women in the research effort. The participatory nature of the research was intrinsically linked to recognition of poor farmers and fishers as crucial agents of change and development, and not merely targets of technological advice. Strengthening and empowering their actions required participatory approaches. The emphasis on indigenous knowledge, on understanding institutions and on practical and sustainable interventions all made it imperative for the researchers and the local people to be jointly engaged in learning. Lessons would have to be convincing and evidence credible for poor farmers or fishers to risk investing in innovations. The best evidence would come from the users themselves.

Second, an interdisciplinary approach to the research was fundamental. The intent was to develop practical and sustainable innovations to address the agro-ecological constraints within the dynamic social and institutional context of resource users' behaviour. Therefore, diagnosis and analysis had to cross disciplinary boundaries. From the outset, it was expected that a wide range of expertise would be called on in each research site. But more than that, it was apparent that the necessity of integrating different disciplinary approaches would require methods which used qualitative and quantitative data, analysis and interpretation. These stretched the conventional practices of any single discipline and required the development of new interdisciplinary tools and methods.

The nature of the research task meant that while a range of comparative and methodological research would be supportive, the fundamental test of this CBNRM approach would necessarily involve long-term, site-based fieldwork.

The research programme was premised on shared learning from experience on the part of researchers and farmers. This was time-consuming: it involved joint diagnosis, analysis, exploration, intervention and evaluation. In addition, it necessarily focused on outcomes, not on analysis. Without specific reference to outcomes in a series of different contexts, little could be concluded about the framework as an innovative approach to the problem of rural poverty and environmental degradation.

These characteristics of the approach to CBNRM were well represented in the international academic discourse of the mid-1990s. At that time, they were beginning to appear in the work of leading rural development practitioners and on the curricula of graduate programmes in the industrialized world. They were spreading rapidly in international-language journals and international organizations. However, in many parts of Asia, these represented a huge departure from the conceptual frameworks, academic preparation and practices of local scientists and development specialists. In the poorest countries and subnational regions where the CBNRM programme chose to focus its research efforts, most of these concepts were completely new. And there were very few examples anywhere of how to integrate and then implement these concepts coherently in practice. Research teams had to build methods, tools and practical intervention strategies while they were digesting and evaluating the relevance of the concepts.

This would be a challenging research agenda anywhere. How reasonable was it to expect to implement this research approach under the difficult conditions of desperately under-resourced local research organizations in remote parts of the region?

It is important to keep in mind the fundamental capacity-building objectives of the programme. First, it was important to characterize the complex and dynamic problems of poor people's livelihoods and their relationship to local ecological degradation. The point of the programme was to build local expertise in addressing this complexity, among researchers as well other actors who were involved. The programme commenced by incorporating emerging perspectives in the literature related to agricultural research, environmental management and international development. IDRC sought to facilitate access to that literature for researchers in isolated and impoverished regions of Asia,[1] but our approach to CBNRM mainly sought to encourage learning by doing.

Therefore, the CBNRM research programme was based less on a preconceived model or formula for intervention than it was on a collaborative learning agenda. The concepts recognized and embraced the complexity of agro-ecological and social systems, while responding to the imperative of action on immediate problems. The emphasis was on building partial understandings and confidence for intervention, but then on iterative learning from those interventions and moving to longer-term issues. Having absorbed some of the lessons from critiques in the literature, the emphasis of the research programme was on practice more than theory. But given the natural science background of many of our partners, the programme particularly made an effort to draw on social science contributions to natural resource management so as to prepare research partners for this kind of work.

Building blocks of CBNRM research

Natural resource management at the local level involves interventions in the resource base. But there are other factors to consider. These include the embedded rights which different people and groups have to use or to manipulate the resource base, the social relations between them which condition the scope of actions which are possible, and recognition of who holds power and how it can be exercised. Therefore, research into this complex system must draw on a broad range of concepts and models from both social and natural sciences as they are applied to agriculture and natural resource management (Ashby, 2003; Sayer and Campbell, 2004). There is an enormous body of literature on which to draw, and we cannot make any systematic attempt to summarize it here. But most of the researchers who became involved in the CBNRM fieldwork approached it from a prior background in natural sciences, and so conceptual and analytical tools from the social sciences were those most frequently needing both introduction and support.

Participatory approaches are essential starting points for CBNRM research. While public participation is novel for some natural resource researchers in Asia, it has long been recognized as a term applied to diverse practices, ranging from the extraction of data to the full engagement of participants in decision-making (Arnstein, 1969). As a starting point when working with researchers who had little previous experience with participatory methods or tools, the programme emphasized collaborative learning and problem diagnosis with farmers through participatory rural appraisal (PRA) methods (Chambers, Pacey and Thrupp, 1989; IIRR, 1998). Participatory research methods take some getting used to on both sides. Practitioners and local people need to become familiar with these practices and to build expectations when they have little experience of this type. But the intention was that over time, using Arnstein's (1969) analogy of a ladder of participation, which sees token consultation at the bottom and full engagement in decision-making at the top, the role of farmers and local people in the research enterprise would ascend to more meaningful and profound levels of engagement. Research proposals were designed so that problem definition would be responsive to local priorities and knowledge, along with technical analysis. A key role of participatory research was to enhance the capacities of farmers themselves so that they became capable of assessing and articulating their own situations (Nelson and Wright, 1995). This meant that participation was not an exercise in merely generating data for researchers to analyse, but was an ongoing and iterative process of engagement, learning and empowerment.

For researchers, this meant learning that participatory approaches are not merely about technique. Indeed, the techniques themselves are easily learned. What participatory approaches are fundamentally about is agency, that is, a perspective on development which emphasizes the role of individuals and groups in applying knowledge, capacity and action to expand their choices in a particular cultural setting. This is a different perspective from one which sees development as being about structure. That type of development concerns itself with systems, organizations, capital or technology transfers, and the ways these interact to generate aggregate outcomes (Long and van der Ploeg, 1994).

Undertaking participatory research is therefore as much about the adoption of attitudes of humility, respect and shared learning in interaction as it is about specific concepts, methods and tools (Chambers 1995; Pretty and Scoones, 1995). These attitudes are best learned through experience, reflection and practice. In particular, participatory researchers require skills in communications, especially listening skills. Unfortunately, these skills are seldom taught in formal academic or professional programmes. When the objective of development research is social and organizational change, research needs to be structured so that all participants gain from the learning process. This demands recognition of inherent uncertainties in the process and commitment to empowering others, reflecting critically on the process and evaluating outcomes. These were all elements which were encouraged through CBNRM research (Vernooy, Sun Qiu and Xu Jianchu, 2003).

In recent years, there has been considerable critical assessment of participatory research in natural resource management (Leeuwis and Pyburn, 2002; Pound et al., 2003; Sayer and Campbell, 2004). Based on a comparative assessment of over 20 case studies, Vernooy and McDougall (2003) suggest five principles of best practice in participatory research. They must:

- reflect a clear and coherent common agenda among stakeholders and con-tribute to partnership building;
- address and integrate the complexities and dynamics of change in human and natural resource systems;
- apply the triangulation principle of using multiple sources and methods, and link together multiple knowledge worlds;
- contribute to concerted planning for the future and to social change; and
- be based on iterative learning and feedback loops where there is two-way sharing of information.

These principles capture well the ideals of engagement, joint learning, collective decision-making and scientific rigour, along with practical action and change, all of which are at the heart of the CBNRM participatory research framework. It is fair to suggest that none of the research projects started with best practices on any of these dimensions. Nonetheless, these principles came to guide the progress which all the projects have followed while conceptualizing and strengthening the participatory dimensions of their research.

In addition to meaningful participatory methods, another foundational building block for CBNRM was the study of resource tenure. The central issues of resource use, control and rights – and, therefore, power – are all encapsulated in the institutions associated with resource tenure. Their importance with respect to the reduction of poverty and natural resource degradation has been discussed above. The central tenet of common property resource theory is that it is not only possible, but empirically frequent, that collective institutions in rural societies are designed to manage resources which would otherwise be degraded by the pursuit of individual utility (Berkes, 1989; Ostrom, 1990).

However, while forests, irrigation systems, fisheries and pastures all appear to be amenable to community management, the devil is in the details. Rights to access and use resources are always linked to power relations. They are inherently bound to shared concepts which give meaning to resource use, as well as the social relations within which these are constituted. Hence, common property research inherently involves not only the study of resource rights and institutions, but also the ways in which they are moderated by culture, social organization, political power and resource values. All of these factors are dynamic and respond to both internal and external change. In the context of natural resource management diagnosis and intervention, it is possible to adopt a prescriptive approach, where you first analyse and then recommend conditions for successful community management of common property resources. Or you can take a historical approach, analysing the ways in which resource tenure, social relations and power have evolved in any given community to generate the contextual pattern in evidence (Johnson, 2004). For the purposes of CBNRM understanding and intervention, each of these research approaches offers value. Choices could depend on context and on strategic objectives.

Resource tenure studies quickly get to the issue of control, which is inherent in the whole notion of CBNRM. Practical measures to redress environmental degradation and strengthen livelihoods require secure common property tenures to respond to the decentralization of authority for resource management or the failure of state management systems. Although they were once typical of traditional rural societies, such tenure systems have been eroded by the state or by commercialization, or are no longer able to deal effectively with the new burdens of conflict and multiple demands on the resource base. The challenges of introducing new forms of collective tenure, or of managing the private enclosure of common property in an equitable fashion, were important issues on the research agenda of CBNRM projects.

These foundational elements of participatory methods and institutional analysis pointed to an area of particular challenge for research partners: the nature of social differentiation and exclusion. Both traditional and modern institutions for resource tenure and management are rooted in social and power relations, and hence in the nature of social and political difference. Such differentiation is structured and expressed differently from one society to another, and may involve a wide range of social characteristics, including wealth, ethnicity, religion and caste. However, a crucial consideration is the role of gender. It was impossible for researchers to structure their enquiry collaboratively with resource users, or to pursue questions of the social construction of rights and power, without confronting gender as a differentiating factor in participation and power with respect to resource management (Agarwal, 2001). In many cases, this was an issue which research partners had not previously considered.

This was not only a matter of gender blindness, but often of avoidance. Researchers who had plenty of field experience or extension training usually were sensitive to the general issues of power, social relations and participation in learning among rural communities. But they found gender issues difficult to address. They often lacked tools for formulating concepts, collecting or analysing data, or even communicating sensitively with both men and women about gender differentiation in natural resource decision-making and utilization. This was an area which, although flagged early on for attention in the research programme, remains challenging (see Beck and Fajber, chapter 15).

None of these building block elements were new. But there were several novel features in a research programme based on such foundations. First was the emphasis on introducing and building meaningful participation of local men and women in all components of research, from problem definition to interpretation and assessment of outcomes. This was not a matter of sacrificing rigour in the research approach, but of ensuring it. The rigour demanded of this research programme was that of effective practice. Results had to stand the test of farmers' fields and practical village life. There is great value in research that expands the frontiers of conceptual knowledge, builds theories for wider exploration and challenges conventional disciplinary wisdom through critical analysis. However, none of these goals were primary objectives of this research programme, which focused on practical outcomes and local change.

By adopting an action-oriented approach, the research programme intended to cross the divide between applied research and practice. Its emphasis on learning by doing as a way to build research capacity using challenging new concepts allowed researchers as practitioners to test theory against local outcomes. By also engaging local resource users as learners, the research was meant to develop models of practice for researchers and professionals, practice which would simultaneously build capacities for local organization, action and continued learning among poor farmers and fishers.

This was also an explicit attempt to combine perspectives on social and natural science problems through an integrated mode of enquiry. It was not merely a matter of building research teams of diverse specializations, but of structuring the programme of research to address issues which lie between and across the disciplinary specializations (see Figure 2.2).

Finally, the research programme was meant to engage governments as well as local resource users. Research projects were structured to involve local government officials in diagnosis of problems as well as in interpreting results. From the outset, policy innovations were identified as valuable targets for the research effort. Taken together, these were the characteristics which set the stage for the cases which are presented in subsequent chapters. But these programming ideals also evolved as research projects were implemented by teams in a dozen different countries in Asia.

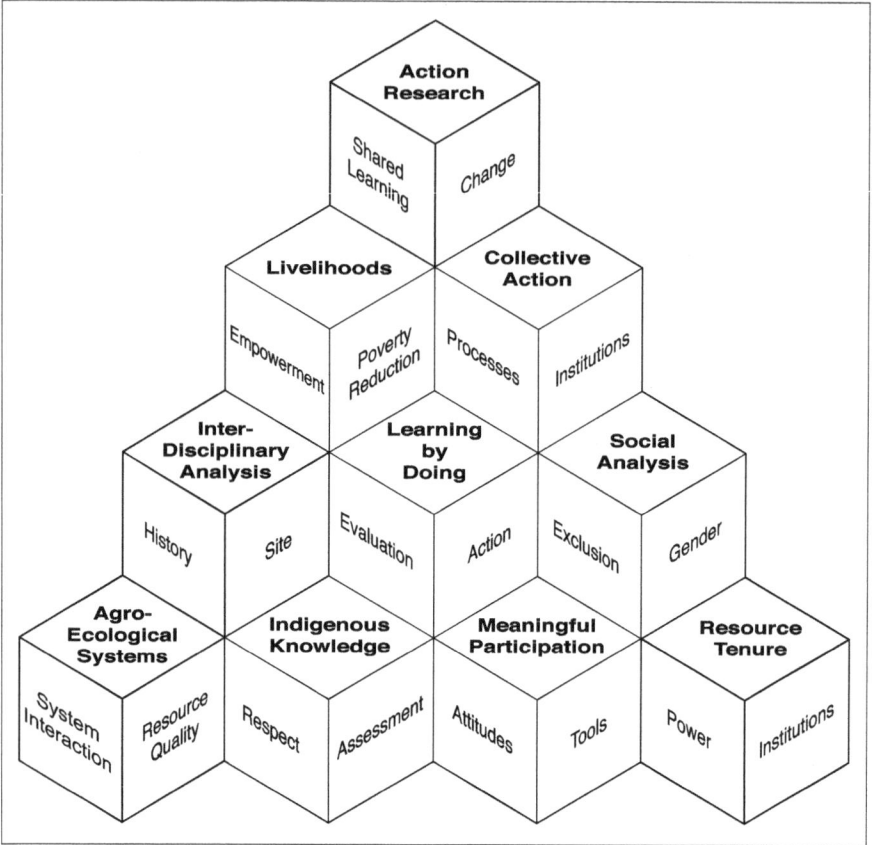

Figure 2.2   Building blocks of CBNRM

A practical framework for action research

A research framework arose not only from these objectives, from the adoption of concepts and models in several disciplines, and from guidelines for implementation which emphasized the characteristics described above. It also matured through the fieldwork undertaken by research partners, including those not represented in this book. Their struggles with practical and conceptual issues helped to refine the initial model, sometimes by simplification and sometimes by elaboration.

One of the first lessons from employing participatory methods in the field was that, not unreasonably, it generated expectations of assistance among local people. Any approach to poor communities by outside expertise is structured in a context of differential power and wealth which itself creates initial expectations, most of which are unhelpful to communication and shared understanding. From their extensive experience, poor communities are generally suspicious of the motives of external interventions. They may have little time, patience or shared vocabulary for explaining to outsiders complex resource, agricultural and social systems which to them are self-evident. Therefore, building positive relationships with local men and women in poor communities meant the research teams had to develop better communications skills. They learned that to build trust they had to set aside preconceived research agendas and start with practical responses to locally perceived problems.

Sometimes this led in directions where the researchers could do little of value. For example, in several of the field sites profiled in this book, villagers were concerned about inadequate local facilities for primary education. The CBNRM research teams were not equipped to address this problem, but could mediate between local communities and NGOs, or government agencies with resources that could be leveraged for this purpose. The research team identified local needs to external agencies, helped local leaders to apply or to meet external criteria, and helped communities to mobilize their own resources. The researchers adopted facilitation roles for local development inputs, which also built trust and shared commitment to their CBNRM research efforts.

This process worked both ways. As the community and its leaders gained confidence in the researchers and their potential to contribute to local goals, the researchers themselves gained greater respect for the strategic capabilities of local people and their leaders. Nonetheless, these processes take time. Expectations on both sides have to be moderate. Building trust and participatory skills is not easily accomplished to a predetermined deadline or a fixed work plan. Project planning had to be flexible and responsive. In the course of implementing the CBNRM research programme, IDRC learned it also had to accommodate reasonable adjustments to project timing and costs.

Another factor which became evident as the research gained momentum in the field was conflict over resource use. Natural resource conflicts are inherent to human valuation and exploitation of resources, and are found everywhere. But these conflicts have become more widespread and more intense as resource demands multiply (Buckles, 1999). Research teams almost always found unanticipated and sometimes complex conflict situations when they diagnosed resource access rights and use in the field. In many cases, they were not well-prepared to address questions of resource conflict. Having established the inequities and abuses of power which frequently lay beneath these conflicts through participatory social and historical research, researchers were no longer able to rely on narrowly legalistic or officially sanctioned solutions. They typically sought to introduce new processes for conflict management, or create new win-win options which would fulfil the mandates of state control yet increase benefits for poor local resource users. This was an important new area of research and practice for the researchers. It required training and the elaboration of new tools and methods. It also required special skills in communication and negotiation, or the ability to foster such skills in others. Developing tools to respond to resource conflicts became an important part of the CBNRM framework, as the research teams repeatedly recognized the frequency of such problems in the field, coupled with the inadequacy of existing institutional mechanisms to address them.

As the researchers gained confidence and experience, and as they were able to demonstrate local successes in addressing natural resource degradation, strengthening local resource rights and improving livelihoods, it became evident to them that these successes needed to be extended to other situations. In many cases, the researchers' first attempts to extend this learning were in response to requests from communities near their field sites, who had seen the improvement in their neighbours' practices and conditions, and wanted to adopt similar measures themselves. This was sometimes a difficult request to address. Researchers are often wary of early positive results and (in good scientific fashion) prefer to wait for validation and repetition before systematic extension. Usually, the teams had limited resources to respond to these requests. But as they became more confident with the methods, and as results were seen to be robust, the researchers recognized that they had to develop better ways to share and extend their lessons. This led to expanding the scale of their innovations.

The research teams approached scaling in two ways: they scaled out especially using farmer-to-farmer and community-to-community extension approaches to reach neighbouring user groups and local government units adjacent to their field sites. In addition, they scaled up by engaging senior government agencies in the elaboration of the methods, and in their replication and adaptation to new conditions. Both scaling out and scaling up research innovations became part of the CBNRM lexicon as the programme evolved, and the reader will find examples of these approaches in the cases.

After gaining experience in the field, and through interaction with local government units, research teams came into greater contact with the policy constraints to local CBNRM action. They learned that local resource degradation was an outcome of complex failures of rights, of conflicts, of power disparities and of inappropriate production systems. But when they tried to design interventions to address the problems they found, they commonly ran into constraints imposed by existing natural resource tenure or management policies. Perhaps there were no opportunities for collective local management of common pool resources. Sometimes there were official systems for community resource management, but these were not implementable due to onerous administrative and technical requirements. Occasionally, the government was one of the parties exacerbating resource conflicts through inept or inadequate implementation of well-intentioned resource policies.

These experiences led most of the CBNRM research teams to explore avenues for influencing natural resource management policies in order to ensure that field-level CBNRM innovations could be put in place. For many of the researchers, venturing into the realm of policy decision-making was another new experience. Policymaking in these countries is far from transparent, and in some cases the mechanisms of policy development were neither obvious nor accessible to the researchers. However, most of the research teams were able to find ways of influencing policy after devoting effort to networking and learning (see Tyler and Mallee, Chapter 17).

CBNRM researchers have come to interpret this general conceptual framework as one of participatory action research (PAR). In this context, the action is not necessarily political action (in association with a particular social movement, for example), but action in the sense of local innovation and change. The main lessons from the research are those which local people can take away and apply themselves to improve their economic welfare, their political power, their social status and the quality of the resource base on which they depend. Learning in this conceptual framework becomes a social process, engaging multiple actors with different interests.

The researchers themselves are only one of the learning groups in CBNRM research. The research process is an iterative one, where scientific and local knowledge are both applied critically to diagnose problems and design interventions. The crucial element of a formalized PAR process is the assessment of interventions by the various actors involved. Were they effective in addressing the problems? Did they generate unexpected consequences? Who benefited? Has resource quality improved? In order to reach some conclusions about what has been learned, actors need to reflect critically on what was being attempted, on the data they have to assess it, and on the surprises which arose along the way. The context is always dynamic: resources, demographics, markets, power relations and policies change with time and require adjustments and adaptations

Table 2.1 Building a practical framework in the field

Lesson	Response
Local expectations easily raised	Build trust and understanding between parties
	Strengthen communications skills
Participatory research takes time	Project planning should be responsive and flexible
Resource conflicts are pervasive	Deal with perceived issues of justice, not just legalistic official solutions
	May require new institutions or processes
Successes need to be shared	Design farmer-to-farmer and community-to-community learning, to scale out
	Engage government officials and extension officers to scale up
Policy can constrain local innovation	Explore enabling policy conditions
	Develop contextual strategies for using research to influence policy and implementation
Different actors measure success in different ways	Design participatory monitoring and evaluation tools; develop monitoring strategies

at the local level. Research teams have developed participatory monitoring and evaluation tools to strengthen this learning process and ensure that various actors formalize their learning (Vernooy, Sun Qiu and Xu Jianchu, 2003). Table 2.1 summarizes the main ways that the CBNRM research framework was adapted and elaborated by research practice.

Applying the framework: case studies from Asia

The CBNRM research framework applied in the cases in this book emerged from a concern with the failures of applied research to reach the rural poor in developing countries. It was based on principles which tried to keep poor men and women central to the framing of research problems, the implementation of projects and the learning which resulted. The framework evolved through application, and was flexible enough to look a bit different in the various site-based studies, in response to the political, agro-ecological, and social contexts, as well as the capacities of the various players.

The collection of cases which follows is representative of the long-term site-based research projects which were the core of the CBNRM research programme over the period 1997–2004. Their methodological commonalities can be attributed to the framework described above, with principles and concepts articulated jointly by the researchers and IDRC, and then elaborated by the researchers themselves during implementation.

The poverty and natural resource contexts in many of these locales were not well-documented in the mid-1990s, in terms of political, institutional, governance and ecological characteristics. Therefore, there was a very limited amount of international literature which might provide relevant background or precedents for any of the sites. In most cases, local studies and background data existed, but these were either of dubious accuracy, or were premised on more traditional agricultural research which was of limited value for CBNRM.

In this context, at the outset most of the projects evolved in unexpected ways. Everyone was in learning mode. Objectives shifted, sites changed, practical difficulties were either overcome or else derailed the efforts. Local researchers also had to deal with the normal challenges of working in any remote part of a developing country. An array of challenges presented themselves: flooding of project offices and computers, unreliable logistics, changing organizational structures and intervening opportunities, and generally low administrative predictability.

At every step, research teams created their own precedents in a field which was new to them, using concepts and methods which were not widely recognized by their peers. This required courage. There was no practical option to learning by doing, and the research teams tried to integrate new processes of collaboration, reflection and integration as well as analysis. The learning process was not smooth, and rough spots remain. But the experiences of implementing and working with this conceptual framework for CBNRM research have generated many insights into practice, as represented in the cases which follow.

Part II
Community-based natural resource management in action

CHAPTER 3

Community-based natural resource management and decentralized governance in Ratanakiri, Cambodia

Ashish Joshia Ingty John and Chea Phalla

Abstract

This chapter describes the experience of introducing CBNRM in Ratanakiri province, Cambodia, through a programme of action research. The research was undertaken in close collaboration with the provincial authorities and linked to the Seila Programme of the Royal Government of Cambodia; a policy experiment on decentralized planning, management and financing of local development. The project helped the province develop procedures for participatory land-use planning, which strengthened the negotiating position of community members in land conflicts with outsiders. At the same time, it helped build the capacity of the government at the provincial and local levels for decentralized natural resource management. This led to agreements on resource management between communities and the provincial government, and to recognition of indigenous people's resource tenure and rights. This was made possible through a combination of field-level participatory action research, along with extensive cooperation with different levels of the government and networking with NGOs and other stakeholders. The strong involvement of indigenous communities in Ratanakiri province also helped the government to begin to understand issues faced by indigenous people and to respond more effectively to their development needs.

Introduction

In 1995, the provincial authorities and the indigenous communities of Oyadao district in Ratanakiri province were informed that a 20,000-ha palm oil concession had been granted by the national government in Oyadao district, which covered parts of several communes, including Somthom commune. The palm oil company started clearing the forest in Somthom and they came prepared to quell any challenge to their claim. Sara Colm recorded the experience of the villagers:

> The company had no relation with people in the village and commune,' said a Som Koul resident. 'They just came here to look for workers to clear the land. Some of the supervisors were good but some were fierce and carried guns. They use guns to intimidate the people.' Another villager from Beang said, 'In the beginning of 1995, twenty company staff came here. Everyone had guns and were dressed in military uniforms. They had AK-47s and rocket launchers. They were looking for workers to cut the forest. They asked the commune to sign and thumbprint a document stating our obligation to look after our cows from roaming or they [the cows] would be shot. (Colm, 1996)

The indigenous communities in Ratanakiri were strongly affected by the government's decisions to grant land or forest concessions without local consultation or consideration of indigenous livelihoods. In the process, the traditional lands and forests of these communities were taken away and control handed to powerful domestic and foreign companies. Somthom was only one example.

Clearing forests for plantation meant clearing sacred areas and land used by shifting cultivators. This made life difficult for Somthom farmers. It was even more difficult for women who gathered forest products. As Seu Chil, a female farmer from Somthom said, 'We are highlanders: our lives depend on the forests and land. Without forests and land, we cannot live. We need firewood, vegetables, fruits, mushroom, and bamboo shoots from the forests. We see the forests as our market.'

Ratanakiri is home to indigenous ethnic minority communities who speak nine different languages. They are animists and practise shifting cultivation. Their livelihoods and culture are traditionally entwined with natural resources, which they actively manage through complex community land-use patterns (Fox, 1996). In the mid-1990s, 70 per cent of the population in Ratanakiri was indigenous. But ethnic Khmer who are Buddhist and mainly paddy (wet rice) farmers are the dominant group in Cambodia, and 98 per cent of the government staff in Ratanakiri belong to this group. The Khmer culture regards shifting cultivation and the culture of indigenous communities with suspicion. Authorities were accustomed to telling indigenous communities what to do and not listening to local, indigenous voices. Corruption was widespread and it was common for companies to offer payments to government officials for their favour. But despite these disadvantages, after three years of effort, Somthom community members were able to negotiate an agreement with the government and the concessionaire to reduce the size of the forest concession by 75 per cent and not to log any more of their forest.

The story of this accomplishment demonstrates a tremendous shift in awareness, initiative and power relations. To understand what happened in Somthom commune, it is necessary to understand the series of events, development programmes and the different projects that helped build new

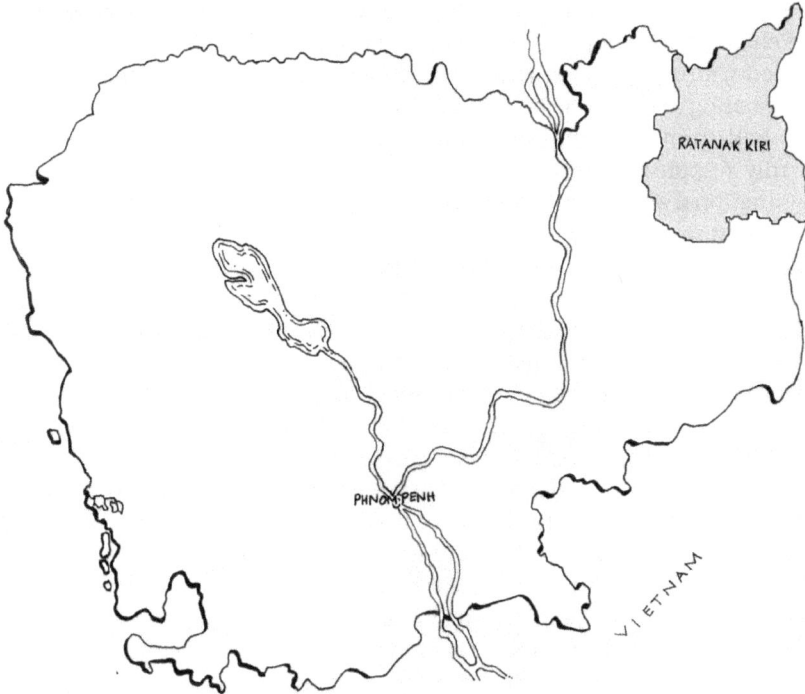

Figure 3.1 Map showing Ratanakiri in northeast Cambodia

relationships between government agencies and community members. This case study highlights an approach to building partnerships for CBNRM. The approach is a balancing act that empowers local communities to negotiate and reinforce traditional land and forest tenure, while also building government capacity for decentralization from national to provincial and local levels.

The context

In 1993, Cambodia held its first elections after more than 20 years of turmoil. As part of the reforms required by the international community, the government agreed to decentralize governance structures and provide more opportunities for local-level planning and decision-making. Known as the Seila Programme, the decentralization and local governance reform processes operated within the broad framework of the government of Cambodia's First Socio-economic Development Plan of 1996–2000. This started as a 'controlled policy experiment' on decentralized planning, management and funding of rural development in five provinces, including Ratanakiri. The projects were concrete investments in the rehabilitation of infrastructure, the establishment of basic services and support for economic livelihoods, but did not at the outset include natural resource management (NRM). To assist the government in implementing the

Seila programme, a support project known as the Cambodian Area Regeneration and Rehabilitation project (CARERE) was formulated by UNDP. Donors have provided strong support to this approach and many donor programmes are now operating under the Seila umbrella. At the national level, the Seila Taskforce works with provincial and district governments and is the body which is primarily responsible for implementing the programme. Technical advisory teams (national and international) are employed by the UN and placed within government structures (see Figure 3.2).

In August 1995, when the Seila programme was preparing to start work in Ratanakiri, a public seminar sponsored by an international NGO opened the debate around development approaches and national policies for indigenous minorities for the first time. As a result of this seminar, the government formed a consultative committee to study issues of indigenous people and to assist in drafting appropriate policies. They emphasized the notion that indigenous people's customary rights should be respected. An international seminar on the same topic in Ratanakiri followed, allowing for strong provincial government participation. These seminars challenged the assumption that central authorities could legitimately make development decisions for indigenous areas without the consultation and participation of local communities. These notions gained public prominence and political support at the national and provincial levels, and later influenced the formulation of the land law and the forest law. In the meantime, a small provincially based research team initiated the Resource Management Policy Project in Ratanakiri with funding from the IDRC. This research activity soon merged with CARERE and became part of the Seila support project to the provincial government.

These events profoundly influenced the Seila/CARERE programme in Ratanakiri, allowing the provincial government to discuss indigenous issues more openly and take advantage of the research unit to experiment with ways to address NRM and governance for poverty alleviation. New field-based information on resource management and customary rights was produced. The provincial government was also looking for ways to gain more management control over natural resources under decentralization. However, at that time, national line ministries were granting large land and forest concessions and declaring national protected areas without consulting the provinces. Indeed, at one point the forest concessions and protected areas approved by the central government in Ratanakiri totalled 115 per cent of the province's territory (Bottomley, 2000).

Ratanakiri was considered by the national government to be rich in natural resources with a very low population, so it was viewed as a prime area for attracting investment. Because it was abundant in forest resources, logging concessions were granted readily. On its rich volcanic soils, industrial plantation concessions were approved. Whether the concessions were for logging or palm oil or rubber or other industrial crops, they fostered widespread clear-cutting of forest prior to any management plans or to plantation development. Other commercial concessions included gem mining, gold mining and fishing.

LEVEL OF GOVERNMENT	ADMINISTRATIVE STRUCTURE	FUNCTION
NATIONAL	SEILA TASK FORCE (different ministry heads)	Policy and Strategy
PROVINCIAL	PROVINCIAL RURAL DEVELOPMENT COMMITTEE (all heads of departments chaired by governor)	Implementation
COMMUNE	COMMUNE COUNCIL	Commune Development Plans

UNDP SUPPORT PROJECT CARERE

Seila Principles: 1. Dialogue 2. Clarify 3. Respect 4. Agreement

COMMUNE COUNCIL

Seila local planning process — COMMUNE → COMMUNE DEVELOPMENT PLANS — Submission for approval by PRDC →

• Agriculture
• Environment
• Education
• Women's affairs
• NGO

Response through different projects based on submitted plans

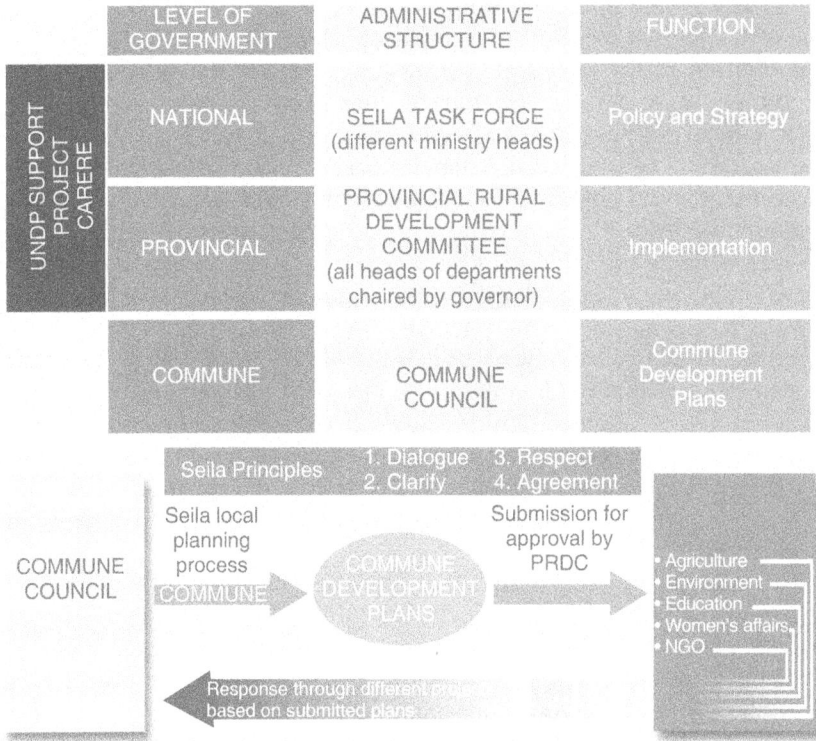

Figure 3.2 UNDP support project (CARERE) helping provincial heads and departments implement projects in response to commune development plans.
Source: Ironside and Nhem, 1998.

Communities were frequently surprised to find that their swidden fields, forests and paddy fields had fallen inside a new concession. In the case of Somthom village, drinking and irrigation water supplies were lost because of an irrigation dam built upstream. It was common for villagers to see logging trucks, guarded by armed soldiers who had been bribed by concessionaires, rolling into their villages and forests. Locals were unable to do much about this situation.

The provincial government did not receive any economic benefits from these concessions as all royalties and taxes go to the national treasury. Therefore, the Ratanakiri governor, Kham Kheun, complained, 'The provincial government must benefit from the logging concessions in order to be able to improve infrastructure in our province.' Perhaps the rampant and illegal destruction of natural resources may have influenced the government to open its doors to donor programmes that would help control such losses. At the time, CARERE project staff also felt that if the provincial government was more engaged in concession decision-making, it would be easier for communities to approach them with concerns about the consequences of large concessions.

In addition to the large-scale concessions, lowland farmers migrated to Ratanakiri in large numbers. Powerful government officials were also procuring land in Ratanakiri. The Ratanakiri CARERE programme manager, Tonie Nooyens, wrote in 1997, 'The situation in Ratanakiri is at the brink of fundamental and irreversible change in its natural and demographic environment. Commercial logging, and clearing of forests by a growing population is changing the ecological balance, triggering a process of degeneration and erosion and putting the predominantly small-holding subsistence farming systems at risk' (CARERE, 1997).

In the context of these events and policies, CBNRM action research was initiated by CARERE/Seila in 1998 to explore ways to provide communities with more secure resource tenure. These activities were initiated with the understanding that tenure security was fundamental to improved resource management, productivity and food security. In accordance with local custom, the research team focused on collective forest resource tenure. The research team attempted to:

- Formalize new collective, not individual, resource tenures (building on customary institutions);
- Build a shared understanding of how to manage and use the resources;
- Identify how to distribute benefits from the resources;
- Ensure secure long-term tenure; and
- Build provincial and local government support for community rights and the enforcement of rules and regulations.

Due to emerging governance reforms in Cambodia, the project became involved in a multilevel dialogue at the national, provincial and community levels. With the support of the project team, Somthom villagers negotiated with the provincial and national governments to reduce the concession area for the community. In this way, they were able to retain their lands and forests.

Empowering communities to negotiate land and forest tenure

The project worked at two different levels, community and provincial. At the community level, rights awareness and empowerment were considered vital starting points because initial contacts with villagers showed they felt helpless to control the destruction of their forest and other resources. They were used to accepting orders from the military and provincial authorities. 'Go and talk to the big people in the province, they are the ones cutting trees, we don't know what to do.' This was a common response in Somthom commune when project team members started discussing the situation with locals.

This prompted the Seila/CARERE prrogramme to undertake a concerted effort to increase people's awareness and understanding of their rights under existing laws, with an emphasis on the fact that it was up to local communities to take actions to address these problems. Members of Somthom commune visited nearby Poey commune, where community forestry boundaries had been mapped to enable the community to prevent commercial logging in their ancestral forests. This practical demonstration showed Somthom community members that even powerful outsiders could be thwarted by community organization and initiative.

After seeing the experience of Poey, Somthom community members expressed a keen interest in working on resource management issues and in particular on the oil palm concession agreement. Villages identified their customary boundaries and the natural resources in them. Then they discussed their problems over these resources. The project team helped build upon the traditional experiences and management systems of the community by formulating management plans and participatory mapping processes. Sol Yuch from Somthom commented, 'As part of our plan we produced a map of our community. This map contains information on the location of fallow forests, spirit forests, agricultural land, streams, and lakes.' Also included on such maps were watershed forests (forest areas protected for drinking water supply), burial forests, village forests maintained as protection from strong winds and forests for non-timber forest product (NTFP) collection. Traditional elders, who are the custodians of the traditional knowledge and who counselled the community in all matters, played an important role in decisions about map features.

Computer-generated maps were produced using information gathered from community discussions and consultations with neighbouring communities. At the insistence of the provincial governor, a global positioning system (GPS) device was used to mark boundaries. Then, using their traditional resource management practices, the men and women in the communities formalized and shared rules to manage the forests and other resources, within identified customary boundaries. These rules included, for example, agreement that swidden plots are not allowed in the spirit forests and that growing more than 2 ha of cashew nuts per family would not be permitted.

All maps and regulations made by the community had to pass through the different levels of government officials. The community presented them first at the commune level, where the neighbouring communities had opportunity to comment, and any disagreements were resolved. They were then presented at the district level, and finally at the provincial level where different line departments and other stakeholders commented and agreed on the set of documents from the community. Finally the governor would sign the maps, rules and regulations endorsing these agreements.

When Somthom presented these documents at the provincial level the government requested the Provincial Conflict Resolution Committee to investigate the situation. The government observed that Somthom's situation involved clearly overlapping and contradictory tenure claims between the community and the concessionaire. Once the committee had verified the maps and traditional boundaries, the province called the two parties together to discuss the situation and come to an agreement. The land-use maps helped the community members explain that they needed the resources for their livelihoods, that they had longstanding customary claims and use patterns in the area, and also that most of the forested areas were rocky and infertile for oil palm cultivation. With the intervention of the provincial government, the community convinced the company that it was not worth pursuing their claim to the resources in Somthom except for the 200 ha they had cleared in 1996. The voluntary agreement of the concessionaire in this precedent-setting case was essential to a successful outcome. It could have been very difficult (and career-threatening) for government staff to force the concessionaire to give up this land.

The maps drawn up by the community were vital to building a convincing case. They showed outsiders and government authorities the boundaries, user areas,and resource management practices of the community. They also demonstrated to the communities that natural resources were not limitless (as in traditional worldviews). The process of publicly reviewing and discussing the maps, complemented by discussions on natural resource trends, built strong consensus within communities – including those community members who were identified as loggers – to protect increasingly scarce forest resources.

After producing maps and formulating the management plans, villagers began to implement them. If problems arose in managing their resources, they were encouraged to solve the problems themselves with minimal support from outside groups. This helped them think through their management strategies and build ownership of project activities. The communities carried out discussions and dialogues with neighbouring villagers and only when the situation was beyond the control of communities did the project staff step in.

To further strengthen community-based activities, communities formed natural resource management committees (NRMCs). These groups reported to the elected commune council and many of their members were also commune or village council members. The NRMCs provided assistance in mapping the community's customary use areas, formulating rules and regulations, and negotiating with neighbouring communities, provincial authorities and outsiders. The NRMCs were composed of elected community members and worked with the traditional elders who advised them. The NRMCs also assisted village authorities, established by the government, to make management plans for natural resources in their commune and ensure that NRM issues were included in their village and commune development plans.

Illiteracy in Khmer reduced the confidence of many indigenous communities. Through non-formal education (NFE) classes aimed at Khmer literacy, sponsored by the action research project, indigenous communities became more articulate. Study tours, drama, role-playing, exchange visits and NFE classes raised awareness and improved the skills needed for participatory planning. The project assisted villagers to travel to provincial or district government offices to engage in discussions with government staff. This allowed them to present their problems and argue their case themselves, and it built relationships so that officials also consulted villagers more frequently.

A continuing influx of people (immigrants and government staff) has exposed indigenous communities to new sociocultural influences. Cultural changes affect a community's social cohesiveness and its pride in its own cultural heritage, especially among the younger generation. By emphasizing the positive aspects of traditional approaches to NRM, the project helped to strengthen recognition and support for indigenous culture.

The community-based plans and agreements with the provincial government were not at first recognized at the national level because there were no legal procedures or instruments to support such activities. However, these planning instruments became quite effective at the local level. As well, other communities went through similar processes to stop outsiders from taking land and forests within their customary boundaries without first consulting community members. For example, in Tinchak commune government officials came and told the community members, 'Whether you accept money or not we will take the land, so it is better you take some money.' After a locally organized mapping process, when the same officials returned to take more land the community showed them the maps and the officials reconsidered their approach. The community had learned the power of using a formal tool (land-use plan and maps) to achieve its political objectives (more secure tenure).

While these agreements were being developed in the field, the national government began reformulating the land law. The CARERE team and NGOs in Ratanakiri realized that to legalize the rights of communities to use their natural resources they would have to lobby for indigenous concerns during the reformulation of this law. The Seila programme requested UNDP to hire a lawyer who would coordinate with the project at the provincial level and assist in drafting the new land law, focusing specifically on issues affecting indigenous people. The communities were involved in an iterative consensus-building process that allowed them to provide inputs to the formulation of the chapter on indigenous communities in the land law. In cooperation with NGOs and other international organizations, the project also ensured communities' participation in important workshops at the provincial and national level.

Similarly, meetings with key policy-makers, donors and community representatives were organized, creating a direct link and open discussion between policy-makers and villagers. Local leaders became increasingly articulate and confident in presenting their case, even to the extent of arranging a personal audience with King Sihanouk (Figure 3.3). A frank discussion between an indigenous villager and the king about sensitive policy issues was unprecedented. The project also hosted study tours for policy-makers during which communities could explain their situation on-site. For example, a second (or deputy) prime minister, Hun Sen, visited the scenic Yeak Loam lake in 1997, the commune where the earliest CBNRM activities had started. After presentations about the CBNRM's work, he promised that, as the most powerful politician in Cambodia, he would protect the lake and surrounding environment for ever (Reibe, 1999).

Figure 3.3   Indigenous representative meeting the king
Source: Yeak Loam Lake Management Committee, 2000.

Direct meetings of the indigenous people with policy-makers were found to be more effective than contacts mediated by NGO representatives or through other official channels. Policy-makers at all levels seemed to appreciate this, probably because it was clear that the indigenous people were speaking for themselves rather than telling the government what they had been primed to say by development organizations. These direct discussions also resulted in breaking down negative stereotypes about minority peoples that were widely held by national authorities.

As a result of the diverse efforts of this project, many other organizations and the indigenous peoples themselves, provisions for collective tenure and customary land use emerged in draft legislation. Later, the government began formulating other related legislation on forestry, community forestry and protected areas. The project used its field experience in Ratanakiri province to provide advocacy groups with evidence to lobby for indigenous considerations in these laws as well.

Building the capacity to decentralize

For negotiations between indigenous communities and government authorities to take place on more equal terms, awareness-raising and community empowerment had to be complemented by building the capacity of provincial institutions to decentralize resource management decision-making. The Seila local government reforms and decentralization processes provided an opportunity with enormous potential to influence the government's attitudes and their approach to working with indigenous people.

The province had to be first introduced to CBNRM as a practical approach. An opportunity arose when the province was looking for solutions for two practical issues. The first was the petition from Somthom commune (see above), which requested the Provincial Department of the Environment to help stop logging in their sacred forests. The second occurred in Ochum commune, where a floating weed was covering the hydropower reservoir, threatening the electrical supply to the provincial town. The CARERE team engaged with provincial agencies presented CBNRM as an option to try to tackle these problems. CBNRM activities were started as an experiment in three communes: Somthom, Ochum and Yeak Loam.[1]

The Provincial Department of the Environment became the lead agency in implementing CBNRM activities, with a provincial core team formed by technical staff seconded from different line departments. This team was trained in skills to carry out participatory land use planning (PLUP) and participatory rural appraisal (PRA) with communities. To support the provincial core team in the field, a commune core team was established, consisting of members selected from local NRMCs. As well, the project set up a supporting geographic information system (GIS) unit to assist the province develop computerized maps. The provincial core team assisted the communities to develop maps, rules and regulations and then set up workshops and meetings at which NRMCs could present them along with their case. It was this provincial core team that helped Somthom commune map its traditional user areas and then present them to the province and other parties. The director of the Department of Environment initiated the discussions on Somthom at the provincial level and was present at the negotiations between the commune, the plantation concessionaire and the government. Pleased with the results in the case of Somthom, the provincial authorities decided to spread CBNRM activities to all the communes in Ratanakiri.

The CBNRM activities were supported by awareness-raising for staff from other line departments. Awareness-building at the provincial level focused on helping the government understand the complexity of indigenous management systems and the rights of indigenous people. Sharing research results from this project and from other researchers (such as from national universities) with provincial agencies helped foster the understanding and appreciation of traditional resource management systems and the agricultural practices of indigenous communities. Such findings were also presented to national government ministry staff. The information was initially received with scepticism by professional staff with deeply-held assumptions about indigenous practices (and a Khmer paddy rice-based cultural background), but similar evidence from multiple sources helped change perceptions. This shift in attitudes was reinforced by direct discussions or meetings with communities and the presentation of resource management maps in the field.

Provincial government officials from the different line departments were also given training on good governance and management through the Seila programme. This introduced new understandings of the relationship between government and civil society. The intention was to help public officials shift away from the viewpoint that laws were intended for government to control society, towards an understanding that laws are intended to help people live together in a mutually agreeable manner. As stated by Hor Hong, director of the Provincial Department of Environment, 'We tried to set up protected sites before, but since the initiative only came from our staff, we failed.' Hong now strongly supports CBNRM and the implementation of community land management and mapping in Ratanakiri. This has earned him national recognition of a gold medal for these efforts.

Provincial line-agency staff came to see their role as more facilitation than enforcement, which represents a radical transformation. Facilitators were encouraged to conduct activities in a participatory manner and were rewarded with increased responsibility. Trust and transparency were important to all parties. The government was kept informed of all activities. Such transparency led to a better understanding of the project's work and eventually smoothed the process of obtaining official approval of local resource management agreements. The Seila principles (dialogue, clarity, agreement and respect) were crucial to this process.

Study tours for provincial staff were not always successful because some participants, who had few opportunities for travel and recreation, tended to prioritize enjoyment over learning. But senior provincial officials and their staff were committed to these reforms. They were compelled to present, defend and explain the project many times during workshops in the province or Phnom Penh (the national capital), and to many visiting delegations. Their preparation for such presentations served to consolidate learning and policy rationales for the CBNRM innovations.

Provincial-level government agencies work under the Provincial Rural Development Committee (PRDC) as part of the decentralization experiment. This body, consisting of the heads of each provincial line department, oversees and coordinates all administrative matters in Ratanakiri. It also takes joint responsibility for any decisions made, which has helped to curb compartmentalized and sectoral thinking. The PRDC was strengthened as part of the government's decentralization efforts. One of the more important issues they dealt with was providing tenure security to indigenous communities. The PRDC also gained credibility and authority over the line departments after receiving external funding through the Seila system. Provincial line budgets were also reviewed to help departments plan their activities in accordance with PRDC priorities for Ratanakiri, rather than wait for instructions from their respective funding ministries in Phnom Penh.

The CARERE project worked with provincial line departments and with the PRDC to develop procedures and tools for implementing CBNRM. The process required a joint learning approach with communities so that they could map their traditional resource use areas and formulate rules and regulations for managing the resources. These procedures had to be accepted by the PRDC before they could be implemented. The procedures allowed all levels of government to comment on the rules and regulations, which were finally signed by the provincial governor. It was clear to all that the community had the right to accept or reject suggestions that were inappropriate or did not conform to their local practices. One study (Ironside and Nhem, 1998) points out that, although the groundwork for community participation had been laid, the work started in the middle of massive forest exploitation. Therefore, the political landscape was not conducive to rapid or definitive NRM reforms. Given the importance of natural resources in Ratanakiri and the vested interests around them, it took time to negotiate these changes.

In 1998, the Seila local planning process for decentralized rural development, which the PRDC followed, showed some serious deficiencies in Ratanakiri. Communities were not including NRM considerations while formulating their commune development plans. For example, in Somthom commune, while the forests were being logged and land taken by the company, the community's annual development planning and budgeting process addressed only schools and health centres. The CARERE project began to assist the PRDC to change the Seila planning process to include natural resource considerations as a priority in their planning efforts. As in many development projects, even under decentralized decision-making it is often easier to build physical infrastructure such as schools than to tackle issues that may imply changes in legislation or require complicated negotiations with the provincial government. The revised planning process allowed communities to raise natural resource issues as part of routine local planning, and required the provincial agencies to respond to such priorities through a government-sanctioned planning process. This allowed Somthom and other communes to include NRM activities in their commune plans in 1999, thus legitimizing resource management activities at the commune (local government) level.

The inclusion of local natural resource issues was a dramatic reform because it stepped into an area that was highly controversial. Up until that time there had been no legal recognition of the traditional rights of indigenous communities over land and forests. All land and forests belonged to the state, therefore, if the government so desired they had the right to give these resources to anyone and all Cambodian citizens had the right to procure land anywhere. Loss of traditional land or forests was not an issue. As part of the inclusion of NRM issues in the local planning process, communities began to focus on the loss of their traditional rights to forests and lands. Once the governor began to approve these local development plans, the government accepted the threat to these rights as an issue. And, once it was officially on the agenda, NGOs and departments could legally assist communities attempting to regain their traditional rights. This paved the way for mapping traditional user areas and developing management plans based on traditional management systems in any community that requested legitimization of their traditional rights. Once these maps and plans were endorsed by the province, they gave the community the right to deny outsiders access to their traditional resources.

The other area where the team helped the PRDC develop procedures was conflict resolution. It became clear early on that conflict resolution was an integral part of CBNRM, especially during boundary demarcation. Land grabbing and illegal or even legal encroachment were common and the resulting conflicts had to be addressed. An important example of this was Somthom, where the resolution of the conflict surrounding the concession paved the way for further community-based NRM activities. The team assisted the PRDC in setting up the Provincial Conflict Resolution Committee whose mandate was to investigate natural resource conflicts, including land grabbing by government officials. When one very senior provincial department director began to expand the boundary of his 50-ha plantation each year by 5–10 metres, complaints from the community led the committee to investigate the issue. The director ended up apologizing to the community, blaming his workers for this problem, and relocated the fence to its original boundary. The conflict resolution committee thus dealt with conflicts that traditional systems could not handle.

Through this action-learning cycle of observing, learning, planning and implementing, PRDC confidence in and support for CBNRM activities increased. As Phan Phirin, chief of the executive committee of the Ratanakiri PRDC, stated, 'Compared to the lowlands, Ratanakiri is still rich in natural resources. I think CBNRM can help protect these natural resources and prevent them from being destroyed further. It is especially important that community members are involved in the project. CBNRM is very important for Ratanakiri.' This new-found confidence allowed the provincial government to host workshops with NGOs at provincial and national levels where different ministries discussed and began to understand issues and clarified the interpretation of laws. This was a significant development at the time because new laws were being created such as the forest law, community forestry sub-decree and land law, which acknowledged indigenous rights and the rights of communities to manage their resources. However, the ministries each wanted to claim their share of resources, so there were frequent conflicts of interpretation between different laws.

It is important to have new laws and policies endorsing both indigenous peoples' and resources' rights. However, many ministries work in isolation and interpret the laws to suit their needs. This leads to considerable tension over how to actually implement new policies at the provincial level.

Thus, in one workshop a representative of the Forestry Administration said, 'According to the Forest Law, the Commune Council has no right to manage forests. This right can only be obtained through a Community Forestry Agreement.' The representative from the Ministry of Interior stood up and emphatically stated: 'I would like all of us to look at the newly formulated

Commune Council Law which states: The Commune Council plays the main role to protect natural resources in the commune. They are the lowest government administrative unit, and therefore, all line departments must strengthen the commune councils to be able to do this.'

Both sides agreed to discuss this further with their respective department or ministry and then respond to provincial authorities. Sometimes the provincial government can do little until national agencies work out their differences. But the open discussion of issues and the creation of opportunities for CBNRM, both in policy and practice, would not have been possible at all just a few years earlier.

Networking

CBNRM is a holistic process requiring multisectoral and multilevel interaction. Therefore, the research team, together with local counterparts in the different line ministries and community groups, linked up with government officials, NGOs and international organizations working in different sectors and levels. Without such networking it would not have been possible to achieve positive results. These other organizations could raise sensitive issues which affect indigenous people's lives with different audiences from those that the researchers could approach. The CARERE team also realized that what had started as a single-action research cycle began to spread into different areas that initiated valuable research cycles in other communities.

These different approaches enabled the government to help deal with the problems it encountered in decentralized NRMs. For example, the national government granted a logging concession known as the Hero Forest Concession, which inadvertently included an important sacred forest area of one community. Together with a number of NGOs, the Seila project organized a provincial workshop where NGOs raised the issue of logging in the sacred forests of indigenous people. This led to a provincial study to identify and demarcate the sacred forests in the concession area and a prohibition of logging in such forests.

This networking required the research team to maintain good relations with both government and NGOs. But trying to balance between the divergent expectations of NGOs and the government was often very difficult. Our group sometimes felt like meat on a chopping block – but with each success, our confidence in the work grew.

The work of NGOs in empowering communities is often more effective because they have highly motivated staff who worked closely with a small number of the communities. NGOs also have the choice to select staff in accordance with their mandate and ability. Our job was to help the government work with a large number of communities testing CBNRM methods in collaboration with line agency staff. Government staff tend to mechanically apply processes and tools through existing administrative structures. In such a project context, project leaders are often unable to select the participating government staff. However, in the long run, because the processes and tools

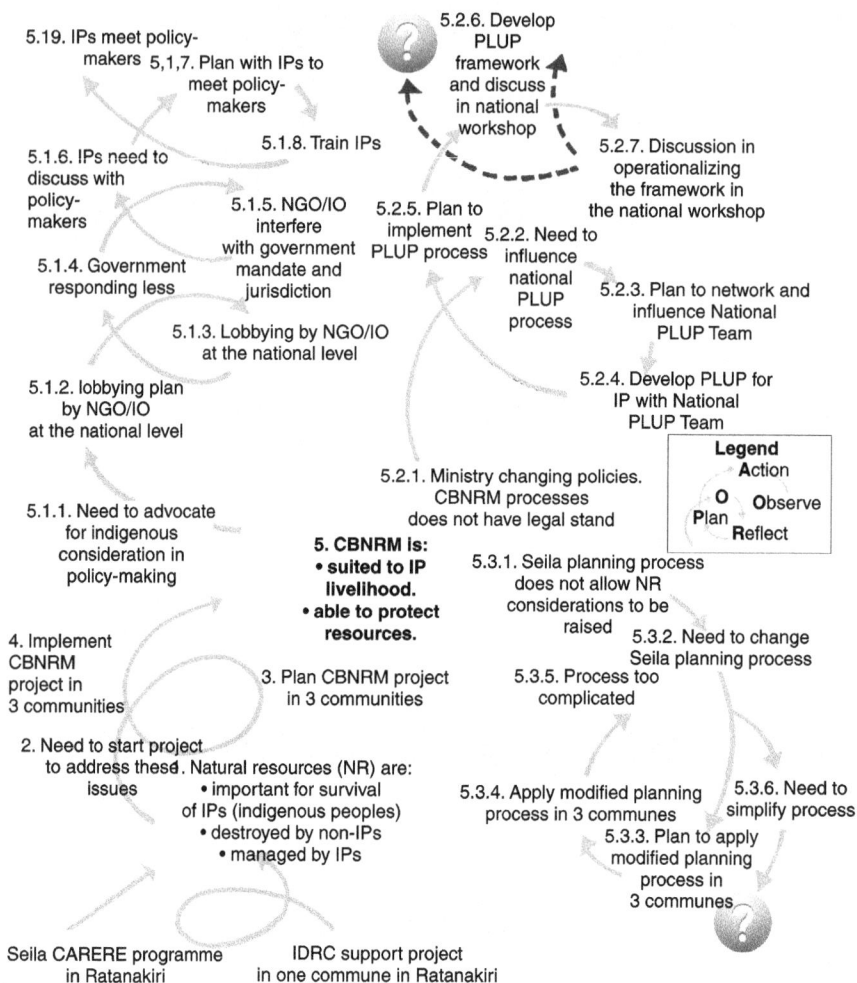

Figure 3.4   CBNRM action research in Ratanakiri (shows action research is not linear but keeps on spreading).
Source: Adapted from Kolb, 1984.

developed by CARERE for implementing CBNRM were matched to the conditions and problems of the provincial agencies involved, they were easier to replicate within the government system. That this has worked is borne out by the fact that lessons and approaches learned in the Ratanakiri CBNRM project are now being scaled up in other provinces under a Seila NRM mainstreaming project.

Role of the research project in a changing institutional landscape

While there was a broad engagement of government and NGOs regarding indigenous rights in Ratanakiri, there was a marked difference in the experience of local planning and negotiations supported by NGOs and those supported by the Seila project team. Communities supported by NGOs were found to be more confrontational in their dealings with the provincial government and less willing to come to terms with it. The government was more willing to deal with communities assisted by Seila, because the negotiations were conducted in accordance with the Seila principles by both sides, and because government staff were themselves involved in project training and implementation.

The merging of the UNDP service delivery governance reform project (Seila) with an action-research project (the IDRC-supported research) brought about an unusual blend of approaches. The Ratanakiri project became a research project to develop innovative procedures to strengthen governance for indigenous people. The processes were designed to suit local needs, and to deal with NRM in a participatory manner. Many other donor activities supported this effort, but the research project played a leading role in several key elements:

- identifying indigenous resource management practices and tenure arrangements to be included in draft legislation dealing with resource tenure, and ensuring these issues were kept on the agenda of policy-makers;
- developing procedures to delineate resource tenure (e.g. the PLUP process for indigenous people), which respected customary rights; and
- delivering evidence and training for government officials to build recognition and respect for the traditional rights of indigenous communities;

The provincial government also actively supported indigenous civil organizations such as the Yeak Loam Lake Management Committee, the Natural Resource Management Network and the Highlanders' Association in Ratanakiri, which all worked to improve the conditions of indigenous people. On some occasions, the provincial government went so far as to provide financial support to these bodies for specific activities. The relationship was ruffled many times by disputes, but these situations helped build respect (e.g. the politically embarrassing issue of the governor's expanding fenceline, above). Overall, the provincial government became more responsive, open and accountable to indigenous communities in the province.

At the local level, communities now had legally recognized maps, rules and regulations that they could use to prevent land sale or the extraction of forest resources. The understanding of resource rights became so widespread that even some communities without CBNRM project activities intervened to prevent outsiders from using their forests. For example, in Chaung commune, local people confiscated chain saws from the military, returning them only after negotiating an agreement that the military would no longer enter their forest lands, even though they lacked the legal force of a recognized local land-use plan.

Challenges

The success of Somthom commune in gaining recognition of traditional resource use and management rights from provincial authorities was a historic moment for Ratanakiri. The provincial government has now replicated CBNRM processes in 20 other communes and is planning to apply them to the whole province. However, with this experience, further challenges have emerged. Simply granting the right to a community to manage its resources does not guarantee that traditional management systems will work in an environment experiencing enormous pressures. Not all communities and individuals can sustain an interest in traditional practices, especially in the face of a changing landscape with multiple and contested interests. For example, in recent years cashews have become a golden crop in Ratanakiri and many indigenous farmers are planting their shifting cultivation forest lands to cashew trees for the higher income these provide. This rapid conversion from shifting cultivation to cashew plantations leads to complicated tenure changes. Whereas shifting cultivation forests were once recognized as community property that could not be alienated, recent trends indicate that this may not be true in the case of cashew plantations. Some individual swidden plots are taking on more of the character of a private property and are sold to outsiders. There are concerns and conflicts within communities about such complicated issues, which pit the rights of individuals to claim private ownership against the rights of the community to protect forest-based livelihoods. Table 3.1 summarizes some of the challenges in implementing CBNRM more broadly in a larger number of communes.

Furthermore, even in communes where CBNRM processes were strong, there are continuing conflicts over the enforcement of local management rules and boundaries. More robust procedures and adaptation are needed to deal with diverging local interests. To assist communities in dealing with these problems internally, the project is working with NGOs and international organizations to establish a provincial Natural Resource Management Network consisting of different commune NRMCs. This network should bring greater mutual support and coordination of resource management activities while providing background support, such as communication materials in local dialects and legal extension information about rights and regulatory reforms A bigger challenge, however, is that some national agencies now question the validity of the provincially negotiated resource-management agreements. Recent regulatory changes put the responsibility for community forest planning, for example, within the Ministry for Agriculture, Forestry and Fisheries. But in Ratanakiri, it has been the Department of the Environment which has led the integrated PLUP and CBNRM activities, and facilitated approval of local resource management plans. Inter-agency disputes at the national level now require additional political effort to resolve.

The Ratanakiri project team, still engaged with local governance reforms and CBNRM research, has also had to reassess emerging policies and leadership at the national level in order to collaborate with agencies that are most likely to

Table 3.1 Challenging situations in various communes

Commune	Situation	Issues
Kalaeng	Has gems that attract many outsiders, i.e. Khmer, Vietnamese, Korean business people and poor gem miners (migrant labourers).	Economic value of the gems outweighs the value of protecting the forest or supporting ecotourism, i.e. NRMCs are involved in selling parts of their land to business people because of its high economic value.
Yeak Loam	Three villages have lost most of their traditional lands with the rapid expansion of nearby Ban Lung, the provincial capital. Villagers face intense cultural and social pressure (proximity to Khmer culture) to change their ways. Needs are constantly changing, in part due to the proximity to markets. Moreover, social cohesion has weakened as people now sell their labour.	One village whose land the other two villages were forced to use tried to tax the other two villages. Although this issue was solved with project facilitation, tensions continue. Also, the committee cannot prevent villagers from selling land to outsiders, which places greater pressure on remaining land for local use.
Ochum	Many indigenous people have come from other parts of Ratanakiri to live in Ochum commune. Many are government workers, i.e. military and police. Absentee ownership of agricultural land has been introduced for the first time.	These people are normally interested in their own plots of land and not in their collective resources and surroundings.

be able to implement the innovations arising from the research work (e.g. PLUP for indigenous peoples, developed in 2004 for implementation by the Ministry of Land Management, Planning and Construction).

After decades of displacement and conflict, and with the widespread reform of all the mechanisms of governance and public administration, the national government is now attempting to classify and formalize public and private tenure for all land resources. To do this, they will use the PLUP process. But there are concerns that the identification of land-use categories locally will also identify the jurisdiction of line departments with respect to different land-based resources. The division of resource jurisdiction could have severe implications for implementing local land-use plans, which have already been approved in Ratanakiri and other provinces for lands that are managed locally as common property based on customary arrangements. Separate line agency jurisdiction over different resources (forests, water, fisheries, agriculture, etc.)

inevitably overlaps in the decision-making of users on the ground, making planning and management interventions very difficult to coordinate.

One option is to secure communal (collective) title for land resources. According to Article 25 of the land law, 'indigenous communities can own land communally under a communal land title', but there is little guidance for how communal titling should work in practice, and what procedures should be used for the registration and enforcement of communal land rights. Seila staff are using the research team's CBNRM experiences to guide research, analysis and feedback to the formulation of the national regulations on communal land titling. This will require addressing many legal ambiguities in the current legislation.

With this in mind, the national level government requested the Seila programme in Ratanakiri to assist in working with indigenous people on piloting the communal land titling processes. Seila staff are using the research team's CBNRM experiences to guide activities which will provide analysis and feedback on the formulation of the national regulations' sub-decree on communal land titling.

The main problem for piloting remains precisely how to interpret the laws at the local and community level. For instance, the Forest Administration interprets the legislation to mean they have exclusive jurisdiction of all forest lands, whether they have trees on them or not (i.e. including fallow forest), while others disagree.

Gains

Although this chapter has pointed out some of the challenges in working on CBNRM, significant gains have also been made beyond Somthom.

At the grassroots level, communities were able to reduce land grabbing and illegal resource exploitation, such as logging, unmanaged collection of NTFP (fruits, medicinal plants, building materials and wildlife) and illegal fishing methods such as using explosives to catch fish in streams. Communities also include natural resource issues in the commune development plans, to which government departments are required to respond and which also provide a good starting point for support by NGOs. Because the government demonstrated it could play a constructive role in helping solve some of the communities' problems, the communities in turn began to put more trust in the government. At the same time, because communities have a better understanding of their rights, they question or complain to higher authorities when laws are broken or proper procedures are not followed.

At the provincial level, the government is more willing to tackle issues faced by indigenous communities, even when this involves politically sensitive issues such as limiting forest concessions. Provincial technical and line department staff have begun to appreciate the resource management systems of indigenous communities. They have the confidence to recognize and hand over management rights to communities, as demonstrated by the fact that to date the PRDC and provincial governor have officially recognized the land-use and management plans of 15 communes.

Provincial officials now listen with more respect to indigenous people when they raise issues. This is a huge shift from the experiences of just a few years ago, when indigenous spokespersons would be humiliated when they spoke publicly because of their limited command of the Khmer language. The provincial government is now more open to discussing laws and legal instruments and even invites the officials at the national level to clarify contradictions, rather than waiting for a national initiative. In addition, it has been active in promoting a uniform interpretation of legal reforms and supporting legal extension services to help indigenous communities know what their rights are. In several cases, the provincial conflict resolution committee has investigated land grabbing by high-level provincial officials and helped both sides come up with a negotiated agreement. Land grabbing and extortion continues in Ratanakiri, but the innovations piloted through action research and adopted by the provincial government have greatly reduced the number of such experiences.

Officials from other provinces who have visited Ratanakiri have appreciated the provincial government's achievements. In one example, after a visit to Ratanakiri, the provincial governor of the neighbouring province of Mondolkiri sided with an indigenous community in his own province when it complained that a community member had sold communal land to outsiders. The sale was ruled illegal, based on the precedent of indigenous collective tenures in Ratanakiri, and the land was returned to the community.

Another outcome of the work has been that provincial authorities are now more tolerant of NGOs and international organizations. Having seen in practice that their support is sometimes valuable, government officials have become more responsive to issues raised by such groups.

At the national level, the research team in Ratanakiri has established strong links to many agencies involved in local government, resource legislation and tenure reforms. The experiences of participatory land-use planning in Ratanakiri have become widely known in the country, and are serving as models for both the Ministry of Land Management and Urban Planning, as well as the national Seila programme. The issue of communal resource tenure and management remains controversial. Future developments will depend to some extent on the resolution of contradictory interpretations of recent legislation. Finally, the policy for indigenous people has been drafted and is being negotiated by different line ministries and departments.

Conclusions and lessons learned

The confidence to make decisions based on good evidence, without consulting national superiors, enabled the provincial government to challenge the concessionaire and support land and forest rights in Somthom commune. In 2000, the provincial governor endorsed the community maps and NRM plans for this commune. Since then, the villagers have used these plans to help them solve other conflicts, including preventing the military from entering their forests. The success of Somthom has been replicated in many other communes in Ratanakiri, and has led to a dramatic change in attitudes, procedures, roles, and policies for the provincial government in NRM.

The crucial foundation of this success has been the action research work undertaken by the project team at the grassroots level. Testing innovations on the ground is essential to understanding complex and dynamic local situations, and to providing credible evidence to policy makers. Learning from innovative local practice is crucial to building the commitment of local, provincial and national governments and the capacity and confidence of communities themselves. With greater understanding and confidence, indigenous communities can explain their own situation to government policy-makers directly. The experience of direct dialogue was very influential in shifting attitudes and assumptions of senior government officials and politicians.

The project devoted substantial effort to networking with government and nongovernmental organizations, international groups and development donors. In an environment of rapid change in policy and governance contexts, the lessons from PAR in Ratanakiri provided timely and relevant evidence for advocacy. In some situations, the project members found that large international donors were supportive in raising issues and pushing agendas which the project or government staff could not. This greatly helped to ensure that national agencies could not skirt awkward issues.

The project was proactive in its approach. The evidence from the field showed the need for changes in local governance. But instead of waiting for national legal authority and regulatory frameworks to be designed, the project used its on-the-ground experience with innovative practices that influenced the design of the emerging legislation.

But this is a challenging working environment. Legal systems are in a state of flux and powerful government agencies are in conflict. Therefore, effective intervention requires a sophisticated and astute understanding of the local culture and political relationships, and of how to navigate in such murky waters. In these circumstances, flexibility to adapt and take advantage of emerging opportunities is important.

Over the life of the research project, there has been a dramatic change in expectations of the role of public services in Cambodia. Widespread governance reforms and the introduction of new democratic institutions, combined with accessible training programmes, have greatly altered the way in which public officials and citizens view the nature of government. The project staff were able to take advantage of these broader trends by providing Ratanakiri provincial officials with new models of professional behaviour based on consultation, public participation and official facilitation. They were able to instil a sense of responsibility towards improved NRM and the issues faced by indigenous communities. This resulted in communities being better able to control exploitation of the resources they traditionally used.

Reforms in Cambodia to make local government more representative, transparent and accountable are mutually supportive of CBNRM activities. Participatory resource planning and management at the local level needs to include not only rights, but also responsibilities and accountability from the community and provincial authorities. Proper sanctions should be in place to ensure that agreements are enforced and procedures followed by community members as well as public authorities at different levels. Public accountability and coordination were greatly facilitated in the Ratanakiri case by the engagement and support of the PRDC, which coordinated implementation by the line agencies.

Our experiences show that CBNRM is not easy and that it takes time and resources. Community empowerment is crucial to successful CBNRM, but at the same time, building the capacity of the government to decentralize and adopt new roles is also very important. CBNRM needs a coordinated multisectoral approach with networking and negotiation at different levels of government. NGOs and international organizations, as part of civil society, are important to counterbalance the power exerted by the government and to provide independent criticism if legal procedures are not followed.

The success of Ratanakiri in influencing national policy and spreading innovations widely in the province has depended on a harmonized approach that carefully balances the many different aspects of the work.

Acknowledgements

We acknowledge the contributions of other team members over the project's lifetime: Kim Srey, Kong Shronnoh, Hou Serey Vathana, Touch Tonet and Lun Kimhy. Others who played critical roles in this initiative but have left the project include Tonie Nooyens, Min Muny, Sang Polrith, Nhem Sovanna, Jeremy Ironside, Graeme Brown, Ken Reibe and Andrew McNaughton.

CHAPTER 4

Participatory local planning for resource governance in the Tam Giang lagoon, Vietnam

Truong Van Tuyen, Ton That Chat, Chau Thi Tuyet Hanh, Duong Viet Tinh, Nguyen Thi Thanh, Nguyen Thi Tuyet Suong, Le Thi Nam Thuan and Ton That Phap

Abstract

Indications of overexploitation and degradation of the rich natural resource base in the Tam Giang lagoon in Vietnam led to a long-term participatory research project to jointly investigate problems and potential responses. Local farmers, fishers and government officials joined the research team in a series of collaborative learning and testing interventions over a period of several years. This initiative generated a new understanding of the conflicts and degradation in the lagoon as they relate to changes in tenure and production systems. The participatory research led to a pilot implementation of a new model for participatory planning and resource co-management in the lagoon. This not only helped resolve conflicts and ensure a more equitable access to the resources, but also improved the prospects for better governance of lagoon resources in the future. Key to this achievement was a common understanding of the community-based natural resource management (CBNRM) approach developed among the stakeholders through the research project. The essential elements included the full engagement of local stakeholders (with emphasis upon marginalized groups), the recognition of customary access rights, and changes to the processes of local planning and resource governance, and to the organization and roles of the key stakeholders. The research team also adopted a new role as facilitators of learning, capacity-building and, more importantly, negotiation and consensus-building among the stakeholders. New locally organized user groups along with leaders of local government played a central role in empowering the community, providing legal support and organizing the implementation of joint plans. The officers of provincial and district government departments adopted a new role, providing technical assistance instead of giving direct instructions. Fishers and farmers participated in lagoon planning based on their improved understanding of problems, benefits and responsibilities, which grew from their ongoing involvement in the research. This chapter describes how participatory research led to innovations in natural resource planning and local governance in the Tam Giang lagoon.

Introduction

Application of a participatory approach to NRM in Vietnam attracted the attention of the government and others primarily because of the failure of conventional top-down measures. Improvements to livelihoods and resource sustainability in a variety of cases in Vietnam and elsewhere in Asia provide an indication of the effectiveness and applicability of participatory approaches (Ferrer, La Cruz and Newkirk, 2001). The participatory approach also provided researchers with a new way of thinking about research. It evolved into far more than the mere analysis of scientific data and technology. Instead, participatory research emphasized people and not things (Brzeski and Newkirk, 2002).

Participatory research has been carried out in the Tam Giang lagoon, Thua Thien Hue province, Vietnam since 1995 by an interdisciplinary research team supported by the IDRC and the Canadian International Development Agency (CIDA).[1] The support provided by the project helped the research team carry out fieldwork with several different communities, to understand the lagoon context and how global and national changes affected people's livelihoods. The application of participatory research was a response to the ineffectiveness of the conventional 'top-down' approaches of technical intervention in resolving problems in complex systems like the Tam Giang lagoon.

As a result of this research, the team and local people identified the fundamental problem as a lack of management control over lagoon exploitation. However, the tools, processes and strategies to deal with such a situation were neither available nor clear. The general opinion of key stakeholders was that any management approach would be ineffective. But this view was based on the failure of the prevailing mechanisms for local planning. These mechanisms were mainly imposed from higher levels of government without the involvement of local stakeholders, and without an understanding of the context and problems. This case demonstrates how research led to new mechanisms for participatory local planning in the Tam Giang lagoon.

> Everybody acknowledges how important the lagoon is. However, no one actually manages and takes responsibility for what happens there. All the different organizations (Communes, Districts, and Departments...) want to have rights, but that is all.
>
> N.L. Hien, Director of Fisheries Department, Thua Thien Hue province

The lagoon context and recent changes

The Tam Giang - Cau Hai lagoon is considered very important to the development of Thua Thien Hue province in general, and to alleviating poverty around the lagoon in particular. Of approximately 300,000 people living on and around the lagoon, many are poor and involved in fishing and aquaculture, or various agricultural activities along the shores. A living standards survey carried out in 1998 showed that the incidence of poverty in these communities varied between 55 and 70 per cent (Socialist Republic of Vietnam, 1999).[2] Approximately 100,000 people depend for their primary livelihoods on fishing and aquaculture, and many others depend on these as a secondary source of income. There are also an estimated 1,500 households living on boats in the lagoon (Vietnam, Department of Fisheries of Thua Thien Hue Province, 2003). These households are extremely poor and heavily dependent on aquatic resources for food and income, and their livelihoods are threatened by various factors, including a declining fish catch and difficulties in gaining access to fishing grounds (discussed further below).

The human and ecological significance of the lagoon extends beyond those people immediately involved in fishing and aquaculture. The lagoon is an important nursery area for inshore and offshore fish species, and thus indirectly supports the livelihoods of people living along the coastal area in the central part of Vietnam. The lagoons of Thua Thien Hue province, their ecological condition, and their capacity to support human development, are threatened by various activities (fishing, aquaculture, agriculture, tourism, transport, and industry development). However, few people in charge of lagoon management properly understand the context of its exploitation.

The 'Doi Moi' reforms, which mandated Vietnam's transition to a market-oriented economy, wrought significant improvements in poverty alleviation and resource management during the 1990s (Socialist Republic of Vietnam, 2003). However, socio-economic disparities also increased (Vietnam Development Report, 2004). One such policy reform that started in 1989 was the allocation of land to individuals. The land laws (1993) recognized legal private rights to the use of land, which had previously belonged exclusively to state enterprises and formal collective organizations such as agricultural cooperatives.

Although the central government still maintains legal ownership, it has issued certificates of long-term land-use rights, which were formalized and presented in the Red Book, or title, to certain legally defined individuals. (The Red Book is the local term for a certificate of title which passes with the land in transactions.) The Red Book, which indicates the purpose(s) of land use, defines the types of land to be allocated (e.g. agricultural lands) and those to be kept under state control (e.g. lagoon and fishery resources). However, recent patterns of lagoon exploitation have rendered existing guidelines on resource use largely irrelevant.

In recent years aquaculture has expanded rapidly (Brzeski and Newkirk, 2002). Fishers who had traditional access rights to specific areas of the lagoon,

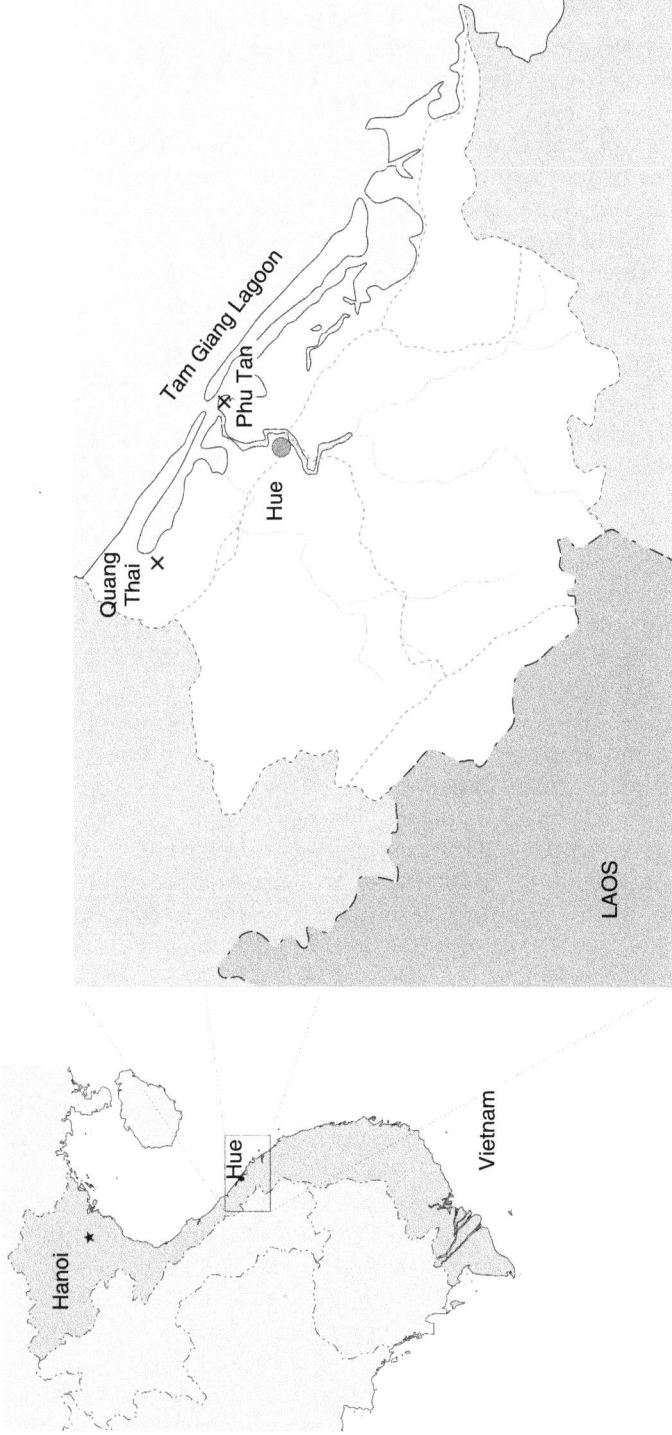

Figure 4.1 Map of Tam Giang lagoon

Box 4.1 Customary access to the lagoon and fishing-gear management

Traditional fishers in the lagoon are grouped according to the type of fishing gear they use: fixed-gear or mobile-gear. Each has different degrees of access to and control of the lagoon. The fixed-gear fishers have had access to specific areas of the lagoon for many years. The existence of the gear itself (including structures clearly visible above the water) indicates that the fishing ground has already been claimed, and that these fishers have exclusive rights to harvest from this area. The fixed-gear fishers collectively control access rights by limiting the number of fixed-gears or by rotating the grounds to ensure equitable distribution of resources among them. This practice may not apply to all types of fixed-gear, nor is the practice necessarily the same for all communities. (Tuyen, 2002)

In principle, mobile-gear fishers may fish anywhere; however, they must not impede potential benefits to the fixed-gear fishers or others using traditional fishing practices. For example, the fixed-gear fishers informally prohibit any fishing activity at the opening of their fish corrals during periods when tides or currents are most favourable for capturing fish. Mobile-gear fishing areas are open to any fisher with priority informally allocated to whomever actually was first to set their gear. Rather than compete, mobile fishers choose an unoccupied area to set their gear. These fishers do not limit their activities to their own commune boundaries, and, in fact, may be unaware of the commune boundaries. (Tuyen and Brzeski, 1998)

such as the fish-trap corral owners (see Box 4.1), have enclosed them with nets. In collusion with commune government representatives, they have been able to secure exclusive rights for aquaculture. Net enclosures and ponds have proliferated in the middle and south of the lagoon, while shrimp ponds and fish pens have rapidly expanded in the northern part. The number of households participating in aquaculture and the number of aquaculture facilities such as fish culture pens per household has also increased rapidly. This wave of lagoon privatization has reduced open-access lagoon areas and widened the disparity between those who have enclosed the lagoon and thus have easy access to lagoon resources, and those who have been excluded from their traditional fishing grounds. Small-scale, mobile fishers have become increasingly marginalized as resources have come under more direct control by the wealthier users or user groups in the community.

While small fishers have always had to compete with wealthier members of the village who own larger fishing gear, recent competition for lagoon resources has reached a scope and intensity never seen in the past. This is because of the sheer number of current users and the many ways in which they are now making claims on the lagoon resources.

The degradation of lagoon resources as a result of this indiscriminate and unplanned exploitation has resulted in declining average fish catches. The total annual fish catch from the river and the lagoon in the province decreased slightly from 3,099 tons in 2000 to 3,088 tons in 2003 (Statistics Office of Thua Thien Hue Province, 2003). However, information supplied by villagers showed that their individual fish catch for all major types of fishing in the north and

Figure 4.2 Illustration of dense net enclosures in the lagoon (drawn by Ariel Lucerna)

middle of the lagoon (except clam collection) decreased by 23–45 per cent from 2000 to 2003. Despite the evidence of increased fishing effort and pressure, small-scale private aquaculture continues to be encouraged by the government because of the high value of export products such as shrimp, crab and certain fish species.

The local government has expressed concern about these trends, but as with most problems, it has chosen to defer the solution to higher levels of government. Meanwhile, the latter has traditionally approached the management of coastal resources by promoting productivity-enhancing technology and capitalization of the fishing industry. Central authorities generally respond to local problems by implementing regulations at the district level without consultation or participation of the resource users, and without regard for the potential impact on the ecosystem. On rare occasions, external consultants and experts may be asked to propose solutions. There had never been an alternative approach to governance that involved the affected communities in a meaningful way.

Participatory research and outcomes

When the research project began in 1995, researchers were just starting to experiment with participatory methods. IDRC provided training on PRA, community-based coastal resource management (CBCRM) and gender sensitivity, among other tools and methods. PRA techniques were employed to get local people involved in assessing current use patterns in the lagoon, and in identifying problems and solutions. At this stage, the project focused mainly on the development of livelihood strategies.

The middle lagoon (Tan Duong village, Thuan An)

In the middle lagoon, the rapid and widespread expansion of net enclosures by fixed-gear fishers led to the marginalization of mobile-gear fishers, already the most disadvantaged group in the community. Hence, the participatory research exercise in this site was initiated to explore options for resolving this conflict. The researchers worked separately with the two groups of users, and then facilitated the establishment of a committee of local fishers, officials and researchers to oversee arrangements in the community. The committee organized the participatory mapping of current net enclosures, as well as the design of waterways on the basis of existing navigation lanes. The representatives also agreed upon the size (length/width) of the waterways after discussion and consultation with the local authority. However, new issues arose in the development of regulations governing the management of the widened waterways. Conflicts became even more heated when the net-enclosure owners refused mobile-gear fishers access to the waterways.

Without consulting the researchers, the commune government acted unilaterally, using police forces, to open the waterways using specific authority provided by a decision of the district government. This decision and enforcement borrowed selectively from the new community plan to open up the waterways at Xa Bac. For example, the community map of the waterway system was adopted. However, the commune government did not adopt any of the procedures for conflict resolution and livelihood provision, intended to increase the fishing area for mobile-gear fishers. After the waterways were opened, the commune formed the respective net-enclosure owners into groups and assigned them particular waterways to manage. There was no support given to mobile-gear fishers in accessing the opened waterways.

The old conflicts grew worse and violence erupted. The mobile-gear fishers had assumed that they would be given access in accordance with the participatory planning agreements, but the local government's unilateral directives meant they were kept out of the waterways by the net-enclosure owners. The latter argued that the opened waterway area was part of their own net enclosures and that the local government had made them responsible for managing the waterways. Therefore, they also had rights to the waterways as well as to the net-enclosure area. Finally, the two groups of users could not even meet to discuss or negotiate because of all the conflicts. The most urgent issue became how to strengthen the fishers' common values and restart negotiations.

Though the waterway conflicts in Tan Duong grew worse, the waterway plan emerged as one of the early examples of local co-management efforts, contributing to the reforms in the fishery law of 2003. The problems in Tan Duong highlighted the problems of the private allocation of the lagoon's surface area and these issues were publicized nationally. The lessons from this experience

Box 4.2   Opening waterways in the net-enclosure area of Tan Duong village

Members of the Government Fisher Joint Committee on Research (GFJCR) were nominated by participants at an open meeting of representatives of the fishing community and government officials. The GFJCR tried to design a plan for constructing the waterway network based on principles which guaranteed benefits to the community and individuals, while preserving a good environment for aquaculture activities, providing transportation and minimizing the consequent damage to aquaculture and aquatic life. Developing a waterway followed a three-step process.
1. Choosing a specific route as a pilot.
2. Trial operation to draw lessons while studying it, thereby assessing the strengths and weaknesses of the pilot route.
3. Applying the experience from the pilot to the establishment and preservation of the entire waterway system.

The GFJCR used three criteria to select a pilot route.
1. The fishers adjacent to the pilot route have a strong say in evaluating what works for the management of their production activities.
2. A key consideration when extending the pilot route is how to minimize any impacts on the cultured area and aquaculture activities.
3. The site is feasible for navigation.

After the analysis of the criteria and ranking of all the routes based on these criteria, the GFJCR chose Xa Bac waterway as the pilot site. The experience in self-management helped fishers to plan and to reach consensus upon where to develop the waterway, quickly and efficiently. Fishers and the GFJCR worked together in the field to identify and set up the route. The regulation for preserving the waterway outlined by the GFJCR and fishers' representatives of Xa Bac aquaculture group consists of five articles.
1. The waterway is considered as public property and a fishing ground for mobile-gear fishers. Those involved in net-enclosure aquaculture are prohibited from fishing in the waterway.
2. Mobile-gear fishers must not cause any damage to net enclosures or poach fish within the aquaculture areas. Anyone who breaks the law will not be permitted to continue fishing.
3. Any action expanding the aquaculture area into the waterway area will be dealt with by the fisher management committee. If a fisher breaks the regulations for a second time, the case will be dealt with by the commune people's committee.
4. The government is responsible for supporting the management committee to properly operate the waterway as well as cooperating to solve in a timely way any problems using this basic principle: 'Do not ignore any case for any reason.'
5. If disputes arise between fishers and the management committee, the commune police are responsible for security and dealing with armed threats or violence. Offenders will be charged and prosecuted.

Source: Phap, 2002.

were also helpful in the later Quang Thai efforts (see next section). It should be noted that the conditions in Tan Duong were more complex than elsewhere in the lagoon. Tan Duong was near the opening to the sea. It was more productive and, therefore, the intensity of exploitation was very high. As well, it was closer

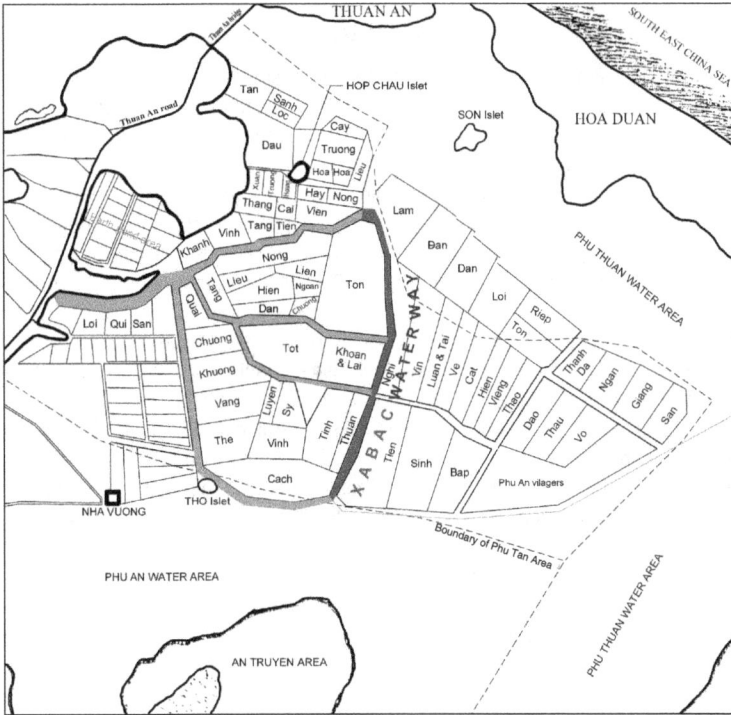

Figure 4.3 Map of aquaculture system and waterway in the Phu Tan area
Source: Phap, 2002.

to the city and more sensitive to market pressures. PAR was much more challenging in this situation. Moreover, with completion of the research in 2000, the local government tried to intervene without sufficient support from researchers and only aggravated the conflict.

The northern lagoon (Trung Lang village, Quang Thai)

Trung Lang village in Quang Thai commune is a mixed farming and fishing community that is isolated from market and administrative centres. The commune includes traditional boat-dwelling households which have decided to settle on the land in the past 20 years. This particular village was among the poorest in the commune. The research team became involved with Trung Lang village through the early promotion of peanut crop production in the village. The success in farm diversification built trust in and credibility of the research team among community members and in local government. This helped address the more conflictual issues related to the management of the lagoon (Brzeski and Newkirk, 2000).

   In the early stages of the research effort, the most critical issue in the northern part of the lagoon was the prevalence of electric fishing and failure to enforce

Box 4.3 Development of livelihood strategies in Quang Thai

Participatory research in Quang Thai started on a small scale by looking at crop diversification in a village with experienced and skilled farmers and good conditions for peanut cultivation (Trung Kieu village). Early successes in 1995–6 were widely adopted, and spread to the neighbouring village of Trung Lang, where many house-holds also practised fishing. Trung Lang had been perceived by local officials as too poor and backward to adopt innovations. In 1998 the research project supported a collaborative activity between the two villages to encourage the transfer of good practices and leadership skills, benefiting 150 households from all socio-economic levels.

A research study focusing on mobile-gear fishers sensitized local officials to issues of equity by pointing out that poor fishers lacked access to government extension and subsidies. The DoF provided aquaculture training and financial sup-port through incentive grants or low-interest loans. But only those who already had aquaculture ponds were eligible for loans and invitations to training courses. As a result, the mobile-gear fishers were effectively excluded. They had no facilities or resource tenure for aquaculture. Pilot efforts to introduce aquaculture training and low-cost fish-pen culture techniques to these groups convinced local officials that by strengthening local organization, supporting agencies could successfully deliver extension and credit services even to marginalized groups in the community (Tuyen, 2002).

an existing ban of it. The fishers used high-voltage electricity to shock entire schools of fish so that they could be easily harvested, but at the same time, they destroyed other aquatic organisms. A self-management committee was established at the village level to organize the villagers to patrol the lagoon. A mechanism for collaboration with local government security forces was also developed. The community ban had been enforced effectively to begin with, but broke down under threats of violence. In one incident, electric fishers from outside the community destroyed fish corrals and threatened the villagers who tried to enforce the ban. This pilot effort brought out important lessons for the local stakeholders about the need for collective action to prevent destructive fishing, and the importance of formal collaboration with local government.

Participatory research in Trung Lang specifically targeted livelihood improvements for the poorest after 1998. The team introduced poor mobile-gear fishers to techniques of raising fish in cages in the lagoon (cage aquaculture), and initially subsidized the capital cost of cages as a strategy for improving their incomes. As a result, fish cages owned by mobile-gear fishers began to proliferate near the shore, and larger fish pens multiplied in the deeper lagoon area. However, as the number of pens increased, conflicts arose because they competed for choice locations.

In 2003, the research team re-engaged after a hiatus of two years in the field research, to update stakeholders on the current situation in the lagoon and problems which could only be resolved through local planning. However, the local government seemed blind to both the conflicts among resource users and

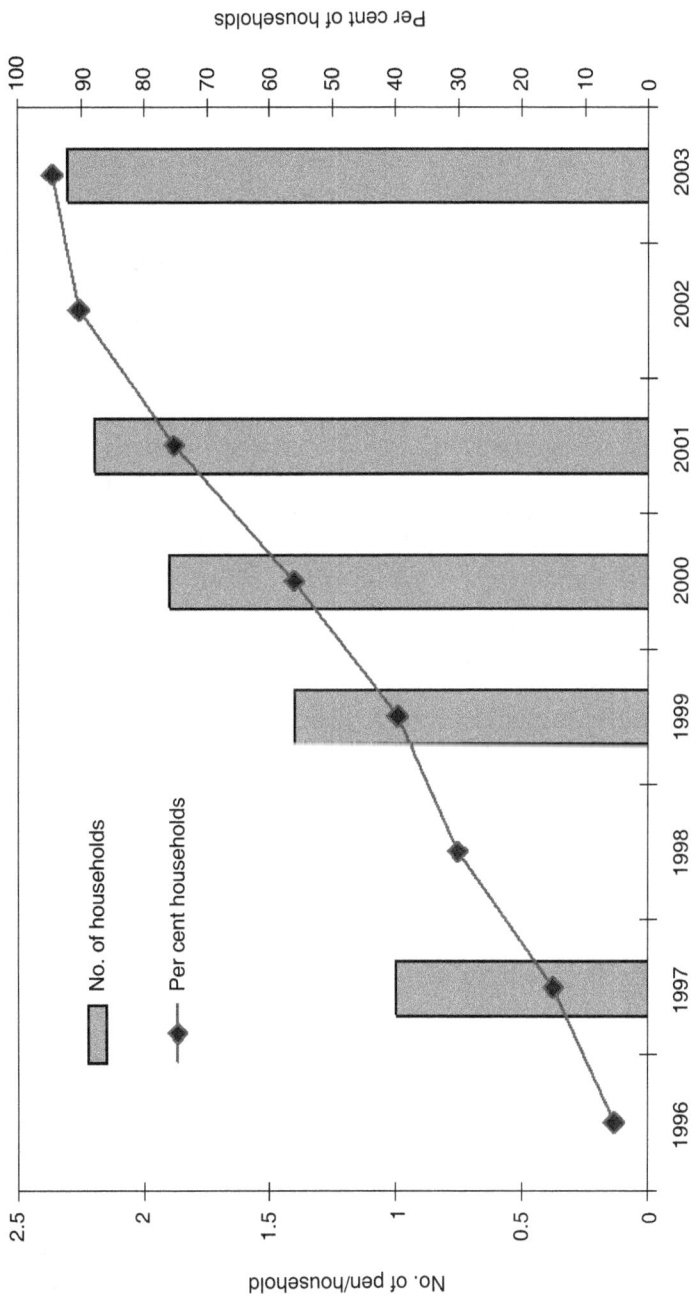

Figure 4.4 Trends of expansion of fish-pen culture in the northern lagoon

the negative environmental impact. This was probably because the prevailing national and local policy was to promote aquaculture with its high returns as being essential to the country's economic development. The growing harvest from fish pens persuaded the government of their efficacy as a pro-poor strategy, and there was little attention to the warning signs of lagoon over-exploitation. Officials assumed that the northern Tam Giang lagoon still had plenty of potential in terms of unutilized lagoon surface area, when compared with the more congested central portion.

An important finding related to aquaculture expansion was that a freshwater macrophyte (locally named *rong*), used as feed for fish-pen culture in the northern lagoon system, was being overharvested. The local people wanted to know the potential amount which could be harvested without damaging the lagoon ecosystem. *Rong* has a close connection with a key aquatic habitat for certain stages in the life cycle of valuable fish species. By providing evidence of this ecosystem link, the research team convinced the commune government that the expansion of fish-pen culture should be limited.

It was more difficult to build awareness of the decline of fishery resources in the lagoon, because summary statistics (which include commercial aquaculture) showed increases in aggregate production, so provincial government officials assumed there was no problem. The research team built its analysis on the villagers' local knowledge and adjusted data to reflect fishing effort, rather than aggregate landings, to illustrate how the fishery resources were deteriorating (see Table 4.1 above). Focus group discussions, however, suggested that the price of most species increased faster than the decline of the catch.

> We don't have to go to market to sell fish or shrimp. The middlemen buy at the boat with prices that are higher today than yesterday.
>
> Fisherwoman in Ha Cong village.

Fishers also explained that the decrease of fish catch was 'the reality of every household. It was due to electric fishing and motorized drag nets catching all kinds of fish of all sizes.' They acknowledged that they themselves used more effective fishing gear and spent more time fishing, too.

Government planning structure and fisheries policy reform

Vietnamese government structure is unified and hierarchical, including national, provincial, district and commune representatives and policy-making bodies. The district is the seat of formal public administration closest to the local level. District offices deliver public services and programming. They combine the responsibilities of several line agencies at the provincial and national levels. District offices are directly accountable to provincial departments, which receive technical and administrative guidance from central ministries and report back to the central government. So, for example, in Figure 4.5 we can see that the Ministry of Fisheries develops the overall national policy and provides regulatory guidelines to the provincial DoF.

Table 4.1 Changes in fish catch per fishing effort unit and income from fishing, 2000–3

Lagoon area	Type of fishing	# days practice/ (kg)	Catch/day 2000 (kg)	2003 (kg)	Difference (%)	Income/fisher/day 2000 (000 VND)	2000 (USD)	2003 (000 VND)	2003 (USD)	Difference (000 VND)	Difference (USD)	Different (%)
North of lagoon	Gill nets	122	2.7	1.8	-30.8	20	1.43	22	1.57	2	0.14	10.0
	Fish corral	253	2.6	1.6	-39.9	19	1.46	24	1.71	5	0.36	26.3
	Drag nets	143	10.2	7.2	-29.7	16	1.14	21	1.50	5	0.36	31.3
	Shrimp Push Nets	85	2.4	1.6	-35.4	15	1.07	16	1.14	1	0.07	6.7
	Tep Push nets	91	1.9	1.4	-23.5	12	0.86	15	1.07	3	0.21	25.0
	Clam collection	86	20.3	22.2	9.2	15	1.07	18	1.29	3	0.21	20.0
	Eel rakes	20	12.5	8.0	-36.0	55	3.93	40	2.86	-15	-1.07	-27.3
Middle of	Gill nets	159	2.4	1.7	-32.1	45	3.21	43	3.07	-2	-0.14	-4.4
	Traps (in net-enclosure)	322	2.8	2.1	-24.0	38	2.71	29	2.07	-9	-0.64	-23.7
	Fishing lights	67	2.2	1.7	-23.1	85	6.07	77	5.50	-8	-0.57	-9.4
	Nets (in net-enclosure)	209	3.6	2.0	-44.2	50	3.57	42	3.00	-8	-0.57	-16.0
	Drag nets	120	2.0	1.1	-43.8	22	1.57	16	1.14	-6	-0.43	-27.3

Source: Field data 2003

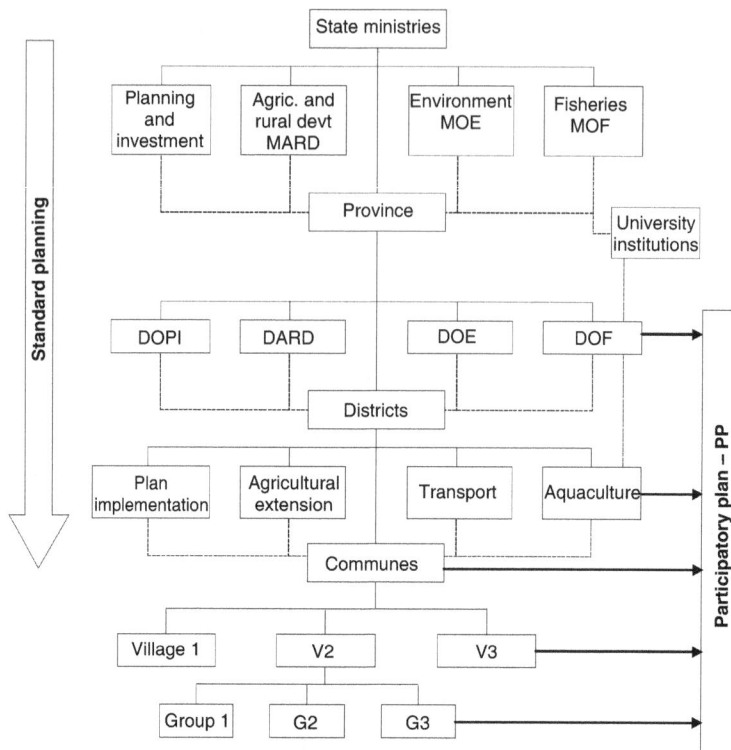

Figure 4.5 Government planning system in Vietnam

It is at the national level that planning requirements for the fisheries sector are determined. The content of fisheries sector plans is prepared by the ministry based on data from provincial agencies. At the provincial level, detailed plans are prepared on the basis of the national policy framework and planning guidelines from the ministry. The plans are approved by the provincial government and then distributed to the district so as to guide implementation. The process is led from above and includes sectoral plans from a wide range of ministries (including Fisheries, Agriculture and Rural Development, Transport, Trade and Tourism, Resources and Environment, among others.) The plans are implemented by district government staff, with the involvement of commune (local) government officers acting under the technical guidance of one of these line agencies. While there are obvious interactions between the sectoral plans when they are implemented on the ground, there is no mechanism to integrate them.

As part of the process of learning for policy reform, the earlier research project experiences in Tan Duong had been widely published and discussed among other research teams and with the Ministry of Fisheries, along with other donor-funded pilot projects. Reforms introduced in the fisheries law (2003)[3] were the government's way of acknowledging that the strategy of allocating resource tenure to households, which worked well in boosting the productivity of agricultural land, was not as effective in the fishery sector.

Instead, the government recognized the need for co-management approaches through which government authorities could work together with locally defined user groups to manage fishery resources. This policy change was implemented by the provincial government in Thua Thien Hue and was designed to develop user groups among local fishers (see next section).

Participatory planning for lagoon use in Quang Thai

Participatory planning for lagoon use was undertaken in Quang Thai two years after the pilot experience of opening the Xa Bac waterways in Tan Duong. The new planning process involved the steps as outlined in Figure 4.6.

In practice, these steps were not separate but integrated. Neither were they strictly sequential, but sometimes took place parallel to each other. Lagoon planning was initiated quite early and developed alongside the learning and awareness-building. Some implementation began while the planning was still in progress. At different levels (commune, village, and user groups), there were different emphases on learning, planning and action. The planning and action should be seen as an integrated process in which the learning was initiated first, followed by the planning. Initial actions were taken to provide a base for learning, further planning, and adaptation. The following sections describe more details of each step.

Participatory learning and awareness-building of lagoon context

Building awareness of the context of lagoon resources exploitation was combined with the application of PRA tools and participatory research processes. Semi-structured interviews were conducted for data collection and to develop a database to facilitate learning and awareness-building. As well, a series of focus group discussions was conducted. Local participants who were involved in the focus groups included core villagers,[4] village leaders and officials from state-sponsored people's organizations, such as the Farmers' Union and Women's Union. Local government (commune) officials were also involved in focus groups. Meetings and discussions were organized for officials and for the core villagers, both separately and together. The outcomes of the learning activities were a common understanding of the context of lagoon exploitation and the need for planning.

The research team supported participatory environmental education. They analysed the community communication network through a training workshop, which addressed the necessity and importance of two-way communication, and the development of information channels and participatory messages. The workshop participants themselves developed a programme for environmental education on lagoon resource problem-solving. Afterwards, the commune officers who were in charge of culture and communication led its

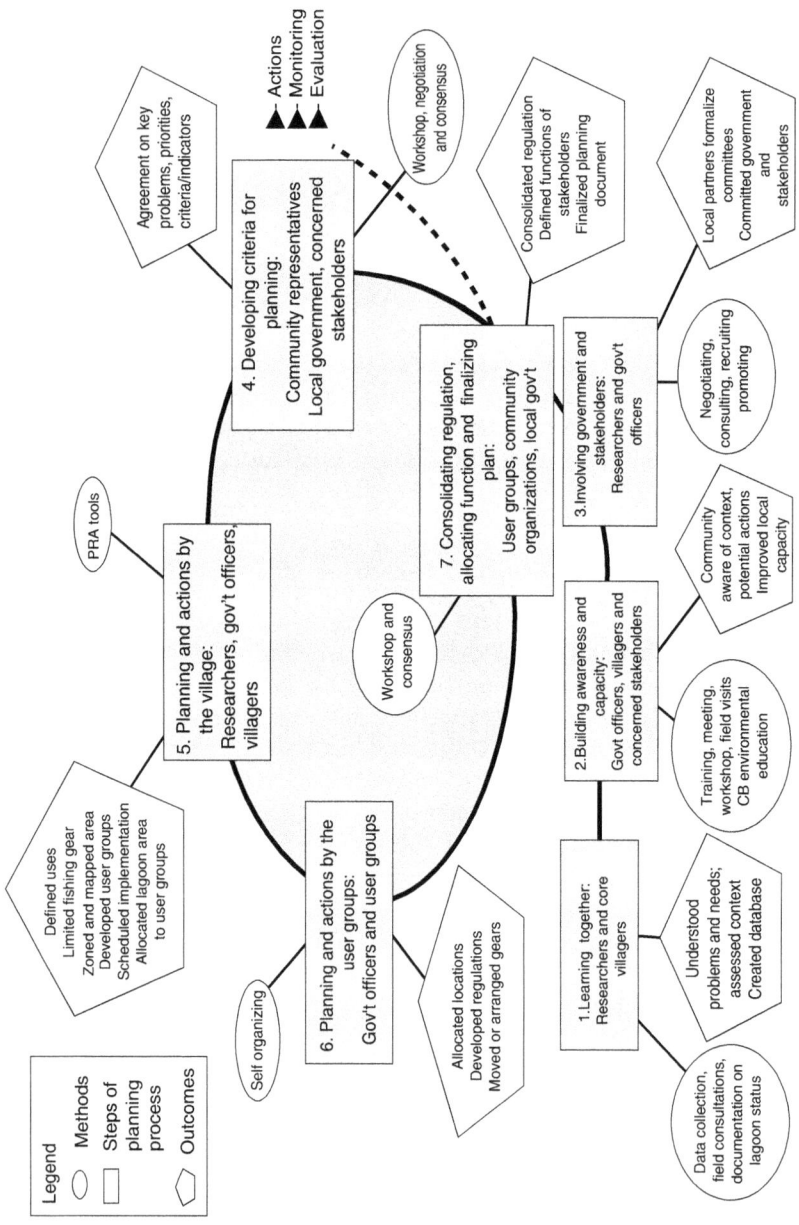

Figure 4.6 Participatory planning process for Quang Thai lagoon

Legend

⬭ Methods

▭ Steps of planning process

⬠ Outcomes

1. Learning together: Researchers and core villagers
   - Data collection, field consultations, documentation on lagoon status
   - Understood problems and needs; assessed context Created database

2. Building awareness and capacity: Gov't officers, villagers and concerned stakeholders
   - Training, meeting, workshop, field visits CB environmental education
   - Community aware of context, potential actions Improved local capacity

3. Involving government and stakeholders: Researchers and gov't officers
   - Negotiating, consulting, recruiting promoting
   - Local partners formalize committees Committed government and stakeholders
   - Consolidated regulation Defined functions of stakeholders Finalized planning document

4. Developing criteria for planning: Community representatives Local government, concerned stakeholders
   - Agreement on key problems, priorities, criteria/indicators
   - Workshop, negotiation and consensus

5. Planning and actions by the village: Researchers, gov't officers, villagers
   - PRA tools
   - Defined uses Limited fishing gear Zoned and mapped area Developed user groups Scheduled implementation Allocated lagoon area to user groups

6. Planning and actions by the user groups: Gov't officers and user groups
   - Self organizing
   - Allocated locations Developed regulations Moved or arranged gears

7. Consolidating regulation, allocating function and finalizing plan: User groups, community organizations, local gov't
   - Workshop and consensus

▲ Actions
▲ Monitoring
▲ Evaluation

implementation. Activities included broadcasting, meetings and seminars. The outcomes were important in sensitizing the community members and preparing them for the next steps in the planning process.

Involving local governments and developing community partnerships

The biggest challenge to the research team in preparing for the participatory planning exercise was to involve local government officials, because they were accustomed only to following central instructions. Therefore, adopting a new and participatory process required considerable learning effort.

The problems with the involvement of local government in participatory planning were twofold: without knowledge and skills, it was much easier to proceed in a conventional way; and there were no formal requirements or incentives to apply participatory planning instead of familiar methods.

The team played a crucial role in overcoming these barriers, using several strategies to accomplish change. The researchers prepared scientific evidence and technical data about resource degradation in order to justify local, participatory planning. Officials from the district and provincial departments of fisheries were informally engaged in cooperation on field activities, analysis and community meetings with the research team to build their confidence and familiarity with the issues. Special workshops were organized and targeted at local government officials in different agencies, to promote a shared understanding of lagoon resource management. Finally, the researchers played an important role in negotiating and facilitating discussions among the various different government agencies involved in the planning process.

The outcomes of these efforts to engage local government were very important in terms of learning for change. They not only made it possible for fisheries departments in the districts and provinces to get involved in planning, but also encouraged government officials to adopt new roles. For example, the team succeeded in getting officials to support community arrangements for opening the navigation space in Quang Thai rather than using the police to enforce a different district regulation. Officials were also persuaded to consider customary and current use rights in reorganizing the allocation of the lagoon area to fish corrals instead of imposing a bidding mechanism provided for in district policy.[5]

The research team was able to overcome the scepticism and suspicion of local government, and encouraged officials to undertake a completely new planning process in part because of the evidence and expertise the team had acquired in several years of prior research on lagoon exploitation and resource conflicts. Another reason was the strong relationships of trust and collaboration they had developed with the involved communities through participatory research. This experience built facilitation and communication skills in the research team, which were essential to the successful introduction of this new participatory governance process.

The involvement of research and government organizations with local village fishers and other resource users proved important in developing new local organizations. For instance, in responding to the fisheries policy reforms, the provincial government was forced to rethink its traditional strategy of allocating areas in the lagoon to individual households. Instead, they had to consider how areas could be allocated to groups of fishers. The problem was that local co-management groups were required to be legally established entities.

There are already a number of mass organizations, which involve most local residents in any village, such as the Farmers' Union, the Women's Union and the National Fatherland Front. These are sanctioned by the national government; however, they do not have the appropriate legal standing to receive resource title under the land law (1993). In a pilot activity, which was approved by the provincial DoF and the district government, a local Fishing Coalition was formally established and constituted as a legal entity capable of holding resource rights. Its members were the villagers who exploit aquatic resources in the lagoon. This new user organization developed a formal constitution addressing membership and procedures, and subsequently played a major role in planning lagoon resource use. An open registration process included all the fishing and aquaculture households, both fixed-gear and mobile-gear, the very poor and the better-off. Membership was defined at the household level, with representation normally by the head of the household, so the organization as constituted by local people themselves is dominated by men.

Another challenge for the research team was ensuring the meaningful participation of women and very poor households in the planning process. In the lagoon communities, women and men are both active in fishing and aquaculture. However, women are more involved in processing and selling products, as well as domestic and farming work (livestock) for additional income. Women from better-off households typically practise both fishing and aquaculture. They also have more opportunities to join in community activities since they have more financial security and spare time.

In the planning discussions, women were not very active and decision-making was dominated by men. The women from very poor households, some of whom practise only mobile-gear fishing, were even more difficult to reach. Men are assumed to represent the different interests in their households, in accordance with traditional practice, power relations in the family and social norms. While the research team has been successful from the outset at engaging even very poor households in the planning process to secure their access to lagoon resources, they also recognize that additional education and awareness-building are still needed to strengthen the representation of women's interests in the process. These activities are being developed as the new local planning procedure evolves.

Consensus on planning criteria

Planning for the allocation of the lagoon surface and access rights started with a stakeholders' meeting and workshop, which involved the participation of core villagers, the Fishing Coalition, the village leadership, the commune government, and representatives of district and provincial departments in charge of lagoon management. With the facilitation of the research team, participants reached consensus on the main problems to be addressed, the purpose and overall strategy, and the criteria for planning. The agreed purpose of resource planning was to reorganize fish-pen culture and fish-corral practices to provide space necessary for waterflows and navigation, as well as a base for improved administration (including registration, licensing and taxation) and more effective enforcement of the ban on destructive fishing. Specifically, the participatory planning aimed to involve the villagers as resource users in the following planning activities:

- determining the fish-pen culture zones and locating them in the local lagoon;
- defining the intended (maximum) number of fish corrals and locating the whereabouts of the fish corrals;
- locating and defining the lagoon space for the navigation lanes and water-way systems;
- community organizing to form appropriate fish-pen culture and fish-corral groups to facilitate community-based management; and
- developing local regulations for resource management based on input from user groups, the village and commune, and in accordance with provincial and district regulations on resource protection.

Three main priority considerations and criteria for planning were also discussed and agreed upon among different stakeholders:

- maintaining access to the lagoon for all current resource users within the local territory;
- respecting customary rights regarding fishing places; and
- sharing any dislocations required for the re-arrangement of lagoon areas.

Participants also agreed to take into account requirements for navigation and resource protection as defined in district and provincial regulations. Feedback from the community led to the consensus that it was difficult (or impractical) to enforce all these regulations fully. However, certain planning measures could be taken to reinforce their intent so as to satisfy the responsible agencies while these regulations were gradually replaced or updated.

Participatory planning and actions at the village level

The research team facilitated development of the plan, using PRA tools such as mapping, Venn diagrams and focus groups to involve the community in learning, generating ideas, proposing strategies and designing plans for lagoon use. The plan was developed in several stages, starting with a preliminary design at the village level and then detailed plans for fish-pen and fish-corral activities. These designs were drawn up jointly by the fish-pen owners and fish-corral owners, the researchers, commune officers and Fishing Coalition representatives. The separate draft plans for fish-pen culture and fish-corral practice were integrated and presented to a meeting of the whole village for review and feedback.

After a consensus among villagers was obtained, actions were taken to strengthen the resource user organizations. Villagers were registered based on the current locations, zones developed for pen culture and rows defined for fish corrals. This led to the formation of resource user groups. Lagoon demarcation was organized by the Fishing Coalition together with representatives from local, district and provincial government agencies. The local government and provincial departments provided technical and legal support through officials who witnessed the field activities. User groups constructed sites and demarcation posts in the lagoon. Meanwhile, the project team contributed consulting services and construction materials for the demarcation posts.

Through participatory planning and action, villagers accomplished several useful results.

- They specified what the number of fish corrals, pens and future limits should be. The community reduced the number of rows of corrals and increased the number of pens and pen zones. The participants defined these in a way that would not increase conflict with the current fish corrals but which would, instead, maximize production, taking account of the lagoon environment, such as depth and currents.
- They defined both the types and number of resource user groups. This was aimed at promoting cooperation among the resource users. All current owners could join in the corral groups and each group would correspond to one row of corrals. However, no new fish corrals or users would be permitted. Meanwhile, all current owners of fish pens could join the pen groups, each corresponding to one pen zone. Newcomers were eligible to join the new zones to be designated.
- They located and designed navigation lanes and waterway systems.
- They defined pen-culture zones, fish-corral rows and waterway systems (using concrete markers in lagoon).
- They mapped all pen-culture zones, fish-corral rows and waterway systems for monitoring.
- They dismantled and removed pen zones and fish corrals in designated navigation areas.

Participatory planning and actions among the resource user groups

All households that practised fish-corral and fish-pen culture were registered with their respective user groups. This guaranteed them access to the lagoon, provided collective protection of their gear and resolution of pollution issues, and brought external and government support, such as extension services.

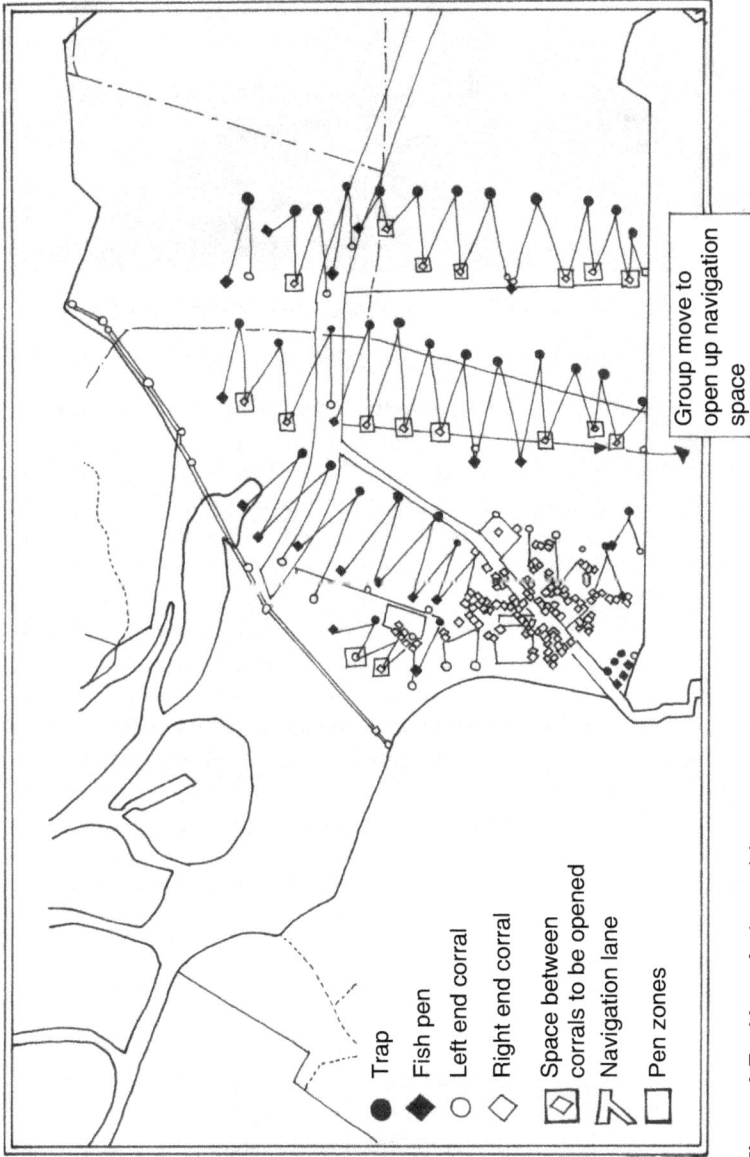

Figure 4.7 Map of planned lagoon use

Trap ●
Fish pen ◆
Left end corral ○
Right end corral ◇
Space between corrals to be opened ⬖
Navigation lane
Pen zones ▭

Group move to open up navigation space

Figure 4.8   Demarcating the pen zones, fish-corral rows and navigation space in Quang Thai lagoon

About 90 per cent of the total 150 households of the village participated in the user groups. The size of each fish-corral group varied from 7 to 15 households, while members of pen groups varied from 17 to 35. There was no specific user group for mobile-gear fishers. However, most of these households participated in the fish-pen culture groups because they practised both mobile-gear fishing and pen culture.

Actions at the resource user group level were led by group leaders who were elected by the respective user groups. They started by designating the location of gears in their allocated zone. For example, the proposed number of rows of pens, the direction of the rows and the space between them were all intended to optimize water current flows, protection and management practices. Places in the pen zone were allocated to group members randomly after the number of pens had been registered. Pens of group members in the allocated zones were then moved and rearranged, and the new locations mapped. In addition, other group regulations and agreements on gear establishment and management were developed. Additional measures for group management and cooperation were still being formulated as this chapter was being written.

Consolidation, monitoring and follow-up

The Fishing Coalition facilitated and reviewed group arrangements, the allocation of locations and places, and the development of regulations. It also coordinated among groups to schedule the moving of pens. Decision-making on user fees and mode of collection, budget management and capital development was remanded to the user groups. The Fishing Coalition has recently developed measures including charging higher fees for people who set up pens outside the designated zones. As long as pen culture is still allowed to expand, newcomers need to be organized in new zones yet to be designated.

Systems for local planning, enforcement, monitoring and reporting are being developed. A continuing role of the research team is to provide technical support and facilitation for a participatory monitoring mechanism with the people of Quang Thai. Its other important roles are identifying means and processes to strengthen local roles in planning processes both at the district level (scaling vertically 'up' in the government hierarchy) and in neighbouring communes (scaling horizontally 'out'). Some preliminary steps have already been taken.

The team is now preparing for planning in Quang Loi, the commune next to Quang Thai. It is also exploring with officers of Quang Dien district and the provincial DoF how to conduct the vertical scaling-up process.

The emerging model for participatory local planning

The new participatory planning process in Quang Thai was not predefined either by government officials or by the research team, but emerged from interaction among resource users and other concerned stakeholders. The process is still evolving as all stakeholders continue to learn from experience and make adaptations. As the research project continues, the research team will reinforce this process of iterative action, learning, planning and adaptation. Figure 4.9 presents the most important features of the emerging local planning process.

Innovative elements of participatory planning

Participatory planning in Quang Thai emphasized the importance and urgency of NRM at the local level. It also succeeded in resolving some of the problems and conflicts that it was supposed to address. This was a dramatic change from the previous planning mechanism. The process tested concurrent planning and implementation, built on local knowledge, organized resource users, assigned responsibility and management authority to user groups and created new roles for users and all levels of government. The planning sustained the livelihoods of resource users because it recognized access based on customary rights, and because community members themselves took action to regulate exploitation and reduce the pressure on lagoon resources.

In terms of problem-solving, conflicts among the fish-pen owners competing for a good location were resolved successfully, though those of newcomers still need to be addressed. All households moved their pen(s) to newly allocated places even without external financial support. It thus became unnecessary to compete with each other. Most users were able to participate in negotiations to come up with collective actions. For instance, when a few households were asked to relocate their fish corrals from the navigation zone, all the group

Participatory Research led to outcomes:
- Identified problems and shared data
- Built trust and community partnerships for effective intervention
- Built awareness of resource system and constraints for participation
- Introduced models of consultation and negotiation to build consensus
- Clarified types of technical assistance and facilitation needed
- Defined questions to be followed up

Participatory local planning

Defined new roles of
- Resource user groups
- Village leadership
- Commune government
- District and province departments
- Research team

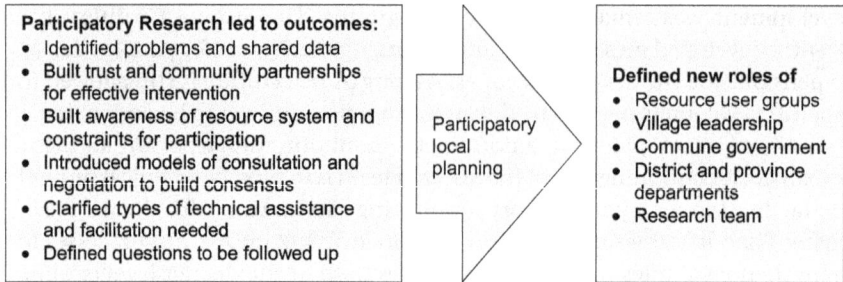

Figure 4.9 The emerging model for participatory local planning for NRM

members decided to move theirs in an expression of solidarity with the affected families.

The planning process also improved the capacity of community leaders to involve people in resource management and community actions. An example was the users' voluntary contribution of time, labour and materials to mark off the exploitation zones, public navigation routes and waterways.

Another positive impact was the support that the process lent to management and governance. It provided the basis for defining new roles and management functions of the stakeholders in further planning efforts. As (co-)managers, the user organizations identify problems, plan solutions and monitor results. Resource user groups carry out collective actions. Commune officials initiate and lead local resource planning. The provincial and district officials provide technical advisers and facilitators to help local people resolve their own conflicts. The researchers design the process, which in turn facilitates learning, planning and negotiations between other stakeholders.

Lessons learned

Key elements of participatory planning

Our experience with the successful introduction and establishment of a new participatory planning process for resource co-management in the lagoon incorporates five strategic elements.

1. The key point is a shared understanding among the stakeholders of the context, problems and planning approach. This came from learning and sharing together in the previous participatory research applications. This common understanding not only assured the participation of the stakeholders, but also facilitated their effective contribution to carrying out the whole planning process.

2. The active and meaningful participation of fishers and farmers is crucial, because they bring their knowledge and experience to the planning process, and because their opinions are respected and valued. They have the most important role in decision-making, but in return are expected to take

responsibility for the implementation of the plan. This is not to be misunderstood as the token consultation of local people in a plan essentially developed by bureaucrats.

3. Strengthening a new community organization, the Fishing Coalition, was very important in order to build the capacity of community actors who would undertake the central roles in organizing and planning resource management. The support of commune government officials, who were able to take leadership of the overall process, was also very important in empowering the community and providing legitimacy to community actors.

4. Participation of the line agencies at various local levels (provincial and district departments of fisheries) was important in providing functional and technical support.

5. The overall facilitating role of the research team was essential to carrying out participatory planning as an innovative process. They were vital to the learning process, capacity building, technical analysis and, most importantly, negotiations among the community groups and stakeholders

The effectiveness of participatory research

The long-term participatory research project was a crucial prerequisite to the planning innovations for several reasons. First, it helped all the stakeholders to understand the context and livelihoods of people, instead of seeing problems in simplistic terms and making assumptions about their causes and solutions. This enabled all parties to recognize the source of the problems and to develop effective strategies for solving them. PAR approaches helped the research team to develop new skills, which proved invaluable in developing co-management solutions. Participatory research also respected the people's knowledge and practices; therefore, it invited local people into the learning process with the researchers. Together, researchers and local people were able to generate ideas to learn and change, and to convince governments at different levels that their recommendations would be practical.

PAR was also an effective tool for developing local partnerships, good relations and trust with the communities. Sometimes problems were not addressed successfully. However, the support formthe development of local livelihood strategies and the involvement of communities in learning enhanced the credibility of the research team and of the solutions adopted.

The team applied PAR for problem-solving. This made the approach adaptive and responsive to the rapid changes in lagoon exploitation. For example, PAR dealt with the new expansion of pen culture. The approach not only provided effective tools for the research team but also for government officials in learning about the context, analysing the situation and designing interventions. The tools were also helpful as a means to facilitate negotiation, dialogue and to share learning among the local stakeholders. This enhanced the involvement of the local government in locally driven initiatives of planning for NRM.

The effectiveness of participatory planning

In Quang Thai, the new participatory planning process was effective in reducing conflicts and improving both equity and environmental quality. This was a different result from the earlier experience in Tan Duong. With less severe conflicts and with the benefit of earlier lessons, the research team was able to adapt participatory research and facilitate successfully a new local planning process. Local government recognized the importance of the actual process involved as opposed to only acknowledging the final planning document with its approval stamped by senior government. Moreover, the participating stakeholders were willing to try new roles, rather than remain stuck in conventional practice. For example, officials from the local government office and line agencies went to the lagoon to witness the demarcation of allocated zones and provide legal recognition, instead of just approving a plan document in their offices.

The planning process was based on local knowledge and meaningful participation in problem-solving, which addressed not only the conservation and ecological issues of the lagoon resource base, but also the economic issues of local livelihoods. Most of the solutions and strategies came from the suggestions of local people themselves. This greatly strengthened local commitment and participation in plan implementation.

The plan recognized customary rights and current (informal) resource use rights in the lagoon, so it did not threaten any groups of resource users. This commitment to resource users greatly increased their buy-in to the planning process, reduced the fear that one group would benefit at the expense of others and lessened the risk of long-term over-exploitation by non-participating users.

The role of the research team in ongoing support for the planning process was crucial. The team introduced the concepts and practices of participatory decisions and adaptive learning, and emphasized to all stakeholders the value of scientific evidence to help achieve equity and sustainability, through several years of engagement in participatory research work. The team's skills in communication and facilitation were essential to gain the support of local government, and to build trust and foster dialogue between stakeholders. The research team maintained its engagement throughout the process of background preparation, planning and implementation, in order to ensure continuity and address technical issues, negotiate conflicts and prevent miscommunications, even as more and more of the leadership for planning and management was being taken by local user groups together with the commune.

The research team did not predetermine the introduction of the participatory planning. This outcome emerged as the dynamics of resource use changed in the lagoon, as all stakeholders came to share a common understanding of the problems, and as they gained experience with new aquaculture technologies and tenure options. The local government and resource users took advantage of the opportunities afforded by the reform of national fisheries legislation to develop an effective participatory planning response.

Everybody had to learn a lot along the way, but learning takes time. Effective preparation for engaging different groups in participatory planning involves time-consuming step-by-step processes, with frequent setbacks and false starts. These steps are crucial to allow the research team, local officials and resource users to understand the context and reach shared expectations for planning. With experience, they can be improved to some extent, but the emergence of effective local participatory planning processes will never be a smooth or rapid process.

Conclusions

When it is undertaken with attention and rigour, PAR provides an effective tool for researchers to involve the community in the learning process about NRM problems and solutions. It facilitates the identification of problems and emphasizes the most effective interventions. Participatory research helps build awareness and trust, and this leads to the sensitization and involvement of the community, government and other stakeholders in local planning for natural resource co-management.

Participatory research made it possible for the research team, the local government and other stakeholders to modify their positions on issues of conflict through dialogue and negotiation. This was key to reaching a common understanding over time of the new processes, roles and actions for lagoon resource management.

The new participatory planning model in Quang Thai not only resolved conflicts and responded to resource degradation but also helped stakeholders to make the changes in processes, organization, representation and roles required to move towards better governance and CBCRM.

Acknowledgements

The research project was conducted with the financial and technical support of the IDRC and CIDA and with special acknowledgment to Stephen R. Tyler and Gary F. Newkirk for their efforts to initiate and guide the project. Acknowledgement is also extended to the reviewers, editors and experts from the 2004 CBNRM writeshop in Tagaytay, Philippines, for their substantive comments, technical guidance, and support in preparing this paper. A number of institutions and individuals have been involved in the implementation of this planning effort: Hue University of Agriculture and Forestry; Hue University of Sciences; Fisheries Department of Thua Thien Hue province; Department of Agriculture and Rural Development of Quang Dien district; and the Commune Government of Quang Thai. The lead author's background is described elsewhere. Co-authors Chat, Hanh, Tinh, Thanh and Suong are all affiliated with Hue University of Agriculture and Forestry; co-authors Than and Phap with Hue University of Sciences. The research team would like to thank all those people who have been involved and who have contributed to this project: government technical staff, faculty members, researchers from participating institutions, local officials and particularly the villagers – the women, men, fishers and farmers from Quang Thai.

CHAPTER 5

Towards upland sustainable development: livelihood gains and resource management in central Vietnam

Le Van An

Abstract

The livelihoods of upland ethnic minorities in Vietnam were traditionally dependent on shifting cultivation and harvesting non-timber forest products. Declining forest cover, government policies banning shifting cultivation and the migration of lowland farmers into upland areas have all led to dramatic pressures on upland communities to adopt new livelihoods. A research team from Hue University of Agriculture and Forestry took up the challenge of working with the uplands communities in the Hong Ha commune of A Luoi district in central Vietnam. The researchers used participatory methods to help farmers experiment with new agricultural production systems and build new farmer-led organizations for mutual support. Results appear to have benefited both men and women farmers, and have attracted attention and support from district extension officials. Based on these successes, the community has negotiated new forms of tenure on restricted forest lands, and increased the area they are allowed to cultivate. Lessons are being transferred to adjacent communities through a variety of mechanisms. We conclude that community-based upland natural resource management approaches should balance long-term resource management sustainability, mainly through resource tenure issues that are typically complex and difficult to resolve, with satisfying the shorter-term livelihood needs of villagers.

Introduction and background

Shifting cultivation is a traditional subsistence practice of upland minority peoples in Vietnam. During the war era in the municipality (commune) of Hong Ha, upland minorities migrated to forest areas along the Vietnam–Laos border. As they resettled their old lands and homes after the war, they were and continue to be faced with new challenges. These include forests that were seriously damaged by war (especially because of use of chemical defoliants), and new government policies requiring them to shift from their traditional swidden agriculture to a more sedentary farming system. According to the government, these policies are designed to protect the forest and provide better services and livelihoods. In addition, most traditional lands and forests were declared a watershed protection area and access to their forests and other natural resources is now limited. Trying to adapt to this new reality is very difficult, particularly because the arable land area per family is small.

To improve forest cover, in the early 1990s the government of Vietnam made efforts to invest in reforestation under national programmes such as 'Program 327', the United Nations World Food Programme reforestation effort and 'the five million hectare' reforestation programme. The government also issued a new forestry law (1991), a land law (1993) and a number of regulatory rulings recognizing and increasing the rights of farmers to land and forest. However, conditions in the uplands – and the top-down operation of state agencies – have contributed to a fragmentary implementation of these policies. These programmes were designed with little local consultation. Local people also complain that benefits often do not reach the local level and, when they do, local officials are forced to follow regulations that simply do not make sense to communities. Government officials blame poor management systems and the limited understanding of local people's implementation problems.

In Hong Ha, most of the land in and around the commune is now under watershed protection and management by the Bo River Watershed Department (a government agency). In practice, this means that local people only have access to about 1 per cent of the total land area for agriculture. At the same time, the population increased from about 300 people in 1975 to 1,200 people in 2003. Combined with the required changes in agricultural systems and the loss of access to resources, upland people have no option but to find ways to improve their livelihoods while using and managing their natural resources sustainably.

In response to these critical problems facing many uplands communes in Thua Thien Hue province and in other parts of central Vietnam, the Community-Based Upland Natural Resource Management project was developed by the University of Hue with support from the IDRC and the Ford Foundation. The project has been implemented by a research team from the Hue University of Agriculture and Forestry. Hong Ha commune was selected on the basis of its social, economic and natural conditions, as representative of the upland situation for many communes in central Vietnam. The aim of the project was to gain a better understanding of the links between poverty, resource degradation and policy, and to test local options to improve agricultural production and build human and social capital. Some recent changes in policy are encouraging. Local authorities have been meeting the researchers and the villagers to discuss various joint resource management arrangements or agreements. One of our ambitions is to make policies work for the poor. This requires involving different stakeholders at district, provincial and even national levels.

The project site

Hong Ha and Huong Nguyen communes are located in the A Luoi district of Thua Thien Hue province, in central Vietnam (Figure 5.1). There are 21 communes in A Luoi, a mountainous area where most local people belong to Pa Co, Ta Oi, Ca Tu and Pa Hy minorities. Hong Ha and Huong Nguyen are two of the 16 poorest communes in the A Luoi district, and among the approximately 1,200 designated poorest communes in the country, according to national poverty criteria. Hong Ha has been the initial research site of the project, since 1998. Huong Nguyen is a new site where lessons learned from Hong Ha will be disseminated in cooperation with different agencies, particularly the provincial Department of Agriculture and Rural Development (DARD). Lessons from Hong Ha and Huong Nguyen will also be used to expand community-based upland natural resource management approaches to other upland communities.

Hong Ha commune has about 230 households with approximately 1,200 people from different ethnic groups, such as K'tu (47 per cent), Pa Co/Pa Hy (28 per cent), Ta Oi (16 per cent), Kinh (7 per cent) or lowland Vietnamese and Bru-Van Kieu. The commune's land area is 14,100 ha, consisting of agricultural lands (180 ha), forestry lands (11,000 ha) and barren hills (2,700 ha). Very little of the forested area is in good condition. In 2002 and 2003, thanks to support from a state agency, about 120 ha of forestry land was converted to new rubber plantations. Most of the forest is under the management of the State Forestry Enterprise or the Watershed Protection Board of Thua-Thien Hue province. People in Hong Ha are adapting to new agricultural production systems in conformity with the local and national policies, as explained above. They also keep some livestock, mainly cattle, which roam freely.

Currently, Hong Ha has a primary school with five classrooms accommodating 250 pupils in grades 1–5, and two kindergarten classes. Children who want to enrol in higher grades must go to Hue City or to A Luoi, far from their homes. Almost 30 per cent of the local people are illiterate.

Hong Ha has a new village health centre but it possesses limited medical and other support services. Due to limited cash income, people usually depend on traditional medicines and health treatments. Only when they get seriously ill do they buy medicines or visit a health centre or hospital. Common health problems include malaria, dysentery, asthma, influenza, miscarriages and premature births for women, and malnutrition among children. Other important problems in Hong Ha when we started our work were a lack of food and food insecurity. People remain extremely poor but we have seen significant changes in recent years.

With a total of 20 ha of paddy field, wetland rice provides the main commodity production and income of the local people. At the start of the project, rice yield was very low, with only 1.9 tonne/ha in 1998. Cassava was the main food crop and was used as staple food. Due to soil erosion and cultivation methods, crop production suffered from low productivity.

Huong Nguyen, like Hong Ha, is also one of the poorest communes in the A Luoi district, but in many ways, people are worse off. Their commune lies adjacent

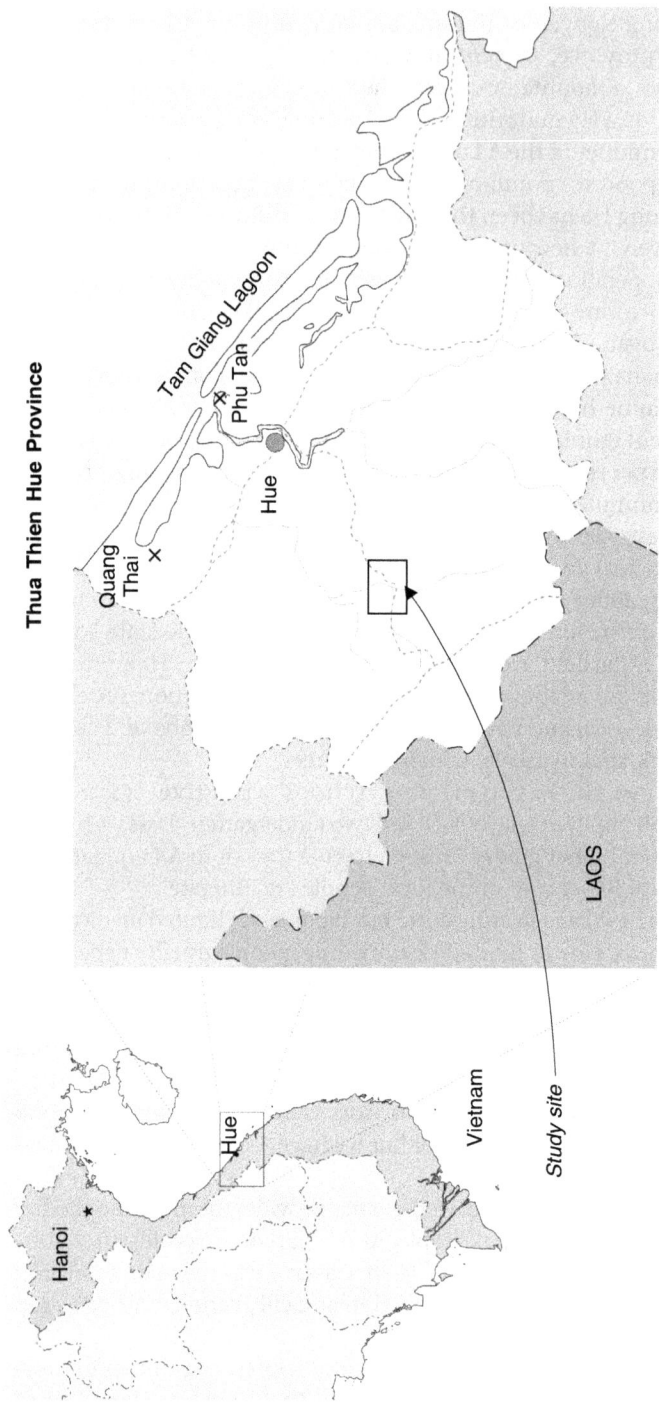

Figure 5.1 Map of Vietnam, depicting its central region and study site
Source: Bao, 2002.

to Hong Ha, along the road from Hue City to the A Luoi Valley. Huong Nguyen was newly settled in 1995 under the government's compulsory resettlement programme. Originally, these people lived in a remote and inaccessible mountain valley and very rich forest area, near the Vietnam–Laos border. When they resettled, they were allocated unproductive *Imperata* grasslands, or wastelands, that needed to be converted to agricultural fields. They were allotted some farming tools and some food to help them begin their new lives. Unlike Hong Ha villagers who moved back to their own homelands after the war, these villagers were forced to resettle. Moreover, to compound their challenges, some time after being persuaded to resettle, the people observed that a state logging company was extensively logging their traditional forests. Outsiders had begun to harvest rattan and other forest products in a non-sustainable manner. They wondered why this was allowed to happen while, in their new homes, they did not have enough to eat. They were told by state authorities that this new life would be better for them and their families. However, many of them wanted to return to their own familiar forestlands.

Our participatory research approach

A farmer's expectations are usually clear and simple: to meet daily requirements such as food, income, health and education. Hence, the project started with trying to improve farmers' livelihoods first. Simultaneously, project participants worked with state authorities to see whether the people's access to forests and other natural resources could be expanded.

They also asked for technical assistance in agricultural production. PAR was used to strengthen participation in the research process, from the identification of problems and possible solutions, to the joint implementation and testing of options. We employed participatory monitoring and evaluation as the work was undertaken (Figure 5.2). Participatory learning approaches were designed to include women and men farmers in all stages of the project.

Development of participatory approaches with local people and stakeholders

It is not easy to get male and female farmers and other stakeholders to participate in the whole process of action research. Participation is usually influenced by traditional top-down approaches to which researchers are accustomed. Researchers normally play all the main roles in all stages of research, from identifying problems to the implementation and evaluation of solutions. The levels of farmers' participation are low or nil. Through our work, we have learned that a good participatory approach requires a variety of methods. These must meet the practical needs of the farmers and simultaneously enhance their confidence. Some of the ways we tried to improve PAR and our CBNRM work are described next.

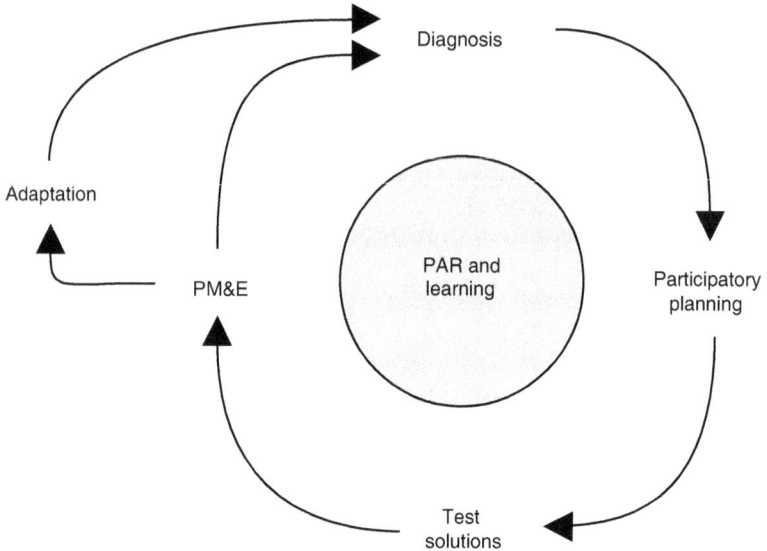

Figure 5.2 Learning cycles in PAR
Source: An, 2002.

The importance of a good initial diagnosis

It is crucial to diagnose the situation and research issues carefully at the beginning of the research process. Meetings with villagers should be organized according to different groups such as women, men, groups of the poor and groups of leaders. Most farmers are more interested in specific aspects of their daily lives and probably less interested in other things. For example, a good rice farmer is particularly proud of his or her production methods but another may be much more interested in cattle, which are looked after with great pride and care. In complicated production systems, one will always find farmers who are experimenting on their own and researchers can learn a lot by working with and learning from them. We were once told, 'If you want to teach a farmer you must first learn from a farmer.' This is something that we began to appreciate more and more. Problem diagnoses by different groups varied a great deal. Rather than leading to confusion, this helped researchers and villagers to understand the complexities of their situation better and to develop further steps for possible interventions (Table 5.1).

Improved criteria for selecting participants

Not all farmers have the same capacity to participate. It is normally easier for wealthy farmers and those who have higher social status in a community to articulate their views and participate more. Women and poor farmers rarely

A female farmer said: 'I never participated in any development activity supported by outsiders because I am poor. I feel that I do not have the ability to do such work for these projects. I am very happy to have attended the meeting organized by the University. I felt comfortable to explain what I need and what I think I can do to improve my situation if I have support from the University.'

Table 5.1 Solutions identified by different farmer groups in Hong Ha

Leaders		Women		The poor		Men	
Solution	Rank	Solution	Rank	Solution	Rank	Solution	Rank
Irrigation system improvement	1	Exchange visits and training in technical production	1	Capital for production and for asset accumulation	1	Rice production	1
Road improvements	1	Pig production	2	Training	2	Fish production	2
Rice production	3	Water for drinking	3	Rice production	3	Training	3
Fertilizers	4	Rice production	4	Cassava production	4	Home gardening	4
Improving home garden	5	Cassava production	5	Pig production	5	Hunting	5
Cash sales	6	Health	6	Health	6	Working off-farm	6
Market access	7	Education	7			Going to market	7
Education	8	Home gardening	8			Tending to animal diseases	8

Source: Farmers' meeting in Hong Ha, 1999.

involve themselves. To encourage participation, community leaders helped the project team to list and classify farmers according to different wealth categories (very poor, poor, middle, better-off, and very rich) and according to a range of social indicators, not just income. Another categorization was based on people's motivations to work with one of several different production groups (we discuss these groups in more detail later on).

Acknowledging different farmer's motivations

Farmers have different reasons for participating in PAR. The usual reason is to improve production and income as well as to gain direct financial benefits. For example, some farmers wanted to be involved in the project's home gardening groups because they offered some financial subsidies for planting materials. However, their real intention was to use project funds for other purposes.

Based on past government-led interventions in Vietnam, farmers often expect financial support from outsiders for their needs. During initial meetings, villagers explain their situation mainly by the phrase 'a lack of'. Lack of money is often the highest priority, based on farmers' perceptions. In our project, we had to proceed carefully to explain that we were not a development agency. We needed them to understand that through participatory action research techniques, we wanted to learn with them and hoped they could learn and benefit from us. A deeper understanding of the situation emerged after many long discussions and many evenings spent in the village.

Upland people are poor and they often conceive of being poor as lacking money. However, many of them do not understand how to invest money loaned from outside agencies, a fact that usually results in them having heavier obligations and losses after such loans. We heard many unhappy stories regarding this situation from them. Hence, a careful analysis is vital. Farmers and village leaders were surprised to find that an outside group wanted to understand their situation and learn from them. This was vastly different from their experiences, where development agencies and government officials arrived already knowing the answers.

The social or economic status of a farmer or individual greatly affects the diagnosis of the problem. CBNRM starts with an understanding of the current situation and the diverse needs of many different groups in a given community. We must develop ways to help different groups overcome different problems, on their own.

Increasing farmers' participation

Using participatory development communication (PDC) methods and tools can improve local engagement in PAR. PDC is a powerful tool that facilitates the involvement of community members through various communication strategies (Bessette, 2004).

We used PDC in a variety of ways. For example, the use of video cameras and the production of leaflets encouraged farmers to participate and helped document new techniques that were applied locally. Project leaders were trained in how to use these kinds of communication tools and media for the benefit of researchers and local people. In the project, farmers were able to learn new production methods more easily with the help of videos on fish raising and livestock feed conservation. This was especially useful for illiterate farmers. An information resource centre was established in the commune, and stocked with a variety of information materials. Farmers said that they liked this manner of supplying information as it made access easier, although it was a challenge to provide suitable resources for low-literacy situations.

When interviewing or working with farmers, the types of questions and manner of talking are important to ensure good-quality participation. In-depth topical studies were used to help better understand their situation and ambitions. Open-ended questions were used to introduce topics and gather general information, but were followed up with probes for specific detail.

We encouraged farmers to form groups with shared interests to hold regular meetings and share information about their activities. This helped build their confidence to participate in other CBNRM activities, and to engage more actively in local government as well as in other types of meetings.

Arranging for adequate time and a proper place to participate

It is very important in the PAR process to consider the time and place of meetings. Most women (80 per cent in our study) noted that they could not attend meetings in the community centre. The centre is usually too far from their homes and is mainly used by community leaders, not by women. They stated that they were uncomfortable in this setting. Organizing meetings near their hamlets facilitated higher attendance and more active engagement. Even when they do not always attend such meetings, they often drop in as observers and then discuss with their friends later what they heard and observed. Researchers and extensionists need to sometimes stay overnight in the community and participate in household farming work. Team members who were able to do this found it a very productive way to learn and to build social relationships – and trust.

Improving the material livelihoods of the upland poor

Upland farmers in Hue and in many other parts of the country are adjusting or adapting both to new realities and farming systems. The policy environment for rural development has also changed dramatically over the last decade. Following the principles of PAR and PDC, our research project started by identifying farmers' needs and how to satisfy them. Meetings were conducted to identify problems and possible solutions. Partial results for some of our earlier meetings are summarized in Table 5.1.

Farmers' learning groups were then formed by inviting farmers to share their own interests and livelihood systems. These groups were built around different agricultural commodities. Each commodity served as an entry point to other linkages in the larger farming system, so the group interests were always broader than their main commodity. Groups included:

- rice production group;
- pig production group;
- fish raising group;
- home garden improvement group;
- cassava production group; and
- forestry production group.

The following section reports on some of the research team's experiences in improving livelihood options among poor farmers in Hong Ha. We focus on the lessons learned in our work with rice and pig production groups, because these are the foundations of their mixed farming system. Pigs are of particular interest to female farmers who see them as a way of earning a bit of extra cash for their other family needs. Extra cash allows them to pay for medicines, administer care when someone in the family is ill, or to buy books or other school supplies. When people in a village are desperate, often they can rely upon social support systems. However, having even small amounts of discretionary cash is extremely important for women.

Rice production group

Each production group initially consisted of no more than 15 farmers. Members began by discussing and explaining the problems they were facing, and identifying possible solutions. The project team facilitated these discussions, using their scientific and technical knowledge to complement the local people's knowledge.

As shown in Figure 5.3, one of the problems identified by the rice production group was low rice yields and productivity. They developed possible solutions, directly addressing the causes of the low rice yields and productivity as understood by them and the researchers. A range of solutions to be tested in their fields were discussed, as shown in Table 5.2.

The group decided to test these options:
- three new rice varieties (TH30, Khang dan, D116), using the local variety as a control;
- various levels of fertilizer application; and
- labour saving transplanting and direct-sowing methods.

In each experiment, between three and five farmers agreed to test one of the three options. The farmer group selected the farmers who would apply the different tests. Other group members participated in evaluation and learning meetings at least three times during the growing season: at the beginning during the planting and experimental design stage; during the growth period of rice; and at harvest time. During each meeting, farmers developed their own criteria to monitor and evaluate results, and made decisions on which varieties were performing well, how much and what fertilizer to apply, and which cultivation techniques to use. The results of on-farm monitoring and evaluation were shared with other rice farmers in the group, as well as with non-members and other production groups. Because of this, the learning process was expanded to other farmers in the community.

Based on the lessons learned from the on-farm experiments, researchers needed to take on facilitator roles to help farmers develop solutions based on their personal situation. Some farmers then could test new technologies, while others could monitor and evaluate the results and thus learn from those testing

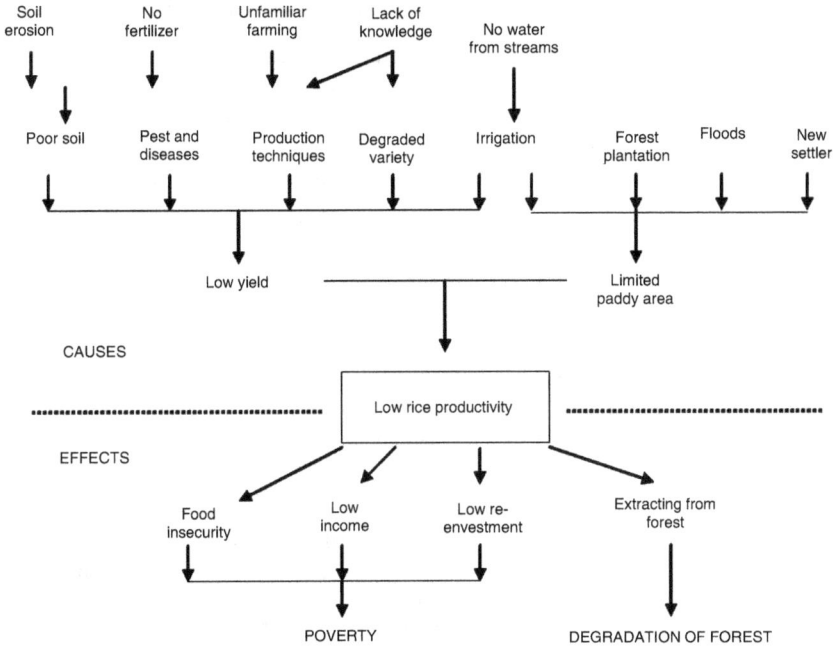

Figure 5.3 Problem analysis as performed by rice farmers
Source: Farmers' meeting in Hong Ha, 2002.

the options. The adaptability of options or solutions to other farmers should also be discussed, with the farmers supported by the researchers. The more familiar farmers become with new technologies and research results, the easier it is for them to share lessons more broadly with others (Table 5.3).

Pig production group

Similar steps of problem diagnosis and formulating solutions were also developed by the pig production group. Due to lack of agricultural land, farmers wanted to try to increase their incomes from livestock production. Some years ago, a number of projects had supported and introduced cattle to the commune. However, this only worked for middling well-off or better-off farmers who had sufficient money to buy better breeds or to pay herders to watch the cattle.

Poor farmers in Hong Ha and Huong Nguyen chose pig production as this endeavour is more suitable to their conditions. Pigs can be fed with farm products, such as cassava, vegetables and other home-grown or collected feeds. Some farmers had kept pigs in the past but their productivity was low. Pig production in upland conditions posed many problems such as low performance, poor husbandry techniques, lack of suitable feeds and diseases (Toan, 2003). Three experiments were carried out by different farmers: raising Mong Cai, a

Table 5.2 Rice production group: farmer-defined problems and solutions (not in priority order)

Problems	Suggested solutions	Farmer capacity	Outside support
1. Poor soil fertility	Experiment with fertilizers for paddy field	Some farmers carry out experiments on their field	Researchers from CBNRM project
2. Production techniques	Training for farmers Farmers visiting wetland rice production	Members of interest groups visit and training	Researchers from university, organized extension training and study visits
3. Degraded variety	Trials with new varieties	Some farmers carry out experiments on their field	New varieties given to farmers Experimental design PM&E
4. Pests and diseases	Sending two potential farmers to courses in Hue; Encouraging services in community	Select two farmers who graduated from secondary school at minimum, and who had experience in rice production	Research project provided money for this training and basic equipment
5. Irrigation	Requesting support from government project	Farmers contribute labour to improve existing irrigation systems	CBNRM project supplied pipe to collect water for one village
		Commune leaders request funding from government programme	
6. Limited paddy fields	Requesting more land for agriculture	Reclaiming available land for paddy field	CBNRM project supported negotiation meeting between the community and other stakeholders

Table 5.3 Rice production group: results of testing options and adaptation rates by other farmers

	1999	2001	2003
Number of farmers growing improved rice varieties and applying fertilizers (# of farmers)	8	110	180
Rice yield; average (tonne/ha) of all farmers	1.9	3.2	4.2–4.5

A farmer, Mrs T, reported that in 2003 she kept six crossbred pigs. She used cassava roots and leaf silage to feed them. Sometimes she also gave them rice bran, fishmeal or commercial feeds. After six months of growth, the pigs weighed 70–80 kg. The pigs looked very good. The farmer liked them a lot, so she did not want to sell. However, when the pigs weighed more than 100 kg, she could no longer supply enough feed to raise them. She and her husband decided to sell the pigs, but the trader offered a very low price (VND8,000 or about US$0.60/kg) while the price in the town market was VND11,000/kg. Her husband went to the town to meet the abattoir staff. They told the farmer that if the number of pigs were enough to fill up a truck, they would come to buy in the village at a price of VND10,500/kg. The farmer told the people in the commune that if they could sell pigs together, they could get a higher price.

local breed of pigs that farmers favour, as mother pigs or as sows; raising cross-bred animals associated with the fattening of pigs for the market; and making green feed (silage) from the widely grown cassava root and leaves.

In addition, two farmers were trained in basic veterinary practices for one month in Hue. This was supplemented by follow-up training in the village with the help of researchers and students. Vaccinations were also applied through veterinary service centres.

Meanwhile, other group members went to the district market centres to gather information on prices of the slaughtered pigs before selling to intermediaries. The farmers decided to sell their pigs together to get a higher price. These activities helped build social capital in the pig production group.

However, not all options or tests developed through PAR were successful. Mong Cai sows were introduced to 10 farmers. The sows produced good piglets in the first year through an artificial insemination service from the university. However, without the support of researchers or students, these sows could not get stud service since there were no boars in the village. As a result, Mong Cai sows stopped producing piglets and villagers decided not to keep sows any longer. Farmers now usually obtain piglets from a lowland commune near Hong Ha where sows produce high-quality piglets. It is anticipated that some of the more successful farmers may eventually invest in a boar or stud service and breed sows, after which time they will sell piglets locally.

Lessons learned

Over the last five years, livelihoods in Hong Ha commune have changed markedly as farmers have adapted technologies and modified both the forms and roles of local organization (interest groups, women's union, farmers' association and hamlet leaders). They have greatly improved their management capacity (collected information, made joint decisions, evaluated outcomes). This has resulted in increased food production and substantial income generation. The lessons learned from these initial experiences are as follows.

1. *How to work with the poor and the disadvantaged groups in community.* Poor and disadvantaged farmers usually do not participate in extension or development programmes because of assumptions about their poor status, low technical knowledge, and capacity to apply new technologies. Therefore it is important for researchers to understand and follow PAR and PDC methods with special attention to the poor. Farmers prefer to work in homogeneous groups where members have similar resource constraints and interests. It is also important that some farmers also want to belong to several groups. As farmers learn from one another and begin to adapt their own production methods, they gain greater confidence, judgement and skills. This helps them respond to new opportunities.

2. *How best to adapt results to other people in the community or beyond.* Research or development projects cannot work with everybody in a community at the same time. In this project, technical interventions were initially tested by a small number of farmers in the different interest groups. Other farmers had the opportunity to learn through the processes of research, communication and farmer-to-farmer interactions. Adapted technologies were evaluated by the farmers, who shared the lessons with other farmers. The role of researchers was generally limited to facilitating the learning process from farmer-to-farmer first in a commune and then at a broader level. Farmers themselves (or perhaps the provincial extension service) need to do this and researchers can only facilitate. The researchers' initial contribution was diverse, given that each group and each farmer had different interests and different resources. Therefore, they adopted or rejected new methods based on their own situation.

   There is little sense in trying to push a technology at farmers if they are not interested. For example, farmers planted new cassava varieties as on-farm experiments, to find the best for cultivation. Some farmers would prefer a particular variety while others differed. The reasons for this could be explained by their points of view regarding yield, market value, or taste, depending on the purpose for cultivation as well as individual preferences.

3. *How to work with other line agencies for the poor.* The results of our research would be more significant if applied and expanded to other areas and supported by additional agencies and policy-makers. In Vietnam, the agricultural extension system has a top-down approach, from central government to grassroots communities. Agricultural extensionists play critical roles in connecting the poor to different line agencies. Agricultural extension agents at provincial and district levels have cooperated in our research project as

The deputy head of the district agricultural and rural development sectors of A Luoi said that results from the CBNRM research are very useful. The agricultural sector of the district will organize farmers from other communities to come to Hong Ha to learn how the poor adapted technologies. The deputy head also announced that a participatory approach will now be applied in planning activities with farmers throughout the district.

working partners. As a result, they are now beginning to use farmer-to-farmer learning approaches in their own work.

These are lessons that are important for agricultural extension agencies to grasp. In the research project, extensionists were given opportunities to participate in PAR processes themselves, as a way to facilitate their learning. Experiences from Hong Ha were shared with other communes throughout A Luoi district in extension meetings. Aside from individual farmer-to-farmer learning, extension meetings provide an opportunity to bring ideas to many other communities and gain feedback. The processes of participatory extension and adaptation with farmers need to be constantly evaluated. Government agencies must learn these processes.

An important tool for extension agencies is the participatory monitoring and evaluation process in which evaluation criteria were developed by farmers with support from extensionists and researchers. Evaluation workshops were organized regularly at community and district levels. In one of the earlier evaluations with both women and men, we were surprised to learn of the very high importance given to farm exchange visits and technical training. Farmers ranked this as their second most important priority (after work on rice). We adjusted our work accordingly. Another priority was that of building social assets in different ways, once basic livelihood needs were more secure.

Building assets

From our work, we have learned that agricultural production is an integral part of CBNRM. Natural resource management in complex uplands production systems requires that both private and collective resources be managed in a complementary fashion. Building assets (which includes access and rights to natural resource use) is essential to the process of poverty alleviation (Ford Foundation, 2002).

Assets as conceptualized in the research project include:
- financial assets such as credit and savings, and financial resources that local people can have the opportunity to access and utilize;
- natural resources in the uplands, such as forests, non-timber forest products (NTFPs), wildlife, land and livestock, which can provide communities with sustainable livelihoods with significant cultural value as well as environmental services, such as a water supply and quality;
- social assets which include the capacity to build productive relationships and organizations between people in the community and with the outside world (or terminate these links them when harmful); and
- human assets, including knowledge and skills, that can be employed to access services, market, health care and other opportunities.

Upland people are often deprived of these assets. Being poor makes people less secure in their livelihoods, and reduces access to educational opportunities, health services and other government programmes. This project has worked with local people to understand their asset situation, support local organizations and build assets of individuals in the community.

In most communes, social assets are constituted by formal and informal organizations. Formal organizations are established to manage community resources according to current government systems, such as the People's Committee of the commune, the Farmers' Association and the Women's Union, among others. These organizations have functions and responsibilities in developing upland communities. The research project has supported and worked with all three organizations very closely as they have long-established relationships with farmers and the poor within communities. Many meetings were held with these organizations to understand their roles, functions, and strong and weak points, and to formulate development plans with them to help build and empower their groups and organizations. Some of the results of this analysis are shown in Table 5.4.

The farmers' production or interest groups discussed above formed their own regulations on how to select members, how to request financial or technical support, and how to work together. (The box illustrates an example of this organization's set of requirements.)

Improving the skills, knowledge and confidence of leaders, individuals in the groups and commune organizations is one of the most important forms of human asset building. Participatory learning and evaluation approaches were introduced and applied by local organizations for their own needs, where users were encouraged to develop their own priorities and plans, and make greater contributions to community plans and activities. Training and study visits were also organized to provide learning opportunities and build confidence, especially in relation to outside groups.

In 2002 and 2003, study visits to China and Thailand were organized for commune leaders and others in their local organizations. They were given the opportunity to learn from innovative upland farmers and commune groups in these countries. The study visits helped create changes in the attitude of leaders, who became more active and motivated and better understood their own situations. As a direct result of our capacity-building efforts, Hong Ha was treated as a special case in the province in order to test different delivery approaches for local government support. The government of Vietnam currently has a special poverty alleviation plan for the 135 poorest communes in the country. Hong Ha is one of these, and will receive financial support (about US$30,000/year) for development activities. Hong Ha is the first commune in Hue province that has gained the autonomy to develop its own plans for spending the money. The community management board of Hong Ha is considered as the best among the upland communes in Thua Thien Hue. Its chairperson now also sits on a national committee for minority people, which provides further opportunities to share local lessons, and provide inputs into policies and programmes at a national level.

As far as financial assets are concerned, the commune Women's Union and the Farmers' Association were trained how to manage small, revolving credit

Table 5.4 Analysis of local organizations

Commune organization	Functions/duty	Strength	Weakness	How to improve
People's Committee	• Responsible for all aspects of the livelihood of the community	• Active leaders (chairman and vice-chairman) • Respected by villagers	• Poor relations with outside • Lack of management skills	• Study visit • Support community proposals
Women's Union	• Supporting member's livelihoods • Family planning and health care • Credit funds for women	• Union perceived as a positive association to join	• Management skills need improvement • Lack of activities to encourage participation of members • Women busy with housework • Women rarely go out of commune • Low education	• Form interest groups • Establish a small credit scheme for women • Initiate study visits • Initiate training programmes
Farmers' Association	• Supporting farmers in their production activities	• Not clear	• No action plan • No fund for work	• Form interest groups of farmers in production • Procure small revolving funds • Initiate training programmes • Initiate study visits

Source: Local organization analysis by villagers, 2000.

Pig-raising group regulations included these criteria

- Membership is for poor women who want to join the pig-raising group.
- Women who borrow money from the group must pay it back after one year. In case of unforeseen events, the group will negotiate case-by-case default arrangements.
- Monthly interest rates on loans are set at 0.6 per cent.
- Monthly meetings are established so activities can be reviewed.
- Training needs are assessed so support can be requested from university or extension facilities/experts.
- The membership selects the leader and credit recorder every year.

schemes with an initial capital investment from the project. The fund started with about 10 farmers in the commune. After three years, 47 women had obtained benefits from the fund, which is entirely managed by local members. With this experience in credit management, both associations submitted a successful proposal for a much larger credit fund from an international NGO. They received about US$20,000 and started work in March 2004.

Improving access to natural resources

In the uplands, local people's access to non-agricultural lands and forest resources is essential to their livelihood. In this section, we discuss access to forests to highlight the third pillar of our work. With over 70 per cent of the country's land area covered by forest (which is often badly degraded) and 20 million people living in upland areas, these resources can play a vital role in Vietnam's development (Quy, 1995; Rambo, 1995). Forest degradation continues due to the expansion of agricultural frontiers and a drive by the government to cultivate export crops. Improper policies or programming and illegal cutting of timber in some cases also challenge the sustainability of forestry resources. Maintaining existing forest or controlling degradation is a major challenge in efforts to reduce poverty and encourage sustainable development of the uplands. (Bao, 1999).

In Hong Ha, the agricultural land base is limited. However, forest lands cover 78 per cent of the land area, while unutilized lands or steep slopes covered by *Imperata* grass represent around 20 per cent. Forests help supply uncultivated foods, income from NTFPs, materials for house construction and traditional medicines for human health care. Sustainable extraction of these products need not degrade forests if they are well managed (Bao, 2002). It is important to note that the forests in the study sites are badly degraded. They have generally not recovered since the Vietnam war years; in fact, recovery has only commenced in a few valleys.

Under the Vietnamese land law (1993), all land belongs to the state. The state can assign user rights to individual farmers or legal organizations for a certain period. All the lands in Hong Ha once came under the jurisdiction of the commune, but now local people are given user rights only to agricultural lands. Forestry lands are managed and controlled by state forest enterprises or government forestry organizations. The Forestry Department of A Luoi district has the authority to check on timber extraction and protect the forest from illegal timber cutting. However, most of the forestlands fall under the provincial-level Watershed Management Board.

Forest policies and management are a major national issue in Vietnam. There are many programmes initiated by the central government designed to protect and reforest using central or local government funds. However, these programmes are often implemented differently in different districts and can create, or exacerbate, local conflicts. Programmes and funds often do not even reach the local level. As well, the duties and responsibilities of forestry departments at different levels overlap and are unclear (Du, 2003). Finally, the number of people available for forest security is insufficient to protect large areas and to stop the illegal cutting of timber.

By the early 1990s, reforestation was encouraged by the UN World Food Programme and national "327" programmes. The barren hills and unutilized lands were used for planting forest with Eucalyptus and Acacia species. The aim of the programmes was ostensibly to increase the surface area covered by forest in the country.

Programme implementation has been problematic. For example, the use of single species such as *Acacia mangigum* or *Acacia eucoliformic* for large reforestation projects and to protect watershed areas has been undertaken. Nevertheless, in large-scale plantations, this species is only useful for pulp production, and provides none of the benefits local people seek from forestlands. Local people are paid for their labour in planting and protecting tree seedlings, but have no rights to use the forests or products. Although the government has issued a number of more recent decrees on forestry and in some cases allocated lands to individuals or organizations, these have not been implemented in Hong Ha.

In general, forestry policies and management have focused mainly on protection, creating conflicts between forest protection and livelihood development needs. In line with this, the government enacted regulations under Decree 178 (November 2001). Unfortunately, this law is difficult to understand and has not been explained to local people. One important article is that local people can annually harvest up to 20 per cent of the total biomass in protection forests; therefore, about 80–90 per cent of the products should belong to them (Sen et al., 2003). In our study, this question was raised with the Watershed Protection Board: how can local people share in the costs and benefits in forest management? Discussion continues with co-management systems, benefit-sharing being our ultimate goal.

Experimenting with co-management and non-timber forest products

As a first step towards possible co-management regimes, the project organized meetings with those local farmers, commune leaders, district extension services and provincial agencies (especially the Watershed Management Board) which are responsible for identifying possible land and forest management options. Using a participatory approach, the group selected NTFPs as one area of high potential. This area could be developed by introducing valuable non-timber species into the existing forest plantation. With support from all the key stakeholders, the research team developed a trial to test the introduction of the Do Bau tree (*Aquilaria crassna*) in the *Acacia mangium* forest plantation. This species increased the density of the protection forest and provided income to farmers. Another experiment was to interplant bamboo in the forest and along the riverbanks to reduce soil erosion while providing a fast-growing cash crop for farmers.

Through these interventions, farmers have been able to increase their income and extend their formal resource tenure rights in forest areas. The lands with *Aquilaria crassna* and bamboo plantation have been recognized and legally allocated to farmers in the commune. The research project demonstrated that the NTFP model plantation did not cause any problems from an environmental perspective and the plantation is now legally recognized by the state.

The NTFP models established in Hong Ha with stakeholder participation are now informing the forest management strategy employed in A Luoi district by the agricultural and rural development sector. *Aquilaria crassna* and bamboo plantations have been recognized by the District People's Committee in 2004 as representing worthwhile production opportunities throughout the district. The budget for the district's agriculture and rural development department includes funds for seedlings and technical support in forest plantation. Lessons learned are also shared with other communities in A Luoi. Therefore, NTFP production is becoming an important element of the provincial agricultural extension service. The Bo River Watershed Protection Board is now using *Aquilaria crassna* as well, instead of only Acacia, in its reforestation projects.

More recently, the project has been working together with several of these government agencies to implement joint forest management where benefits and costs are shared between the government and local farmers. This is an important new research avenue that we will explore further. In meetings with A Luoi district officials, research on participatory forestry management options has been proposed by local government. The researchers hope that in the next several years options of co- and joint management forest tenure will be tested in A Luoi.

Conclusions

Commune leaders have told the research team that this CBNRM approach is very different from other projects. In the past, the ideas, priorities and local knowledge of commune leaders and other local people were mostly ignored by rural development experts or agricultural extension services. Giving poor farmers, including women, the opportunity both to improve their understanding and to work on their interests, as this project has done, builds confidence and skills among locals. Our experience suggests that poverty reduction in the heterogeneous upland areas of Vietnam is much more effective when it employs participatory tools and fosters adaptive learning.

We can summarize the key conclusions of the action research project in Hong Ha and neighbouring Huong Nguyen communes. First, improving their livelihoods is the first priority of the upland poor. Not all farmers have the same interest and capacity to improve their production and income generation, so participatory approaches must make special efforts to engage all local people, especially the women and poor. Second, successful new technologies and institutions can best be disseminated by structured farmer-to-farmer learning activities, and by extension agencies that use participatory tools and methods.

Third, the key lesson learned from forest management in Hong Ha is that resource and land tenure must be identified clearly, along with other rights and responsibilities for forest protection, in order to ensure that there are local benefits. The direct involvement of different stakeholders from various levels of government is vital for learning, building consensus and resolving conflicts. The final goal of CBNRM is to achieve better natural resource management options in which the local community plays an important role. Increasing access to resources and building assets of upland people for collective action help to build social equity. Long-term resource management options should be balanced with the short-term needs of local people and other stakeholders.

Acknowledgements

The author acknowledges the extensive contributions to the research and preparation of this chapter made by other research team members: Hoang Thi Sen, Le Quang Bao, Le Duc Ngoan, Ngo Huu Toan, Nguyen Thi Thanh, Nguyen Thi Cach, Nguyen Minh Hieu, Nguyen Phi Nam, Dao Thi Phuong, Le Quang Minh, Nguyen Xuan Hong, Hoang Huu Hoa, Tran Minh Tri, Truong Tan Quan, Le Thi Thuy Hang, Tran Ngoc Liem and Nguyen Khoa Hieu.

Financial support from the IDRC of Canada and the Ford Foundation in Hanoi is gratefully acknowledged. The author would also like to thank Dr John Graham, IDRC senior program officer; Dr Charles Bailey, representative of the Ford Foundation in Hanoi, Vietnam and Thailand; the Department of Agricultural and Rural Development of Thua Thien Hue province; the Agricultural Extension Centre of Thua Thien Hue, the Forestry Department; the Watershed Management Board; the People's Committee of A Luoi district; the Department of Agriculture and Rural Development of A Luoi district; the Department of Forestry of A Luoi district; the People's Committee of Hong Ha commune, and farmers in Hong ha and Huong Nguyen communes.

CHAPTER 6

Co-management of pastureland in Mongolia

H. Ykhanbai and E. Bulgan

Abstract

This chapter describes and analyses participatory action research (PAR) undertaken by the Ministry of Nature and the Environment of Mongolia (MNE) to promote community-based pasture management in the country's changing policy environment. Stakeholders in pasture and natural resource management (NRM) are faced with a triple challenge: how to continue unlearning a centrally planned economy and society, how to handle changes given the economic and political opening up experienced in the country, and how to develop a herding and pasture management system that is sustainable under the current socio-economic and ecological challenges.

With weak central and local governments, the sustainable management of pastureland as a common property resource requires the participation of all stakeholders in strong herder organizations. This can be facilitated through co-management agreements supported by appropriate policies linked at national and local levels.

Co-management processes establish effective roles and responsibilities of stakeholders. Over time, such processes should help avoid the degradation of pastureland. In the case of transitional economies, the implementation of CBNRM approaches requires time so as to establish the legitimacy of the concept as well as supportive policies. To some extent, the Mongolia case supports theories about collective action in the CBNRM literature, although questions related to exclusion remain unanswered.

Background

Grasslands in Mongolia make up approximately 82 per cent of the land area and are currently home to 25 million head of livestock and 172,000 herding families. Nomadic livestock producers are the backbone of the Mongolian economy, and in 2003 livestock production accounted for 45 per cent of employment and 19 per cent of gross domestic product (National Statistical

Office, 2003). More than these numbers indicate, herding is a way of life for Mongolians and is rooted in the country's long history.

In Mongolia, grasslands have always been controlled by the government. Until 1921, pasturelands were under the control of feudal officials, clans and tribal groups. But the pasturelands were used in common by herders according to their livelihood needs, following wide-ranging seasonal migrations of animal herds and herder families.

Animal husbandry was linked with the socio-economic conditions of the time and the needs of society. For example, during the Genghis Khan period (13th century), the Ministry of Horses regulated nomadic pasture because of the importance of horses for imperial military purposes. During the Manchu Dynasty (18th century), camels were important for their use in caravans along the Silk Road trade route of Central Asia. At present, goat populations are increasing because of the high price of cashmere wool on the international market.

During the Soviet era (1921–90), citizens had almost no right to own livestock. They worked for the state and used pasturelands to herd state-owned animals for salaries. Another change began in 1992. Mongolia moved from the centralized, Soviet-style management system towards a more market-oriented one, where private ownership of animals was reinstituted. As state enterprises failed and unemployment increased, herding became an easy-entry livelihood option. Between 1992 and 1999, the number of families involved in herding more than doubled, and livestock numbers increased by some 30 per cent (National Statistical Office, 2003). For the first time in Mongolia's history, in 1999 the number of livestock in the country reached 33 million. In this ongoing transition period to a market economy, because of the weak arrangements between herders and local administrations coupled with the lack of an appropriate management system, pasture conditions are deteriorating rapidly and overgrazing is a common problem.

Historically, herder groups used different pastures or areas for spring, summer, autumn and winter grazing. It was a system developed and adapted to meet local climatic variations and livelihood needs. Herders moved their animals and camps throughout the four seasons, and it was common for a small group of herding families (*khot ail*) to move together to a new seasonal pasture. Within a given season, there were also shifting and rotational systems, which meant animals grazed in different areas in a seasonal pasture, as agreed by customary groups of herders and local governments. Figure 6.1 further details this scheme. During the Soviet era, full employment was guaranteed to herders, and some elements of the customary systems were maintained. In the post-Soviet period, herders are no longer state employees. Few remnants of the customary system remain, and there is increasing pressure on the fragile environment from new, unemployed entrants and herders wishing to increase their herd sizes to maximize profit. This has increased environmental degradation, poverty and an inability to adapt to climatic extremes.

Currently about 70 per cent of herders have herds of fewer than 100 animals. These herders own only 25 per cent of the national animal population, so 75 per

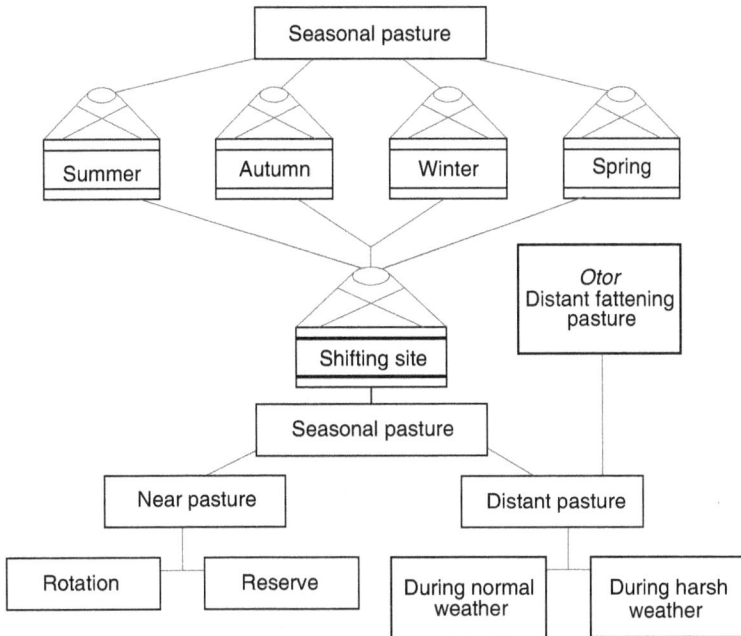

Figure 6.1 Customary pasture shifting scheme
Source: SUMCNR, 2003.

cent of the national total is owned by only 30 per cent of the richest herders. A herder who has less than 100 animals is considered poor (National Statistical Office, 2003).

Pastureland ecosystems in Mongolia are fragile, highly susceptible to degradation and slow to recover, primarily due to the cold, dry climate. Some estimates show that more than 76 per cent of the pastureland is subject to overgrazing and desertification (MNE, 2003). The degree of degradation is also drastically increasing year by year. Why is this? Poor management or increase in herder families and animal numbers? Climate change? Do we need to reinstitute traditional methods of herding and grasslands management, or intensify agriculture? There is no single answer.

In the post-Soviet era, disagreements on pasture use between stakeholders have increased. With the increase in herd size in the 1990s, there has also been an uncontrolled concentration of animals around water sources, settlement areas, hay lands and seasonal camps, combined with an ongoing degradation of pasturelands. The unprecedented scale of recent *dzud* or severe winters has had a devastating impact on the livelihoods of most herders, particularly new and inexperienced ones. These consecutive *dzuds* during 1999–2002 resulted in a combined loss of over 10 million animals, or over 30 per cent of all livestock. Almost 12,000 herding households were left with no animals, and a further 18,000 were left with fewer than 100 animals (Ykhanbai et al., 2004). It seems that in the near future, overgrazing will continue to be a serious environmental and economic problem, given the very harsh and fragile climate of Mongolia. Change is needed.

Tragedy of the commons

A very important reason for the current pastureland degradation is herders' desire to satisfy their immediate economic or livelihood needs. Herders want to increase the size of their herd as a means of survival and for profit maximization in competitive market conditions, where herding has low entry costs compared with other livelihood opportunities. According to the new constitution of 1992, there is no legal base for ownership of pastureland in Mongolia under which an individual has the right to exclude others and to regulate the use of the resource. Rights to the resource under the existing state ownership of pastureland, which includes controlling access and regulating use, are vested exclusively in the government. As the state's capacity for effective monitoring and management of all pastureland is limited, an open-access situation has been created, in which everybody's property is potentially nobody's concern.

This appears to be a situation of Hardin's 'tragedy of the commons' (Hardin, 1968). In this situation, a better pasture-management system could avoid pasture and ecosystem degradation. The 'tragedy of the commons' argument is that individuals have no regard for common resources except to maximize personal gain. Hardin illustrated this point by envisioning a pasture that is open to all, in which each individual herder is motivated by self- interest to add more and more animals, leading eventually to overgrazing and degradation (Hardin, 1968).

Historically, however, pastureland in Mongolia was not open-access but a common property resource in the sense used by Ostrom (1990). Common property resources exist where one person's use subtracts from another's use, and where it is often necessary, albeit difficult and costly, to exclude other users outside the group from using the resource (McCay, 1999; Ostrom, 1990).

According to Ostrom (1990), there are many enduring indigenous institutions, which for centuries have ensured the sustainable management of natural resources. Under the right conditions, interdependent resource users can organize and govern themselves to obtain continuing joint benefits despite the tendency for opportunist behaviour such as free-riding.

In Mongolia, the community management of pastureland and other natural resources is becoming important, because individual herders now absorb the risks of pastoral agriculture, rather than the government as during the Soviet era. This suggests a strong argument for co-management approaches to pasturelands and herd management, because individual herders need to cooperate and work together with their groups and with other stakeholders to ensure future sustainability. These approaches could build on past customary practices, but also must take account of current political and economic reforms and the opportunities these create.

Project objectives and study sites

A research project to develop alternative institutions for pasture management (the Sustainable Management of Common Natural Resources or SUMCNR project) was developed in 2000 and supported by the IDRC. It has been implemented by the MNE, in cooperation with the Ministry of Food and Agriculture, the Research Institute of Animal Husbandry, the Mongolian State University, the Gender Centre for Sustainable Development and others. The primary objective has been to develop new ways to improve the livelihood and livestock management opportunities of local communities. This has been achieved through more efficient, sustainable and equitable use systems for pasture and other natural resources by jointly designing and developing co-management options and appropriate improvements for pastures and other natural resources. As well, appropriate policy options for natural resource management have been studied and tested with input from herders and local and higher levels of government. Figure 6.2 illustrates the various activities discussed in this case study, including the linkages between them.

Project activities

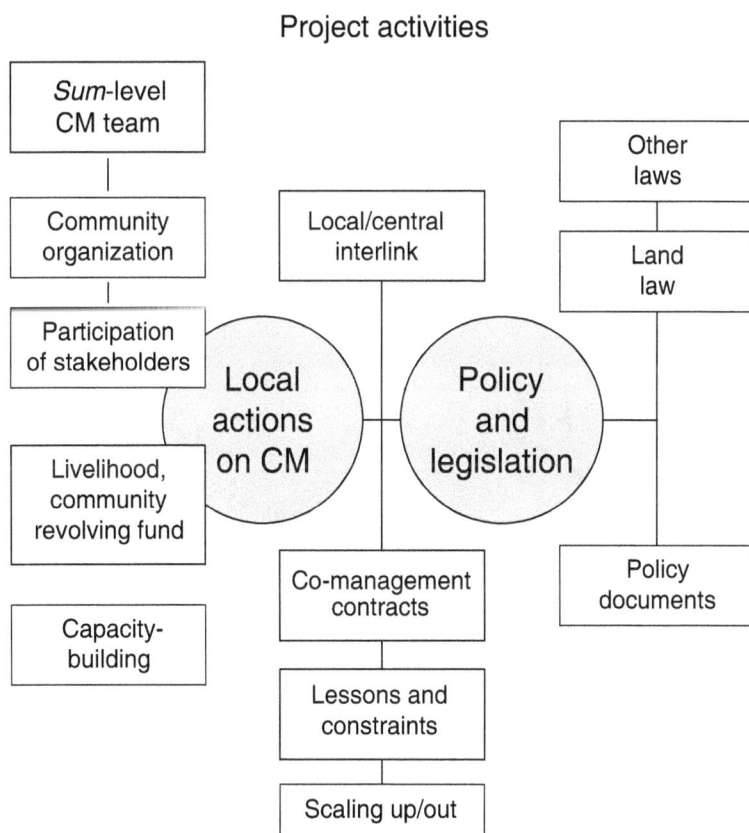

Figure 6.2   Project activities and the case study structure

The MNE was founded in 1987 and is responsible for overall policy formulation and coordination relating to the management of natural resources and the environment. One of the most important issues is how to deal with desertification and natural resources degradation. The involvement of the MNE in pasture management is relevant because of its role in sustainability policy, and the protection of pastureland and other natural resources.

Mongolia's vast land area is divided into five ecoregions: desert-steppe, steppe, mountain-steppe, steppe-forest and forest. The project addresses the challenge of environmental degradation through a combination of participatory and action-oriented field research in three *sum*, or local government districts. They were selected because they were considered representative of all the herding systems, as well as the three main ecoregions (steppe, mountain-steppe and steppe-forest) and the different forms of social organization. The three tested the feasibility of co-management arrangements in different settings. The study sites were chosen in part because the multidisciplinary project team was familiar with them. The team was made up of eight women and seven men, most of whom were born and spent their childhood at one or another of these sites with their herding families.

The *Khotont* study site represents the steppe-forest ecosystem and its diverse ecosystem components – forest, water, grasslands and wild life. There are good relations among herder households and a tradition of community coherence. The herder population originates from the major Mongolian ethnic *Khalkh* group.

The *Deluin* study site represents the mountain-steppe ecosystem. Here, customary pasture division systems by seasons were maintained through the Soviet period. There was higher interest displayed among herders in operating co-management systems because of the extensive degradation of this area's

Figure 6.3 Map of project study sites

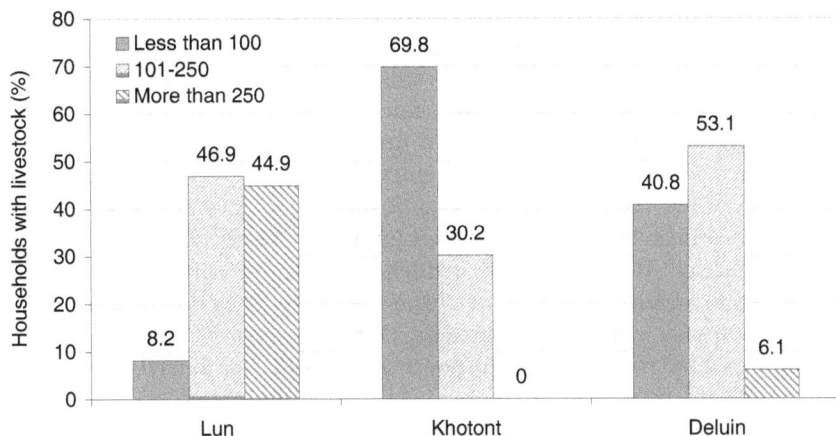

Figure 6.4 Proportion of households in different herd size categories at each field site, 2003

Source: Tserenbaljir, 2003.

pastureland. Local groups are organized around kinship relations and the population is made up of the minority ethnic *Kazakh* group.

The *Lun* study site represents the steppe and prairie ecosystems, and due to its closeness to the capital city has a higher concentration of animals. Herders display individual market-oriented behaviour and originate from different geographical locations throughout the country.

In each study site, the number of animals varies seasonally from approximately 1.2 times to about 2.3 times the pasture's carrying capacity. Wealth-ranking analysis was carried out in the study sites prior to the implementation of co management arrangements. The research showed that almost 70 per cent of herder households in the Khotont study site and 40 per cent in the Deluin study site were considered poor, having fewer than 100 animals per household. In contrast to these groups, about half of the herder households in the Lun study site have more than 250 animals, and are considered richer, as depicted in Figure 6.4. Their average annual income was roughly four to seven times higher than the poor households.

PRA was used as the main method for the study. Various PRA tools, such as focus group meetings, oral testimonies, mapping of herd movements, seasonal diagramming and semi-formal interviews were used for qualitative analysis. These tools were very effective in sharing information between stakeholders. PRA was coupled with other methods such as semi-structured field interviews, household surveys and gender assessment study.

Working for co-management

Respected herders were the entry points for the project team to begin local discussions. After the first PRA meetings and discussions, herders on their own initiative consulted with each other about the possibility of forming a community organization. Up to then they had all managed pasture individually. In further meetings, members of the project team outlined the advantages of community cooperation, organization and co-management. After hearing this, most herders formed a community organization. An unexpected result was that women became very supportive of co-management. After long years of top-down governance, their voices could now be heard. In fact, originally only men attended meetings, but later on women joined, spoke out and took part in decision-making. At first, the rich herders were not so willing to join the community organization and co-management system. They thought they had nothing to discuss with the poor herders. They were uneasy about the idea of sharing their good pastures with the poorer households which were occupying pastures of lower quality.

To facilitate the establishment of these new organizations and investigate suitable conditions for pasture co-management, the project suggested a working definition of community as a social entity made up of herders who lived in the same area, watershed, mountain or valley; who had pastures close to each other; and who were willing to modify their customary pasture management system for current conditions. Each community was a relatively homogeneous socio-economic group (herding together in one *khot ail*, a group or camp of herders) based on social or ecological (sharing the same watershed or mountain valley) conditions. Otherwise, the communities had not been defined in any formal or official sense prior to the project.

One of the main priorities of the herders was to keep their local and familial connections, a need which was recognized and supported by the project. Some herders joined community organizations later, after they understood that the new management organizations encouraged participation of all herders, regardless of their wealth or opinions.

Both rich and poor herders were interested in reducing environmental degradation and increasing economic benefits. But there were also some differences between rich and poor. The latter were the most interested in being involved in CBNRM. This is because they needed to improve their livelihoods, secure pasture, participate in decision-making and reduce the costs of herding animals through cooperation with others. Wealthier herders were interested in maintaining positive social relations and hiring labour for agriculture production. Some wealthy herders, who were unwilling to participate in the community organization at the beginning, joined later, after discussions and negotiations with the *sum* management team.

CBNRM proved to be a process whereby herders learned how to represent themselves to senior officials in local government, and strengthened their engagement in governance by participating in decision-making on pasture and NRM. By joining the community organizations and co-management arrangements, herders and other stakeholders became aware of one another's views, aspirations, opportunities, and the collective potential for local development and NRM.

Setting up co-management teams

Sum-level co-management teams were established in all study sites to act as local umbrella institutions. Their aim was to facilitate and monitor co-management arrangements among concerned stakeholders. At a later stage, they also began to handle the scaling-up of co-management activities in the *sum*. A team consisted of 8–15 persons, headed by the *sum* governor, and included representatives from herder community organizations, local government officials, NGOs, schools, private companies and the project team. The team usually meets twice a year or as necessary. It coordinates *sum*-level co-management through consensual decision-making processes.

At the start, PRAs and other meetings allowed individuals and other stakeholders to better understand one another and work together. During the PRA exercises, local problems were prioritized and solutions identified by local herders. Communities also mapped their pasture management practices, the location of seasonal pasture, water sources, natural resources and infrastructure. The PRA exercises were strongly supported by herders, as these were their first attempts to identify and represent ecosystems with which they were already very familiar and locate key resources. This exercise allowed herders to feel that they were the real 'owners' of the pasture and ecosystem in their environment.

In most cases, after the PRA, herders better understood their environmental and socio-economic problems as well as the need to jointly protect and manage their degrading pasture and natural resources. Most of the herders enthusiastically agreed to cooperate, viewing co-management as one way to solve this problem. Another reason why herders, especially women, supported co-management was that it filled an unmet need to be involved in community social activities and services. During community meetings, people could meet each other and chat, get community help when someone was sick or needed money, or learn the best practices of herding, farming and livelihood improvements from each other.

One of the constraints to herders' participation in the community meetings was the distance that they had to travel, up to 15 km. This was particularly challenging in terms of women's participation during the winter season, because they could not travel that distance with their children. In future, in order to organize, communities need to plan meetings well in advance so that the right time can be chosen for women and other herders. Advance notification also needs to be planned so that women and other herders can organize their work.

As of summer 2004, more than 15 communities or herder groups exist in the project study sites, with about 13–32 herding families in each group. New groups are being formed through the facilitation of research teams or, sometimes by *sum*-level co-management teams as the research project and scaling up continue.

Based on the experiences in earlier stages, the research project team has produced and distributed a guidebook for local government and herders on the establishment and facilitation of community co-management organizations.

Increasing accountability and transparency

The election of a community leader, vice-leader, secretary and accountant was on the agenda of the first community meeting. It was very important and exciting for the people to elect their own leaders. Households that wanted to join the community were registered, and the community was usually named after the mountain or river where they lived. The election of community leaders was important, because future community successes or failures depended on how they would facilitate joint activities of the group. The election process supported greater accountability and transparency.

Prior to the election, the project team consulted with local governors and elders about potential group leaders. However, the community members themselves strongly favoured an election process. In most cases, a man was elected as community leader. The election was usually done by secret ballot but, in some cases, by show of hands at a public meeting.

Women's groups

In pastoral agriculture, women and men play important, but different, roles. However, women's roles and participation in natural resource use, decision-making and implementation have been undervalued. In many cases, in research and policy-making, women's knowledge and abilities are neglected.

Project interventions on co-management have been designed with a major role for the community, including for women as a separate, disadvantaged group. Women's groups were established in all communities to help increase their participation in decision-making for NRM. The establishment of women's groups facilitated the promotion of gender equity in NRM and created an environment to support women's participation in the co-management of natural resources. It also encouraged women's initiatives to protect natural resources according to inherited knowledge and customs.[1]

> Women have clear roles in natural resource management. By establishing a women's group, they can join and share opinions, make joint decisions, and help each other. (Female, secretary of community organization)

Later on, women's groups helped the community leaders to organize income-generating activities among women, such as handicrafts, felt-making and vegetable growing; to provide venues for mutual learning (teaching skills to other community members, learning from other communities, organizing various training activities on sustainable livelihood options and NRM); and to undertake participatory monitoring and evaluation (PM&E) of the community's co-management efforts.

Community revolving funds

When the community organizations were established, herders agreed to create community revolving funds (CRF), which were made up mainly of contributions

> **Box 6.1 Community revolving fund**
>
> Fund can be loaned to individuals or groups in the community.
> - 50–60 per cent is used for financing community projects;
> - 20–30 per cent can be used as emergency assistance for the members;
> - 10–30 per cent is used for training, experience sharing, and community meetings;
> - Beneficiaries can apply for interest-bearing loans; and
> - Funds help stimulate a community's joint activities.

by members of the community. The contributions took the form of animals, such as several sheep or goats, cash or cashmere. In each case, the project contributed some cash and provided organizational advice. These revolving funds are used by the communities to organize activities targeted at such issues as improving women's income generation, and to support poor members. Currently, communities have CRF of up to MNT2 million (US$1,725) each.

Co-management agreements

Co-management focuses on partnership arrangements between government and the local community. It represents a decentralized approach to decision-making that involves user groups as partners or co-equal decision-makers with government (Jentoft, 1989; Pinkerton, 1989; Berkes et al. 1989).

CBNRM is people-centred and community focused, while co-management focuses more on a partnership arrangement between government and the local community. Figure 6.5 illustrates the relationships.

Co-management actors can be classified as primary and secondary, and on this basis are accorded different roles and responsibilities. Primary actors are herders, communities and local governors. All others such as non-community herders, economic entities, schools and so on are classified as secondary.

Based on the results of discussions and negotiations among the primary actors, three co-management contracts were devised: between the community leader and community members; between the *bag* (subdistrict) governor and the community leader; and between the *sum* governor and the community leader. These are outlined in Box 6.2.

Co-management contracts allow herders and other stakeholders in NRM to assume clear obligations, roles and responsibilities. One of the most important aspects of the co-management process was clarification of and agreement on the boundaries of pasture areas or the geographical sizes of the community pastureland.

As part of the project interventions, several communities entered into contracts with the local government on pasture use. In these contracts, boundaries for seasonal pasture were clearly agreed on, using topographic maps. Then all regulatory measures, responsibilities of protection and use rights were transferred to the community.

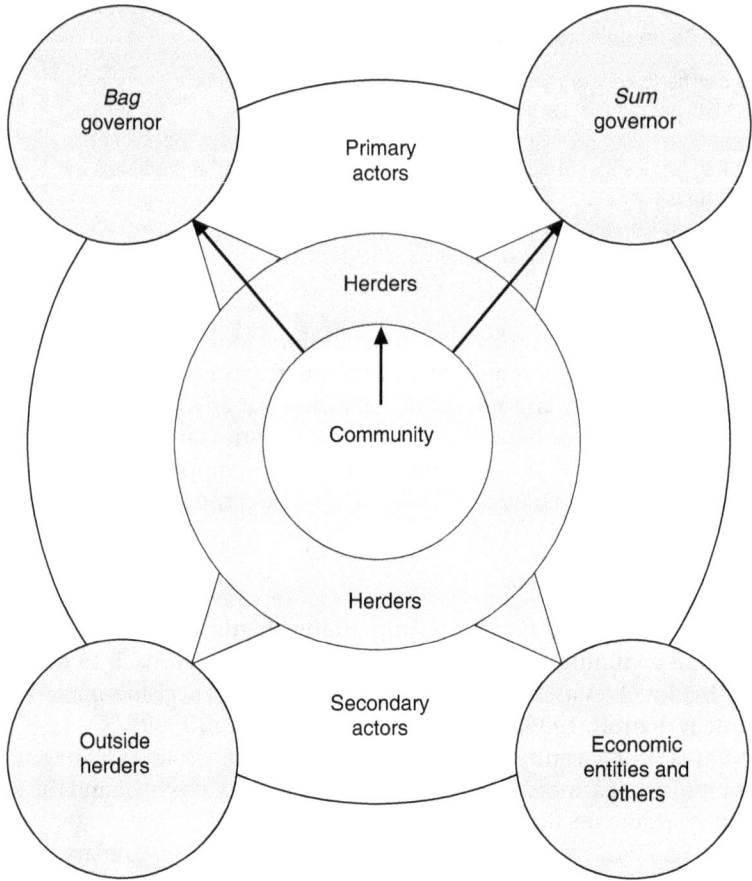

Figure 6.5 Co-management actors (stakeholders)
Source: adapted from SUMCNR, 2003.

Geographical size and distance of herder movement between seasons also differed according to the specific ecosystem, with the main determinant being grass yield. There was a longer or more distant movement when grasses were shorter or when yield was lower, particularly in the mountain-steppe ecosystem of the Deluin study site.

After one year, all initial co-management agreements were revised and re-approved in the communities, taking into consideration the recommendations of the women's groups. The ideas and perceptions of women were included so as to promote gender equity. As women defined their views on co-management agreements, they started to become more actively and meaningfully involved in the community decision-making around natural resource management, as shown in Box 6.3.

Box 6.2   Contents of co-management contracts

The rights and responsibilities of community members, *sum*, and *bag* governors are stated in the contracts. The roles and responsibilities of all stakeholders, as agreed upon in previous community meetings and discussions, are also included. Local governors agree:
- to approve community rights to exploit and allocate certain pasture areas according to the laws and regulations;
- to link more effectively the *sum*'s economic and social policy with community activities, and to support their sustainable NRM and livelihood activities;
- to define community pasture borders in the *bag* and to discuss this during the people's representatives meeting at the *bag*; and
- to regulate exclusion of outsiders to the community pasture area, in communication with other governors.

The community members agree:
- to follow community rules and regulations;
- to follow community decisions on pasture use; and
- to work in close connection with other members and to exchange experiences.

The agreements are valid for four years and are assessed annually at the stakeholders' meeting.

Box 6.3   Women's views on co-management

A survey was conducted among 461 women from 220 herding households in nine communities. When asked for their perceptions of the goals of co-management, they said these were:
- to cooperate with the common goals;
- to plan their activities;
- to improve and share knowledge on NRM and sustainable livelihood opportunities;
- to appropriately use pasture and other natural resources;
- to improve herding management and the productivity of animals;
- to improve their livelihood and income; and
- to learn the laws and rules related to herders and pastures.

Source: Odgerel and Naranchimeg, 2004.

A questionnaire survey conducted in late 2003 revealed that respondents, who were members of the co-management groups, were highly satisfied with the revised co-management agreements and with the new roles and performance of key local government officials in the new co-management system (Enkchimegee and Tsendsuren, 2003).

Participation and equity issues

One of the main objectives during the implementation process was the participation of all stakeholders in NRM. Stakeholders' equal participation in the planning process is crucial on several levels.

- It provides a venue where stakeholders' voices can be heard and included.
- It supports herders' and communities' initiatives.
- It ensures that the varied knowledge of different stakeholders is included in planning and implementation.
- It contributes to joint planning for the efficient use of labour.

Participatory assessment of the roles and responsibilities of the stakeholders and their inclusion in co-management agreements are important for successful co-management.

> Our goal is to extend the community activity not only within that area but also to other regions of the bag. We are also making agreements with incoming herders from other areas to limit their access to that community pasture area. (A *bag* governor)

The establishment of NRM groups as communities has become a principal activity to emphasize ecosystem sustainability. They also promote change at a broader level, that is, that they should not only concern themselves with pasturelands to the exclusion of other natural resources. Today, herders are not only responsible for their animals and pasture. They are also an important unit of rural development and NRM. Therefore, communities in all study sites implement improvements in forest, wild life, plant and water resources management. Co-management contracts in the community were developed and enforced for the sound use of water wells in the pasture. In the steppe-forest ecosystem, communities agreed to have co-management contracts among forest and water resource stakeholders.

Community-based co-management arrangements allow local resource users to make participatory decisions about pasture boundaries and use which can be defined both by season and by geographical features such as valleys, mountains and rivers. These were traditionally used to define seasonal herding arrangements. According to co-management agreements, pasture in a community area is managed under a common property regime, but other communities or outside herders can be excluded, especially for crucial winter and spring pastures.

As this is a source of potential conflict, it means that there is greater need for communication among stakeholders.

Disagreement in the community

In most cases, disagreements in the community are related to periods of seasonal pasture use. Some herders want to remain in autumn or spring pasture at a time when the majority would prefer to move to allow pasture to regenerate. To resolve disagreement on this, the project team facilitated several discussions and meetings with all stakeholders, to agree on the best way to pasture animals for the community as a whole. Researchers discussed with herders how important it is to shift the pasture during the vegetation-growing period, and to take part in collective decision-making. This was supported by most community members;

the minority had to accept the majority decision in order to stay in the community organization. Hence, they have started to make annual plans and to agree on the timelines for seasonal shifting of pasture. Over the long term, communities will need to make these decisions by themselves.

Disagreements between herders within and outside the community organization

There are local households which choose not to join the community organization. These include newcomers, wealthy households which control their own pasture and those who have misunderstandings or disagreements with others. They live in the same area, but are not involved in the co-management activities and thus their exclusion reduces the effectiveness of community decisions on pasture shifting or other joint activities. For example, when the community decides to move to distant pasture, such herders either refuse to move, or in some cases, allow outsiders to use community pasture in exchange for payment.

However, after some time (one or two years), when most of the herders are involved in co-management, when non-participants see others receiving its benefits, they do not want to be left out. Some awareness-building activities also help these herders to understand the importance of co-management. These activities include co-management meetings, visits of the project team and local governors to their homes to explain co-management benefits, and community-day activities which are held annually in study sites in order to exchange experiences among the communities and herders.

Another type of disagreement arises between the community and its neighbours. Neighbours are often afraid that the community might take their pasture. As a result of better communication and awareness-building, they can understand what the new co-management groups will do, and become reassured.

In cases where newcomers settle in an area without the community's permission and arbitrarily occupy pasture, pressure is exerted on herders and on local authorities. The project facilitated several discussions on the relationship between community and non-community herders. It also became necessary to include local government officials. The new land law allows herder groups to enter into contracts with *sum* governors for the exclusive communal use of winter and spring pasture only. Therefore, in co-management contracts between communities and local governors, a special article was included on how to settle issues of access to community pasture for non-community herders.

Relations with authorities

Good communication between herders and local authorities is key to co-management. One case where this is evident is the use of distant *otor* (emergency winter pasture) for herders, which is regulated by agreement among the governors of the neighbouring *sums* and *aimaks* (provinces). Sometimes herders ignore these regulations. One case occurred during the winter of 2002–3 when some herders from the Tsagaan-Uul community of Lun *sum* moved to an *otor* in the neighbouring Tseel *sum* because of the bad grass yield in their area. This was based on an agreement made only between herders of the two *sums*. But in the middle of winter, the herders from Tsagaan-Uul were forced to return to their original area because the agreement made among the herders was not supported by local governors. As a result, the herders of Tsagaan-Uul suffered more losses than others in the same community who had not moved their herds.

Capacity-building – training and livelihood activities

The research team's engagement with herder communities started with an assessment of their natural resource and social conditions. This quickly led to community interest in co-management experiments, and also to the identification of the need for training and capacity-building in support of new co-management efforts.

Training efforts included introducing local leaders, both men and women from herder households, to PRA methods and later to PM&E tools. General awareness-raising and educational efforts were needed to link local problems to the concepts of natural resource and pasture management. This led to extension advice on techniques such as seeding degraded pasture or hay lands and reforestation. Training in livelihood opportunities was also arranged, especially at the request of women. These included vegetable growing, raw materials processing, handicrafts and sewing.

As groups became more active, they required training and support in group processes such as running meetings, financial and other management procedures, and formalizing new kinds of groups such as a council or a women's group. Although the research team provided technical advice in some areas, and helped establish a pasture and natural resources database in each study site, much herder learning evolved through experience-sharing during intersite seminars and meetings, farmer-to-farmer exchanges, community information days and exhibitions, and exchange study-visits to other regions to compare experiences.

There is strong support for improving the capacities of newly established community groups in a 'bottom-up' manner.

> I agree that we should also think about other income sources, rather than increasing animal numbers. We will have to involve other herders of our *bag* in our community activity, if they are willing to join us. (A community leader)

> I attended the felt-making training in Darkhan city. I learned to make good-quality felt and felt handicrafts using new equipment. I think that it is a very effective way of gaining additional income. (A woman herder)

The action research on co-management carried out by the team has gone hand-in-hand with research about economic diversification and improvement of livelihoods (Ykhanbai et al., 2004). During PRA in the early stages of the research, community members defined their preferred options for additional income as improving dairy production, felt and felt products, and planting vegetables. Exploring additional income sources is important because such funds can diversify the herders' livelihoods, reduce poverty and reduce pressure on pastures, which indirectly addresses ecological problems.

In cooperation with the research team, pilot communities in the field sites are carrying out a number of action-research experiments. These include growing potatoes and vegetables; collecting and processing medicinal plants; and improving the processing quality, diversity and marketing of animal-derived products, particularly felt, wool and cashmere, furs and leather. Products include tapestries, clothing, slippers, hats, gloves, socks, home decorations and boots.

Policy and legislation

Several national policies and laws affect CBNRM and the co-management of grassland resources. Many laws and regulations support the devolution of decision-making on pasture use and the leasing of natural resources to citizens, economic units or herder groups. With ongoing concern about land degradation and desertification, the government is also providing economic and regulatory incentives for improved pasture management, such as credit and taxation policies. Official support has been directed mainly to cooperatives and private companies, but is now being made available to herder groups as well. However, the many separate and inconsistent laws and regulations make it difficult to develop integrated ecosystem management practices. This is being addressed through policy and legal reforms to unify natural resource management, including the new land law and water law. The project team and herder groups have made substantive contributions to the drafting of these laws.

The land law was approved in 2002. The project team proposed ideas to the working group which was drafting the land law, including suggestions on how to include aspects of pastureland co-management in the draft law. Proposals included provisions for the long-term leasing of pastureland by the herder groups and the establishment of a legal base for co-management contracts on pasture use. Some of the team's proposals were eventually included in the final legislation after an extensive revision process.

Provision 53.2 of the new land law allows long-term pasture use agreements between herder groups and the state, rather than leasing, if they have jointly defined roles and responsibilities with local government to ensure sound use and to restore and protect degraded grasslands. Balance is needed between conflicting longer-term sustainability issues. Leasing arrangements that promote the herders' investment in pasturelands need to be balanced with political sensitivities related to control over these lands. In cooperation with communities and local governors, the research team continues to experiment with principles related to specific pasture use contracts.

Under the land law, if herders and local governors cannot arrive at a consensus decision, a higher-level governor or the central government arbitrates disputes.

Also, the central government defines the location of reserve *otor* pasture in the case of *zhuds* (hard winter, characterized by extreme cold and heavy snows which prevent animals from foraging effectively), which can include protected areas for temporary use.

The project team also participated in the drafting of the pasture use payment law and the water law. In the new pasture use payment law, the team recommended higher fees for pasture use around heavily degraded areas, such as near the cities, settlements and water sources. For the water law, the team brought forward the recommendations of herder groups themselves for the establishment of participatory watershed management committees.

Linkages between local planning and national policy-making

During 2001–4, linkages between NRM policy and planning activities at local and national levels were strengthened as the project facilitated flows of information on natural resource policy-making.

Local regulations and policy implementation link local issues to national plans. Provisions to support community initiatives for the protection and sustainable use of natural resources were included in the National Action Plan to Combat Desertification, which was revised and approved in 2003; the Rural Development Policy (approved in 2003); the National Forest Action Programme (revised and approved in 2002); and the National Water Policy Reform Programme (approved in 2004).

Regular engagement with herder groups in the project sites enabled the project team to discuss drafts of national policy and legal documents with them to facilitate feedback on strengths and weaknesses. In the absence of other systematic mechanisms for public input, these suggestions from local herder groups were often influential in revisions to the draft documents. For example, the implementation of the law on expenditure on environmental protection and natural resources restoration from natural resources use taxes (2000), drafted initially by the project team at the request of MNE, was evaluated by herder groups, government representatives and local politicians. This law covers the reinvestment of taxes gathered from natural resource use for the protection and restoration of the particular resource. The income from the taxes could be one of the main sources for financing local co-management activities. However, at present the funds do not reach the communities, or the *bags*, *sums* and *aimaks*. Although policies and laws are becoming better on paper, there is a risk that de facto improvements remain elusive. The government needs to transfer the funds fully to the local authorities in order for them to support local co-management strategies.

Extending results

The efforts of the research project in selected areas of each field site have resulted in roughly 20 per cent of all the herders in each *sum* belonging to herder groups and supporting the experimental co-management agreements. The project team plans to involve more herders and other stakeholders in co-management activities, in response to mounting requests for support in forming new herder groups in every one of the *sums* in which we are working. This expansion will strengthen the effectiveness of existing groups, and is one of the objectives for the next phase of our ongoing research programme.

Changes and outcomes

As a result of introducing and implementing co-management procedures with local herders in pilot sites, a number of significant changes have been observed.

The most important has been the introduction of new cooperative processes and mechanisms between herders, local governors and other stakeholders, even though some external facilitation is still required. Herders understand the benefits of cooperating with one another and with new regulatory institutions, because the effectiveness of management depends on their joint actions. All stakeholders have started to realize the importance of sound use of natural resources, and their new roles and responsibilities are clarified under the co-management agreements. Herders more freely express their ideas and opinions with other stakeholders, which supports the concept of joint decision-making. By being part of a community, herders are beginning to realize their strength, which lies in their influence upon *sum* or *bag* governors, as well as their contribution to the formulation and implementation of resource management policy. Participatory research methods to define and assess the problems are novel to both the team and to local herders, and have played an important role in demonstrating the value of collaborative and participatory NRM mechanisms.

New CBNRM institutions have been established at the local level, and the organizational capacity of communities has increased. In three years, the number of organized communities in the three project sites has increased from three to 15, and new groups are being established regularly. Community members' knowledge and skill in applying group processes, management and learning have increased, and women have gained confidence through their involvement and application of tools such as PM&E. Women's groups have also started to share their experience with other communities. As a result of implementing new livelihood activities, direct economic benefits from co-management are being reported.

Customary pasture management practices have been introduced, along with innovative approaches derived from research and extension efforts. Pasture quality in areas of intervention appears to be improving, although this is difficult to measure in such a short time. Before the introduction of co-management, herders in the study sites were not very enthusiastic about protecting natural resources; they were only thinking about their individual benefits. But now, three years after the introduction of co-management principles, the local people's knowledge and understanding of NRM dynamics have improved, and even when acting as individuals they now make better-informed decisions. Responses to an independently conducted survey at the end of 2003 show that approximately 87 per cent of community members think that community joint efforts to shift and rotate seasonal pasture have improved overall pasture quality. About 60 per cent of community members in all study sites are now able to estimate the pasture carrying capacity by themselves, as a result of project and community training that has enabled them to make better management decisions (Enkchimegee and Tsendsuren, 2003).

Ecosystem and management changes in the study sites are monitored and evaluated by herders through various methods, one of which is through regular comparisons of photographs by season and under specific ecological conditions. But it remains challenging to measure the actual impacts of pastureland improvement efforts because of the effects of broader trends, such as climate change and desertification.

Preliminary evidence suggests that these interventions are leading to improved livelihoods for herders in the study sites, which saw income increase from 9 per cent to 67 per cent during the last three years. Through protection and improvement of community hayfields, establishment of hay and fodder funds, and preparation of additional fodder for the winter season, community herders in project study sites have reduced animal losses by 6–12 per cent on average.

Challenges

Despite the general enthusiasm among the herders in the study sites for the evolving co-management arrangements, the research team has identified a number of challenges to spreading the CBNRM concept. These are areas which require ongoing effort and innovation at the local and national levels.

Herders are almost totally dependent on animal husbandry as their only income source. Combined with the lack of local or national pasture management systems, this situation creates a strong incentive for individual herders to raise more and more animals to raise their income and welfare. Even in the pilot sites, herders are still struggling to develop a sense of shared interest in co-management of pasture and natural resources. Engaging a high percentage of community members may require an extended time period, probably 5–10 years. During the previous 60 years, herders followed instructions from the state. They now find it difficult to accept responsibility to solve problems independently and to apply new management techniques.

Legal and administrative systems are not yet structured to recognize local voluntary organizations which are not formed solely for the purpose of profit-making. In the transition to a market economy, legal reforms have been almost entirely oriented to privatization. The status of pastureland as falling under exclusive state ownership also poses some challenges to ensuring long-term tenure rights for herder co-management groups. The legal framework in Mongolia is changing, and the research lessons are influencing those changes. But even so, information about such changes reaches local herders only gradually.

Recent reforms which favour decentralization and privatization, and enable co-management are not widely recognized.

Public administrative structures are sectoral and disconnected. NRM bodies are only responsible for one area: the animal husbandry sector manages pasture resources; the hunting sector manages wild life; the forest sector looks after forests and their restoration. At the local level, there is now increasing recognition of the linkages between different resources and their respective management strategies. However, formal decision-making has yet to integrate across sectors in a way which supports co-management interventions.

The new *sum*-level co-management teams do not yet have sufficient capacity to effectively implement the co-management procedures which they are developing, and there are no official sources of technical support or extension for them. One of the key issues the co-management teams grapple with is the question of the exclusion of new entrants so as to protect pastureland and enforce co-management agreements. And finally, the effectiveness of co-management and other CBNRM approaches is premised on familiarity with participatory approaches and transparent decision-making processes, both of which are radical concepts and departures from historical practice. Project researchers, herders and local governors are still learning about these approaches and the skills needed to implement them successfully.

Lessons learned and conclusions

In Mongolia, the current capacity of national and local governments for pastureland management needs to be strengthened, both in terms of policy guidance and extension for resource users. We think that there needs to be more visible and appropriate policy support for building on communal arrangements, where the resource is held by an identifiable community of users who can exclude others and regulate use. This means that inside the community, pastureland will be used as a common property resource. However, where non-community herders are concerned, their inclusion will be regulated through co-management arrangements. These will be made by the community along with local governments and other stakeholders, according to the legal rights and responsibilities of the stakeholders.

If co-management is supported by all stakeholders, then it can overcome the 'tragedy of the commons'. For this to happen, new roles and responsibilities of stakeholders need to be clearly established. Outside facilitation has been required for some time to promote collective action within the communities.

The experience with implementing pilot pasture co-management arrangements in Mongolia has had a generally enthusiastic local reception, and has engaged local government officials in new roles and responsibilities. The success has come as a result of the involvement and participation of a high proportion of herders in the local pilot sites. This has required building awareness and shared understanding about NRM and local problems. It has required transparency, collective decision-making and broad participation across different social groups, including women, elders and youth. Successful local interventions required the establishment of joint co-management agreements by all stakeholders at multiple levels of government. Methods adapted from participatory research experiences in our project have proved very useful in the Mongolian context for promoting the co-management of pasture and other natural resources. Feedback on policy and regulatory reforms has also been very useful in drafting new legislation.

Community-based management of pasture resources can be more effective when integrated with management of other natural resources (forest, water, plants, biodiversity), because of the interrelations between them. This is more important in the case of the steppe-forest (Khotont study site), and the mountain-steppe (Deluin study site) ecosystems, where herder groups also want to be engaged in forest and biodiversity management.

One of the lessons learned from comparing the different study sites is that herders who live in an area with limited pasture capacity or far from market and government services (such as Deluin and Khotont) are more committed to trying CBNRM approaches than herders who live close to the city and market centre (Lun). These approaches may not be suitable to the same extent in all areas. We have found that co-management arrangements work more effectively when there are strong local social relations (such as in the Khotont study site) and clearer community boundaries (as in the Deluin study site).

This action research project has been characterized by extensive learning among all the stakeholder groups engaged in the project. Herders in the study sites, for example, learned to participate in decision-making for pasture and NRM at the community level. They shared ideas and thoughts with other stakeholders and became able to estimate the carrying capacity of their seasonal pasture. They learned to evaluate community activities using structured PM&E techniques, followed community arrangements for seasonal pasture use and introduced pasture-shifting and rotation methods. They also developed new livelihood opportunities such as growing potatoes and making felt products.

Local governments learned to work closely with herders and communities, to pay more attention to herders and other stakeholders, and to link their requests to local policy-making. Researchers learned to carry out participatory action research with herders and other stakeholders, use PRA and PM&E methods, and to facilitate the planning and implementation of policies, programmes and innovative technologies by local people and multiple levels of government.

Acknowledgements

The authors would like to acknowledge B. Minjigdorj, B. Biniye, Ts. Odgerel, B. Naranchimeg and all other research team members of the Sustainable Management of Common Natural Resources in Mongolia project, along with R. Vernooy, J. Graham and Tony Beck for their valuable contribution to writing this case study.

CHAPTER 7

Exclusion, accommodation and community-based natural resource management: legitimizing the enclosure of a community fishery in southern Laos

Nattaya Tubtim

Abstract

CBNRM is normally practised within a co-management framework. It often deals with managing common property collaboratively among different groups who possess diverse worldviews and agendas, which raises the potential for significant conflict. This case study deals with a CBNRM project intervention that involved unexpected exclusion, but in a way that did not limit the success of the project. Rather surprisingly, the exclusion occurred without creating significant conflict.

The case study involves enclosure of a communal backswamp previously accessible to 17 communities, through the establishment of an exclusive regime by a single village in southern Laos. The enclosure was an inadvertent consequence of a CBNRM project intervention. This chapter examines the perspectives of officials, villagers and a researcher on the transition of the property regime in the context of development and associated legitimizing discourses. It explains how the enclosure in this case was achieved with relatively little social friction, and aims to encourage practitioners to recognize different perceptions of key actors on various points.

Introduction

CBNRM has become a popular strategy for organizations working on rural livelihoods and sustainability. The tone of most literature in the field is that CBNRM has an inclusive approach and involves peaceful collaboration among various groups – the project, officials and villagers. But in fact, CBNRM does not necessarily arise from shared interests. Each agent involved has its own agenda, and the process of establishing collective resource management must deal with this reality. Despite the collective nature of CBNRM, its implementation can lead to some groups being excluded from being able to use resources. This does not always cause conflict because it can be legitimized by the actors involved. However, it should not be overlooked when cases are documented.

This chapter does not detail the methods or formal results of the research study in this particular case, nor does it describe the research project's activities. It describes the story of an incidental outcome from the research team's interventions in studying small-scale fisheries in southern Laos. It emphasizes that CBNRM is not necessarily a consensus-based process and that it can function as a platform enabling different views to coexist.

The case is about changes to the property regime of one backswamp in southern Laos. The property regime of the backswamp shifted from an inclusive one, where it was accessed by many communities, to one where it was used exclusively by a single community. This change resulted from a CBNRM research project intervention. A surprising outcome was that the exclusion did not create serious conflicts between the communities. The description of the case relies on observations, conversations and stories shared with key participants on all sides of the issue during my work as a field research adviser to the project funded by IDRC from 1997 to 2001.[1]

Setting the scene: the case and local realities

The Lao Peoples' Democratic Republic (Lao PDR or Laos) is a post-socialist, one-party state. After the failure of collectivization, in 1986 the government declared the new economic mechanism designed to accommodate a market orientation (Evans, 1995). Laos has traditionally based its development on natural resources; therefore, common property has been very important for local communities in Laos. This has been especially true for the poor. Over time, several relevant policies were developed on NRM, such as land and forest allocation to village communities, decentralization and the encouragement of production for market surplus. These policies have guided the development of market-oriented growth. Since 1986, there have been changes at all levels during this period of policy transition in Laos.

Traditional Lao communities have an agricultural subsistence base and rely upon common property resources. Apart from farming private land, local communities rely upon the area's natural resources for household consumption and income. These common property resources include forests, rivers and streams. From these areas, villagers gather wood and fencing materials, as well as their daily food, which includes fish, some insects and wild vegetables. The poor have limited private land and depend on these resources, which have very limited commercial value but are accessed across village boundaries.

Villages share other ties, too. Neighbouring communities know each other quite well and marriage relationships cross village boundaries. People rely upon each other and participate in various shared activities other than farming, such as planning for and celebrating festivals. Hence, individual communities are interwoven in multilayered ways.

In 1997, I started working with the Indigenous Fisheries Development and Management Project (IFDMP). My task was to work with local communities in collaboration with local officials at both the provincial (Provincial Livestock and Fisheries Office, PLFO) and district (District Agriculture and Forestry Office, DAFO) levels. We surveyed diverse aqua-ecosystems and people's livelihoods in Sanasomboun District, Champassak Province, in southern Laos (see Figure 7.1). The study revealed that fish catches were declining in all types of natural water bodies – rivers, streams, rice fields and backswamps – because of the pressure of an increasing population, improved fishing gear and the rising commercial value of fish. The project's focus was changed to Small-scale Wetland Indigenous Fisheries Management (SWIM). SWIM narrowed its focus to small-scale water bodies such as wetlands. This was because the villages already had rules for

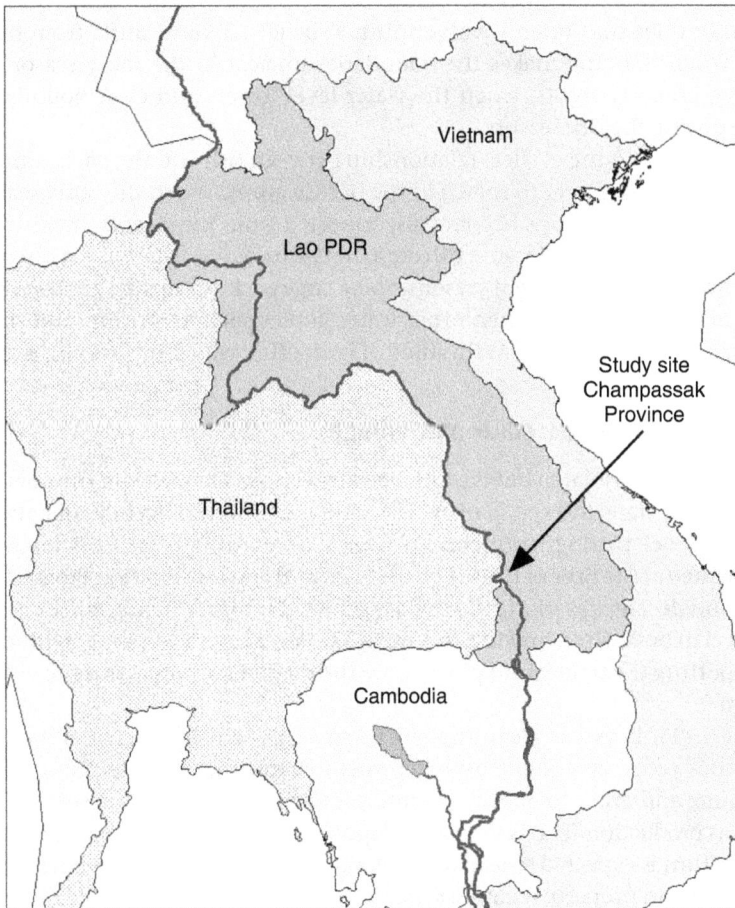

Figure 7.1 Map of Laos and study site in Sanasomboun district, Champassak province

these resources and the size was manageable at the local level. SWIM started the process of participatory action research. Its co-management approach aimed to increase fish catches to improve people's livelihoods.

Farming initiatives in these villages included wet rice crops, raising livestock (including pigs and poultry), fishing and some home gardens. Even though the market economy had been promoted for some time, it had not yet reached this rural area because of geographical barriers, poor infrastructure and lack of money.

Laos wetlands management

After studying how people used and managed their small wetlands or backswamps,[2] project members found that their management systems were not only complex, but also that they varied by locality and season. Tenure of most backswamps is de facto, where there is no legal approval but rather a set of customary rules that often involve spiritual beliefs. Tenure shifts from open access, when flooding makes the boundaries unclear in the rainy season, to exclusive property rights, when the water level lowers and clear boundaries emerge during the dry season.

We also studied the cyclical relationship between fish and the backswamps. Fish come from the river to spawn in the backswamps. When the rainy season ends and the backswamps become disconnected from the river, some fish are trapped in the shallows. Because fish are a mobile resource, fishers must discover where they are in the different seasons. Some large backswamps are good sources of fish in the dry season when other water bodies such as streams and small backswamps have dried up. At this time of year, other wild foods are also scarce.

Relationship between state and village

The village is not isolated but is influenced by various factors from the outside, including the state and the market. The state is a powerful agency that affects the local level through policies and laws. Two influential policies were implemented at the time of the study: the Land and Forest Allocation Programme (LFAP) and decentralization, which have affected resource management at the local level in both direct and indirect ways. The key actors that play a significant role in putting the policy into practice are the district authority and the village committee.

Since 1993, Laos has been implementing LFAP, which clearly defines and demarcates property rights. The government claims that LFAP leads to secure land tenure and thus provides an incentive for people to move from subsistence to surplus production. This is seen as an important step to facilitate marketization, which in turn is expected to lead to development. LFAP categorizes all resources into three main property regimes: state, community and private. State property includes national protected forests and rivers. Resources such as streams, natural ponds and forests are defined as the common property of the village. At the village level, paddy fields and residential areas are formalized as private property.

Maps are drawn and neighbouring villages are invited to confirm the village boundaries. A map showing the boundaries is posted at the entry to each village (see Figure 7.2). As a result of LFAP, rights in each different property regime are confined to the designated geographical areas.

Vandergeest (1996) explains that LFAP encourages territorialization because the state uses mapping and territorial delimitation to formalize and legitimize resource tenure. This agenda is also interpreted as 'state simplification' (Scott, 1998). The state can regulate resources more easily when they are mapped and categorized than when they are under complex property regimes. This is especially true when the common property regime uses customary practices that are only understood by the people in each locality. However, clearly defined property regimes are not only the state's agenda. Communities can use them as well to make claims, particularly when economic incentives can be applied to resources. But even where resources are mapped as a certain property type, they can be used in overlapping ways, especially if there is no pressure from scarcity or commercial incentives.

LFAP is more progressive than Thai law, which only has private and state property regimes and where villages cannot own or manage communal resources. Laos may be different in this regard because the government does not have the resources or capacity to enforce rules that are more restrictive. However, even though the Lao government recognizes common property regimes, these are only defined within the administrative boundaries of a single village. In addition, government authorities still have the authority to intervene in how communities manage their resources. For example, the village must get district recognition or approval every time it wants to change the management rules or obtain benefits from communal resources, such as selling timber for electricity.

In the late 1990s, a few years after the economic crisis in the region, the national government implemented a policy of decentralization, to respond to fiscal pressures and macro-economic imbalances. The government made up a slogan, *Kwaeng pen Yudtasaat, Meuang pen Ngobpamaan, Ban Jadtang Patibat*, which translates as 'The province plans while the district finances local development plans and the community has to participate, contribute, and implement.' It forces local villagers and authorities to increase their self-reliance in development at the provincial, district and village levels. This kind of decentralization is not designed to devolve power to the local level. Instead, it allocates administrative functions, especially financial responsibility, to local authorities (Fisher, 2000). This policy has eased the financial constraints of the central government, but the government still reserves the exclusive authority to plan (through its provincial line agencies) and make decisions about local-level policies and development directions.

Lao village committees consist of four groups: the village heads and village party; respected elders; mass organizations (for example, women's unions, youth organizations, village patrol units); and a technical group including the forest caretaker, village doctor or village veterinarian.

Figure 7.2 A board showing the village boundaries
Photo: N. Tubtim.

These village committees can represent both the state to the community and the community to the state, depending on the context. Even though full participation in a village meeting is the ultimate decision-making mechanism, the village committee is influential in the affairs of the village. The village heads do not have absolute power, but they can raise issues and initiatives, bring these topics to village meetings, facilitate the meetings and conclude decisions from the meetings. Most issues and initiatives are first discussed in the village committee, and then decisions are made in the village meeting.

In my experience working with several villages in rural Laos during the past decade, the village committee is very influential in directing decisions. This is because many people do not bother to participate in sharing ideas, but instead choose to follow the decision made by the majority. They also tend to be quiet in public and more active in the informal sphere. People discuss and gossip about the failure of some collective activities. However, ordinary villagers may not express their opinions at a meeting, especially when the topic or decision discussed does not have any direct impact on their families.

Policies do not come into force at the local level overnight. People become informed about them at the village level through the meetings and training sessions that the state arranges for the village committee. People also do not implement policies until they have some experience with what they mean in practice. Two examples of this are the policies that people implemented only after they mapped the resources in their village or after they enclosed Nong Bua. However, some policies simply endorse what is actually everyday practice, such as exclusive rights over an individual's rice fields. Development discourse can facilitate the acceptance of new policies such as an exclusive property regime for productive management.

The case

Our CBNRM case started organically. The project was not originally intended to initiate interventions, but while studying wetlands management, we raised local expectations. While I was being amazed at the complexity of the backswamp fisheries, the villagers, district and provincial staff asked me the typical Lao question: 'You have been walking in and out of the villages and asking many questions; what are your findings and what is next? Will you do some development? What about giving villagers some fingerlings?'

As I have done in previous projects in Laos, I replied that this was a research project and that we did not have many resources at our disposal. However, I knew this was not a good answer for them because it did not show what direct benefit they would gain from our research. They expected something concrete to come out of the project, especially when it involved a foreign expert.

This reaction is understandable because Laos has very limited development resources. Therefore, the government has placed a priority upon infrastructure development while leaving most development activities at the village level to international organizations. These included NGOs and donor organizations such as the UNDP, the Swedish International Development Agency (SIDA), the Japan International Cooperation Agency and Canada's IDRC. The notion of project, or *kong kaan*, in Laos, when it involves foreign experts, clearly implies the expectation of both new knowledge and investment in facilities or infrastructure.

On reconsideration, I thought that the request from the district was not unreasonable, and that a small project such as ours could afford it. The more important rationale was that it would be a good opportunity for the project to demonstrate support for the local initiatives of both officials and villagers. In this way, we could meet our goal of encouraging the co-management of communal resources and improving food security through low-cost development activities. We decided that our project would give 10,000 fingerlings bred by the provincial fishery station to each backswamp, at a cost of approximately US$100. With financial support from the project, PLFO offered training in fish nursery and fish breeding practices.

The case was interesting because there was a range of rules and tenure differences in the four backswamps we studied. Three were roughly 2–6 ha in size, while one was much larger. Also at issue were the spiritual beliefs held by local people. These placed restrictions on particular types of fishing gear as well as limitations on who could fish and when. The three smaller backswamps were used exclusively by a single village, even though there was some provision for other fishers (usually relatives) to fish on a single day in the dry season. All fishing was for household consumption, so few fish were sold. In contrast,

Nong Bua is a comparatively large backswamp of 28 ha (see Figure 7.3). It was the only one of this size in our project, and there were no restrictions on use. Therefore, fishers from outside Kaengpho district, where Nong Bua is located, could come and fish here. In fact, this backswamp was used by 17 different communities. The only prohibition at Nong Bua was on certain fishing gear, based upon a spiritual belief.

The project-supported fish stocking began after the rainy season finished in late October. The communities introduced new management rules prohibiting villagers from fishing between stocking time through to the end of the dry season in April or May. This allowed fish to grow for about five months so that people could catch bigger fish and obtain a higher yield. Harvesting in all four backswamps now changed its focus from subsistence-based household fishing to a carefully managed harvest system. All fishing was prohibited until an agreed opening date near the end of the dry season. At that time, the village committees fished for some time, and all proceeds from the commercial sale of the fish went to a collective community fund. (In all cases, this period was followed by a stretch of individual, household-based fishing.) The villages used their community fund for communal purposes, such as maintaining temples, schools and roads. In the absence of sufficient income, some villages levied a fee from each family for these purposes. Other income-generating activities included organizing festivals, which would draw paying visitors, or selling some other community resources, such as fishing rights or wood in their forest.

Fish stocking did not create problems for the three backswamps that were exclusively used by a single community. For Nong Bua, however, the project intervention led to the exclusion of communities that had previously held access rights.

The Nong Bua exclusionary situation

Nong Bua is located inside the boundaries of the village of Kaengpho, a medium-sized village that had 111 households and 662 people in 1999. It is situated on the left bank of the Sedone River, a tributary of the Mekong River (see Figure 7.4). Nong Bua is surrounded by rice fields that Kaengpho's villagers use. Prior to the stocking of fish, the property regime of Nong Bua was inclusive all year round. People from other communities could fish here at any time, although they did not bother during the wet season when fish were abundant everywhere and people were busy with farming. There was only one management rule, which prohibited specific types of fishing gear based upon the belief that these would offend guardian spirits.

At the end of the flood season, many fish are trapped by filter traps (*tawn*) set in 18 channels that connect the backswamp to the Kaengpho villagers' rice fields. The catch supplies families with enough to preserve as fermented fish for their households' annual consumption. During the dry season, especially between February and April when fish are concentrated in a small area, Nong Bua becomes an important source of low-cost protein and secondary income for people in

Figure 7.3   Nong Bua, one of the four study sites
Photo: N. Tubtim.

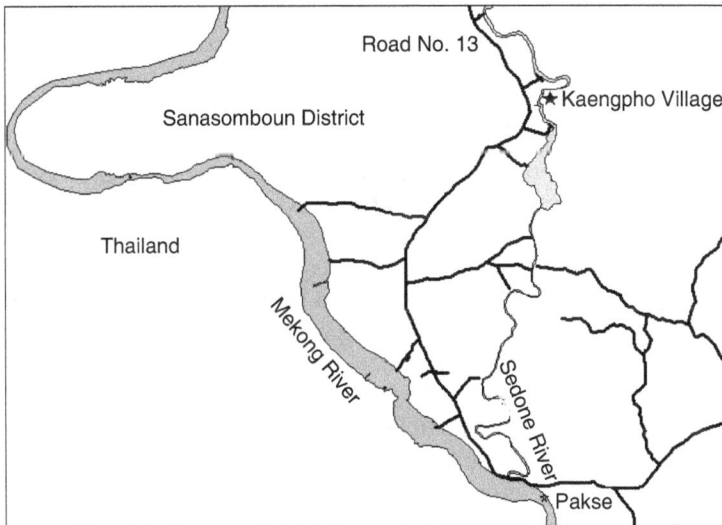

Figure 7.4   Map of Kaengpho village area

these 17 communities surrounding the backswamp. During this time, most other water bodies dry up, so food that is abundant at other times of the year becomes scarce.

The furthest community from Nong Bua is about 1–1.5 hours away by bicycle or on foot. On a daily basis, some fishers from a couple of communities sold fish caught from Nong Bua to buy rice. Many villages have their own backswamps, but they are small and dried up during the dry season. Some of these wetlands are far from the villages and are not connected to the rivers, meaning that there is not much fish. Therefore, only Nong Bua was readily accessible and had ample fish, so people from many communities preferred to go there.

Nong Bua is believed to be protected by two fierce female guardian spirits, *Maetho Kammai* (a female widow) and *Nang Waan* (a female spirit who likes sweets). People have found house posts and some pots in the backswamp that they connect to the tale of *'Phadaeng Nang-Aai'*, a common legend of widow spirits living in big natural ponds in Laos and the northeast of Thailand. People pay strict respect to the spirits. Certain fishing gear and activities are prohibited.[3] Those who suffer from an unidentified sickness or who die are believed to have broken the rules. At one time, almost 100 animals died and people believed that the spirits had been offended.

One elder in Kaengpho explained to me that worshipping the spirits is the last resort in treating illness when modern and traditional medicines fail. If the patient recovers after this, however, the cause of the sickness is often traced to an offence to the spirits of Nong Bua. Because of this type of event, the Kaengpho village committee once sent letters to the surrounding communities who came to fish in Nong Bua. They asked the outsiders not to break the rules because they feared that if they did, problems and sickness would befall the people of Kaengpho.

Those who break the rules must appease the spirits by offering gifts to the village shaman. The offering consists of two pigs (a black one and a white one), a piece of cloth, a bottle of whisky, a *khouai yai* (phallus or large timber carved in the shape of a penis) and some dessert. This is quite costly for villagers. Because of that, some people have recently switched from pigs to chickens for their offerings. During this case study, I saw one of the large phalluses at the spirit house located near the backswamp.

Kaengpho people told me that in the past the situation was more serious than now, because back then they could not even build a house near the backswamp. Now, new houses are being constructed closer to the backswamp because the original residential area is crowded. However, the community has to worship the spirits first to ask for their permission. As for the prohibited fishing gear, the restrictions remained in effect at the time of my study.

Around May each year, when Kaengpho people worship the village spirit before the new crop season, they include the two guardian spirits of Nong Bua in this village annual ritual. Commonly, people think that there are both good and bad spirits in nature. Some readers might think that this was just a belief of people that was not based on scientific evidence; however, these beliefs are common in Asia and they determine people's behaviour to some extent. In the case of Nong Bua, this belief was shared among people in both Kaengpho and the surrounding communities. It was more effective in influencing user behaviour than many legal rules that the government has tried to implement in the area.

Enclosure of the backswamp

After stocking fish in Nong Bua, Kaengpho people claimed exclusive rights over Nong Bua and prevented the 17 surrounding communities from fishing there. Kaengpho people maintained the belief that guardian spirits prohibited the use of certain fishing gear and added an additional rule forbidding the use of gill nets. More importantly, they prohibited other communities from fishing in the dry season. Kaengpho people still fish during the dry season, but only use hooks and lines.

When I asked why other communities were excluded, I was told that they did not enclose Nong Bua in the rainy season. However, it was widely understood that during that season other communities do not fish in Nong Bua in any case because fish are abundant and they use other closer locations. Therefore, I think people tried to find an answer to please me.

Kaengpho used the money gained from communal fish harvesting under the new management to help fund a new primary school in the village and to buy fingerlings for re-stocking the next year. The project was considered successful by the villages and the district authorities. However, it does not mean that everybody agreed, especially if they happened to be from the excluded communities. Nevertheless, the enclosure did not cause a lot of conflict between Kaengpho and the excluded communities.

Nong Bua legitimization process

The legitimization of the situation in Nong Bua started immediately after villagers got to know that they would receive fingerlings as a direct result of the project. Kaengpho villagers organized a meeting to establish a community fishery committee to set the new management rules. Afterwards, they invited DAFO to attend the meeting so they could offer comments. As a result, changes were made to some details in the new exclusionary rules. DAFO then announced the new management regime for Nong Bua to the other communities. These steps were required because villages do not have authority over one another. Therefore, they needed approval from a higher authority which would endorse the new arrangement. This process is followed in Laos whenever a change in management rules is made.

When fish were stocked during the first year of the project in Nong Bua, I was delighted that officials and villagers had initiated the intervention on their own. In addition, on the first fish release day, I was amazed to see the elaborate decorations adorning the area near the backswamp. As well, time was spent feasting and hosting invited guests from the province and district, as well as representatives from neighbouring communities. Monks were also invited to chant, after which the district head made a speech, emphasizing how this type of project represented a good opportunity for village development.

A village party member of Kaengpho then announced Nong Bua's new property regime, suggesting that its management goals included both the community's development and its collective benefit. Following these speeches, the district head released the first fish, after which other officials did so too, including project staff, representatives from other villages, and lastly, Kaengpho people (see Figure 7.5). It is a common tradition in Laos to make events very formal, especially in ceremonies involving government officials and foreign project researchers.

The ceremony on the fish release day was part of the legitimization process. The enclosure of Nong Bua was endorsed through this ceremony by the officials' speeches and the presence of invited guests from the project. This was a way of giving authorization to the new claim. Simultaneously, the participation of representatives from neighbouring communities was automatically a sign of their acceptance of Kaengpho's new exclusive management of Nong Bua.

Before the fish release, the new property regime of Nong Bua had been announced to the excluded communities through the district. Therefore, apart from the ceremony, the Kaengpho village committee itself had never communicated directly with the other villagers to describe the new rules. There was only one confrontation between Kaengpho and the excluded fishers from

Figure 7.5 Fish being released in Nong Bua by villagers and district officials
Photo: N. Tubtim.

the other communities in the first year of fish stocking. A group of fishers from one village came to catch shrimp and fish in Nong Bua. When the Kaengpho village committee could not convince them to leave, one of the members of the committee fired a gun into the air to chase away the intruders. The excluded group of fishers reported to their village head and the district. However, although DAFO received this report, they did not do anything about the incident.

After that, there were no direct arguments between Kaengpho and the other communities. This is partly because the culture of rural Laos avoids direct confrontation on conflicting issues. Although this behaviour helps ease problems at some levels, it does not mean everyone agrees with the outcome. Because of this community incident and how it was dealt with, there was much teasing, gossiping, and arguing back and forth among residents of the other villages as well as third parties such as traders and students. As a researcher who asked many questions, I was privy to much of this gossip and teasing. However, complaints faded out over time and eventually most people supported Kaengpho.

Some Kaengpho elders told me that at first they were not confident of their exclusive claim. They were not afraid of the other communities because they felt they had support from the district and the project, which also meant the provincial authority. What mainly concerned the elders was that the change might upset the spirits. However, their fear disappeared three years later.

In 2000, Kaengpho sold fishing rights for one day only to fishers from other communities to overcome the problem of weeds that had become invasive after the enclosure of Nong Bua. Prior to the exclusion, weeds were fairly controlled by the number of fishers who tramped around in the backswamp. In this one-day event, 200 or so people from many villages, including the excluded communities, came to fish in Nong Bua because it had many more fish than other neighbouring wetlands. The event was envisioned as a kind of ceremony and festival with feasting, whisky, music and dancing, so people thoroughly enjoyed participating. This was another step in the legitimization process, too, because when the excluded fishers bought tickets to fish in Nong Bua, their action acknowledged Kaengpho's rights over Nong Bua.

However, the most significant event of the day was when the spirits intervened. The first indication of their presence came in the morning. Villagers were surprised to discover that over half of the fish collected on the previous day for the feast had disappeared from their cage in the backswamp. Moreover, at the close of the day, a normally shy pregnant woman in Kaengpho greatly altered her usual character by speaking to people and laughing loudly, and by drinking a big glass of whisky and smoking a cigarette. She said that she was *Maethao Kammai*, one of Nong Bua's guardian spirits. She said that the festival atmosphere was fun, that she had released fish from the cage and she would help look after Kaengpho people. The elders and shaman interpreted this to mean that as long as everyone in the village agreed and worked collectively, the spirits would protect everyone. As a result, this case became a confirmation for the Kaengpho people, proving that what they were doing was accepted by both the spirits and other communities.

In the next section, I describe how the Nong Bua situation is perceived from the perspective of a researcher, local officials and villagers. They explain the exclusion based on their different worldviews. I will also explain the roles of the researcher and of the CBNRM processes in this context.

People's differing perspectives

The following stories are taken from my many discussions with local officials and different groups of villagers through the project's life from 1997 to 2001. These stories do not necessarily represent facts, but they convey underlying messages that the officials and villagers needed the outside researcher and project representative to understand. These descriptions were their views at the time of the study, but might have changed after the project finished.

Different views

When I asked the head of DAFO whether the new property management at Nong Bua was appropriate, he said, 'There was no *kaan jad kaan* (management) before.' However, I had a different opinion. I thought that the strict prohibition of some fishing gear based on spiritual beliefs was a kind of management in itself. He explained:

> *Kaan jad kaan* has to have a kind of proper rules. The rules from spiritual beliefs did not help people manage the resources better, instead they obstructed development. In the Nong Bua case, the backswamp had lots of weeds but superstition did not allow people to separate out an area for harvesting fish so it made a big problem. Anyway, this will be changed gradually when people see the benefit from management and development.

This statement illustrates that the officials view management as a formal arrangement intended to facilitate the efficient use of those resources that can foster development. It is a common belief among orthodox Lao socialists that superstition is one of the primary obstacles to Laos's progress. An elder told me that after the socialist government came to power in 1975, the government commanded people to destroy their spirit houses. However, after the country adopted new economic mechanisms in 1986, the government gradually softened this approach.

Another related point is that officials wanted to devise a simplified, standardized type of institution to manage development because the state has difficulty working with a unique set of rules in every community. This is what Scott (1998) means by 'seeing like a state'. There is also the issue of language and culture. The term *kaan jad kaan*, which applied to socialist views of development, could not be used in relation to the prohibitions attributed to spirits.

It is interesting that even though the Lao officials did not support the Kaengpho people's belief in superstition, they let them keep the rules regarding guardian spirits and arrange a ceremony to ask permission from the spirits before releasing any fish. One reason was that these beliefs and ceremonies did not conflict with their agenda of formalizing property regimes through the land and forest allocation and productive management policies.

Regarding productive management, officials both at provincial and district levels congratulated me on the success of the project. They explained:

> Fish stocking in the backswamp was a low-cost input but it initiated a good idea for village development that later people could adopt by themselves. People should start producing for surplus. Our government does not have sufficient development budget. Today even the district has to look for our own sources of money to pay our staff.

Later the district and the province helped Kaengpho by mobilizing additional resources. They organized a fish release at Nong Bua in celebration of provincial wildlife conservation day, where the province subsidized the fish fry. They convinced the district education office to support Kaengpho by providing some construction materials for the school. The research project also provided money for the school. Because of the decentralization policy there was no state or provincial budget for school construction, but officials were able to pool small amounts of additional funds from various sources based on the community's initiative. Moreover, officials stated that these kinds of development activities should become a model for other communities.

The concept of a 'model village' is well known in Laos. The Lao government has few resources for rural development at the village level, so examples of villages that initiate development activities or of farmers who can produce a higher yield of rice become a way for officials to encourage people and communities.

However, Kaengpho people did not want to become the sort of model village that the district wanted to promote. The village committee said:

> It is not good to show to the other villages that we are better than them or they should follow us. In fact, we want to ask them for understanding that we did not have other resources for development like the others have. If we do not do this (enclose Nong Bua), we will never be able to have this school for our children.

This interpretation reflects the tradition that Lao villagers try not to put themselves above their neighbours. Culturally, Lao people are more inclined to modesty and to seek sympathy. Because Kaengpho people still had to relate with their neighbours, they probably thought it would be better to express positive feelings.

As a researcher, I began to understand these varied viewpoints, although I was still concerned about the exclusion, as it seemed to be unfair to the excluded fishers. However, officials and Kaengpho people had different opinions. The Kaengpho village head explained:

Kaengpho does not have a proper school, no road, and no electricity while the other villages do. So, the project helps us to be able to keep up with the development of the others.

This means that Kaengpho also legitimized their claim based on equity with other communities, while pointing to differences in infrastructure development. I should note here that Kaengpho was no poorer than the other communities in terms of livelihoods; for instance, they had as much rice as their neighbours. However, Kaengpho villagers did have less infrastructure, and this is how development was understood locally. District officials did not object on the point of less development, but they felt that development could not happen evenly, at the same time. They explained that villages were not equal: some had resources and *kwam samakkee* (solidarity), so they could mobilize collective activities better than those that did not have such facilities. This made sense from the local officials' position of encouraging development at the village level under conditions of severely limited resources.

Shared views

I also discovered some shared opinions that sprang from customary practices, development discourse, exclusive management, the villagers' capacity for collective action and socialist values.

Both Kaengpho residents as well as those in other villages believed in guardian spirits. Moreover, the excluded people knew about the spirit's possession of the pregnant woman. Their shared beliefs helped formalize the exclusive ownership of Kaengpho over the backswamp. The district officials also heard about this and chose not to oppose it. This was perhaps because the belief did not obstruct their vision for new management of Nong Bua.

As to development discourse, the officials considered fish stocking to be an investment. Therefore, it would not be useful to open up access to everyone, as had previously occurred, because:

To reach development, the villagers had to put something back into the resources so that people could gain benefit from the resources. People should not just take from nature. Resources might be enough for subsistence, but with increasing population and the need for development, they will be used up quickly.

Village heads of the excluded communities also recognized that it would be a shame if benefits to the community were lost when the project ended. This is a familiar situation in rural Laos, where benefits disappear once projects are finished. Both local officials and villages prefer projects that support sustainable productivity improvements. In order to gain concrete, ongoing benefits from fish stocking, Nong Bua needed exclusive management.

One member of the Kaengpho village committee said they considered allowing other people access if they used certain types of fishing gear such as hooks, to ensure only big fish were caught. However, the committee decided not to do this, because:

> It is impossible to monitor everyone. If Nong Bua is partly opened for the others, they may cheat and this might lead to conflict within and between the communities more often. Therefore, it was better to displease the others once rather than feeling paranoid, and distrust each other forever.

Everyone whom I interviewed from the excluded communities agreed to exclusive management. They thought it would be easier to manage the resource under one administrative authority because costs and time for such events as meetings, for instance, would be reduced, particularly if benefits from the resource were small. People knew of a collaborative fish-stocking project where two communities owned a backswamp, but the project ended after a year. Afterwards, one family in the village got the concession to operate it. The village head explained that mobilizing people to work collectively was not easy and sometimes created more problems than it was worth.

In the case of the exclusive management of Nong Bua, the excluded villages were able to accept the change for two main reasons. First, the Kaengpho village committee had a good reputation. Second, the collective mobilization linked well to socialist ideology, which emphasizes action for common benefit (*suan ruam*).

The village committee explained that the new management of Nong Bua was intended for the benefit of the whole village and for the children, because as a result of the project the village could build the school. In fact, some of the village's poor gained a larger proportion of the benefit, especially the women. After Nong Bua was enclosed, these women could catch some shrimp and buy fish from the other fishers in the village for trading. The women were able to sell them to Kaengpho families who did not often fish and to outside communities, but now without any competition from the excluded villages. This benefited only select individuals, so it was not mentioned as an incentive for the project's acceptance, nor was it in the district's declaration. This information was related to me as a researcher, but not shared with the other communities. At the same time, according to the village head, he and other wealthier members of the village gave up benefits because the new rules prohibited the use of their costly but effective gill nets. These decisions added to the village committee's good reputation and their claim demonstrated their commitment to collective benefit.

Elders and village committees from the excluded villages responded positively to the collective benefits, noting, 'If they had excluded us for their individual profit, it would not have been so easy.' The excluded group might not want to accept the new regime but they still had to present the image of supporting 'socialist' development. This moral value is well accepted in socialist rural Laos. However, the idea of collective benefit refers exclusively to a single village.

The exclusive management of Nong Bua fit well with LFAP's goals. Even though the programme was implemented formally in Kaengpho in 1999, only two years after the initial fish stocking, the idea of formalizing property regimes and creating incentives for productive management had been with both local officials and villagers for quite some time. This does not mean they aimed to enclose and exclusively manage every resource located inside village boundaries. Procedures vary depending on the characteristics and value of the resource in question, and after considering whether it is possible or worthwhile to enforce management rules.

People in the area tend not to prohibit neighbouring villagers from collecting food from nature for their own household consumption. Nevertheless, when a particular resource becomes scarce or valuable in the market, village boundaries can be easily brought into play to claim exclusive rights. In the case of Kaengpho, the reaction from the excluded group did not challenge the village ownership of Nong Bua or the jurisdiction of the guardian spirits. Some people attempted to return to fish, claiming they were following the usufruct right that they used to have. However, this argument failed when district officials chose to ignore their complaint.

The implementation of LFAP in areas where people have permanent farms with clear individual ownership such as at Kaengpho has not led to conflicts as are experienced in situations where shifting cultivation has been practised. Rather, it has helped to reduce conflicts between communities in some ways. Many village committees in the area told me that since LFAP was implemented in their villages, there were fewer arguments about resource access and management than before. In the past, people could raise reasons for using some resources in other villages and access could not be denied very easily, because good relations among neighbours had to be maintained.

After a few years, members of excluded communities stopped complaining about the exclusion for a number of reasons. Initially they tried to voice their complaints in the name of the entire village, but in fact, their own village head did not support them. Village heads are part of the state administration and in situations like this they tend to side with the state. At the district level, meanwhile, officials ignored the complaints in order to demonstrate to the excluded groups that they actually supported Kaengpho. Opposition finally collapsed after villagers (and in particular a very vocal leader who was opposed to the project) discovered they had personally obtained benefits from fish stocking, because some fish from Nong Bua appeared in their own rice fields during the wet season.

On the one hand, the local officials and Kaengpho villagers were able to work together on the new exclusive management of Nong Bua even though they did not base legitimization on the same issues. On the other hand, even though the villagers of Kaengpho and the excluded communities did not completely agree about exclusion, they shared the same perspective on development and the belief in superstition, proving that they held common ideas, too.

Conclusion

CBNRM is not a process in which people agree on everything. However, it can be a way for them to work together to meet different objectives. The real power of the experience comes from this collaboration.

Collective resource tenure as part of CBNRM can lead to exclusion, but it may not necessarily lead to conflict if all the participants accept the exclusion. It is also possible that while some will want it, others will accept it reluctantly, while still others might oppose it, depending on material circumstances and discourses of what is or is not legitimate. In this case, exclusion was a subtle process of making a claim over Nong Bua in the context of legitimizing development discourses and spiritual beliefs. The exclusion was accepted because, while the project was trying to meet its agenda on CBNRM, it was also facilitating the implementation of government policies, as projects in Laos are expected to do.

Exclusion was not a goal of this research project. However, the new property regime was initiated because part of the project agreement entailed the support of fish stocking, and afterwards, project members had little control and had to limit themselves to providing technical support. In addition, it was only the foreign researcher who was concerned about the enclosure, while the local people and officials focused on different issues. This case shows that researchers should be aware of and reflect on their roles in the process of CBNRM, especially where projects could lead to exclusion.

Part III
From local action to policy impact

CHAPTER 8

Building networks of support for community-based coastal resource management in Cambodia

Kim Nong and Melissa Marschke

Abstract

This chapter examines the role of one PAR team in creating relationships to support CBNRM. Relationships, in this case, occur at various scales (international, national, provincial and community) and take place in various forms such as through partnerships, networks or facilitation by the research team. The chapter highlights the role of such relationships, including an analysis of why creating networks is a key strategy for facilitating CBNRM. Field stories about stolen fishing gear, water conflicts and mangrove logs shed insights into these processes. Unless adequate networking mechanisms and facilitation support are built into the CBNRM processes, community management plans and maps alone will do little to enhance local livelihoods or engage critical provincial and national actors.

Introduction

In part as a response to declining access to natural resources, community-based management (also known as community fisheries, community forestry or CBNRM) has emerged in Cambodia. Although approaches can vary, communities are establishing management plans and territorial claims, often with support from NGOs or government agencies. In comparison with a handful of sites in the late 1990s, in 2002 there were an estimated 162 community fishery sites and 237 community forestry sites in Cambodia (McKenney and Prom, 2002). Many of the community forestry and fishery sites in the country have an elected resource management committee (also known as a community fisheries or forestry committee) that is responsible for guiding resource management activities. This growing community emphasis in resource management appears to be a departure from past practices in Khmer villages, which were based on technical leadership from government institutions and informal regulations directed by village and commune leaders.

Much of the initial community-based work, which began in the 1990s, was experimental because community members, NGOs and government facilitators needed to understand just what resource management could look like on the ground. These initial experiences have contributed to the proliferation of community-based management processes – or at least fragments of them – throughout Cambodia. Examples include approaches to government decentralization, land management activities and increasingly formal community forestry and fisheries programmes. However, it is difficult to get a sense of what it really takes for CBNRM to work once plans are finished, maps made and documents approved. What issues are community resource management committees solving and what support do they require?

Cambodian rural households typically depend upon a diverse range of income sources, including those derived from a combination of common property resources such as fish, forest and water sources. However, access to these depends upon where a household is located and what livelihood opportunities the household is able to harness (Helmers, 2003). There is limited research that only hints at what it really takes in practice to enhance livelihoods, solve conflicts or increase access to resources for rural dwellers. Households and village-level institutions already do implement a variety of resource management strategies, including using forests as buffers from wind and storms. However, lessons from older CBNRM projects suggest that resource management strategies can more easily be enhanced when there is appropriate support that exists beyond the village level for community involvement in CBNRM. Perhaps greater consideration of Cambodia's cultural context[1] is necessary while working on CBNRM. In this country, village-level institutions often cannot engage in resource management practices such as patrolling or enforcement activities without some form of higher-level support.

This chapter tracks a specific case (Marschke and Nong, 2003) in which it is argued that both bottom-up and top-down strategies are needed to successfully bridge knowledge gaps and bring different players together to support CBNRM processes. Specifically, the chapter examines the role that one project team, Participatory Management of Mangrove Resources (PMMR), has taken in creating relationships to support CBNRM. Relationships, in this case, occur at various scales (international, national, provincial and community) and take place in various forms. These include partnerships, networks and facilitation by the PMMR team. This chapter highlights the role of such relationships, including an analysis of why creating these types of networks is a key strategy for facilitating CBNRM. Field stories relating to stolen fishing gear, water conflicts and mangrove logs shed insights into these processes. Unless adequate networking mechanisms and facilitation support are built into CBNRM processes, community management plans and maps alone will do little to enhance local situations or engage critical provincial and national actors.

The PMMR team and coastal villages

The PMMR team, funded by the IDRC, is composed of government staff at the national and provincial levels who come from various technical departments. This is an action research project, which means that team members are engaged with other stakeholders in CBNRM research. The lead institution is the Ministry of the Environment (MoE), and the provincial team is interdisciplinary. The PMMR provincial team members come from the Department of the Environment, the Department of Fisheries, the Department of Rural Development and the Department of Women's Affairs. This research team works directly at the village level, more recently with local-level resource management institutions.

Because team members belong to different institutions, partnership building could only begin once the PMMR research team had a better sense of what actually was happening (or not) within their own institutions as well as at the local level. For example, after the project team had worked together for the first few months, the original name of the project, Community-based Mangrove Management, was changed to the current name, Participatory Management of Mangrove Resources. This happened because the team felt that the term 'community-based' could potentially alienate government partners since they are not community members. Figure 8.1 explains why this research team chose to build partnerships at different levels. Team members found themselves taking on multiple roles in this action-research process, from learner to facilitator to researcher to trainer. However, perhaps more than any other role, the team considers itself a bridge connecting those with typically less power with those with more power to discuss, and potentially solve, coastal resource management issues.

Most of the PMMR team's village-level work takes place in a handful of immigrant fishing villages in and around Peam Krasaop Wildlife Sanctuary (PKWS) as shown in Figure 8.2. Many of these households were displaced by internal conflicts and economic disasters in other provinces, and so they migrated into this area with the hopes of taking advantage of lucrative resource extraction activities. Most households have learned to harvest various resources, after other income-generating activities collapsed, such as charcoal production and shrimp farming. As resources such as mangrove trees and fish declined, some villages requested support from the PMMR team to help them with resource management initiatives. Although the team initially spent time doing a series of environmental education activities in these villages, they did not help villagers to organize themselves or create resource management plans unless villagers specifically requested help.

The PMMR team's main focus is to research how local-level resource management institutions can engage in resource management and how local livelihoods can be enhanced. The team has worked hard to establish good relationships and cooperation with all governmental levels, and to aid this, the PMMR team facilitates between the national government and local people. In

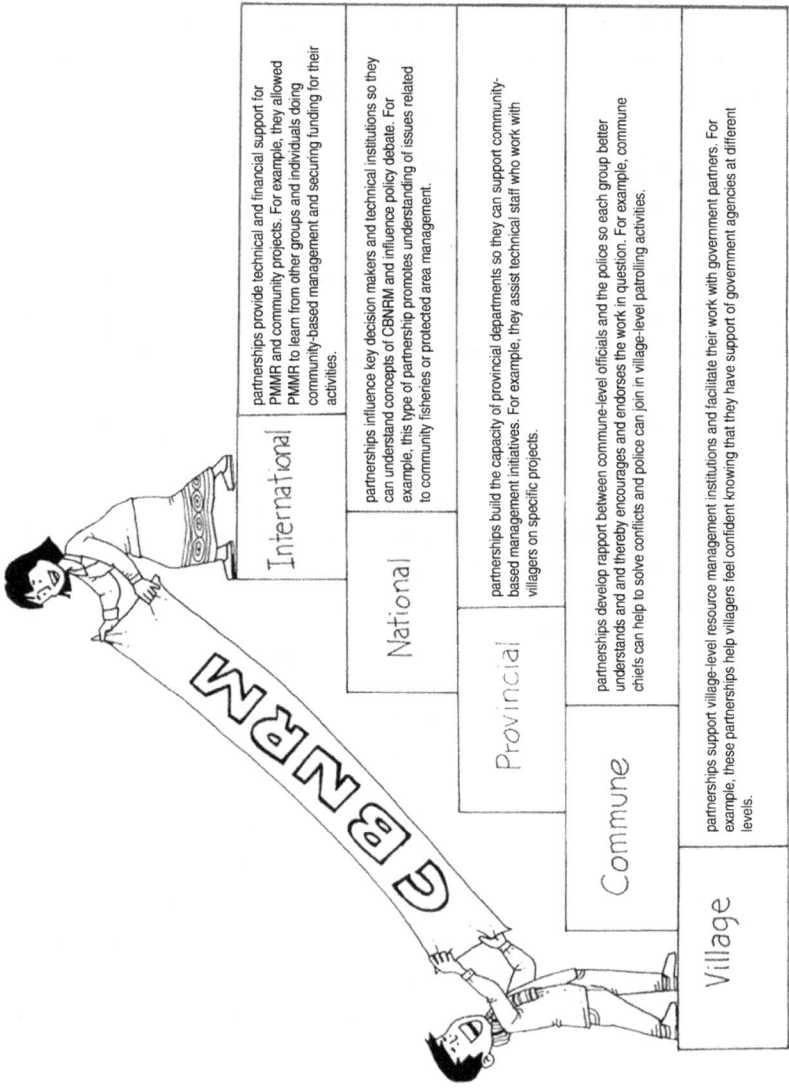

					partnerships provide technical and financial support for PMMR and community projects. For example, they allowed PMMR to learn from other groups and individuals doing community-based management and securing funding for their activities.
International					partnerships influence key decision makers and technical institutions so they can understand concepts of CBNRM and influence policy debate. For example, this type of partnership promotes understanding of issues related to community fisheries or protected area management.
	National				partnerships build the capacity of provincial departments so they can support community-based management initiatives. For example, they assist technical staff who work with villagers on specific projects.
		Provincial			partnerships develop rapport between commune-level officials and the police so each group better understands and and thereby encourages and endorses the work in question. For example, commune chiefs can help to solve conflicts and police can join in village-level patrolling activities.
			Commune		partnerships support village-level resource management institutions and facilitate their work with government partners. For example, these partnerships help villagers feel confident knowing that they have support of government agencies at different levels.
				Village	

Figure 8.1 Why PMMR builds partnerships at different levels

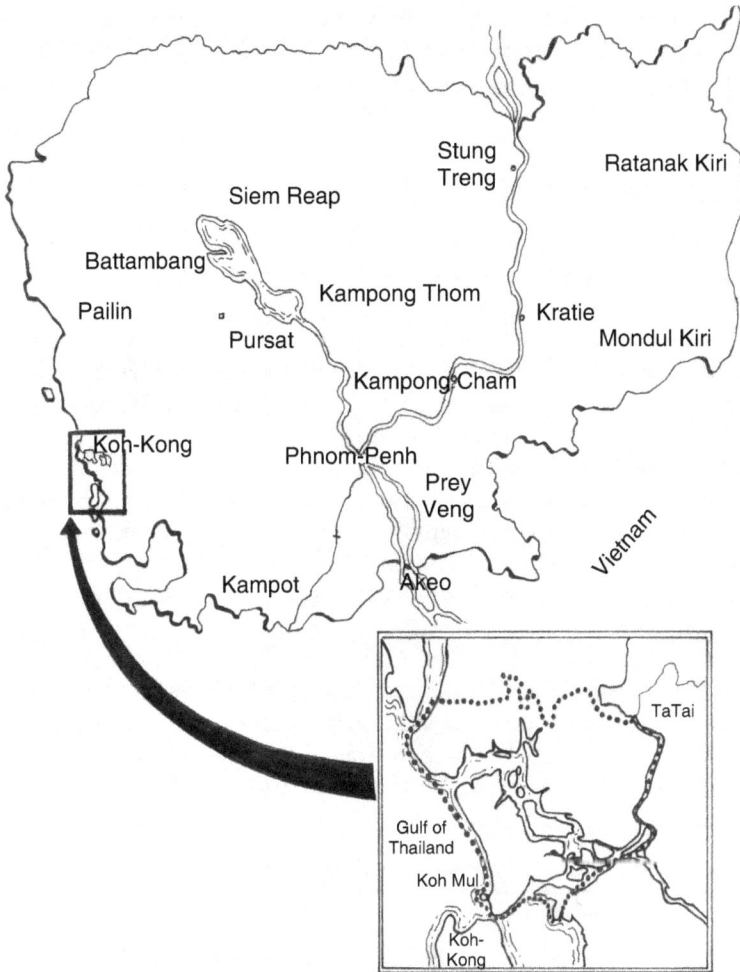

Figure 8.2 Location of the Peam Krasaop Wildlife Sanctuary in Cambodia

order to build the capacity of provincial and local authorities, the PMMR team has held many training courses and sent provincial and local leaders to participate in training courses on mangrove forest management in Thailand. Local villagers have been sponsored on study tours to other areas in Cambodia where local people are also working on CBNRM. In adopting an action research approach, much of the team's learning has come from working directly with villagers on resource management issues, and from networking with partners to help them to better understand CBNRM processes. It is argued that much of the success of this research project is due to this explicit orientation to learning with partners versus implementing blueprint plans, regardless of how the latter may be developed. Perhaps, in part, this learning orientation was in reaction to individual experiences of team members while working with or watching NGOs and government institutions facilitate time-consuming and complicated planning processes led by a small number of people. Such processes sometimes resulted in plans that were not accepted by villagers.

International and regional partnerships

The PMMR project began in late 1997. This was a time when only a few donors were working on community-based management in Cambodia, when CBNRM as a concept was very new to all participants. Much of the initial emphasis of earlier projects was upon community forestry. The PMMR project did not quite fit into this dialogue, given that the team was working in mangrove fishing communities with many in-migrants. Consequently, at first a national–international dialogue was critical while national-level staff sought to understand CBNRM concepts, and while international advisers started to comprehend the unique Cambodian context. Networking with other IDRC partners, therefore, was an important first step in PMMR. It allowed everyone to learn what was involved with community-based management, and to learn participatory, analytical and other skills related to researching resource management issues.

Project advisers who visited from Canada or who lived in Cambodia have held multiple roles with the PMMR team, being friends, facilitators, trainers, questioners and sceptics. As the CBNRM work unfolded, from the PMMR team's perspective it was essential that there was a dialogue among national and international members regarding questions and situations that arose. Although

Table 8.1 Partnerships with PMMR: enhancing a movement

IDRC partnerships
Dalhousie University, Canada; LeaRN CBNRM Networking Project, Philippines; Tam Giang Lagoon Project, Hue, Vietnam; IDRC, Ottawa, Canada; Coady Institute, Antigonish, Canada

Regional partnerships
Songkla University, Thailand; Mangrove Action Project, Thailand; Can Gio Mangrove Reserve, Department of Forestry, Ho Chi Minh City, Vietnam; United Nations Environment Programme

National partnerships (government/NGO)
CBNRM Case Study Writing and Networking Initiative; CBNRM Network (IDRC projects, quarterly meetings); Oxfam America; Oxfam UK; Community Fisheries Development Office, Department of Fisheries; Coastal Coordinating Unit, Ministry of Environment

Strategic Koh Kong partnerships
Coastal Zone Management, DANIDA; Seila NREM Mainstreaming, Koh Kong; American Friends Service Committee, Koh Kong

---

Source: PMMR, 2004.

initially advisers played a critical role in helping to shape the project, with time this shifted into local staff taking the lead. Therefore, the role of project advisers evolved over time. Now, in a supportive context, their role is to challenge team members to help them to reflect and learn more from their experiences. Table 8.1 lists these PMMR partnerships.

Networking in Asia and Canada

Similar to the PMMR team's relationships with project advisers, the team's experiences with regional networking evolved over time. Networking in the region and through international study experiences always seems like a good idea. In fact, several national staff participated in university courses in Canada. Comments such as 'we need more training', or 'we need to build our capacity', are common, especially when embarking on a research project that demands an analysis of complicated situations. Hence, PMMR team members were exposed to several training events, both in the region and in Canada.

> My first trip to Canada, learning with other students, was really hard. I had been so excited to have the opportunity to learn from others, but I found it really hard to follow the ideas or to share very much even though I had a lot of field experiences. I really had to make an effort to speak and to get people to listen to me.
>
> Ouk Li Khim, a national PMMR team member

However, training, study tours and international courses alone are not enough to understand CBNRM concepts. It takes continuous practice, reflection, more training and then refinement before experiences can be synthesized and fully understood.

At times, workshops, meetings or projects with regional IDRC partners have created a cooperation that actually felt forced, like something that PMMR was obliged to participate in. At other times, team members have been genuinely excited by such opportunities. Team members' skills in English might be considered adequate, but none is particularly fluent. It takes serious effort to respond to e-mails, read documents, search the web or contribute to discussions. Regional networking takes away from local work. However, regional interaction can provide the spark that helps people really grasp what they are doing. Over time, the research team began to appreciate the value of such networks and the potential that the learning brought. 'Sometimes I need to hear outside ideas, even if I don't fully understand them, to consider if these may help me in my work,' noted An, a provincial team member.

Over time, the PMMR team became more sophisticated in ensuring that they could benefit from these sorts of exchanges. For example, when the team wanted to initiate a reflection session with local institutions, they knew they did not have the time to design an in-depth training programme. They contacted a Philippine CBNRM networking project called Learning and Research Network for CBNRM (LeaRN). This group designed an approach that would enable the team to learn more about participatory monitoring and evaluation approaches. For LeaRN, it was an excellent chance to learn about a new context and to adapt their skills. After LeaRN facilitated a training session in Phnom Penh, the PMMR team was able to adapt the lessons so that they could facilitate an appropriate village-level reflection session (with support from LeaRN). Such a networking approach, which enables both partners to learn, results in greater appreciation for context and differences. Moreover, it builds a pool of resource people in the region who can contact each other, long after projects end, to work through other issues.

PMMR team members have linked with other networks too. In August 2003, they hosted a workshop in Koh Kong for fishers from Thailand, Sri Lanka and Cambodia. Although Cambodian fishers had participated in such exchanges previously, it was the first time that the network had come together in Cambodia. The workshop was hosted by the PMMR team in collaboration with local resource management institutions. The emphasis was on fishers learning with each other. One fisher from Siem Reap province who attended the Koh Kong workshop noted:

> While sometimes this is a new way of thinking for us, but if we think about our homes and what we do, it makes sense that we have to take care of the fish and the forest. I am just very sorry that those with power do not see the importance of this. (Marschke, 2004)

For this fisher, such exchanges created an understanding of environmental issues and the reasons why villagers play a role in resource management. Exchanges help broaden views, incorporating complicated issues that concern government officials, community members and international experts. Networking can also create unexpected opportunities such as securing additional funding, learning new skills and solving a problem.

Understanding the national policy context

Since Cambodia is a strongly hierarchical social context, having high-level political support for NRM activities is essential. That is, one needs to engage with policy-makers in ways that are both formal (laws) and informal (official endorsement). Consider the fisheries reform. In October 2000, the prime minister of Cambodia visited the provinces and heard about conflicts between fishers and fishing lot owners. He immediately announced the release of 8,000 ha from the 84,000 ha under commercial fishing lots in Siem Reap province. By February 2001, the government had agreed to release 536,000 ha from the fishing lot system for local community management, which represented 56 per cent of the entire area under commercial fishing lots in Cambodia (Evans, 2002). Although no law was in place to support such a reform, the prime minister wields enough power to mandate such a change.

It is perceived by many government officials that villagers have a low capacity or limited skills and experiences for resource management. This, in part, is related to the hierarchical nature of Khmer society. The challenge, therefore, is to break down negative perceptions while getting higher-level officials to support CBNRM processes. The PMMR team has had to consider how to present CBNRM concepts, especially to those persons who can make decisions to support – or not support – community involvement in NRM.

Exchanges with government institutions: national and provincial partnerships

A direct benefit from extensive networking during meetings, study tours, field visits, workshops and socializing is the strong support all PMMR project team members derive from national and provincial government organizations. For instance, higher-level officials are willing to give their support to village-level resource management activities, even though there is no legal framework to mandate such activities. That is, each local-level resource management institution, known as a village management committee (VMC), has created a management plan, which includes rules and regulations along with an area to manage. These plans are recognized by appropriate technical institutions and by the provincial governor, as well as by the Minister of the Environment, for those villages found inside a protected area. When dealing with resource issues, it helps the VMCs to know that they have support for their work, whether it is to stop illegal activities or to try different village-level initiatives.

By enhancing decision-makers' understanding of CBNRM concepts, the PMMR team has had a significant influence in the MoE and in Koh Kong province. Between 1997 and 2004, the PMMR team organized a series of workshops and strategic field visits with national and provincial government officers whose mandate was to develop coastal resources and local livelihoods. This strategy involved consistently bringing key decision-makers to the field and facilitating an exchange between villagers and government officials. Table 8.2 outlines the strategy.

While the PMMR team has hosted multiple workshops and study tours, written reports and papers, and encouraged villagers to speak in many venues, the annual televised field visit from the MoE and other high-ranking officials has been the activity which has contributed the most to promoting the work of the communities. These visits, combined with annual mangrove replanting activities, were what the villagers remembered as most significant. In fact, some activities facilitated by the PMMR team have been particularly useful for villages while others have been insightful for government staff. This is why engaging in a range of strategies is an important aspect of the research team's work.

Initially, the PMMR supported villagers to plant mangroves in exchange for rice. After several years, the provincial governor began supporting this activity personally, and it appears that support for mangrove replanting continues to grow. In 2004, a National Assembly member pledged his support for the communities to replant mangroves in exchange for rice. Sok Net commented, 'Did you hear that Tia Bun (a National Assembly member) will support our

Table 8.2 Creating relationships with strategic government officials

Year	PMMR objective(s)	Action(s) facilitated
1997	Introduce the minister and provincial governor to mangrove fishing communities.	The PMMR organized a field visit for the Minister of the Environment and the provincial governor so they could see the mangroves and better understand the livelihood of several villages in PKWS; the PMMR objectives for fieldwork were expressed at this point. **Outcome** Key stakeholders began considering coastal environmental issues and the role of resource management by government institutions.
1999	Provide a forum to discuss mangrove conservation issues. Invite high officials to see mangrove degradation in PKWS (during the 1998 election period).	• The PMMR invited representatives from MoE and the provincial governor of Koh Kong to participate in a workshop discussing coastal resource management from the perspective of provincial government officials. • The PMMR organized a field visit, especially to show the recently degraded mangroves near Koh Kapic village. **Outcome** • More government officials agreed to stop obtaining money from the destruction of coastal resources, and to participate in the conservation and protection of mangrove resources. • One district chief who was heavily involved in resource extraction was removed from his position by the provincial governor.
2000	Facilitate a field visit with the minister and the Canadian ambassador to get endorsement for CBNRM.	Since it was challenging for the PMMR to get support for CBNRM among local government officials, another strategy was to get top-down support. Hence, the PMMR invited the Minister of the Environment and the Canadian ambassador to visit the project site. **Outcome** The PMMR team's work was supported by key officials. This helped get more support from local authorities and provincial technical departments. As a result, local communities gained more power and the right to be involved in CBNRM.
2001	Show decision-makers or government officers the CBNRM process in PKWS.	The PMMR arranged for the delegation of high officials of the government (Minister of Environment, Minister of Fisheries, member of the national assembly, representatives from USAID) to learn from the local community in PKWS about mangrove resource management.

Table 8.2 (Contd)

Year	PMMR objective(s)	Action(s) facilitated
	Set up open forum between high government officials and local communities.	This enabled villagers to share their CBNRM issues with high officials, communicate where more support was needed and allow for an exchange of ideas. **Outcome** The CBNRM concept was better understood by key officials in the government of Cambodia. Much of the legal framework has since been reformed to support local communities in natural resource management.
2002	Monitor the local community's involvement in CBNRM. Disseminate the idea of local community development to donors.	The PMMR team and the VMCs organized a field trip for members of the MoE and the provincial governor to demonstrate the results of the project and to help them understand the need for their community development. **Outcome** • Every year the provincial governor gives rice to the local community for its mangrove replanting. • Outside organizations began to invest in the village, e.g. for schools, pagodas, wells, clinics, etc., and villagers feel confident to negotiate these types of interactions.
2003	—	National elections, with campaigning. Not suitable to bring campaigning politicians to endorse VMC work (since the VMC is not meant to be a political organization, such messages would be confusing).

Source: PMMR, 2002.

mangrove replanting? He will provide 15 t of rice for us, and 5 t for Koh Kapic [a neighbouring village]. I'm really pleased.' Net, although not a member of the VMC, participates annually in mangrove replanting activities. She was pleased that a high-ranking official would consider supporting her community.

Sometimes additional attention can lead to conflicts among the VMC members or in the community. For example, unknown to the PMMR, the MoE issued a certificate of dedication to key villagers working on community-based management in various protected areas. The provincial director of the environment nominated one VMC member from Koh Sralao who was given this certificate. Other villagers became angry because they felt that the entire committee worked on community-based management and that one person should not be favoured unless it was the VMC chief. The provincial director of environment never thought to ask the PMMR team or the VMC members before making this appointment. In addition, he did not consider the internal ramifications of what he perceived as a nice gesture. The PMMR team, therefore, held group sessions with government officials encouraging them to think about the implications of their deeds before acting. Also, they were asked to consult VMC members so that people would not have bad feelings about one person being singled out, but rather feel proud that someone in their village had been recognized.

Local authority cooperation

In Cambodia, local authority refers to administrative units that conduct various government functions. Provincial, district, commune and village administrative units all fall under the Ministry of the Interior. Any community-based management initiative requires both support from and participation by local authorities, especially endorsement for activities at the village and commune levels. Of note is that commune powers increased with the 2002 elections. If civil society movements emerge without local support, conflict can arise. Therefore, the PMMR team took the approach to involve local authorities wherever possible to ensure smooth operations at the village level. This provides village institutions with a line of communication, apart from the PMMR team, when they wish to solve their conflicts.

However, the following story indicates the challenges of getting local institutions (police and the VMC) to cooperate to solve resource management conflicts:

Dom was acting as the temporary head of Koh Sralao's VMC, since the VMC head was exploring livelihood opportunities elsewhere. Stolen fishing gear is one of the biggest challenges fishers face, and sometimes the VMC is asked to help solve thefts.

Sareun, a crab fisher from Koh Sralao, came across 40 empty crab traps near his fishing ground. No one claimed these traps during the time he was out fishing, so he decided to take them himself. When he returned to the village, he talked to Dom. They decided that most likely someone had stolen the traps and subsequently left them. They agreed to leave three traps at Dom's house and the rest with Sareun, and to advise the villagers that some crab traps had been found. They documented what they were doing and thumb-printed the paper to make it clear that Sareun did not steal these traps.

A month went by, and no one claimed the traps. Sareun decided to sell the traps to someone known as Po who lived in a neighbouring village. This exchange took place at a communal fishing ground called Chrouy Pros Bay, used by both villages. A few weeks later, the original owner happened to see his crab traps and reclaimed them. He was quite upset that someone from a neighbouring village had his traps and went to the police. The police hauled Po in for questioning.

Sareun quickly called Dom, the VMC chief, to explain to the police what had happened. However, the police dismissed Dom, saying that this was a matter for the police to handle and that he should not be involved. The police thought that the fisher, Po, had stolen the traps and should be fined.

After an intense exchange of words between the police and Dom, Dom realized that he needed some help to negotiate this situation. He called Rathana, a PMMR provincial team member, to help solve this conflict.

Rathana met the police and Dom to help them find a solution. Since the police are meant to cooperate with the VMC on issues relating to NRM, Rathana encouraged each side to explain their story. He emphasized that fishing gear theft is complicated, since gear often is exchanged through many hands. Eventually, a solution was found. The original crab trap owner got his crab traps back and Po got half his money back from Sareun. It was not a perfect solution, but it was considered fair. More importantly, it was agreed that in the future the VMC must work directly with the police and notify them if stolen gear is found.

Theft of fishing gear is a constant issue in fishing villages. The police are in on this. The villagers steal from each other. The VMCs make mistakes in how they handle these situations. These days, PMMR staff are acting as facilitators and are an important option for villagers to turn to. Smaller conflicts generally can be solved locally, but sometimes require outside facilitation. The VMCs need adequate support to help them solve issues related to resource management. If not, the CBNRM process will fall apart.

Community partnerships

The PMMR team was welcomed in the villages because it is composed of provincial and national staff, and because Khmer culture demands deference to authorities. Over time, this relationship has changed from one of formality to one of cooperation. Villagers initially agreed to anything that the PMMR suggested, even if they never planned to do anything about it. For example, villagers agreed to do monthly garbage cleanup but never did unless the PMMR team came to the village. After five years of thinking about waste management issues, however, one village has now devised its own waste management system, and is in the process of trying it. Over the years, villagers have become more comfortable in expressing their views and in connecting with the team, either at their provincial office or even in Phnom Penh. Meanwhile, the team realized that there was much to learn from villagers, and that each field visit brought some new learning or insight. Notably, the current approach evolved over several years of field visits, training and exchanges.

To date, four VMCs have been elected by villagers. These committees, to varying degrees, play a role in helping villagers with livelihood issues and coastal environmental protection. Importantly, they work together not only to identify and prioritize their problems, but also to experiment with different solutions. The VMCs engage in multiple activities including mangrove replanting, stopping illegal fishing and hunting, forming strategies to prevent loss of fishing gear, waste management, conflict resolution in the community and village infrastructure development (school, pagoda, bridge, road). Table 8.3 shows the key characteristics of the VMC in Koh Sralao.

Table 8.3 What one VMC did: the case of Koh Sralao village

Year established	2000
Legal status	Informal. The management plan and management area are supported by agreements with the provincial governor and the Minister of the Environment.
Management issues addressed	Illegal fishing from within and outside the community, mangrove cutting and charcoal production, fishing gear theft, declining resources, waste management and other community issues.
Examples of management strategies	Solving theft through innovative solutions (painting crab traps, patrolling); supporting local teachers.
Reasons for villagers' support	Key villagers are involved in the committee; strong leadership is respected; people believe the committee is working on the village's behalf and see good results; village leaders openly support committee.

Source: Adapted from Marschke, 2003.

Some VMCs appear to be able to run activities on their own, using the PMMR to help with conflict resolution or for financial support. Others struggle to carry out activities or find solutions and require greater facilitation input from the PMMR. Committee members all volunteer their time. Some may initially join, thinking it will enhance their power in the village or for other reasons. However, those who remain engaged see this as an opportunity to learn with outsiders and believe in what they are doing. 'I want to help my community. We are really poor. We know that when the mangroves increase, this will help the poor fishers a lot, especially in the rainy season,' comments Wayne Som Sak.

The PMMR team often finds itself acting as an anchor, facilitating potentially sticky situations. The following experience highlights the need for facilitation, to ensure situations do not become explosive.

Water is an issue in Koh Kang village: there is no ground water supply on this tiny mangrove island, and fresh water is brought by boat by a middleperson from an upland area. With support from the PMMR team, the VMC decided to build two water-holding tanks in the village. A contract was made with the middleperson to sell water at a slightly reduced cost because water could be pumped into one tank, saving the time involved in water delivery. The tanks were placed at opposite ends of the village, with the caretaker of the holding tanks getting access to free water supply. Two women from poorer households, who were active in the VMC, were chosen as caretakers.

This system has been in place for several years now. However, the PMMR team has helped to negotiate several internal squabbles within the village. For example, several people complained to the team that the caretaker only sold water to members of the opposing political party. These people were connected to the village chief and the ruling political party and the situation happened around national election time (July 2003). The PMMR facilitators felt that this case was related to politics and suggested that it could only be resolved through a group discussion, open to everyone.

PMMR team members went to the village to learn more. The caretaker was quite upset and wanted to meet the people who accused her of not selling water. Facilitators encouraged both parties not to cause conflicts. Then, a meeting was called to remind people that the VMC work was not political and that it was designed to help the entire village. Interestingly, the villagers who had complained privately were unwilling to bring this issue up with the entire VMC. While PMMR team members have monitored the situation since, everyone seems clear that politics cannot be brought into water selling, and no more complaints have been heard.

Having additional water-storage tanks built in the village and having water subsequently being sold at a reduced price has helped to ease life in Koh Kang. Those villagers who cannot afford water tanks can access water at a reduced price, while those who have water tanks can get their water pumped directly at a slightly higher cost. As with any resource management system, internal conflicts will ensue. Successful management occurs 'not because there is an absence of diversity, conflict, and power struggles, but through established mechanisms for negotiation and resolution' (Sick, 2002).

Since the PMMR project research team is only temporary, it is critical to encourage permanent conflict resolution mechanisms. For now, the team serves as a moderator, offering a valuable learning experience to team members and to those involved in resource management. An important lesson is that each situation needs monitoring. In Cambodia at least, community-based management work often ignores the influence of local politics. It is important that CBNRM initiatives are seen as politically neutral so that all villagers can feel comfortable to participate. It is equally important that government facilitators do not spread their political beliefs to influence who participates in resource management at the local level. What needs to be fostered is the notion that technical departments have a role in supporting local resource management institutions.

Stopping charcoal production: using the networks

Just like fishing gear theft, stopping illegal charcoal production represents another ongoing battle for villagers and provincial officers. In the 1990s, many villagers came to the area to produce charcoal because mangrove wood burns well, producing a high-quality charcoal, which is sold to Thailand. This system was complicated, with intermediaries reaping most of the benefits and poorer persons cutting the mangrove trees and producing the charcoal. Various government-supported crackdowns began in the mid-1990s, with the most significant in 1999. By this point, it was clear to villagers that producing charcoal was not a secure option for them, and most people switched to fishing.

When the VMCs in the area began producing their resource management plans, stopping illegal activities such as charcoal production and dynamite fishing was included. Each community tried to make its plan for coastal resources protection and conservation. Before the establishment of the VMCs, local communities were afraid to stop illegal activities, especially those supported by powerful persons. However, the situation described below shows the growing confidence of the VMC in its resource management work.

> In May 2002, the VMC in Koh Sralao detained one boat carrying mangrove logs. This boat did not have permission from the VMC to cut trees. According to the regulations, mangrove trees could be cut for house construction by villagers only with permission from the VMC. However, the boat owner was related to the provincial police commander. Therefore, after the VMC had confiscated his logs, he called the provincial police. The provincial police called the provincial PMMR team leader, who reminded them that the provincial governor was the one who had signed the management plans of the VMC, and that the VMC was stopping illegal activities. The PMMR member asked the police to work with the VMC to solve this issue while reminding the VMC that it had the right to solve this conflict. The VMC was able to negotiate with the boat owner to pay a fine and sign an agreement saying he would no longer carry out illegal activities in the area.

This action set a precedent of vital significance, particularly because the boat owner had connections to the provincial police, an organization far more powerful than the VMC. The VMC needed the support of the PMMR team especially to remind it that it had the right to stop this activity. It was up to the VMC to negotiate how to solve this problem. Without the signature of the governor and the facilitation support from the PMMR team, it is debatable whether this could have proved successful. There are many issues in CBNRM development, but capacity-building and cooperation among relevant stakeholders on coastal resource management are key priorities. Sometimes the task of including multiple stakeholders is exhausting but the support generally proves beneficial over time. The successful mangrove resources protection in PKWS comes from strong cooperation and participation among interested stakeholders who support CBNRM both directly and indirectly.

Conclusion

Field stories, whether about negotiating crab trap theft, illegal mangrove cutting or the politics of selling water, help to illustrate why it takes active facilitation and extensive networking (in this case from the PMMR team) to ensure adequate support is in place for community-based management. The Khmer saying '*neak mein knong*', which literally translates as 'person with back', refers to the idea that someone with greater power is supporting them. Thus, there is a role for donors and international consultants to play in these processes, just as there is for high-level officials. Such backing and political support are a key ingredient for successful community-based management, since project partners also need to know that their work is supported. Yet when it comes to actually implementing CBNRM on the ground, it takes a team of people committed to problem-solving and working consistently on issues with different partners. Most importantly, it takes villagers who are willing to take risks and dedicate their time to resource management activities. The PMMR team's experience shows how critical such support or backing is at national, provincial and local levels to ensure that CBNRM processes can be carried out.

The PMMR experience illustrates the active role that one project team has taken in facilitating partnerships to support CBNRM. Is an external agent required, in the Cambodian context, to mobilize and stimulate a successful CBNRM movement? Backing beyond the village level is an important aspect of CBNRM in Cambodia. Villages are constantly negotiating and renegotiating livelihood and resource management issues, with or without CBNRM networks. Perhaps the value-added benefit that external agents can bring in enhancing (or creating) such partnerships is to create platforms to potentially address CBNRM issues at multiple levels. This is particularly apt because many things cannot be handled at the village level alone. We believe that this support does not need to come from an outside project or NGO. It can also be fostered within, and even between, government departments, if there are a few motivated individuals able to mobilize themselves and others located in strategic positions.

The activities in this case study are described in terms of networking and facilitation. However, in this case the real transformation is in the perceived nature of rural development work and the role of senior government agents. The importance of village-level involvement in resource management is acknowledged. The transformation of perceptions has occurred through team members and partners who are involved in multiple PMMR project activities. It would now be hard for project staff to continue on to any other project or agency and not approach rural development as a more participatory, adaptive learning exercise.

CBNRM is a long-term process, and is challenging to negotiate in a context where short-term needs are also pressing and immediate. Thus, it is important to work on facilitating short-term solutions (such as solving fishing gear theft) and long-term ones (such as creating lasting conflict resolution mechanisms). From the PMMR team's perspective, taking the time to bring partners on board, and repeating messages and sharing lessons consistently is an important part of CBNRM. Trust-building takes time: partnerships do develop, especially when the goal is working towards a common objective. Therefore, CBNRM work is as much about changing attitudes as it is about changing practices.

Although many local authorities may have low technical skills in NRM, they know their local situation well. Provincial technical departments are mandated to help local authorities with resource management. The PMMR members come from provincial departments, and tend to have stronger skills from their extensive fieldwork than others in their departments. The intention of the PMMR team, therefore, is to continue building capacity and support for CBNRM within technical institutions and local authorities, so that village institutions can be adequately understood and appropriately supported. Working with a project that helps to facilitate learning and thinking is an important aspect of CBNRM.

We believe that training in project planning and implementation is not so critical. What is vital is helping people to solve their own problems and to think for themselves. This is a subtle but crucial difference. We advocate the use of networks to support a flexible and responsive approach to rural poverty reduction, rather than a document-driven approach.

CHAPTER 9

Scaling up community-based natural resource management in Guizhou province, China

Yuan Juanwen and Sun Qiu

Abstract

This chapter highlights two lessons from a multidisciplinary research team's experience in adopting a CBNRM approach in Guizhou province, China. The first lesson is that a CBNRM approach needs to be adapted to Chinese practice when attempting to work with multiple-level local government agencies, which are organized in a top-down structure. The second lesson is that one of the innovative and powerful elements of the CBNRM approach is the creation of a platform allowing villagers to voice their ideas, needs and interests, and to provide input to government-led programmes. An effective scaling-up strategy requires a diversity of action-oriented initiatives to allow government staff to become familiar with the strengths, challenges and advantages of CBNRM, experiment with the approach and adopt it in policies, programmes and projects.

Introduction

A research team at the Guizhou Academy of Agricultural Sciences (GAAS) has worked for nine years implementing CBNRM in Guizhou province, China. This experience proves how CBNRM can be used collaboratively with the government of China to improve the livelihoods of large numbers of rural people.

During the initial years, this project addressed NRM issues at the local level. Using participatory appraisal and action research tools, the team described and analysed both household and community-based management practices; evaluated the impact of economic, socio-cultural and agro-ecological factors on the natural resource base in the villages; and identified constraints and opportunities for technical, organizational and policy interventions aimed at improving livelihoods and the sustainable management of land, water and trees.

During the first six years from 1995 to 2001, the research involved only six villages. Therefore, the positive impacts on livelihoods and NRM in rural communities were largely overlooked by various levels of government. Like many other projects which have worked well with local communities, the grassroots successes and approaches were not integrated with local government processes, programmes and projects.

It should be noted that in China, 'local' encompasses several levels. The smallest unit of local organization is the village. Although a 'natural village' is a long-standing separate settlement, it is not a unit of government. The administrative village (commune) is an official unit defined for administrative purposes, frequently including several natural villages. Communes typically have leadership and committee structures that attend to community issues and interact with senior government agencies, but they have little administrative autonomy. Above the commune is the township, which is the lowest level of formal public administration. The level above townships is the county, which in many respects is the most powerful unit of local government. This has been a key unit of public administration through centuries of imperial history. In China, a county may include rural and urban settlements, and have a population of well over 1 million. Above the county is the prefecture, followed by the province. In this study, we refer mainly to the village, township and county levels of local government.

By 2001, trying to scale up the CBNRM approach in Guizhou province became the research team's logical next step (Sun, 2001). What has the GAAS team achieved so far? How have their accomplishments been realized? What elements of the CBNRM approach have contributed to success? What have been the challenges? What experiences and lessons have emerged from the project? In this case, we focus on these questions by describing and reflecting on the scaling-up action research that we have carried out since the end of 2001. However, before doing so, we will introduce the research site and summarize research carried out before that date.

The setting

The work started in Kaizuo township, located in the north of Changshun county, 60 km from Guiyang, the capital of Guizhou province. Guizhou, which is located in the southwest of China, is a karst (porous limestone) mountainous province and one of the poorest provinces in China. About half of its population belongs to ethnic minority groups. These groups mostly inhabit the mountainous rural areas where they manage complex production systems consisting of irrigated and rain-fed rice fields, less productive uplands and grasslands, forested areas and so-called wastelands.

In the period during the 1950s called the 'Great Leap Forward,' much of China, including Guizhou, was deforested to fuel local steel-production ovens. Most of the wastelands now found near villages were once forested. Regenerating them has been a slow, difficult process. Apart from these unproductive wastelands,

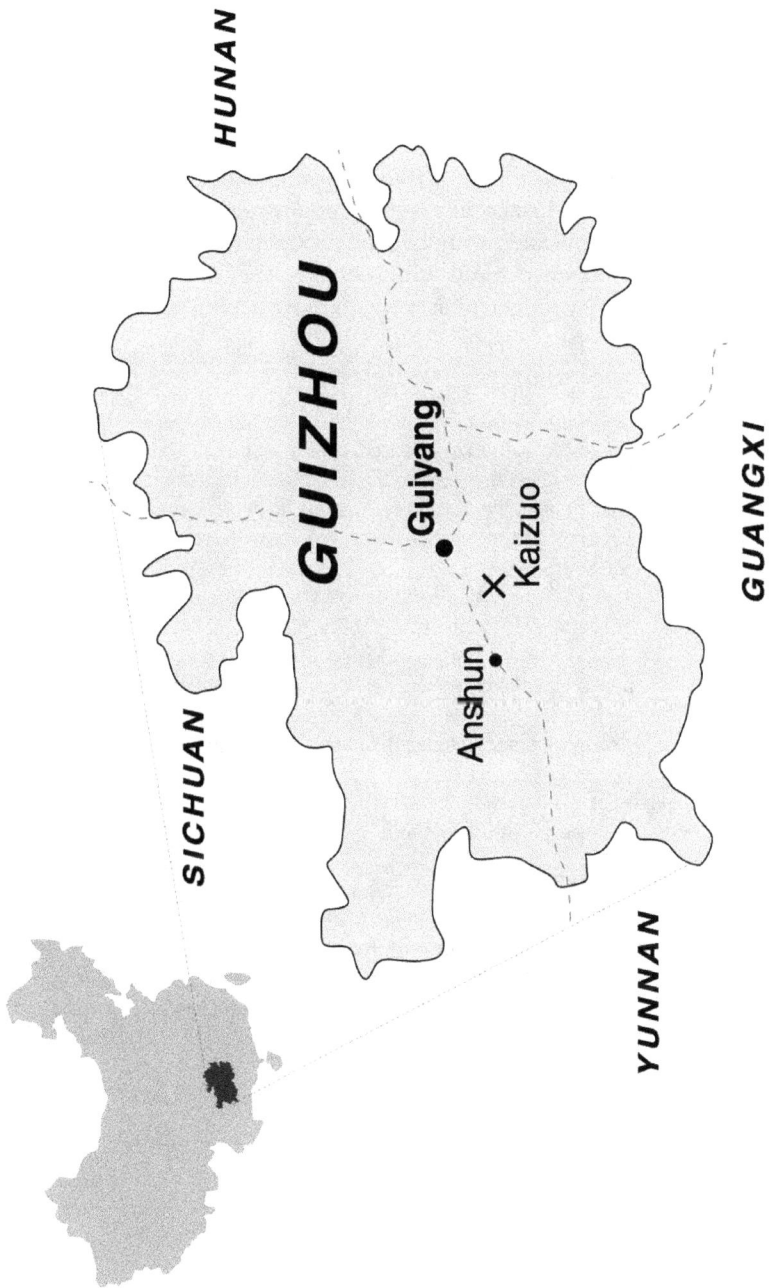

Figure 9.1 Map of China indicating Guizhou and research site

villagers are facing serious problems such as degraded forests, overgrazed common grasslands and water resources that have been affected by barren hillsides. Chronically low crop yields are the result. Introduction of improvements such as crop diversification has proved to be complicated.

Like farmers in other rural areas in Guizhou, those in Kaizuo make their living from fragile natural resources. Most farm lands are rain-fed and the few irrigation systems that work are small-scale, serving up to 10 households at most. Some of these systems fell into disuse after the commune production system collapsed, and they have progressively deteriorated since then (see Box 9.1 for a brief description of the changes following the demise of the commune system). Nobody took responsibility for the irrigation systems and no rules of use were defined. Although Kaizuo has seven pumping stations for irrigation, according to the township leaders only two are properly functioning.

The region's staple foods are rice and corn. Diets are poor and health problems abound. Nowadays, many younger villagers (men in particular) go to the city to

---

Box 9.1 Rural resource tenure and management

Since the early 1980s, China experienced rapid economic transformation from a centrally planned economy to a market-oriented one. Because of the economic reforms, the commune-level collective production system in rural China collapsed between 1980 and 1982. Under the commune system, farmers were organized to work collectively on farmlands and to manage water resources, forest and grasslands according to commune instructions. In turn, the commune received production orders from the central government. The state kept a tight control of natural resource use and management through its centrally planned economic system. After the breakdown of the system, both paddy and upland farmlands were contracted out to individual households under the household responsibility system. Meanwhile, the forests, grasslands, wetlands and water systems became the 'commons,' lands that were owned and managed collectively by the community or village.

Effective management mechanisms for sustainable NRM did not emerge overnight. The government made an effort to clarify private-use rights and tenure, but current laws, including the revised constitution, regard all natural resources as the collective property of local communities. Rural households cannot lay claim to these resources and have little or no incentive to develop new, collective ways of managing them, despite the potential benefits from such arrangements.

Furthermore, state laws and regulations are frequently too general to address daily or minor violations and the social dynamics that underpin them. This is why sound village regulations and folk or customary agreements formulated by farmers have a special significance and impact on CBNRM.

As a result, China's natural resources have been drastically degraded. To address issues of resource degradation and biodiversity, the Chinese government has recently developed some strategies. However, these have not had the desired results because of insufficient human resources to implement them and because the programmes are neither community-focused nor people-centred.

Source: Sun, 2004.

Figure 9.2 The landscape of the project site
Source: Yuan et al., 2004.

work and this is causing a serious labour shortage in the busy season. Villagers normally work together to complete every household's fieldwork in a rotating manner or to engage in other village activities. The formal education level in both villages is low and the dropout rate for children is high, especially for middle-level students. The average land holding per head is 23.7 mu (15 mu equals 1 ha), and as mentioned, land utilization is very low. The arable land resource per head varies from 3.8 mu to 2.6 mu. Water resources are scarce and difficult to access because of the karst topography. The villagers – mostly women – must fetch water from some distance. They must wait for the rains to irrigate their fields naturally. In comparison, artificially irrigated fields, where they exist, bring high yields (Chen et al., 2002; Zhou et al., 1998).

Putting CBNRM into practice: insights from the first six years

Getting started

Before 1995, GAAS researchers had done a lot of agricultural research and extension work, but many of their activities proved unsuccessful or unsustainable because they focused on the technology and overlooked the socio-economic aspects of their work. For instance, when they did extension work for hybrid varieties of rapeseed, they did not notice that internal migration was causing a labour shortage. Hence, despite investing serious efforts and resources in the extension work, farmers only adopted and used the new varieties for a short period of time. When the extension work moved to another topic, farmers abandoned the new varieties. In 1995, a multidisciplinary research team at GAAS started a research project to address these problems. The team decided to introduce and practise a CBNRM approach in two villages, Dabuyang and Xiaozhai, in Kaizuo township of Changsuan county. Four other villages were added later when the research team expanded its field-based learning sites.

CBNRM provided an alternative approach to addressing NRM concerns. In particular, a major theme has been supporting both the formal and informal organization of farmers, empowering them by enhancing their capacities and promoting a supportive institutional environment. The GAAS team formulated three main hypotheses to guide the research.

- Local institutions are essential for sustainable NRM.
- Capacity-building of farmers is the basis for institutional development.
- A supportive environment for collective action of local communities is key for developing sustainable community-based institutions.

With input from and participation of villagers, the team facilitated the implementation of a number of research interventions and monitored and evaluated their impact.

Local institutional development for sustainable resource management: building on local knowledge and practice

The villages have a tradition of creating local regulations to manage the community, including how to deal with theft, crop destruction and security problems. Yet in discussions with the villagers, the team learned that there were no such regulations concerning NRM. Accordingly, the project researchers facilitated a series of village meetings with a view to filling this gap. Specific persons and groups were designated to enforce the new regulations. Dabuyang formulated water, road, cattle and forest management regulations, whereas Xiaozhai formulated rules governing water and forest management. Regulations were drawn up by the villagers themselves and accepted at village meetings, thereby giving them the force of customary law. As a result, villagers followed the rules as best as they could. Villages also formed resource management groups which monitored the effectiveness of the regulations and were supported by the research team.

Farming technology options were provided and farmers and researchers tested them on fields. For example, farmers tried planting fruit trees and mushrooms and intercropping with crops such as maize and wheat or rapeseed and maize. Cross-farm visits were organized to analyse the experiments and share experiences.

A participatory approach to infrastructure-building at the community level was designed with a particular emphasis on integrating livelihood improvements and innovative management processes. Male and female farmers were involved in the decision-making, design, mobilization of resources (labour, materials and funds), construction, operations and maintenance. For example, in one village, a 200-year-old drinking-water problem was solved by the construction of a village-managed drinking-water system. Government technicians had given up on this problem, declaring that the village did not have enough water resources in the first place; however, the old-timers in the village knew better. Moreover, after the water system was constructed, villagers drew up a set of standards and rules to define the rights and obligations of users. Water meters meant that individuals paid by use and the management group used those revenues for maintenance and other village priorities.

After three years, visible improvements began to be observed in the pilot villages' use and management of their water, arable land, forest and wasteland resources. Significant changes in incomes resulted. However, the more important accomplishment of the project was giving women and men the opportunity to participate actively in managing these resources. This was a vast improvement over the traditional rural development approach. As one villager remarked,

> We have not held a community meeting to discuss community affairs in a long time. The government usually makes the decisions for us. Now that we have begun to organize to manage our resources, we are seeing more and more benefits.

With hardly any effort on the part of the researchers or the villagers, some nearby communities started to find out what was happening in Dabuyang and Xiaozhai. On their own initiative, they visited the project sites and, seeing the improvements for themselves, wondered if the same assistance could be given to their communities. Some local government officials also came to observe the progress made in the project sites. This prompted the researchers to think about the possibility of expanding the coverage of their project to other villages.

Deepening our understanding and expanding our efforts

In 1998, the project expanded to four new villages (Dongkou, Chaoshan, Guntang and Niuanyin), to validate the experiences and lessons gained from the original two project sites (Dabuyang and Xiaozhai villages) and to deepen the team's understanding of the CBNRM approach. The team members felt that they had only begun to understand CBNRM ideas and practices. In the next three years, the team worked on several issues and innovations. At the same time, they continued to monitor health, nutrition and environmental conditions in Dabuyang and Xiaozhai. In the four new villages, participatory analyses of resource management systems, including a study of gender roles, were carried out and constraints and opportunities for interventions were identified. The research team also broadened the involvement of key stakeholders, actively including local and provincial-level administrators and policy-makers.

In the next three years, the team undertook many more activities such as clarifying property rights to forestland, infrastructure development and participatory agricultural technology testing. Just as in the first phase, villagers were involved in all aspects of these projects, including identification of needs, project design, implementation and maintenance. Investments, which were partly supported by the research team, were small compared with most government projects. A significant addition, however, was the use of PM&E. This process helped the villagers to better monitor and maintain the introduced systems because problems or issues that could undermine the project's sustainability could be identified early and addressed while the system was installed or began to operate. It also stimulated a critical reflection on the whole process of participation, including the action research decision-making process (Vernooy, Sun and Xu, 2003).

Villagers reported that one important result of the project and its approach was increased community cohesiveness, which helped villagers identify and solve many other problems. Increased numbers of community groups, especially women's groups, became organized and so women's voices became more prominent. As well, self-learning groups grew in importance. Meetings became more lively community events at which issues could be discussed. This broke with the past, when everyone simply had to listen to government officials deliver instructions, and the villagers rarely met to develop a new activity. Thanks to the innovations introduced by the research project, they have learned the value of discussing their affairs, needs, priorities and problems. Now they identify ways to change things collectively that they themselves consider appropriate. This represents a remarkable change.

During this phase, the team also made modest efforts to involve government agencies in the project. Because it was being implemented within the government's jurisdiction and many of the project's activities were normally done by the government, the team made an effort to let the local authorities know about what they were doing. For instance, they invited township or county officials to village meetings, study tours, training and other activities. Government officials seldom attended these events. Their own internal incentives did not encourage involvement, and they felt no ownership of any of the project activities or even the project itself. Some officials, however, began to recognize the merits of the approach and said they wanted to learn more.

Many visitors from government and NGOs visited the six villages and met leaders and farmer groups to discuss the work and CBNRM approach. They expressed their appreciation of the efforts and could see clear changes. However, few government projects adopted successful elements of the CBNRM approach in their own activities or planning. This contrasted with neighbouring villages that readily adopted or adapted some elements. Despite this government attitude, we continued to explore the possibility of getting government involved as a partner in order to spread the approach and benefits further, as well as to make the government more responsive to rural people. In particular, we thought that the following three principles could be scaled up:

- building and strengthening villagers' knowledge and skills are a sound basis for effective NRM;

- increasing villagers' participation, especially that of women, in the entire management process (decision-making, design, implementation, maintenance, monitoring and evaluation) is critical;
- local NRM groups and locally formulated regulations are the key institutions.

Trying to scale up CBNRM experiences and processes

In 2001, the research team realized that the project's initial success would remain small-scale without the greater involvement of the government. But given the complexity of the governmental system, particularly its many levels and multiple institutions, the team had a difficult time deciding how and at what level to deal with this challenge. In China, the government is stratified in five levels: national, provincial, prefecture, county and township. There are many line agencies and so-called special programmes. There is often a lack of coordination or even interaction among all the different government units. Sometimes, serious conflicts exist.

The government system is heavily bureaucratic and decision-making is top-down. There is very little space for villagers to influence policy-making and policy implementation. The government has a preference for large-scale demonstration projects because they are perceived to generate quick economic gains. Environmental considerations remain mostly of secondary priority or are ignored altogether. The diverse ideas, needs and interests of female and male farmers are not taken into consideration in this type of intervention. Although the central government is developing more people-oriented programmes, projects and activities, these do not include monitoring and evaluation guidelines for tracking outcomes. Projects are often evaluated only when constructed or completed and not during their operational life. Local conditions are ignored and failures are common. In addition, the performance evaluation system of government officials in China ensures that they are only accountable to the higher ranks of government. They are not accountable to the people with or for whom they work, such as farmers. Despite official government instructions, when officials visit villages during government-led projects, they barely interact with villagers. Instead, they tend to 'watch the flowers from the horse's back', as the saying goes.

To design a strategy for scaling up our CBNRM approach, the team reviewed the literature on the topic. We also held a participatory planning workshop with NGO staff, government officials, donors and research team members. Before the workshop, the team carried out an evaluation of its work with villagers inside and outside the research site (Vernooy, Sun and Xu, 2003: 124–47). Six interrelated questions guided the strategy: Why scale up? What should be scaled up? For whom should we scale up: that is, who will actually use our methodologies and approaches at different levels? Who should implement the scaling-up process? When to scale up? How to scale up? The workshop helped the team to reflect on its previous work. Later we also met with other IDRC project teams to see how they were approaching this aspect of their work and compare their procedures with our own ideas and efforts.

Following the workshop, the team experimented with a methodology combining a horizontal and a vertical strategy, as Figure 9.3 demonstrates. From a horizontal viewpoint, the project focused on community-to-community interactions to build a strong social base, for example, through farmer-to-farmer or villager-to-villager extension. The aim was to strengthen the villagers' organizational capacities socially, economically and politically. Vertically, the project aimed to promote government and community cooperation and multistakeholder partnership development. As well, it helped facilitate recognition of community-based institutions for NRM, and to change the government system and operations so that they could become more responsive and dynamic. In fact, the goal was to change the way in which government works with villagers. Our hypothesis was that both strategies are required in the Chinese context.

Meanwhile, the team was encouraged because the government adopted a policy supporting poverty-alleviation planning, an autonomy law and other people-centred guidelines among the participating villages during the research project (Sun, 2001). These are examples of how policy direction from the national and provincial levels helped reinforce the local participatory institutions which the project sought to scale up.

Three types of action research projects were identified as testing grounds for CBNRM-based partnerships with the government. All represented a mix of vertical and horizontal elements. In each case, however, the township officials were key implementers in adopting a CBNRM approach, while the project team acted as facilitators, mentors, coordinators, trainers and researchers. This was a challenge in the Chinese context, as it represented a radical change from past practice, and introduced new roles for both government staff and researchers. At the time, we chose to concentrate on investment types of projects because they are the most common type of service provided by line agencies in agriculture and village development. Three experiments in participatory institutional and organizational development were conducted:

1. Small-grant projects (financially supported by the research team) that were fully managed by the community. This was a wholly horizontal scaling out, because villagers learned from one another about group management and how to implement and monitor this type of project. Villagers set priorities and managed funds (which only covered part of the actual costs) themselves, according to rules and regulations developed in a series of meetings. The township officials agreed to this approach and committed themselves to assisting the villagers in several tasks. Four roads were built to link the villages to their market, one animal bank was established to help poor farmers acquire animals, two water-systems were built and one mushroom production activity was started.
2. Projects supported by small grants that were provided either by the research team or by the government. This project type combined horizontal

---

Vertical approach

Scaling up within the government system
- Cooperating with line ministries to integrate CBNRM elements into government projects.
- Advocating CBNRM to higher-level government via mass media, exposure of provincial officials to the project site, and networking with other organizations in the province and China.

Methods:
- institutionalizing within the local government system (township, county and higher levels);
- networking; and
- advocacy.

Horizontal approach

Scaling out through grassroots and area expansion
- Facilitating farmer and villager-led extension.
- Facilitating township government to practise CBNRM approaches through small-grant projects in more villages.
- Area expansion by the local government from six villages to the entire township.

Methods:
- farmer- and villager-led extension;
- village networking; and
- institutionalization within local government system.

Figure 9.3 Strategy for CBNRM scaling-up processes in Guizhou province
Source: Sun, 2001.

and vertical strategies. Township and county officials assisted villagers to implement the various activities. A CBNRM approach was integrated partially, in that some CBNRM elements were employed. Since the project had some counterpart investment, the project team had a say in how the project was run. This type of project included three biogas projects, two water-system projects, one potato and corn experiment, and one animal bank.

3. Projects supported exclusively by the government, but integrating some elements of CBNRM. This type combined vertical and minor horizontal elements. Township officials collaborated with county officials to assist the villagers to implement activities. A CBNRM approach was employed in a limited manner, such as in the implementation and management process. This type of project included one forest station, one terraced orchard and one water system.

After two years of efforts, the horizontal scaling out proved to be easier than vertical scaling up, with the exception of the institutionalization process within the township system. The scaling up turned out to be more challenging than the team anticipated. The three following examples illustrate the difficulties and limited successes in introducing more community involvement in policy-making and rural development in China. These examples offer an insight into daily action research practices aimed at changing the ways government officials, farmers and researchers think and behave.

Road construction: improving market access and introducing collective management

Huabian is a village with 63 households and 250 people. Compared with other villages, the community spirit there is good. Totally without government support and despite low household incomes, villagers installed a road lighting system several years ago. This is impressive as it is the only village in Kaizuo that has such a system. The Huabian village leader participated in the 'CBNRM scaling up' workshop in March 2002, together with village leaders from the whole area. They debated the development of their villages in a lively manner. The Huabian village head was inspired by the efforts and enthusiasm of some of the other villages to manage their community resources collectively and sustainably. Upon his return to Huabian, he immediately called a villagers' meeting to discuss how they could follow these examples. One week later, the village leader submitted a proposal to the township officials to build an improved road as a means to increase their market access. The villagers soon raised 7,000 yuan (over US$1,200) for the proposed work. Project team members and township officials met several times to discuss the proposal and to define a response. It was decided to offer Huabian 7,000 yuan as counterpart funding. After the busy planting season, the villagers started the road in July and took less than two months to finish 1.26 km of construction. After its completion, villagers formulated clear management regulations and so far, the road has been maintained very well (see Figure 9.4).

The example is instructive for several reasons.

- Exchange visits are extremely effective in horizontal scaling-out processes. Villagers normally have poor access to information and opportunities. Widening their horizons and seeing inspiring examples motivate new local initiatives.
- Village organization and community spirit are crucial while adopting a CBNRM approach. In most places in China, village spirit has been decreasing steadily since the land-reform policy of the late 1970s. How to reverse this trend is now the challenge.
- Because of village leaders' political and social position, they can play a key role in scaling out.

Extension of biogas production: adapting technologies and learning to negotiate

In early 2002, the project team and township officials of Kaizuo approached Changshun county to try to encourage its officials to integrate a CBNRM approach, or some elements of it, into their projects. The county leaders agreed and committed to experiment with the new approach in five of their projects. One of these involved the dissemination of biogas production technologies with construction subsidies to individual households. The biogas project aimed to reduce indiscriminate collection of firewood, which contributes to forest degradation, by providing local communities with alternative fuel sources. In 2003, 16 households in Chaoshan village were trained in biogas production technologies with support from the Changshun Agricultural Bureau (see below).

In implementing this project, Changshun county followed the provincial regulations which govern such projects. The first rule was that 70 per cent of households in each natural village and 70 per cent of the natural villages in each administrative unit had to be involved, on the assumption that the project would only be technically successful if at least 70 per cent of households used the gas produced. Additionally, each household was required to raise three pigs, in order to generate the amount of manure needed to produce the gas.

For the poor villagers of Chaoshan, these requirements were rather difficult. For one thing, the biogas system was not easy to build (see Figure 9.5). Second, acquiring and raising three pigs was more than most villagers could afford. In general, the central government encourages provincial officials to consider the local situation in implementing project guidelines flexibly. But unfortunately Guizhou officials decided to apply the criteria strictly. They tried to help the project along by building the biogas facilities and supplying pigs to the demonstration farmer sites. However, the county could do this only for the demonstration units. Others were left wondering where they could procure pigs.

The project team proposed a more flexible approach. Team members and township officials negotiated with the county leaders and were allowed some flexibility in doing extension work in Chaoshan. Sixteen households were helped to build a less expensive locally adapted biogas production system that worked very well. Villagers who could not afford to raise three pigs were asked to collect cattle manure instead. As a result, several villagers opted to build the biogas system and regretted not having built one sooner.

Notwithstanding this encouraging development, challenges remain. For instance, the government is primarily concerned with construction and pays little attention to maintenance. The villagers have had a hard time buying supplies to replace broken parts of the biogas facility. The project team and township officials discussed these concerns with the county bureau responsible, which promised to address them, but no response was forthcoming.

This experience made the team realize several points. Government project proposals must be studied very carefully and creativity must be used to find ways to encourage the government to practise or adapt one or more of the core CBNRM elements. Negotiation skills are very important for starting a CBNRM initiative. Government officials continually need to be coached on what they stand to gain from supporting successful projects that work well for farmers. They need to understand what works and what does not work and why. As well,

Figure 9.4 Improved roads link villages to markets
Photo: Ou Guowu.

Figure 9.5 Constructing a locally adapted biogas production system
Photo: Yuan Juanwen.

Figure 9.6 Villagers terracing the land to establish an orchard
Photo: Yuan Juanwen.

we need to encourage the adoption of a new performance incentive system that recognizes continuing and sustainable success on the ground.

Establishing a terraced orchard: the pros and cons of partnership building

An orchard project in Kaizuo township delivered by the Changshun County Agricultural Office offers more insights into the challenges of integrating CBNRM into government programming. Approximately 25 ha of terraced orchards were established on wastelands in 2003 (see Figure 9.6).

At the beginning, staff at the Changshun Agricultural Office in Kaizuo township, project team members and three natural villages were supposed to work as partners to implement this project and to involve villagers in decision-making, implementing, management, monitoring and evaluation processes. The team and township officials worked together, holding several villagers' meetings to decide where to locate the orchard, how large it should be, which varieties of fruit to test, when to start planting and other related orchard development activities. Project team members also brought the villagers to visit some successful terraced orchards. At first, everything went smoothly. The villagers finished terracing the land and digging the holes. But at the stage where seedlings had to be purchased, the county officials acted unilaterally, in violation of their agreement. It was known that officials could benefit personally by purchasing seedlings from a particular company at inflated prices. The project team members insisted that the seedlings should be purchased together with village representatives in order to control this, but the government officer responsible said he had already wired the money to the company in accordance with their seedling purchase agreement. The project team was forced to pull out of this activity because they could not ensure reasonable financial oversight.

Later on, county officials contracted out the orchard road and pond construction, but the quality of the work was poor. In addition, during the planting season, the company provided a poorly qualified technician to teach the villagers how to plant trees. Government officials did not provide further technical support once the orchard was established. The villagers had no idea of how to do the pruning or how to apply the correct amounts of fertilizer. The officials promised to do something, but no training was offered. County government officials, even when confronted by the imminent failure of their investment in the orchard, and even when responding to specific requests, seemed unable to adopt supportive and participatory extension procedures.

This is a common problem. Government officials pay close attention to establishing orchards because officers in charge can only get successful performance reviews if quantitative targets for areas of orchard established are met. But there is no incentive to provide technical training or to look into questions of orchard maintenance and improvement. As a result, the success rate for these types of projects remains low.

Meanwhile, after visiting other project sites the villagers were inspired to formulate local agreements based on their own customs to manage their orchard. For example, one villager was fined 50 yuan when her cattle went into the orchard, even though the poor state of the seedlings gave others the impression that the orchard was abandoned or had failed.

In the winter of 2003–4, the county government supported a 25-ha terraced orchard in another village. The difference was that this project was implemented by the township officials without direct county involvement. This time, the villagers were more involved in the process. The villagers built the orchard road and pond themselves and also had a say in the purchase of planting materials. So far, this orchard is doing well. The survival rate is higher and the fruit trees are growing well.

The story tells us that:
- government officials' personal interests can strongly influence CBNRM projects;
- transparency and accountability are very difficult to achieve in the current administrative system; mismanagement of funds is common;
- partnership building is not easy; power abuse is common and breaking promises is easy for senior officials; there is no monitoring mechanism to prevent this;
- the lack of practical extension support constrains the effectiveness of scaling up;

- even though the full and meaningful participation of villagers in government projects has a long way to go, some encouraging signs are appearing; the government has begun to respect villagers' opinions and, in this last orchard case at least, to pay more attention to post-seedling management;
- villagers' capacity-building efforts are bringing good results;. 'farmer to farmer' extension visits and learning help convince villagers to manage their natural resources.

Progress made so far

Among the research results at the Kaizuo project site there are some successful experiences, but also some challenges. In terms of progress in scaling out, the township government has included scaling out of the CBNRM approach in its 2004 work plan. There are now 29 out of 37 villages in the township involved in testing CBNRM approaches. In these villages, a total of 30 management agreements have been approved and results are promising. Management regulations have proved effective in conserving resources and improving productivity, and have been enforced locally Township officials and villagers are beginning to have more dialogue. Participating township officials are starting to change their attitudes. Officials have also begun to integrate gender perspectives into their daily work. In villagers' committee elections this year, for the first time, township officials required that all four administrative villages should select at least one woman for the village committee, something that has never happened before. Three women were selected in the four villages. This represents a good start to including women in decision-making.

The institutionalization of CBNRM at the township level remains a challenge, although more and more officials are beginning to adopt some aspects of the approach. One township agricultural extension officer said: 'I only used to do what my superiors asked me to do. Now, I begin to hold villagers' meetings to discuss with them and try out some new things.' One of the township leaders said: 'After we adopted the CBNRM approach, many management activities were done by the villagers. The government has been released from some tasks. The villagers now take care of themselves. The villagers benefit more.' (Shi and Shi, 2003)

The villagers are becoming more confident and are approaching local officials more frequently to solicit funds for community development priorities. Such priorities are defined after long discussions. Villagers, particularly the women, are beginning to initiate some activities to strengthen their capacities and improve their lives. The most important change is that more opportunities and options are created for the villagers. As well, they are more assertive in managing their natural resources, claim ownership of the process and carry out or at least attempt sustainable management practices.

In terms of scaling up, despite the frustrations in dealing with individual county-level officials and agencies, the team's efforts to introduce and demonstrate the approach have been successful in capturing official attention and support. In December 2003, the Changshun county government directed the county's Poverty Alleviation Office (an agency with a large discretionary programme budget) to adopt the CBNRM approach in all its poverty alleviation activities. One of the county leaders noted: 'The CBNRM flower is already blooming in Kaizuo and now we hope that it will bear fruit in Changshun.'

CBNRM was selected as one of the most significant approaches to government programmes and actions by the Changshun county government. Several county agencies such as the Changshun Planning Bureau and Changshun Science and Technology Bureau are also demonstrating their willingness to try the CBNRM approach in their own programmes. Overall, dialogue between county officials and villagers is increasing. Villages are gaining confidence and assertiveness as they use CBNRM tools to identify their priorities for development, and county officials are increasingly willing to respond to local initiatives. Recently, two villages approached the county government on their own and received support for two village construction projects.

Changes are also happening at the prefecture, province and national level. The prefecture governor asked the project team to provide some lessons and reading materials about CBNRM. Township officials have also advocated adopting the CBNRM approach. The provincial government has gradually recognized CBNRM and provided funds to support the project. The provincial poverty alleviation offices invited the team to do a consultancy and provide training to the officials who are working with the poverty alleviation line agencies. Project-team members have succeeded in getting funds from the Guizhou Department of Science and Technology to scale up the CBNRM approach. The Ministry of Science and Technology from Beijing has visited the project site, has evaluated the work and is planning to support the team in scaling up the CBNRM approach at the national level. Some of the work detailing the approach has been published by the influential national magazine *Outlook Weekly*.

These outcomes are contributing to improved livelihoods for villagers, to villagers' and particularly women's stronger roles in decision-making about natural resource use and management, and to a gradual shift in the power relationships between villagers and government officials. Through nine years of efforts, the natural resources, living conditions and welfare of villagers have been improved in Kaizuo township. There are now about 9,000 mu of forests that are growing well. Except for sticky rice varieties, 90 per cent of rice crops and more than 60 per cent of maize crops are high-yielding hybrid varieties. Nine new drinking-water systems and four new irrigation-water systems benefit approximately 550 poor households. Another 500 households were helped by the construction of eight new roads, which allowed people access to market and other services. About 1,000 mu of fruit trees and crops (including strawberries) are growing well and realizing good returns. Other alternative, income-generating activities are being pursued, such as mushroom production and virus-free potato cultivation. Four villages representing 230 households are running their own animal bank and thus avoiding high-interest loans and the difficulties associated with accessing micro-credit.

Conclusions and lessons

Through our action research efforts we have found that scaling up CBNRM in China is a difficult endeavour. Government officials lack motivation or incentives to adopt CBNRM even though they recognize its usefulness. There are no CBNRM agencies or policies in the country, although many government agencies have recognized that their programmes are ineffective and are looking for ways to change approaches to planning and service delivery. There is a lot of talk about poverty alleviation, which is a crucial government priority, but precisely how to implement successful programmes remains a big question. Four line ministries and the poverty alleviation office of Changshun County have tried to adopt CBNRM in their projects, and Kaizuo township has been using this approach to administer small local development grants. However, this does not mean CBNRM has been integrated into the government system. The responsible officials did experiment with CBNRM, but only in selected projects and activities while continuing with traditional approaches in the rest of their work.

One of the more obvious reasons why this remains challenging is the prevailing system of performance evaluation for government officials, which still emphasizes quantitative targets. In the recently modified Chinese constitution, the phrase 'people-centred' is included in descriptions of the role of government. Now the central government requires that officials should have the 'right perspective and assessment' of their achievements, in relation to practical and enduring improvements in people's lives. This is encouraging and offers more potential for scaling up a CBNRM approach. But the challenge remains: how to change institutional arrangements, policy-making mechanisms and daily practices of government in order to create space for meaningful community participation in NRM.

Horizontal scaling out is easier than vertical scaling up. Villagers and township officials are more directly exposed to the effective results of CBNRM. Township officials have more frequent face-to-face interactions with villagers than do county officials, and are more accountable to them in many ways. As a result, critical reflections follow more easily. Their work attitudes have started to change and their abilities to use facilitative and participatory methods are improving quickly. Also, their work results are easily recognizable and they get strong support for effective results from villagers. Officials feel a sense of pride when they can successfully tackle these difficult poverty and NRM problems. All of this is creating a more fertile working environment for CBNRM to flourish. But the county officials' stereotypical bureaucratic attitudes and exercise of power remain strong. They fear that adopting the CBNRM approach could bring more risks and threaten their interests.

Cross-village exchange visits are very effective for horizontal scaling out. Villagers readily interact with each other, listening and observing, and trying new things. In particular, women are very active and eager to take on new ideas and put them to work.

Here are some of the things we have learned in rethinking and adapting CBNRM to the Chinese reality.

There is still not much space for the meaningful participation of villagers in government programme delivery. Local men and women can participate in government projects to some extent as long as the interests of government officials are not threatened. Several government officials commented: 'If we give all the decision-making power to the villagers, what are we going to do? We will lose our jobs!'

It is vital to improve the organizational skills and confidence of villagers and village leaders. Villagers, in particular women, usually do not have a chance to communicate directly with officials. CBNRM approaches create opportunities for villagers and government officials to collaborate, but local people still lack the confidence to express and defend their ideas. Therefore, leadership training and capacity-building in many different forms are important. The process of engagement in CBNRM itself has many leadership and capacity-building benefits, if properly facilitated.

Integrating the CBNRM approach into the government's daily activities is critical. Although several line ministries of Changshun county have been trying to adopt CBNRM in their projects and the Kaizuo township has been implementing CBNRM in several small-grant projects, it does not mean that CBNRM has been fully integrated into the government system. This stage marks the start of the integration process. How to engage local officials more fully remains a challenge. One township official said: 'I am interested in being involved in CBNRM activities, but there are so many important tasks I must finish otherwise I will have problems in passing the annual evaluation.'

It is important to provide more opportunities for township and county officials to learn participatory approaches in experimental programmes. This research project engaged a small number of officials at both township and county levels in active project management committees. However, we found that aside from the committee members themselves, few officials became involved in the pilot activities. And at the county level, where line agency staff were involved, many officials changed jobs during the course of the pilot and were unable to complete their CBNRM learning. In order to build experience and capacity, we need a commitment from senior leaders to long-term assignments, and to engaging more staff in these participatory pilot efforts. However, because such officials have limited experience with participatory approaches, it is not easy for them to appreciate the importance of supportive project management.

Changing the attitudes of senior officials at the county and township levels is critical to scaling up the CBNRM approach (Yuan et al., 2004). Leaders play a vital role in creating opportunities, in coordination, human-resource inputs and other resource inputs. If staff want to attend scaling-up or learning activities, they must get permission from their superiors, but senior officials are too busy to learn much about these innovations themselves. Supportive senior officials are crucial, but to gain their support, we must convince them that CBNRM offers them more benefits than risks.

Coordination with different line agencies is important. The research team realizes that their coordinating role has become increasingly complex and coordination must be approached more strategically. The team assumed that since senior county officials agreed to support the project, they would also coordinate the project efforts at the line agency level. However, this assumption proved unrealistic. Officials are always busy and frequently unavailable when needed. This issue of line agency coordination needs more analysis and an effective strategy.

Partnership-building needs to be based on a set of negotiable and non-negotiable criteria including both government standards and CBNRM principles. In implementing government projects, officials tend to adhere strictly to government standards and criteria (such as for biogas production systems, reforestation and orchard development, as described), rather than consider other success factors. They do not want to take the risk of being accountable to the villagers or to hand over leadership and decision-making to them. The research team realizes that they need to be better prepared to deal with the politics of government operations and programme delivery. There is a need to compromise, facilitate and negotiate. To accomplish this, we must be clear on each project's negotiable and non-negotiable elements, so as to find space for integrating the CBNRM approach.

Anticipating the different interests of various stakeholders is crucial. The government has a preference for large-scale projects that give officials more attention and recognition. The team needs to raise issues of feasibility and how to measure real success. The technical feasibility of a project might be clear from the government's perspective, but associated social, gender and organizational aspects are often not considered. A clear example is the biogas project. The team is now consulting on how to address difficulties in reaching the required number of household participants and how feasible this might be considering the village reality. As well, we recognize that it is crucial to be flexible when dealing with different village situations.

Strengthening the team's advocacy and other skills is required. Most of the team members are researchers from natural science disciplines who are unaccustomed to public speaking and lack experience in policy advocacy. They have had to develop skills in communications, negotiation and diplomacy. Moreover, they have had to adopt new roles, not only as researchers, but as trainers, negotiators, communicators, advocates, mobilizers and mentors. This requires skills training as well as graduate studies in diverse social and natural sciences.

To conclude, an effective scaling-up strategy requires a diversity of action-oriented initiatives that combine horizontal and vertical elements. In addition, it is crucial that government staff become aware of the strengths, challenges and advantages of CBNRM; and that they are encouraged to experiment with the approach and to adopt it in policies, programmes and projects. This is a time-consuming and extremely challenging process.

Acknowledgements

This chapter is inspired by and builds on Sun (2004). We would like to acknowledge the contributions to the research of Chen Deshou, Zhou Pidong, Ou Guowu, Wei Xiaopin, Vicky Bautista and Norie Garcia, Kaizuo township officials and villagers and Changshun county officials. We also wish to acknowledge the funding support of IDRC and the Ford Foundation.

CHAPTER 10

Walking the extra mile: from field learning to natural resource management research and policy in Bhutan

Sangay Duba and Mahesh Ghimiray

Abstract

Historically in Bhutan, research and development on natural resources was sector-specific, commodity- and discipline-focused and researcher-led, with little community involvement. The Renewable Natural Resource Research Centre (RNRRC) of the Ministry of Agriculture, located in Bajo, piloted a watershed CBNRM project. Its focus was to improve resource productivity as well as people's livelihoods through integrating NRM with the participation of local communities.

This case study relates how CBNRM and PAR in the field influenced changes in the community, at the Bajo research centre and more widely in Bhutan's agricultural research sector. In the community, the CBNRM approach led to improved resource (water, forest, soils, crops) productivity and enhanced benefits from these resources. Communities also strengthened social assets and local institutions for planning, implementing and monitoring resource management. At the RNRRC Bajo, the focus of research programmes moved towards more holistic and integrated methods that fostered team learning and responded to community needs. Two examples of water and forestry problems in the watershed illustrate this novel research process and the lessons learned. Based on the successes of this programme, CBNRM approaches have been adopted nationally in the research system and through a national CBNRM policy framework.

Context

Bhutan is a landlocked country in the eastern Himalayas between India and China. It is characterized by high mountains and deep valleys, rising from an elevation of about 100 metres to over 7,550 metres. As a result, the country has a highly varied climate, topography and biodiversity. A forest cover of over 72 per cent represents a large and valuable pool of natural resources for the country. Over 80 per cent of the population depends on mountain agriculture and livestock for their livelihood. Use of natural resources, especially forest resources, remains an essential component of Bhutan's livelihood and culture (Royal Government of Bhutan, 2002). Buddhism is the dominant religion of the country, and serves as the foundation for Bhutanese values, institutions and culture. The king is head of state, with governance devolved to an elected Council of Ministers.

Forest and water resources are under state ownership and management with little community involvement Royal Government of Bhutan, 2002). Individual households own an average of 0.8 ha (2 acres) of agricultural land planted with rice, maize, wheat, fruits and vegetables. Although food insecurity is not a widespread problem, there are instances of seasonal food shortages. Farming households augment their income through such off-farm work as afforded by construction sites or logging, and collection of NTFPs such as mushrooms, ferns, bamboo and rattan.

Over the years, an increasing population and additional demands on resources has led to relative degradation of the country's natural resources such as forest, pastures and NTFPs. The overall forest cover is good but the quality of forest in some areas is poor due to harvesting of preferred species, replanting programmes that have not worked well, firewood cutting and grazing pressure. As government and communities search for more income-generating opportunities, some of the NTFPs have recently become commercially important and existing policies are inadequate to meet the extraction pressure (Henderson, 2003).

Historically, the government has been the service provider and development has been top-down in approach, with communities expecting and depending on government interventions. Bhutan has decentralized development to *dzongkhag* (district) and *geog* (administrative block) levels since the 8th Five Year Plan (1997) so as to engage people in development planning and the management of natural resources (Royal Government of Bhutan, 1999). The government is now promoting bottom-up planning and decentralized approaches to community development, including NRM. However, with limited experience in community participation, the implementation of this goal has been challenging. In 2002, the mid-term planning exercise involved communities of all the 202 *geogs* in defining their development needs and aspirations for the first time in Bhutan.

Renewable natural resource administration

The Ministry of Agriculture (MoA) is responsible for managing the renewable natural resources (RNR) sectors of agriculture, livestock and forestry. Recognizing their interdependence, the government of Bhutan integrated them under one ministry in 1992. The research and extension components of the three sectoral agencies were merged for some years with the aim of more directly linking research to development implementation. However, it was felt that sector-specific technical departments were ineffective in delivering services as they did not have direct control of their extension personnel in the field (Royal

Government of Bhutan, 2003). Recently, these sectors were restructured again as separate line departments, which do not always work in unison. The newly formed research council continues to integrate the three sectors, but operates separately from the line departments.

Bajo research centre and team

The RNRRC at Bajo is one of four such centres in the country under the Council of RNR Research of Bhutan (CoRRB), MoA. It has the dual mandates of coordinating national level research on field crops (for example, oil crops, grains and legumes) and catering to the research and development needs of its five districts at the regional level. Other centres located in different regions of the country have national mandates for livestock, forestry and horticulture.

Historically, our research approach at Bajo evolved from a focus on single commodities, to one of farming systems (RNRRC Bajo, 1995) and then to integrated NRM. Organized and systematic agricultural research began in Bhutan only in 1982 when the Centre for Agricultural Research and Development (CARD) was created. In 1984, the team at Bajo, in collaboration with the International Rice Research Institute (IRRI) and with support from Canada's IDRC, developed a research programme to improve rice production through the introduction of new varieties and management techniques, in order to address the food security needs of the Bhutanese. Consistent with findings elsewhere in the world at that time, it became evident that constraints to increased yield had complex and interrelated causes. The next phase of research focused more on the development of farming systems technologies and strengthening the human capacity of the MoA (RNRRC Bajo, 2000d). Under the farming systems research programme, the research team emphasized cropping systems and on-farm enterprises.

In this earlier work, farmers had little involvement in setting research priorities, planning or implementing the results of research. In addition, most researchers from Bajo were trained only in natural sciences. They had not been trained to work directly with communities, to ask about their perspectives, or to consider some of the social aspects related to the livelihoods of the people. At that time, these ideas were very new to conventional research (RNRRC Bajo, 2000a).

Starting approximately a decade ago, staff at the research centres were exposed to concepts of participatory research through learning by doing and on-farm methods in trainings and workshops, as well as through interactions with donors and visitors. Recognizing the need to work directly with farmers, the Bajo team decided to integrate participatory approaches in their research programme, and was one of the first organizations in Bhutan to do so. Initially, this work was primarily on-farm, and the team soon realized that they were neglecting the linkages to other natural resources that were often managed by farmers or communities in different ways (RNRRC Bajo, 2000b). For instance, given the valley type of agriculture in Bhutan, forests provide livestock fodder and organic

Figure 10.1 Women collecting leaf litter for use as cattle bedding
Photo: RNRRC Bajo.

materials for fertility development, in addition to regulating the availability of water for farming. The research programme on farming systems primarily studied private lands and did not consider the farmers' reliance on common resources, such as forests and water, which helped them to meet their livelihood needs.

The research team at Bajo realized that there was a need for greater understanding about farmers' use of and dependence on resources beyond the farm, and for comprehending the resource interactions at a watershed level. The team had been exposed to concepts in CBNRM, emphasizing community participation in planning and the integrated management of natural resource use. At the same time, during the years 1996 and 1997, the Bhutanese government was implementing changes towards decentralization and plans for local participatory RNR management processes.

In collaboration with communities which were facing problems of limited resource productivity and poverty in Lingmutey Chu, a nearby watershed, the Bajo research team planned a pilot project employing a multisectoral and integrated approach, linking crops, livestock, forests and water, and aiming to enhance overall productivity. In this work, we wanted to improve linkages between farmers, researchers and extension workers to expand the scope of research from solely on-farm to include broader resource systems, and to also include the participation of local communities (RNRRC Bajo, 2001). The team had begun to recognize the importance of community participation in any development activity, in diagnosis, planning, implementation and evaluation.

This CBNRM project took place over two phases from 1997 to 2004, and was jointly funded by IDRC and the Swiss Agency for Development Cooperation (SDC).

The research team consisted primarily of natural scientists: soil scientists, water engineers, horticulturists, foresters, entomologists, livestock specialists and agronomists. In the later stages of the project, one social scientist joined the team. CBNRM and participatory approaches were new, not only to the research team but also to the farmers. Members of the communities were interested in participating in the research programme because they hoped the team could help them find solutions to their natural resource problems, in addition to providing them with material and other support.

Lingmutey Chu watershed

Lingmutey Chu is a small watershed with an area of 34 km^2, with about 6.3 per cent under agriculture. The watershed consists of seven villages with a total of 170 households distributed between elevations of 1,300 metres and 2,170 metres. The total population in the area is about 1,000, with a nearly equal male:female ratio. Most people belong to a single ethnic group from the western part of Bhutan, except in Nabchhe village, where migrants from the eastern part of the country resettled in the 1950s (RNRRC Bajo, 1997).

Forest cover varies from poor in the lower watershed, to moderate and predominantly *chir* pine in the middle region, to good deciduous forest in the upper watershed. Farmers depend on forests for fuel, timber and other forest products (Figure 10.1). Agriculture is the major source of livelihood in all villages. Wetland irrigated cropping dominates, except in Nabchhe village where dryland farming is practised. The main cash income sources are potato and chilli, seasonal vegetables, beaten maize and wild mushrooms. In general, soils are slightly acidic with variable organic carbon, total nitrogen and available phosphorus (RNRRC Bajo, 2001). Farmers also gain income from wage labour on other farms in the villages or at nearby construction sites.

Seasonal food insecurity is a problem for between around two and four months before harvesting crops. Households overcome these shortages by borrowing food from their neighbours and exchanging labour for food. Sometimes grain debts accumulate when people are unable to repay their debts due to such events as a bad harvest season or misfortune in the family. Other major problems are low and unstable crop yields, declining soil fertility, shortage of irrigation water for rice cultivation, scarcity of animal fodder in the winter and losses from pests or wild life (RNRRC Bajo, 1997).

Learning to walk: implementing participatory approaches

The research team approached these challenges by combining participatory methods with more conventional science. These processes were new, so the team learned by doing, implementing tools learned while training in the field.

At the outset, the team used participatory methods combined with traditional survey methods and natural science research – for example, measurements of hydrology and soil fertility – in order to understand problems as well as community needs. PRA tools such as participatory mapping, wealth categorization, transect walks and focus-group discussions were used extensively. A baseline participatory diagnosis was carried out involving all the communities at the beginning of the project. Both male and female community elders and senior household members participated in the diagnosis. Thereafter, focused and topical PRAs were undertaken to achieve more in-depth understanding and interventions.

During PRA exercises, farmers categorized themselves into different wealth groups depending on the resources they controlled, such as land, labour and livestock (RNRRC Bajo, 2000c). Formal surveys were used to understand and document issues and practices of soil fertility and nutrient management. Similar studies on participatory forest management and resource use were also done (RNRRC Bajo, 1998).

The centre collaborated with farmers in conducting on-farm research in conjunction with on-station research. On-farm research included participatory variety selection for rice, maize, wheat and vegetables; soil nutrient management using a farmer field school approach; and livestock fodder management. Farmers' capacity development was another important aspect of the project. The centre trained farmers on new varieties, technologies, agronomic practices and new crops such as asparagus and oak mushrooms. The project team also worked with community members and facilitated the development of local institutions for resource management and savings.

After an in-depth participatory analysis with local users, resource use patterns, management issues (such as access and control) and conflicts became clearer to both researchers and community members. Subsequently, interventions were developed by the communities themselves, and facilitated by the research team. On-farm technical interventions evolved from suggestions by both farmers and researchers, based on their knowledge and experience elsewhere.

> Never in my life was I consulted… I was always asked to do… This is the first time that people are asking my views on our needs – Farmer Ap Wangda, 68

The team, equipped with information on the wealth categories of farmers, developed different interventions that were based on the wealth group and targeted at the poorest of the poor. Areas of interventions included soils improvement, irrigation management, fodder improvement, forestry plantations, cereals and horticulture, institution building and skill development.

Our work covered a number of resource management areas. However, only the water and forest resources are presented here as examples to illustrate the participatory research process in planning, developing and implementing interventions, and to highlight key learnings for the research team. Similar processes were also followed for other sectors.

Water management in Lingmutey Chu

In the late 1980s, the government of Bhutan developed a national irrigation policy that emphasized the infrastructure and maintenance of irrigation canals. The government provided one-time support for canal maintenance and required beneficiaries to form community-based water-user associations (WUAs) to sustain maintenance (Brand and Kamtsho, 2000). All households using canal water for irrigation and other purposes were members of a WUA. The WUA guidelines called for households to raise funds for maintenance, and to keep accounts and book-keeping practices up to date. However, these expectations were quite different from community norms and while WUAs continued to exist in principle, they did not function. In Lingmutey Chu, problems of water scarcity, conflicts over water use and demands for maintenance support by the communities opened up opportunities for the research team to initiate participatory water management research with the communities. The research aimed to understand and analyse issues concerning water use and management, and to develop sustainable options for improvement through participatory processes.

Diagnosis began in six out of seven communities in the watershed, using focus-group discussions, participant observation, interviews and PRA tools such as resource mapping, seasonal calendars and transect walks. Two water engineers spent three months camping in the upper watershed and walked the fields daily to listen, observe, learn and analyse traditional water management systems. Previously, water scientists were university graduates who had little or no grounding or knowledge in participatory methods and approaches. They had fixed ideas and technical solutions to problems without any consideration of local perspectives and needs. After staying in the communities, our team's scientists learned by observing exactly what locals were doing, how farmers expressed and defined resource constraints. Then they were able to relate local problems and terms to scientific terminology. Because they stayed in the communities, the scientists grew to understand the particular perspectives involved, which helped them to adapt their technical expertise to the reality the villagers experienced.

Water shortages

One important issue that emerged was the problem of water shortages during the June–July rice transplanting season. Discussions took place regarding the probable causes. The Lingmutey Chu River starts in the upper watershed and runs through to downstream villages and fields, providing irrigation to all the communities. River flow depends on the monsoon season in July and August. However, farmers usually transplant rice in early June, before the onset of monsoon rains. Farmers downstream are faced with a water shortage during transplanting, a task that cannot be delayed without threatening flowering and seed maturation.

The team worked with the WUAs to develop potential interventions. These included supporting community members to improve existing irrigation structures, using less water-intensive irrigation practices for rice cultivation and trying rapidly maturing rice varieties that could be planted late in the season when more water is available. To improve canal structures, the research team provided hardware, such as concrete pipes, cement and other materials, to improve lining and conveyance efficiency. Meanwhile, the communities provided labour for maintenance work. Since canals often run through steep and unstable terrain, it is common for frequent landslides to wash away parts of the canal. The team assisted one community to select grass and tree species and plant them in the eroded areas. *Melia, dodonia,* poplar and two local species were planted (RNRRC Bajo, 1995–2001). There were several positive results to this. Slide-prone areas were stabilized and the flow of irrigation water to the fields improved, resulting in a saving on labour while the productivity of the land was maintained. As well, fallow lands that had become idle due to over-sedimentation problems were returned to cultivation, and farmers in the lower watershed adopted rapidly maturing rice varieties. As a result, the WUA has been greatly strengthened. It conducts regular meetings, and members attend training programmes and lead monitoring of water canals.

However, not all trial interventions were successful. For example, farmers and research team staff conducted on-station and on-farm trials of intermittent irrigation for rice cultivation, as a water-saving technique. While this technique improved water-use efficiency by 30 per cent, it did not address the issue of shortages during the transplanting season. The trials did result in suppressing the aquatic weed, shochum (*Potamogeton distinctus*), which is otherwise difficult to control. Although research both at the station and on-farm trials was technically successful, farmers did not adopt the technology. One reason was the difficulty of water control for intermittent irrigation in a rotational water-sharing system. Water was not available at the precise time it was needed for effective intermittent irrigation. The research team realized that although an experiment may be technically successful, it may not be applicable or appropriate in the context of the farmers' own management systems.

Water conflicts

A study of farmers' water rights and the sharing system between communities and within farms was undertaken concurrently with an analysis of the farmers' water management practices. A crucial issue that emerged unexpectedly was water-use conflicts between upstream and downstream communities, even though within each community there was relatively equitable access to water (Brand and Jamtsho, 2000).

Water-balance studies confirmed that the water supply is inadequate during transplanting throughout the watershed. But studies also revealed that the water consumption of many farmers was higher than what is technically required for rice cultivation. Traditional water-sharing rights were not based on equity and efficiency, but on two principles: first come first served; and upstream users can divert all the flow into their irrigation canal regardless of the need of downstream users. This forces downstream users to use seepage or tail waters from the canal. The right to use as much water as they like does not give upstream users any incentive to improve the efficiency of their water supply system. As a result, over half the water was lost in the water supply canals. Water rights within the village were defined by several factors including a household's contribution to religious ceremonies, their ancestors' participation in constructing the canal, the size of their landholding and participation in canal maintenance. These factors are interdependent and their relative importance varies from village to village (Brand and Jamtsho, 2000).

In the past, these communities took this long-standing dispute to the local courts, which always ruled in favour of the traditional arrangements.

The team first held separate discussions with both upstream and downstream communities about the inequity associated with access to water resources. Based in part on exposure to various participatory approaches and conflict resolution mechanisms, the research team conceived of a role-playing game as a tool to prompt dialogue between two of the communities and also to enrich researchers' and farmers' knowledge of the situation (Gurung, 2003). Initially, we encountered many challenges in facilitating this process because community members were highly sensitive about the issue. This was particularly true with the upstream community, who did not wish to change the status quo. The team was aware of the inequity in the water rights systems and was uncertain how to transform this unequal power relationship for the benefit of the disadvantaged communities. Role-playing exercises helped break the barriers of communication and facilitated the different communities – and the researchers – to understand and appreciate the issues and perceptions related to shared resources. In the end, the upper community did release water to downstream farmers, and permanent mechanisms for resolving water allocation disputes are being put in place at the time of writing.

The water research team leader brought the issues of inequitable sharing in traditional water systems to the national Agriculture Policy and Planning Division. A policy was developed to promote the principles of equitable access to water resources because this is a common problem in other watersheds. The draft was presented to the communities for feedback. After seeing the emerging policy support for entitlements by the community in the lower watershed, the community in the upper watershed relented and became more willing to negotiate. The communities continue to negotiate water allocation through a new consultation forum at the watershed level, a mechanism introduced by the research project team.

The experiences in Lingmutey Chu have been vital in formulating the national water policy and the Water Act. Bhutan now also has initiated a national and interministerial water forum or partnership approach to its water resources and management. In the future, upper watershed users and managers of water resources may be compensated by downstream users. For example, hydro-developers and other users may need to compensate upstream communities for their role in protecting and managing watershed resources.

In this case, the role of the researchers changed from that of scientific and technical experts to facilitators and coordinators, who aimed to link different institutes, organizations and individuals in order to solve problems and meet community needs. The team also came to recognize the importance of and potential for policy to address these issues. The team realized that adding local perspectives increases the complexity of the problems, which sometimes defy solution. For example, water shortages still exist, as do community tensions on sharing this crucial resource. However, the efforts made during the project have had positive impacts towards resolution, and have raised community awareness of the underlying issues.

Community forestry in Lingmutey Chu

The Bhutan Forest Act of 1969 nationalized forest management with the objective of protecting natural resources from illegal loggers and enabling the government to generate needed revenues through the sale of timber products. Local communities only had limited rights through permit systems for the collection of fodder and fuel wood. In 1979, King Jigme Singye Wangchuk initiated community forestry in principle when he commanded the Department of Forestry (DoF) to prepare a programme on social forestry to involve local people in planting trees on their own private or village land. In 1993, the DoF decentralized participation in forest conservation and management along with the private and community forestry programmes to *dzongkhag* (district) authorities for implementation. The Forest and Nature Conservation Act of 1995 replaced the earlier act, and a full chapter was devoted to social forestry, which provides a legal basis for community participation in forest resources planning and management. However, although the policy and frameworks have been put in place, community forests have not been widely implemented.

In part, the DoF embarked on implementation slowly because it was unconvinced that communities had the capacity to manage the resources and feared that over-exploitation would result. There were no examples of official community forestry practice in Bhutan aside from customary management regimes. In addition, most forestry officials were trained to operate under conventional centralized management practices, and had not been exposed to participatory community forest management practices. At the time that the research work in community forestry began in Lingmutey Chu in 1997, it was among the very first community forestry schemes in the country.

A participatory diagnosis was conducted in the watershed to understand people's perceptions of forest resources management and assess their interest in community forestry programmes. This process also offered an opportunity for the research team to clarify forest rules and regulations that were unclear to the community. To begin to understand forest degradation, the research team and community representatives assessed the quality of the forest in terms of resource availability, general health and potential to supply various products. Through a forest-function mapping exercise, community representatives identified various functions and zones in the watershed forest. Locally important sites such as streams, religious sites, areas of steep erosion and other areas of interest were mapped and identified as zones requiring protection, while potential areas for exploitation were mapped as local-use areas. This enabled the preparation of a management plan to incorporate local concerns for forest protection, conservation and use. The communities also conducted a forest-demand assessment to estimate the demand for various forest products in the next 10 years. Conclusions were discussed during presentations to the whole community and enabled the development of a forest management plan for local use.

The resource assessment revealed several common problems faced by communities in the lower watershed. These included degradation of forests close to the village, shortages of fuelwood and timber, long-distance travel for women to collect preferred fuel species, scarcity of preferred timber species, shortage of feed and fodder, and diminishing access to forest resources. The upper communities, which are closer to forest resources, only expressed concerns regarding shortages of winter fodder. Access to major forest products was equitable among households in each of these communities.

Every village was very interested in establishing their surrounding forest as a community forest, provided that their benefits and rights would be guaranteed. But all communities expressed reservations about managing the entire watershed forest as a collective community forest. They were concerned about the labour and time demands of additional management responsibility, and they doubted that benefits would be equitably shared. Some communities also worried that a new community forest management regime would limit existing access and tenure rights. For example, lower communities consisting of relatively new settlers feared they would lose their access rights to nearby forests that were claimed by the upper community as ancestral lands. However, in the interest of protecting their forests from exploitation by outsiders, all villages agreed to designate their surrounding forest as a local community forest and to gradually work towards a watershed level management regime.

Establishing community forestry institutions

The establishment of a community forest user group (CFUG) is a prerequisite to formalizing a community plantation or forest under the Forest and Nature Conservation Act of 1995. As a pilot initiative, the research team worked with communities to facilitate the formation of two CFUGs in the lower watershed in the Matalumchu and Omtekha communities. These initially included all households in the communities, and each group appointed six community leaders, at least one of whom had to be female, to form the CFUG committee (CFUGC).

As a starting point, the CFUGCs decided to establish a multispecies and multiple-use type of community forest on degraded areas close to the villages.

Degradation of areas near the homestead and surrounding fields is a major concern among local communities in the lower part of the watershed. Soil erosion was already a big problem because extremely large gullies had formed near the villages and community lands. Initially, communities doubted whether they would be granted ownership of their forest plantations. The team discussed the issue with higher authorities and was assured by the divisional forest office that collective ownership and user rights would be given to them.

The communities selected species for firewood, timber and livestock fodder. The research team provided information and resources on additional fast-growing leguminous species that could be useful for community needs. The community established a community forest nursery to generate planting materials for successive years. Each household contributed an equal share of work for fencing, digging pits, planting and watering the plants. To date, a total of 37 ha of community plantation has been established on degraded areas surrounding Omtekha and Matalumchu villages (Figure 10.2). Over 27 species are growing, and grasses are being collected for livestock feeding. There are now two active CFUGs in the watershed. In collaboration with the research team, the communities developed by-laws based on national social forestry guidelines. The CFUG regularly meets and monitors the plantation. Farmers were happy with the plantation because they did not have to travel far to collect grasses for livestock. The research team, however, feels the growth rate of species like cypress and other broadleaved species could be higher and they are working with farmers to augment productivity. As tree growth continues over coming years, the farmers will benefit more substantially.

The CFUGs and CFUGCs initially appeared enthusiastic and cooperative. The Omtekha CFUGC in particular was dynamic and well organized. However, tensions arose between members, in part because of inequities in power and social relations in the community where prestigious, influential, and better-off community members influenced the function of the groups and implementation of community forest activities. Some households dropped out and female members of the CFUGC left.

Some critics have argued that CBNRM processes mirror social hierarchies in communities and exacerbate inequity in access to resources (Beck and Nesmith, 2001). Although it is intended that all households have equitable access to forest resources under CFUG management and existing guidelines, poor households were not able to contribute the required inputs such as labour. Negotiating for more equitable processes within the CFUGs in the context of these broader power relations within the community is very difficult. The team is still faced with the challenge of how to support more equitable processes given the strong social structure and hierarchies in communities. Occasional but repeated visits by research-team members were found to be helpful in mediating and diffusing tensions among the members. However, the CFUGs have not yet developed rules to strengthen engagement and resource access for the poor, and to sustain women's participation. These issues are still being

Figure 10.2 CFUG monitoring community plantations
Source: CBNRM Project RNRRC Bajo, 2001.

discussed and will become more critical as these forests begin to reach maturity and as use levels intensify.

Farmer groups and forestry officers from other parts of the country have visited the watershed to share the experiences, successes and concerns of these forest user groups. This has helped support community forestry and user group formation processes in other parts of the country.

There are now 23 CFUGs established in Bhutan and others are in the process of being established. These are important beginnings to a new approach to forestry management in the country. With shared responsibilities and benefits between communities and the DoF, we are hopeful that the community forestry movement will result in better forest management practices and that communities will be also be able to share benefits in a more equitable manner.

Project impacts in the community and beyond: changes in doing research

Overall, the project led to a number of positive changes in the community, as evidenced in the above cases. Aside from resource productivity improvements, communities strengthened their social assets and local institutions for planning, implementing and monitoring resource management. Several institutions such as the water and forest user groups were formalized to enhance resource-use efficiency and collective action. These groups have strengthened social cohesion more broadly. Groups are now uniting, identifying resources and working together towards common community goals. For instance, the Matalumchu group constructed a road for their village through loans acquired while using their own collateral. In Dompola, a savings group was established, the first of its kind in the country. Communities have a stronger and more active voice in seeking advice from the Bajo research centre and support from local government. They have gained a better understanding of water and forest policies and their local significance.

The impacts of the project go beyond positive livelihood changes at the watershed level, and have transformed the way that the research centre at Bajo operates. As the two case examples in water management and forestry illustrate, the RNRRC reoriented its research agenda to reflect community priorities, rather than the interests of the researchers. This responsive approach and close collaboration with communities was a new experience for the research team. During implementation, the team attended numerous training and capacity-building activities, both inside and outside the country, on social and institutional aspects of NRM, thus improving their capacity to integrate social aspects into the research programme. The researchers began to investigate problems in a new way, using a more flexible approach to address resource problems, respond to community needs and work closely with community members.

The project's integrated approach also altered the research planning process at the centre. Staff from all sectors and subsectors (crops, livestock, forest, integrated pest management (IPM), socio-economics and water) now discuss their plans together and explore opportunities for synergy. Hence, a more integrated planning and implementation of research occurs. More emphasis is placed on participatory technology development, participatory plant breeding and variety selection and the need to build on farmers' knowledge and practices.

Overall, the Bajo research team learned some key lessons.

Learning by doing means walking the talk. When the government of Bhutan's Minister of Agriculture was appointed recently, one of the first things he did was to walk to remote villages in the country because he wanted to learn from them and officials in their own settings. Many people talk about the importance of participatory approaches in NRM, to the extent that it has become common rhetoric in universities, research institutions and among donors or extension agents. However, very few put these concepts into practice. The team learned that it was only through practical implementation that they could start to understand what participatory approaches and integrated CBNRM were all about. There is a need to readjust both research and implementation priorities in a cycle of reflection, learning and action.

The researcher must take on a role as facilitator. This is very challenging and difficult, even more so if one's background is in the natural sciences. Also, some aspects of the project such as community forestry involved a larger number of stakeholders, including government agencies, local government and perhaps neighbouring communities. Working with such diverse groups is time-consuming and complex, requiring constant negotiation and adjustments to keep everyone comfortable and on board.

Participatory research is essential for relevant research. Through participatory methodologies, the research team realized that research priorities should address community needs and concerns if they were to be relevant and actually improve farmers' lives. Local needs were identified early, which improved the research process. Interventions addressed community priorities and were more relevant in their social and physical contexts. This led to increased adoption of technological and institutional interventions among farmers. The process also enabled community members to have a better understanding of, and a stronger say in, resource policies.

Building rapport with communities is crucial for meaningful work. CBNRM approaches require time to build meaningful participation and partnership between researchers and communities. No matter what tools are used, farmers will only express their feelings gradually. Commitment, sincerity, trust and professionalism on the part of the research team are key factors in building rapport. The team learned that time and patience is required to implement participatory approaches because of the intensive nature of work that requires frequent visits and interactions. Research programmes should be willing to support this and allocate additional resources if the approach is to be followed nationally. This can involve trade-offs for time spent on other work.

Linking both participatory and conventional research approaches is necessary. It is important to complement participatory research in communities with conventional research in order to explore new technologies and options. After working on the station, the project team was able to introduce technical knowledge and research results related to crops, soil fertility, soil erosion control, water, feed and fodder. This knowledge was subsequently integrated into the design of interventions to address the community's needs and resource problems. While it is important to understand and build on local knowledge and institutions, scientific knowledge is also crucial to enhancing productivity and improving management. It is an ongoing challenge for the research centre to balance time and resources for participatory research in the watershed and conventional research on-station.

Understanding traditional resource management systems, practices and local institutions is critical. Intervention strategies that improve efficiency, equity and sustainability need to build upon existing institutions, arrangements and systems. At the same time, it is also often appropriate to introduce new ideas, concepts and technologies to these traditional systems to encourage adaptive management. New institutional mechanisms that address resource management issues are essential both within and between communities, such as the watershed-level forum where water-related conflicts were discussed and resolved. Scientific information can be used and presented to aid in discussions and facilitate dialogue. An example of its application was the hydrological validation conducted to assess whether there was enough water available in the watershed for all the communities. External interventions are sometimes appropriate, such as developing clear policies on resource use to help increase the bargaining power of disadvantaged communities. Addressing inequities and working in the context of complex social relations can be challenging, however, as evidenced by the experience with internal conflict in the CFUGs.

Implementing integrated approaches to resource management is challenging in practice. Research team members continue to feel more comfortable working in their own sector. It is very messy to go beyond one's primary area of expertise and try to understand the complex interactions between resource sectors and the social institutions that are involved. The team discovered that training within and outside Bhutan, exposure to other projects and resource persons such as consultants and donors, and also gaining the support of superiors were all important to build their confidence. Training in participatory methods, conflict resolution and facilitation skills were especially useful for the team.

Sharing CBNRM experience is important. Sharing project experiences with other agencies and farmers, either through cross-visits or farmer-to-farmer extension, created an awareness and further understanding of CBNRM, both vertically and horizontally. This took place at all stages of the project, even while the team and communities were in the process of learning. We involved interested institutions and individuals in visiting and cooperating in our work, and during the training and capacity-building activities organized by the centre. These actions all helped the team expand and share experiences which could later be adapted to other parts of the country. Developing a critical mass of people with CBNRM background has also helped change mindsets, which has contributed to the development of the national CBNRM framework.

Scaling up the CBNRM approach

RNRRC Bajo was the first institution in the country to pilot a watershed CBNRM project. The Lingmutey Chu case had profound impacts on research and development in the RNR sector in Bhutan, well beyond the Bajo case. Interested visitors from around and outside the country were impressed by the lessons and experience gained from this project. Senior ministry officials visited the project and gave political support for the CBNRM effort. Project staff who had gained experience working in Lingmutey Chu later moved to other RNR research centres and championed the CBNRM approach in their activities. Other CBNRM learning projects were developed and implemented in other parts of the country.

As Bajo project staff moved to other government offices, they continued their work on CBNRM, creating a pool of CBNRM advocates in various places. A national-level workshop on CBNRM in Thimphu brought together resource management policy-makers, managers, researchers and extension staff from different departments and agencies. The workshop unified research and field experiences on participatory, integrated NRM. To better understand the experiences of CBNRM in different contexts in Bhutan, the group commissioned a synthesis of field experiences which emphasized the need to draft a CBNRM framework as a key strategy for sustainable resource management. Additional case studies on CBNRM and common property resources (forests, NTFPs and water) were also commissioned. Based on these experiences, a national CBNRM policy framework was drafted and discussed at various levels, with the support of several international donor agencies.

The framework provides guiding principles and suggestions for community action to improve the management of common pool natural resources in Bhutan. It also provides guidelines to operationalize CBNRM programming in research and in policy adjustments which may be needed in the future. The framework advocates CBNRM approaches and programmes that are deeply rooted in the field lessons of the Lingmutey Chu watershed project, including:

- recognizing the importance of full community participation in the planning and management of resources for effective improvements in farmer livelihoods;
- strengthening social assets in communities;
- conducting field-based action research; and
- networking and sharing experiences.

The policy framework incorporates an action plan for CBNRM, emphasizing institutional arrangements, action research, networking, policy and programme integration and capacity-building aspects, among other factors. The MoA has implemented a number of these recommendations, including the establishment of a national-level coordination unit, where the Bajo research centre continues to play a leading advisory role. The ministry initiated a set of 10 action research projects on CBNRM in forest, water and watershed resources at sites across the country. A regional CBNRM workshop was organized in November 2003, involving over 80 participants from Bhutan and eight Asian countries. The meeting was highly successful in terms of sharing experiences and improving understanding about CBNRM of policy-makers, researchers, extensionists and lecturers in Bhutan and other countries. The action plan is ongoing and we are working towards the institutionalization of CBNRM approaches throughout the ministry and the sectoral departments in research and development.

Conclusion

The CBNRM research by the RNRRC Bajo team has dramatically changed the way that the centre approaches the whole process of research, including problem definition, methods, programming, and links to policy and extension. This work has enabled the research team to tune programmes to community realities so that research processes lead more directly to improvements in resource productivity, livelihoods and social assets in communities. The team has recognized the value of participatory methods to address resource management issues, but believes that CBNRM can be most successful when used in conjunction with conventional research and technological know-how in NRM. As CBNRM is more widely incorporated in the research system in Bhutan, emphasis must be placed on ensuring that young scientists gain skills in participatory research and build commitment to shared learning.

Experiences such as Lingmutey Chu provide concrete examples of how communities can participate directly in decisions about the sustainability and productivity of their own resource base. These experiences guide the implementation of decentralized NRM policies. Bhutan's National Framework on CBNRM provides the basis for a participatory approach to resource management, which helps identify clear strategies. However, this is an ongoing process. Challenges still exist in the realm of institutional support and implementation. These will continue until we all 'walk the extra mile' to bring about a reality in which communities can fully participate and be entrusted with responsibility in managing their own natural resources.

Acknowledgements

The authors acknowledge with appreciation the other members of the project team: Doley Tshering, Thinlay Gyamtsho, Gyambo Tshering, Yeshey, Aita Bhujel, Yonten Gyamtsho, Rinzin Dorji, Dawa L. Sherpa and M.P. Timsina. This research was supported in part by grants from the IDRC and SDC.

CHAPTER 11

Strengthening local voices to inform national policy: community forestry in Cambodia

Phan Kamnap and Sy Ramony

Abstract

This chapter details the key strategies through which the Community Forestry Research Project (CFRP) addressed opportunities for policy reform in community forestry in Cambodia. The research project's engagement in national forestry-sector reforms and its contribution to forest governance processes evolved from three different approaches. The first was the action research of the CFRP team in the field to formalize and improve the local community management of collectively held forestlands. The results of this work were highlighted in order to strengthen local voices. The second approach cultivated multidisciplinary and multilevel cooperation between different actors in community forestry in Cambodia. Recognizing the value of the roles and relationships held by different actors has been central in facilitating a stronger role for communities in forestry-sector reforms. Third, links were created between field learning and institutional and policy development to bridge the gap between community and national levels.

In October 2003, villagers discovered poachers cutting timber from their recently formed community forest in Toupcheang, Koh Kong province, Cambodia. There had been a longstanding problem with armed outsiders entering the forests in their community and logging valuable luxury-quality timber. Community members said: 'Please leave our forests alone and find somewhere else to do it.' However, with the power of guns and threats, the poachers cut timber virtually uncontested, saying 'We have the guns, you don't,' and, 'You should think more of the safety of your families than the trees.'

Previously, some of the villagers had visited communities managing forests in Ratanakiri province, where they heard stories of conflicts between villagers and concessionaires and saw widespread forest degradation and local organization to oppose it. Motivated by this experience and frustrated by tensions with poachers in their own forests, the Koh Kong villagers began to consider how community forestry might benefit them. They began negotiations with a concessionaire company, whose representatives agreed that it would be possible for some of the concession forests that were located close to their villages to be managed by the villagers.

Together, the company and villagers developed rules and regulations for the forests and with the help of provincial forestry officers were able to convince the district governor to approve them. After receiving this official support, the power dynamics shifted in favour of community members. In cooperation with the military, community members confronted the armed poachers, presented the signed document and secured the transfer of these poachers into custody. This experience demonstrates how community forestry in Cambodia offers an opportunity to increase the security of local livelihoods and legitimize collective action by local user groups.

Background

Community forestry (or CF) appears to present an opportunity for improved forestry management. This chapter describes how the community forestry research project has worked to generate wider understanding of this option.

Cambodia is predominantly a rural country with an annual income per head of US$310. Cambodia still lacks much of the infrastructure and growth opportunities of a modern economy. Forests are essential for the daily lives of most Cambodians and play a critical role in maintaining the ecological balance and productivity of farming and fisheries, peoples' main sources of livelihood. This fact, coupled with the growing population, means that the vast majority of Cambodians will continue to rely heavily on forests and other natural resources for the near future.

Box 11.1 History of community forestry in Cambodia

Cambodia borders Thailand, Laos, Vietnam and the Gulf of Siam. Historically a powerful nation centred at Angkor, modern Cambodia was devastated by war (1967–75) and the Khmer Rouge regime (1975–9). Since the 1990s, Cambodia has been engaged in a process of reconstruction, including the introduction of broad governance reforms.

Following the re-establishment of a sovereign government in 1993, forest concessions were introduced as a primary instrument of forest management and government revenue. Between 1994 and 1997, the government granted more than 30 concessions covering over half of Cambodia's forests.

The government also established a conservation-oriented system of protected areas that affected 23 per cent of Cambodia's forests under the Ministry of the Environment (MoE). However, the forest sector in Cambodia generally refers to forests under the Forestry Administration (FA) and has not included forests managed by the MoE.

Before 1970, forests in Cambodia belonged to and were managed by the state through a centralized Forestry Administration (FA), using a system of forest reserves with some concessions. However, between 1970 and the early 1990s, this administration lost effective control over the forests during the civil war and Khmer Rouge regime. Central management was replaced by a regional structure under which forest resources were primarily controlled by provincial authorities. However, while authority shifted from the central to regional and provincial levels, the state maintained a central role in forest policy and management (Savet and Sokhun, 2002).

In the early 1990s, Cambodia had the most intact national inventory of primary and natural forest in Asia. When postwar reconstruction began, under the United Nations Transitional Authority in Cambodia (UNTAC), the country's forest resources represented a major national asset that could have become an important and sustainable base for livelihoods and for the environmental health of the country. However, during the mid-1990s, Cambodia experienced some of the highest deforestation rates in Asia. Forests provided an important source of revenue for both the government and others, both legally and illegally. Many areas of forest were cut to feed one side or another in the slowly fading civil conflict in the countryside.

The political, economic and institutional environment in Cambodia also began to shift substantially with the re-establishment of national self-government in the early 1990s. National policy favoured private-sector development under a new market-oriented economy. Many forest or land concessions were granted to large domestic and international companies, by different authorities and without clear legality, coordination or public disclosure. This resulted in a frenzy of logging, conflicting claims and general confusion.

In the late 1990s, efforts were initiated that are still ongoing to reform the forest sector and related policies. Most early reforms focused on improving the performance of forest concessions as a means to achieve more sustainable forest management. Concurrently, the FA and the government were increasingly concerned about the small share of timber revenues they were receiving from the concessionaires.[1] When it transpired that many concessionaires were logging at rates exceeding sustainable levels, a public outcry ensued. Global Witness[2] and other organizations succeeded in drawing the attention of important donor groups and the outside world to the plight of Cambodia's forests. Because of these pressures, the FA and the Cambodian government began to rethink their forest policies.

A number of important steps in the reform process were adopted, including:
- identification of priorities and recommendations for forest-sector reform;
- new legal instruments such as the Sub-decree on Forest Concession Management (1999), a revised Forestry Law (2002) and a Sub-decree for Community Forest Management (2003);
- preparation of a model Forest Concession Agreement including Codes of Practice for Forest Harvesting, a Forest Concession Management Planning Manual and community forestry guidelines, which include community

forestry agreements and community forest management planning requirements;
- establishment of an independent forest crime monitoring office reporting
  to government and the FA; and
- cancellation or renegotiation of over 80 per cent of forest concessions
  based on mandatory compliance requirements that had not been met, including the preparation of long-term, strategic forest management plans
  consistent with international standards.[3]

While these steps represent important progress in forestry reform, the
processes have also lacked transparency. Broad and genuine participation was
absent. Real progress in forestry reforms is viewed by some as being substantially
less than appearances and certainly less than the potential. As with all policies
and programmes, constant reassessment is required, while keeping in mind
that implementation processes are often difficult to administer.

The evolution of community forestry: an alternative pathway

Community forestry in Cambodia evolved and expanded in a relatively
uncoordinated way, with support from various groups and through different
mechanisms. A few small-scale community forestry projects commenced in the
early 1990s. Forest communities undertook the projects themselves, with limited
support from NGOs. As a result, community forestry projects gained momentum
and expanded rapidly throughout Cambodia. Recent surveys identified over
176 such initiatives, spanning a wide variety of local and institutional contexts
across the country.

The total area under community forestry remains relatively small (about
90,000 ha, mainly in degraded forest areas). However, it is significant, because
these types of projects represent the only forests in Cambodia under active
forest management. This is in stark contrast to the millions of hectares allocated
to forest concessions that were damaged heavily by poor logging practices.

Early community forestry groups were successful. They proved that forests
can regenerate and bring tangible benefits to the lives of local people, particularly
when they are managed in a sustainable way by local communities. Their success
invited the wider adoption and promotion of community forestry approaches.

Box 11.2 Community forestry

Community forestry (CF) represents an effort to support and empower communities
so they can continue their traditional uses of forest resources and encourage
sustainable practices. CF harnesses local knowledge and skills in forest management and ensures that communities have a stronger voice in the forestry sector's
decision-making process. CF focuses directly on meeting the needs of rural people
through strengthened local governance of forest resources. CF contributes directly
to major strategic policy objectives such as sustainable socio-economic development, integrated rural development and decentralization, as well as sustaining the
productivity of forests.

A variety of NGOs (such as CONCERN Worldwide, Oxfam and the Coopération Internationale pour le Développement et la Solidarité,CIDSE) have actively embarked upon support for community forestry practices. However, their strategies and efforts often were poorly coordinated with other groups. Some major donors have also supported community forestry projects, notably a large FAO project in Siem Reap province and another located in Ratanakiri province. The Seila Programme also supported community forestry development.

The CFRP was formed in 1999 and was structured around multi-institutional collaboration between different levels of government and by different actors that include representatives from civil society. A prime goal is to give stronger voices to local communities. Three national institutions have collaborated in steering and implementing the project: the MoE,[4] the Forestry Administration (FA)[5] and the Forestry Sciences Faculty of the Royal University of Agriculture (RUA). Through the research project, these national organizations collaborated with each other, with provincial and local government agencies, NGOs, commune councils, village groups and local forest user groups. In some cases, the research team also worked with forest concessionaires and the military. A number of the research project's activities promoted a broader understanding of forest governance. CFRP joined with others to establish consultation mechanisms and build capacities for a pluralistic policy and institutional environment for community forestry. Key initiatives included:
- building a national community forestry network and broad alliances;
- supporting working groups at different levels;
- collaborating with other projects or groups in this sector; and
- engaging in and supporting a multistakeholder process to draft national community forestry legislation (creating a sub-decree).

CFRP has contributed to forest-sector reform and to governance processes through three main strategies. The following strategies form the structure for this chapter.
1. Strengthening local people's practices and voices in forest management and expanding their practical understanding of community forestry in different forest conditions;
2. Developing multi-institutional and multilevel approaches that recognize and value the roles and relationships of different agencies and organizations in community forestry, and which contribute to inter-institutional learning at many levels; and
3. Creating links between field learning and institutional and policy development that allow actors to understand and influence policy processes, such as the community forestry sub-decree and community forestry guidelines.

These concepts and approaches are illustrated in Figure 11.1.

Project start-up and site selection

When the project started, the concepts of community forestry and PAR were new to most team members. Although some of them had forestry degrees, they

Field-based
learning

Community forestry
action research
and learning
cycle

L

R

Learning continues
and knowledge is built

L

A

The action-reflection and
learning cycle is continuous

A

R

Participating researchers, actions and
learnings differ by site

R & L

CF begins

Links from field to
other levels

Networking

Learning and sharing lessons

Learning and
governance
processes

Drawing in other partners

Capacity-building

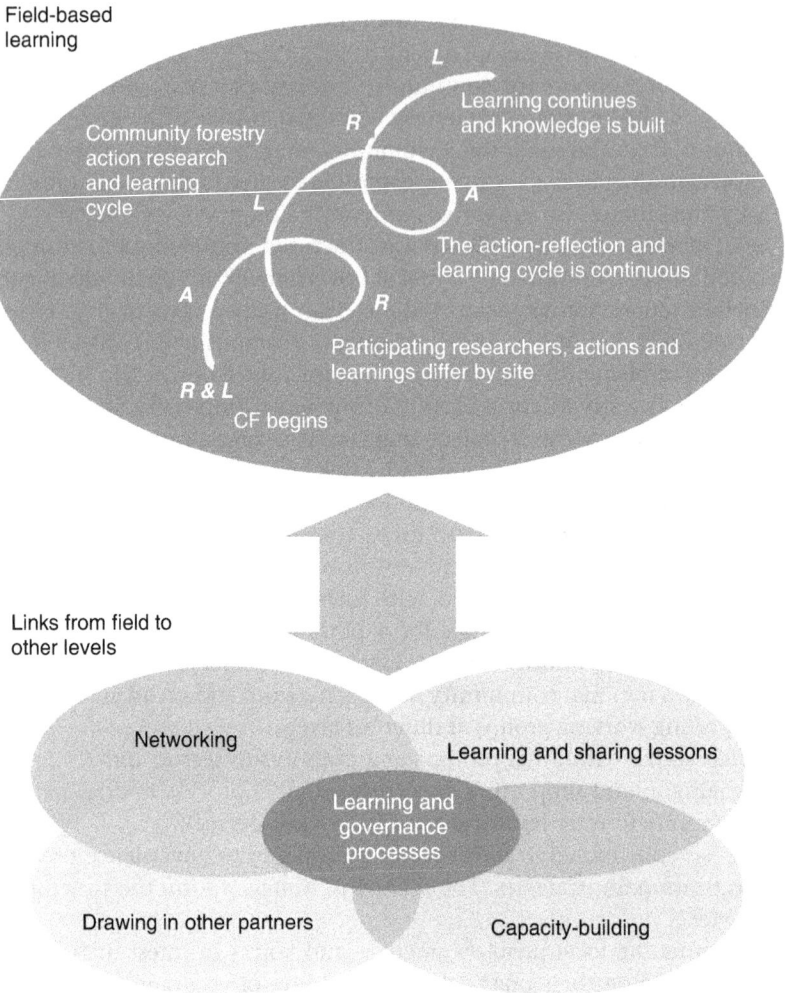

Figure 11.1 Diagram of a community forestry action research and learning cycle

had been taught little about community forestry. To begin building understanding and awareness, teachers from the RUA and others who were involved in the project were invited on field site visits. Here they viewed some of the early successes of other community forestry groups. They became enthusiastic about the natural regeneration possibilities for degraded forests when they are managed by community groups. Team members noted the degree to which regeneration could provide quick returns to households and noted how mixed tropical forests are highly valued by villagers. In addition, they saw how forests can regenerate with minimal investment costs. Team members wondered why it was necessary for governments to borrow money from development banks in order to re-establish natural forests.

PAR was adopted as a key strategy of CFRP, aimed at expanding practical knowledge of forestry rooted in experiences from different forest conditions and different institutional or economic settings. The project strategy was to promote a learning-oriented approach to forest management, in contrast to a conventional rule-based approach.

CFRP has five research sites, as shown in Table 11.1. The five sites include those inside protected areas and forest concessions; one straddles a protected area boundary; and two sites are considered 'typical' under FA administration (in neither a protected area nor a forest concession). In one of these latter sites, the forests are degraded while in the other their condition is still relatively good.

The site-based research teams in the CFRP are all multidisciplinary, originating from various organizations including NGOs. Community members also participated. Each team was led by ministerial and departmental representatives at the national and provincial levels.

Strengthening local forest management practices in Chumkiri

This chapter highlights outcomes from the Chumkiri site, in a commune where both agriculture and forest resources are crucial to villagers' livelihoods. People in Kampot province are among the poorest in Cambodia. During the Khmer Rouge era, forests here were logged extensively in order to support the military. Even though peace was officially restored before the commencement of the Chumkiri project, a strong military presence continued. Until recently, both

Table 11.1 Location and characteristics of CFRP research sites

Research sites, province	Forest description	Forest Jurisdiction	Field partners
Chumkiri, Kompot	Hillside degraded forest adjacent to agricultural lowlands	CF in FA jurisdiction	CIDSE and FA, district agriculture office
Kompong Kor, Kratie	Degraded ex-concession forest adjacent to villages on the Mekong River	CF in FA jurisdiction	KAFDOC and FA
Sre Ambel, Koh Kong	Upland, forest still in good condition	CF located within Samling forest concession	AFSC/ISLP & FA
Kompong Seila, Koh Kong	Slightly degraded forest adjacent to Bokor National Park	CF in MoE and FA jurisdiction	FA
Boeng Per, Kompong Thom	Upland forest within the buffer zone of Poeng Per Wildlife sanctuary	CF in MoE jurisdiction	Provincial Environmental Department and Park Office

Figure 11.2 Map of CFRP research sites

local people and outsiders treated the forests in Chumkiri as a resource that could be logged and used for firewood and other needs. As such uses continued, the quality of the forests steadily declined.

The action research cycle that the team followed typically began in discussion with village groups about the condition of the forest and other natural resources. Im Maredi (one of the CFRP members at Chumkiri and a local FA official) reported,

> I learned a lot from the traditional forest management practices of local people. They already have clear ideas on the proper management of private forests and I appreciate also their active participation in community forestry.

When reflecting upon these early visits and experiences, team members felt it was important to arrange a study tour for villagers to other parts of Cambodia to learn about positive community forestry experiences. By visiting, discussing and solving problems together, villagers enriched their understanding of community forestry, and assessed its value in terms of their own situation. At this early stage of the work, Kim Noun, a Chumkiri elder, stated:

> This is the first time that I saw a forester come to work with the local people. So far, I have never seen this before and am surprised at how closely he is working with the people.

Box 11.3 Damnak Neakta Thmorpoun Community Forest, Chumkiri district, Kampot

In Chumkiri district, several dozen villages occupy the broad Chumkiri valley, which is bounded by mountains on the east and west. Most people are engaged in subsistence livelihoods, based on agriculture and natural resources. Rice is a staple crop. Forests are especially important to local livelihoods, because they provide products that people use directly and are part of the agro-ecosystem on which local communities depend.

Before 1980, the mountains of Chumkiri were rich in forest and other natural resources. But by 1998, they had become heavily degraded, destroyed mainly by illegal logging, but also by unregulated collection of firewood and NTFPs, and by forest land-grabbing activities conducted by private owners. Forest ecosystems changed from healthy, semi-evergreen forests to degraded deciduous forest. The loss of forest cover led to wild life depletion, erosion and sedimentation of the rice fields. Once abundant NTFPs such as wild fruit, wild vegetables and rattans became scarce. Little timber was available for house construction, forcing villagers to spend one or two weeks away from home in distant forests where they faced a greater danger from malaria. Such impacts affected both men and women. Men usually collect the timber, while women collect NTFPs such as firewood, bamboo, bamboo shoots, mushrooms, wild fruits, vegetables, traditional medicines, vines and rattan.

Local people in Chumkiri were concerned about problems associated with forest degradation, but they felt powerless to address them. Although several villages received rural development assistance from an NGO (CIDSE) or from provincial agencies, these efforts did not extend to forestry issues. Following a participatory assessment conducted in three villages by CFRP in early 2000, local people asked for assistance to improve forest resources. In early 2001, villagers in the three communities agreed to establish a community forest. They undertook community forestry boundary demarcation, formed a management structure, prepared community forestry regulations, and received recognition from the technical agency and the provincial governor.

With this mobilization and recognition from authorities, the local community has prevented almost all illegal logging and outside use of their forest resources. Community forestry committees have conducted awareness-raising events among community forestry members, children and neighbouring villages, and have resolved conflicts in peaceful ways. In 2003, the local community drafted community forestry management plans to submit to technical agencies for review and official recognition.

Although most of the area in Chumkiri is degraded forest, a few older residents have managed to preserve small private forest areas. One was a former forester during the French colonial times who maintained a private forest area near his house so that he did not have to go far to collect firewood. He sometimes lets poorer households access this area for firewood. As someone with more financial resources, he has some influence among other villagers. Therefore, it helps that he actively provides support, shares information willingly, and serves on the Community Forestry Committee.

There are several research activities involved in forming community forestry groups and in developing management plans for the community's forests. The different steps, which are neither mechanistic nor sequential, are set out in Figure 11.3. In terms of community organization, the research team helped to facilitate the election of a community forestry management committee. Candidacy was based on criteria such as willingness to serve and time available, literacy, and popularity of and respect for candidates. In addition, the team hoped to find women who could participate.

Action research and learning processes involved participatory land-use mapping, negotiating agreements on boundaries and forestry sites, forest inventories, and local studies on forest resource use and management options. It was relatively easy to conduct forest assessments in Chumkiri, where the forests were already in a state of degradation. There the main task was to help all the villagers understand the value of establishing a community forestry group and to build commune support for the initiative. After this, the community identified areas to be managed as community forest and agreed on rules and regulations for their management. Finally, the local commune and district were asked officially to support the group.

Once the community forest management group was formed, meetings and lengthy discussions formalized the group. In the first site, this process took more than a year, but in subsequent sites, the process has been accomplished more quickly.

Because policy provisions for community forestry had not been finalized at the national level, all the community forest groups operated under ad hoc provisional recognition. The first step in acquiring recognition occurred at the commune level (a commune is the lowest level of formal government structure and includes several villages). Local community forestry groups must receive support from their village in order to secure commune council approval. These groups then apply to district and provincial FA officials, who can endorse proposals for the approval of district or provincial governors respectively. The team discovered that field visits by officials facilitated this process because villagers could demonstrate their management knowledge and ability. During the process, the team learned the effectiveness of shared learning between one site-based research team and another. In all five of the research sites, there are now formalized community forestry groups with official recognition by district or provincial governors.

Local outcomes

Action research on community-based management of forest resources has resulted in a variety of outcomes in the sites where CFRP is active. The basket of outcomes is a result of local adaptive capacity and local empowerment processes generated by PAR, in contrast to more traditional research approaches.

To structure the process of community forestry development and planning, CFRP research teams have begun to test a 'principles, criteria and indicators'

Community forest implementation: benefit and cost sharing, monitoring, conflict resolution, enforcement.

Forest management plan begins to be developed.

Establish local CF rules and formal approval.

Further village discussions.

Boundary demarcation.

Share CF concepts.

Village study tours to learn more and share more.

Share research finding with villagers.

Initial field research.

These steps were not conducted 'mechanically' at research sites, but were flexible, based on the local condition and stakeholders involved.

Learning continues and knowledge is built.

The action reflection and learning cycle is continuous.

Participating researchers, actions and learning

CF begins.

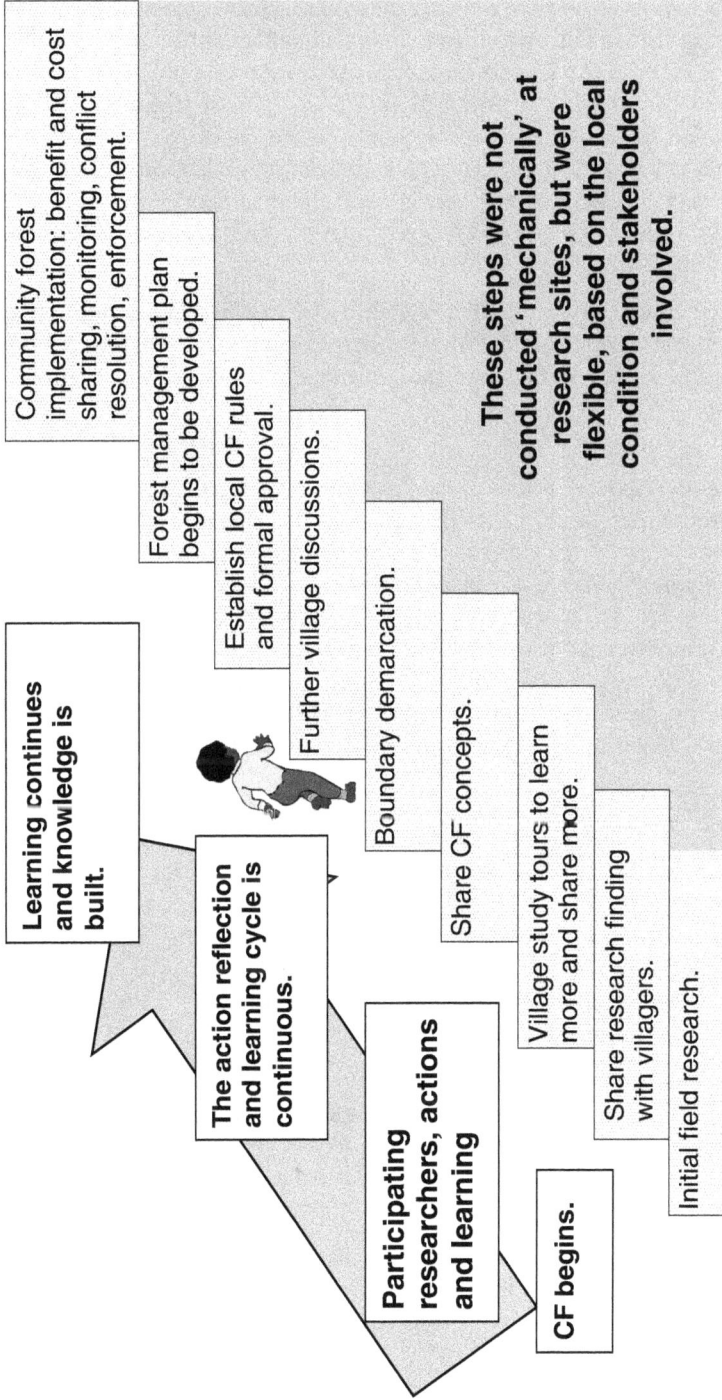

Figure 11.3 Steps in helping to establish a community forestry group, to procure formal approval at a local level, and to implement a management plan

(PCI) framework with local communities, which has led to very positive results. This approach provides tools to measure the sustainability of forest management by examining three main dimensions: the well-being of the forest, the well-being of the community and its members, and supportive policy conditions. While the PCI framework is primarily intended to assist communities plan community forestry activities, the project has also been working with FA officials at different levels to see if this methodology can satisfy their approval standards for community forestry agreements. We use these categories of forest well-being, community well-being and related policy conditions to report outcomes in Chumkiri below.

> I believe that our Community Forest members can protect these trees. Before, this forest was degraded and during the dry season it was not green. But now the forest has recovered and we can see green and yellow even during the dry season.
>
> Noun Siv, a villager from Chumkiri

Once the degraded forest came under community management, improvements in forest productivity and quality became evident. Villagers in some parts of Chumkiri now travel for only half a day to collect products from newly regenerated forests, whereas previously they would have had to travel for between seven and 10 days. An indicator of forest health has been the growing abundance and diversity of wild life. The increased population of wild pigs has even led to problems in Chumkiri where they destroy crops and villagers are prevented from hunting by local regulation. This is an instance where local policies and regulations will need to be reviewed in keeping with changing realities.

Improved food security through increased rice production is an unexpected benefit in Chumkiri. As the forests regenerated, the productivity of fields located near the forests rose, and crop yields increased. Soil erosion was reduced in the forest where runoff and erosion had damaged fields and impeded farming. In addition, other forest-based food sources are contributing more to community members' diets. Bamboo shoots, mushrooms and wild fruits are becoming more abundant and accessible. For the first time in 2004, after three years of management, community members were able to harvest significant quantities of bamboo for sale. Now, selective harvesting of poles is being considered.

> If they (management committee) are not able to participate in writing up plans, whatever results will not be practical.
>
> Chun Sara, CFRP member from Provincial Forestry
> and Wildlife Office of Kampot Province

> If we do not have a proper management plan, then anyone can cut trees in our forest. Soon the forest will be destroyed again.
>
> Tep Ant, Chief of the Community Forestry
> Management Committee of Chumkiri

The cohesion of the community has been strengthened through increased collective activities under community forestry. In Chumkiri, the community forestry committee organized the pooling of finances and supplies to allow the poorest five families in the village to construct housing. Voluntary participation through contribution of monthly fees for the support of the committee has increased, while the proportion of contributing households has also increased from approximately 50 per cent initially to 80 per cent by early 2004. Community awareness of the importance of firebreaks as well as participation in their maintenance has also increased. Finally, a multiplier effect has resulted whereby community forestry activities have spread from the core communities to other villages in the commune.

In the past, there was extensive illegal use of timber and NTFPs by outsiders. In the Chumkiri project site, illegal use of the forest has stopped completely, due to community patrols and better recognized boundaries. There is greater understanding of penalties related to illegal forest activities and communities can now enforce these with the support and sanction of forestry officials.

Complex local conflicts relating to forest use could be addressed, but only after the community forest regulations have gained a measure of legitimacy and credibility. The crucial step was the support of the FA office at the district and provincial level, which leads to official recognition and the signature of the provincial governor. Chumkiri was able to use the legitimacy conferred by this approval to successfully challenge even the military, when outsiders bribed a local officer to ensure access to firewood collection in the newly designated community forest.

The introduction of community forestry improved the regulation of forest use and ensured local people could enjoy some benefits from the forest. The condition of the forests has improved in terms of diversity, cover and the diameter of the trees, and there has been a notable reduction in soil erosion and the sedimentation of rice fields. The community forestry management plan now being prepared will divide the forest into three zones: timber, rotation and bamboo. This next step will strengthen local management and the sustainability of forest resources.

Forest well-being has been enhanced in all five research sites. Community-based management and the enforcement of approved forest boundaries has halted open access and over-exploitation of local forest resources, enabling forest ecosystems to begin recovery. While community forestry is unlikely to result in re-establishing primary forest conditions, it has initiated recovery towards a forest ecosystem that provides many important ecological functions and services.

The team noted that discussions among different communities were often instrumental in prompting local communities to adopt a community forestry development project in their village-level development plan. For instance, now that the Chumkiri community forestry group has become well established, they have hosted 28 visits from official groups (as of 2004). Hosting is often tedious and costly for communities. In Chumkiri, the team and villagers ask visitors to contribute to their community fund to help compensate for their time.

Multi-agency and multilevel approaches

The research project has not only led to local impacts, however. Throughout the project, careful structure of the research teams and strategic engagement with related organizations have allowed the project to have far-reaching effects on the attitudes and knowledge of government staff, development organizations, and university faculty members and teachers.

Community forest management also includes functional linkages to government at all levels, from local through district, provincial and national. Donor support has often translated into stronger links at the national level. However, there is a shift towards more support at provincial and district levels of government.[6] A pluralistic policy and institutional environment for civil society has been actively encouraged and strengthened by advocates, donors, practitioners, NGOs and communities. Many community forestry advocates recognize the need for engagement with the FA and for creating the enabling policy and institutional environment required.

Historically, the Ministry of Agriculture, Forestry and Fisheries (MAFF) and MoE have not always seen eye-to-eye on forest management issues. There have been tensions resulting from unclear mandates and competing jurisdictions. The research project brought staff from these two key national institutions together, and at times also involved their provincial counterparts and staff of the RUA. Their goal was to develop an awareness of forestry issues and realities at the local level. Interagency collaboration such as this will be essential to promote policy dialogue and institutional reform in community forestry.

The same applies at the commune, district and provincial levels. Local departments' activities have considerable impact on local communities and in promoting good forest governance. These groups' institutional capacities require strengthening so that learning can be shared among different groups. Because of its multi-institutional composition, the national project team has been helpful in facilitating communication and understanding between different groups. Likewise, at the local level the different partners who worked together in the field began to reach understanding and agreement on shared issues and concerns.

Effective interagency cooperation and learning involves line departments, the Forestry Faculty of RUA, local communities, field implementation agencies and partner NGOs. All were key to the success of this project. The project's structure, strategies and activities demonstrate organizational learning approaches that have strengthened the institutional environment for community forestry. The field experiences of the multidisciplinary teams and of national staff, who have worked with provincial and district level counterparts as well as communities to pilot and evaluate community forestry schemes, have played an important role in influencing policy outcomes. The value of the participants' experiences and expertise has not been lost on the project's three parent agencies. For example, these agencies involved CFRP members in policy discussions when important decisions needed to be made. Research outputs, such as reports, presentations, case studies and briefs have not only assisted the ongoing discussions, but also have won recognition of the value of community forestry practices.

Partnership leads to community forestry expansion

Cooperation in community forestry requires changing conventional resource management practices, acquiring new skills, building or establishing new partnerships and overcoming the distrust that often exists between different stakeholders. Managing forests, including the community management of forests, involves many stakeholders whose interests may vary because they are represented through organizations with different mandates and goals. No single organization can effectively undertake community forestry, from national to local levels and across all types of contexts. The research project has highlighted the value of partners as well as interinstitutional and multisectoral coordination. CFRP has been involved in multiple partnerships among government and NGOs involved in rural development. For example, in Chumkiri, CIDSE became a major partner. It helps implement rural development programmes such as rice and livestock banks, credit and road-building.

Prior to joining CFRP as a partner in Chumkiri, CIDSE expressed little interest in forestry activities. However, based on the lessons from this project and requests from other villages for community forestry assistance, CIDSE incorporated forestry into its programming in Chumkiri. The research team continues to provide technical support to CIDSE's forestry programme.

Community forestry is also spreading to other sites and government agencies. In Kampot province, the local FA officials are beginning to consider ways in which to increase community forestry initiatives elsewhere, because of the province's degraded forests and the success of Chumkiri. Community forestry may be possible under the Seila programme. In Boeng Per, local commune councils have made similar requests for support from the national research team so that they can adopt community forestry approaches in protected areas. Based on these and other cases, the MoE, the ministry responsible for permanent nature reserves in Cambodia, has begun to adopt a people-included approach to parks and forest conservation.

One of the ways in which the project has achieved a wide impact has been the presentation of reports in both English and Khmer at various meetings and workshops. Research findings and results have been presented and discussed among key partners, institutions and stakeholders, as well as with donor representatives at review meetings. Throughout the project, documents, reports, brochures and posters in Khmer and English were used as tools to inform relevant stakeholders. These publications and other dissemination activities have successfully attracted a wide interest in the project's fieldwork and results.

The experiences and lessons learned at the field level have also influenced course and curriculum development in the forestry faculty at the RUA. CFRP strategically included university faculty and students as part of the research team. These team members have used their experiences to enrich their teaching, and as a result they are sharing PAR and community forestry practices more actively. The close involvement and collaboration of teachers in field-based research means that important new material is being incorporated into university courses and curriculum design.

Along with other faculty members, the dean of the Faculty of Forestry has been an important member of the team. So far, 16 students from the RUA have received financial and field support from CFRP. Their thesis research findings have also been a valuable part of the overall research and, in some cases, theses have been incorporated into course materials in forestry and environmental programmes.

Creating links between field learning, institutions and policy development

Viewing the work of CFRP in a forest governance framework provides illuminating insights on how to situate the work and approach. This framework focuses on three main types of groups: enabling agencies, service providers and user groups (see Figure 11.4). The importance of power relationships among the different actors is at the core of this governance perspective. Viewed from this angle, the experience of the research project brings out the basic relevance of building good working relationships and maintaining good communications among different organizations in order to garner the necessary acceptance and support for policy changes.

At the start, CFRP realized that the FA authority under the MAFF would continue to be extremely important before reforms could be achieved. Therefore, the FA became involved in community forestry research and dissemination at all levels. The research team identified and invited key policy-makers to sit on our management committee. We involved them in our work and learning, and they and other top officials visited our field sites on many different occasions. We believe that they learned a lot about community forestry as a management approach during our discussions with community members. Now we are seeking formal approval for local community forestry agreements under the recently passed community forestry sub-decree. Therefore, we are assisting communities in developing formal forest management plans for FA approval under the new legislation. At the same time, we are continuing to involve senior ministry staff in the work of the project. Learning from the different forest research sites helps explain how the FA is implementing new regulations. Research evidence, reports and field visits help villagers' voices to be heard in the ongoing discussion on policy implementation.

Dialogue and interaction between the national, provincial and local levels has been encouraged in our work. This has been one of the most significant

Enabling agencies

National level:
MoE, FA, RUA,
and partners

Linkages, power and
relationship

Voice, power and
relationship

**Service
providers**

Relevant Policy:
Forestry law, CF Sub-
decree, environmental
law and draft Protected
Area Sub-decree

**User
groups**

Provincial level:
FA, environment
department and
NGOs

Local level:
Local community
and authorities
(commune
council)

Linkages, power
and relationship

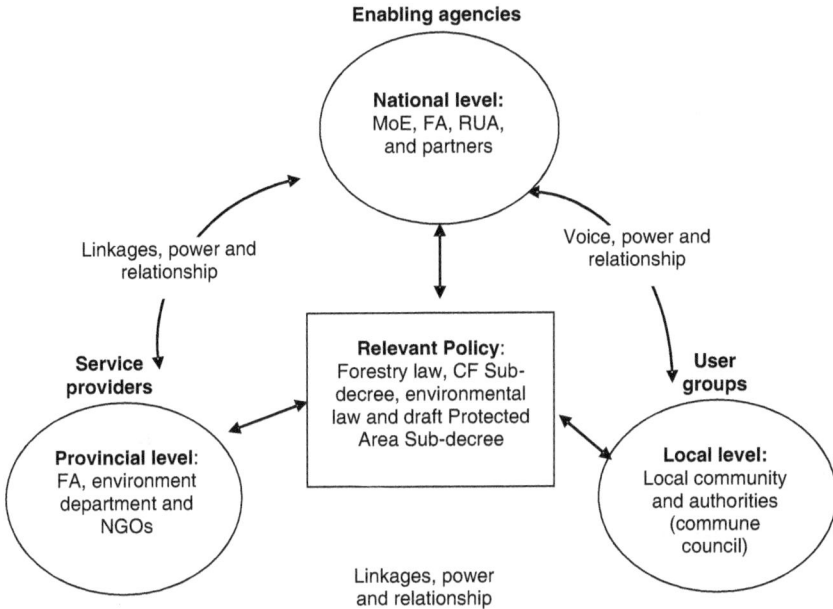

Figure 11.4 Beginning to understand forest governance, interinstitutional linkages
and power relationships

challenges that CFRP has faced. In practice, the realities of policy implementation
often mean that policy adoption at the national or provincial levels does not
easily translate to the grass roots level. Nor are the needs and experiences at the
local level generally taken into consideration by higher levels. CFRP attempts
to bridge this gap by operating at and between these levels.

The research team has established a number of specific links between field
learning and institutional and policy development processes, including the
formulation of sub-decrees (*anukret*) for community forestry and protected-area
management. We were also involved in developing guidelines (*prakas*) for
community forestry management planning, a proposed national community
forestry programme, forestry curriculum reforms and the participatory land-
use planning process. The team's field research and experimentation provided
policy-makers with first-hand information about the problems at the grassroots
level, as well as feasible options for policy implementation.

I have learned a lot from the field experiences of CFRP and it has been very
useful in formulating policy related to community forestry such as the Community Forestry Sub-Decree and Community Forestry Guidelines. It is expected that in the near future, it will play a role in formulating draft community forest agreements, community forestry guidelines, draft forest community management plans and other important documents.

Lao Sethaphal, CFRP member and Deputy Chief of the
Community Forestry Office of the FA

CFRP has attempted to foster a pluralistic policy and institutional environment for community forestry by promoting and supporting various multi-stakeholder mechanisms. This involved both vertical learning between the field, district, provincial and national levels; and horizontal learning among communities, commune councils, local government agencies, NGOs, and other local stakeholders. Such linkages provided the less powerful stakeholders with platforms for voicing their concerns and opinions.

Community forestry sub-decree consultation process

Although community forestry expanded significantly from the early 1990s onwards, this occurred without any specific national policy or legal basis. Several efforts to formulate a national policy foundered due to differences and disagreement among important stakeholders, particularly between the FA, MoE and NGOs. Recognizing the need to resolve the impasse and to move forward, in May 2001 Chan Sarun, then undersecretary of state of MAFF, called for the formation of a multistakeholder task force to undertake a consultative process in drafting a revised community forestry sub-decree, to establish a specific national policy and legal basis for community forestry.

The research team members were involved in the drafting process in several ways. Some were included in the task force and directly involved in the drafting exercise. The team also had working relationships with a number of the key stakeholder groups represented on the task force, including FA, MoE, NGOs, Seila and forest concessionaires. As well, the research team actively supported local consultations during the drafting process. Such consultations were important in order to ensure an inclusive and transparent process, rather than one that happened behind closed doors. The research process and ensuing documentation showed that community forestry user groups could manage and regenerate forests under their own control. As a result, these groups demonstrated they had a meaningful role in the consultation process.

The consultation process undertaken by the task force engaged different stakeholders in the formulation of the draft community forestry sub-decree. In February 2002, the multi-agency task force for developing the sub-decree successfully completed its work and made its submission to the FA. This was the culmination of more than six months of consultations. It was the first time that forest-sector legislation had been formulated with an extensive consultation process. Formerly it was achieved via centralized experts. Local communities became active participants in this consultation processes. In practice, consultation involved brainstorming subjects to be included in the draft chapters and articles, which in itself was a key entry point for local voices. Communities were both able and enthusiastic to express their concerns and suggestions. This was a landmark because up to that time officials had been sceptical of the role villagers could play in the drafting process.

These consultations set a precedent in being the first open public consultations in any FA policy-formulation process.

This is the first time that I have had a right to say what I think and to give suggestions on what are our needs from the community forestry sub-decree formulation.

Sya Sam, a villager in Tbeing Pork, Chumkiri,
who was involved in the sub-decree consultation process.

The community forestry process proposed in the draft legislation mirrored this kind of consultation. It suggested that all proposed regulations be discussed first at the village level, then at other appropriate levels in the decentralized administration. Under the provisions of the sub-decree that was formally approved in December 2003, the entire village has to be consulted throughout the community forestry planning and authorization process. After community agreement has been reached, relevant technical departments and local authorities can become engaged. A finalized local community forestry regulation must not only win the approval of community members. It must also be recognized and accepted by the commune council, the district governor and the provincial forestry office, before the approval of higher officials can be given.

The sub-decree clarifies the roles and responsibilities of the various government bodies with respect to community forestry. In addition, it represents a significant advance in protecting the rights and interests of communities, and in promoting decentralization, poverty alleviation and providing an adequate legal framework for community involvement in the sustainable management of forestry resources.

The sub-decree allows community forestry organizations to be established and to manage forests wherever there is forested land. This potentially allows community management of all forested areas under the jurisdiction of the FA. Based on the sub-decree, a community forestry group has the right to plant, manage and harvest forest products and NTFPs, and use and sell timber from selected tree species based on a community forest management plan approved by the FA.

Communities under a Community Forestry Agreement may harvest, process, transport, and sell forest products and NTFPs in accordance with the following conditions: Harvest of forest products for selling or bartering shall not be allowed within the first 5 years of approval of the Community Forest Management Plan. If the Community Forest has been operating with a Community Forest Management Plan prior to the passage of this Sub-Decree, then the moratorium on harvesting forest products shall be considered from the date of approval of that Community Forest Management Plan. (Article 12 of Community Forestry Management Sub-Decree)

In theory, the sub-decree is supportive of community forestry, but at the time of writing this chapter no group had managed to receive official approval or to obtain an approved community forest management plan. Therefore, the CFRP team feels that it has only made partial progress. The sub-decree, however, has only recently been approved, so the FA is still exploring implementation options. One of the most difficult issues is the list of requirements for forest management plans. When the FA initiated the new forest concession management system, it required that a forest inventory be conducted prior to approval of a management plan. The process demands the use of expensive equipment and elaborate statistical calculations, which are beyond the capacities of most local communities. The technical difficulties involved in drawing plans and planning processes have meant that traditional methods are still primarily used, which the FA does not consider satisfactory for the task. Therefore, the research team faces a challenge in bridging the gap and facilitating consensus on what type of management plan might be acceptable to both parties.

Mainstreaming natural resource management into Seila/PLG planning processes

The Seila local governance reform programme is now undertaking efforts to mainstream NRM. Villagers and commune councils can request help and support for the establishment of a community forestry group or similar resource management initiatives. When this occurs, local governments and provincial line agencies are obliged to attempt to meet these requests. When this approach was initially considered, Seila and staff from the Cambodian UNDP programme, Partnerships for Local Government (PLG), visited many different field sites and began to conceptualize ways to incorporate community forestry into their programme. Seila staff are line department officials at the national or provincial levels. Accordingly, they wanted to visit sites to learn what mainstreaming NRM actually involved, so they could consider how to adopt this approach into their work.

Likewise, officers from the Danish International Development Agency (DANIDA), which has launched a mainstreaming project in NRM under Seila, visited one of the CFRP's research sites. Using this approach, Seila is beginning to set up procedures so that they can satisfy the demands of commune councils who request community forestry practices. CFRP's work with villagers and partnering with line agencies successfully demonstrates it is possible to support forest user groups. Their work also proves the costs do not need to be prohibitive, which is an important consideration for nationwide programming.

Future challenges

The CFRP team's success in informing communities about national policy was made possible by its field-based research and learning processes. Research outcomes in the field translated into support for community initiatives as well as documentation. Another reason for their influence was the multi-agency and multilevel nature of the learning processes. Other important outcomes of CFRP work include contributions to the sub-decree process and to university curriculum development. Finally, direct links between field, policy and governance processes provided an opportunity to extend the impacts of the research. However, despite the project's successes, it has not been without its complications.

On close examination, the NRM policy environment in Cambodia provides both opportunities and challenges for researchers. A key question is how we can be more effective in linking our work to policy processes, while at the same time meeting important grassroots needs. The legal framework now recognizes decentralized forest management by communities and their customary rights to use forest resources as a viable option. However, laws remain fragmented and inconsistent, with conflicting statements among ministries. As our understanding of this legal framework deepens, implementation at the local level is expected to become clearer.

Clarity depends on an iterative process of field learning, multilevel and multisectoral learning, and of building stronger linkages between the various policy levels. One interesting challenge that has emerged at the community level has raised the concerns of forestry officials. Although villages with community forests can quite effectively conserve their own forest area, there is a tendency for them to exploit and degrade other forests outside their own protected boundaries. This is a challenge that requires further research and policy measures.

Perhaps one of the more important challenges will come when the new Community Forestry Sub-decree is tested and implemented. There has been resistance to reform from within the forestry sector in several of the countries in the region. Real commitment at the policy-making level is often questionable. The draft sub-decree has been revised significantly, but it is hard to pass judgement on it before it has been widely tested in the field.

The CFRP has an ongoing and important research agenda related to the forest policy reform process in Cambodia. As the new sub-decree is implemented, the research team will continue to build trust, support and commitment from all stakeholders in its study sites and elsewhere in the country to evaluate and improve CBNRM.

The next step in this process is to study the changing structure of local and provincial governance with respect to forest administration under the new legal framework. Conclusions emanating from this work will be shared with local forest users and village leaders to help them determine successful approaches to propose to government officials. The research team also plans to investigate internal conflicts and exclusions within forest user groups, with a view to identifying emerging problems and social issues in the implementation process.

The research team will continue to promote and respect the plural views of stakeholders for collaboration and networking. It will also build on its successful iterative-action research strategy to help local communities develop innovative but practical community forestry management plans.

Acknowledgements

Many thanks to Stephen R. Tyler, John Graham, Hein Mallee, Doug Henderson, Regan Suzuki and other IDRC officers and participants in the writeshop in Tagaytay, Philippines (May 2004), who provided tremendous support and helpful advice for this chapter. Very grateful thanks to local communities, field partners, local authorities at CFRP research sites, CFRP research teams, as well as the project coordination and steering committees of MoE, FA and the Royal University of Agriculture. They significantly contributed to strengthening local livelihood conditions through promoting CBNRM. The CFRP research project was supported jointly by IDRC and RECOFTC in Phase 1, and by IDRC in Phase 2.

CHAPTER 12

Harmonizing ancestral domain with local governance in the Cordillera of the northern Philippines

Lorelei C. Mendoza, June Prill-Brett, Bienvenido P. Tapang, Gladys A. Cruz, Arellano A. Colongon, Jr, Victoria Lourdes C. Diaz, Ma. Cecilia San Luis and Alicia G. Follosco

Abstract

Over time, and despite official state policy on the national patrimony, the people of the Cordillera controlled their territory through indigenous land tenure systems and customary resource management rules. They managed their internal affairs with minimal state intervention. Finally, in 1996, the Philippine state recognized native titles by enabling the formal issuing of a domain or Certificate of Ancestral Domain Claim (CADC). These certificates required the preparation of an Ancestral Domain Management Plan (ADMP) by municipal governments, despite the geographical and administrative contradictions between such levels of government and customary land and resource management entities. This contradiction served as a focus for participatory research into how to harmonize customary management structures with the requirements of the new CADC process. The research led to CBNRM approaches being used in planning. The research team devised a two-step strategy. The first step was to get formal recognition of the domains within the municipality so that they could be recognized as key planning units. The second step was to help three selected *ilis*, or traditional communities, to identify the issues and activities to include in their management plans.

Introduction

In 1996, the government of the Philippines gave formal legal recognition to the ancestral domain claim of the municipality of Sagada in Mountain province, located in the Cordillera Administrative Region. This gave Sagada the right to exercise customary resource tenure and management practices. This represented a watershed in the long struggle that Philippine indigenous cultural communities had fought to compel the Philippine state to recognize native title.[1] The case represented a dramatic reversal in the state's attitude toward indigenous people's land rights. The Cordillera Studies Centre (CSC) of the University of the Philippines Baguio had worked for some time on these issues of customary land tenure and ancestral domain.[2] The policy change provided an opportunity for our team and partners to look more closely at the implementation of NRM devolution to customary, community-based institutions.

We launched a three-year participatory research project in March 1997, entitled 'Ancestral domain and natural resource management in Sagada, Mountain province, northern Philippines'. It is usually referred to as NRMP 2. We focused our attention on the following issues of policy implementation, which guided the design of the project's activities and priorities:

1. ensuring local peoples' participation in the identification and delineation of their ancestral domains and lands;
2. formulating ecologically and economically sound management plans (see Box 12.1);
3. enabling the recognition of the *ili* (see Box 12.2) as a planning entity in the preparation of the ADMP; and
4. strengthening coordination efforts among government agencies towards achieving development goals in an area covered by the award of an ancestral domain claim.

Historically, the Cordillera was not effectively colonized until the 19th century. Residents of these areas had already evolved enforceable rights to types of property regimes before the colonial state declared all lands as part of the public domain under the Regalian doctrine. The American colonial government

---

Box 12.1 Ancestral domain management plan

As mandated by national legislation, an ADMP contains three main sections.

The first consists of basic information on the indigenous peoples, including members and head individual, the land area covered by tenure instruments and a list of the tenure instruments.

The second is a description of the community in terms of such things as its demographic profile, economic organization and socio-political institutions. The area of the ancestral domain must also be described, including such factors as location, topography, accessibility, importance of resources and land uses.

The third is the strategic resource management plan. It must delineate such items as the community's resource management vision, goals and objectives; envisioned forestland use and resource allocation; assessment of resource usage; environmental and socio-economic impact indicators; and proposed financing and marketing strategies.

The first section of the ADMP was already submitted in the application for the CADC. Sections 2 and 3 required more inputs. This is why NRMP 2 organized its project activities to assist the indigenous peoples to fulfill these requirements.

maintained the primacy of state law over customary land tenure for half a century, and it was adopted by the independent republic in 1946.

On 15 January 1993, the Department of Environment and Natural Resources (DENR) issued Administrative Order (DAO) No. 2, which specified the rules and regulations for the identification and recognition of ancestral domain and ancestral land claims. This government policy intended to preserve and maintain the integrity of ancestral domains and ensure recognition of indigenous cultural communities' customs and traditions. In addition, it sought to identify and delineate ancestral domain and land claims, certify them and formulate strategies for their effective management. Specific documents were required to support any community's application to the CADC, including ethnographic accounts of the community's local history and sociocultural profile.

The municipality of Sagada was granted its certificate in 1996. In November 1996, the DENR issued Administrative Order No. 96–34 entitled 'Guidelines on the management of certified ancestral domain claims'. It contained the basic steps in the preparation of the ADMP. The plan is meant to ensure that the management of diverse resources and land uses within the domain is in accordance with traditional processes and customary laws.

The ancestral domain of traditional communities

Through our research, we wanted to demonstrate the feasibility of using the traditional village or *ili* as the appropriate entity to exercise rights over an ancestral domain. The *ili* is a pre-existing community where people are accountable to one another through long-term associations of mutual dependence and trust. As an autonomous social and political unit, it is also closely tied to the specific landscape and natural resource features of the area inhabited and used by local residents. *Ili* members follow the rules and practices of their indigenous property systems and manage the natural resources in their ancestral domains and lands (Prill-Brett, 1994, 1995). Such accountability may be expected in long-established communities or *ilis* that continue to apply the

---

Box 12.2 The *ili*

The *ili* is an autonomous sociopolitical unit which controls and makes use of the resources in its surrounding geographical area. A council of elders exercises decision-making authority over village welfare and controls the *ili*'s common property resource. This control follows the rules of the indigenous tenure system. Members of the *ili* establish their rights as citizens through birth, marriage and permanent residence. As citizens, they must abide by certain obligations and can exercise specific rights. Usually, citizens who migrate outside the community are still considered members of the village and have the right to exploit common property resources. However, the longer such villagers remain outside the community, the weaker their rights. These rules are typical of most of the mountain province communities, including those of Fidelisan, Demang, and Ankileng in the Sagada project site.

rules of the indigenous property system over their ancestral domain (see Box 12.2).

Variances are expected because not all indigenous communities maintain customary practices for management of common property.[3] Some traditional communities have a long settlement history that spans several centuries, which allowed for the establishment of a strong attachment to a territory or domain. Newer communities have been established by people's migration within the Cordillera region. These do not have a tradition of common property regimes.

The legislative reforms (DAO No. 2) define possession and occupation as the primary requisites for formal recognition of an ancestral title through the issuing of a CADC. By themselves, these two basic requirements do not distinguish indigenous communities in terms of concepts of territory and territorial control. Instead, they are indicators that relate to the sustainability of common property resource management (as distinct from private cultivated lands, see Ostrom, 1994; Agrawal and Ostrom, 2001). The maintenance of the domain despite outside threats, such as the rule of exclusion, proves the territorial and cultural integrity of the responsible group.

Because the DENR was keen to fast-track and implement the awarding of CADCs, it granted certificates to municipalities rather than the traditional community or *ili*. This procedure simplifies the application process because the politico-administrative system of the country legally recognizes the *barangay*[4] and the municipality[5] but not the *ili*. However, neither the *barangay* nor the municipality is necessarily equivalent to the sociocultural definition of *ili*. Because of this, it can be difficult to identify the unique cultural community that is entitled by custom to exercise rights over an ancestral domain. Therefore, a key element of the research was to assess how the *barangay* might address sociocultural identification in its ancestral domain administration. Conversely, our research also assessed how the traditional *ili* could manage the legalistic and administrative requirements of ancestral domain definition and planning.

Figure 12.1 shows Sagada, a municipality that included several traditional communities or *ili*. Despite this, it was awarded only one certificate. The project identified nine *ilis*, which are delineated on the municipal map. The smaller units within an *ili* are the *barangays*.

The *ili*, not the municipality or the *barangay*, is the customary unit for resource management. However, traditional communities have no formal place in the planning processes that accompany the formulation of the ADMP. DENR drafted a circular[6] that intended to formally recognize pine forest stands in Mountain province that were managed by families, clans and communities under customary laws and practices. This circular encouraged the research team to pursue the proposal to use the *ili* as a management and planning unit for the Sagada management plan.

The development of an ADMP for the *ili* encourages us to reconsider the indigenous resource management practices of traditional Cordillera communities. Indigenous property regimes could be reasserted within the state's governance framework. In Sagada, the development of the management plan

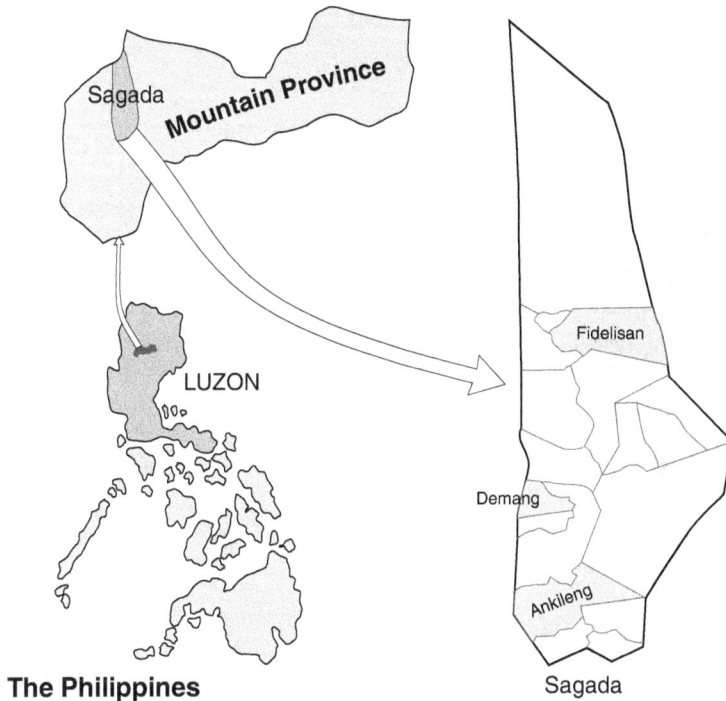

The Philippines   Sagada

Figure 12.1 Map delineating the municipality of Sagada including its *ili*s

would benefit and empower communities by reinforcing their customary laws on resource management.

Formulating the ADMP

The awarding of a CADC to the municipality of Sagada required that an ADMP be formulated as quickly as possible. The management plan included specific activities and land-use guidelines that fell within the customary management rights of the community. The DENR's acceptance of the plan would subsequently precipitate the legal recognition of community rights over resources in the ancestral domain. Government projects would then have to conform to the plan within ancestral domains. The formulation of the plan was considered imperative because of the growing resource competition in the area, which primarily emanated from tourism.

Aided by CBNRM tools and techniques of participatory action research, activities encouraging the formulation of ADMPs were undertaken for three of the nine *ili*s. This strategy tested the *ili*'s methods and processes, which meant that incorporating changes into the remaining *ili*s would be much easier later on. During these exercises, the research team acted as the facilitating entity. The *ili*s were Fidelisan, Demang, and Ankileng, as shown in Figure 12.1. Respectively, they represent the northern, central and southern agro-ecological zones of Sagada.

Social arrangements governing natural resource use

Research commenced with the description and analysis of social arrangements that govern natural resource use. Although Sagada's nine *ilis* may be considered long-established indigenous communities with defined property regimes, we recognized that they are not at all homogenous. Figure 12.2 displays transects for the three villages showing land use, agricultural systems, resources and products, and issues in NRM. We address similarities and differences in resource management practices between Fidelisan, Demang and Ankileng *ilis*, below.

The management plan attempted to respond to common and *ili*-specific concerns in Fidelisan, Demang and Ankileng. The heterogeneity of these communities' agro-ecological and social contexts gave rise to a variety of livelihoods, resulting from the differences in resource endowments and incentives to utilize them. As a consequence, various stakeholders had divergent interests in the management of natural resources.

Figure 12.2 Transects for Fidelisan, Demang and Ankileng *ilis*

Fidelisan transect

Elevation	1,300 m	1,200 m	1,100 m	1,400 m	1,700 m	1,800 m
Land use	Residential, agricultural, pine forests, lake	Residential, agricultural	Mining, river	Pine forests	Watershed/ pine forests	Mossy forests
Agricultural system	Rice, commercial backyard	Backyard, fruit trees	Gold	Pine forests, agroforestry	Pine forest	Oak species, wild fruits, medicinal plants
Resources/ products	Rice, fruits, cash crops	Livestock, root crops	Timber, temperate vegetables, subsistence crops	Timber, fruit trees, fast-growing species	Timber, temperate vegetables, subsistence crops	Medicinal plants, grasses, orchids, water
Issues	Land conversion to agricultural and residential use, depletion of soil nutrients, reduced yield, forest fires, erosion	Depletion of soil nutrients, reduced yield	Threat of river pollution and erosion of agricultural lands above the mines	Land conversion to agricultural and residential use, depletion of soil nutrients, reduced yield	Forest fires, stray animals	Loss of biodiversity, hunting and collection of forest products

Demang transect

Elevation	1,550 m	1,400 m	1,500 m	1,600 m	1,650 m	1,750 m
Land use	Pine forests, agricultural	Residential, agricultural	Residential, agricultural, pine forests	Pine forests	Pine forests	Pine forests
Agricultural system	Pine forests, orchard, root crops, commercial temperate crops	Backyard, fruit trees	Rice, commercial temperate crops, backyard	Pine forests, orchard, root crops, commercial temperate crops	Pine forests, orchard, root crops, commercial temperate crops	Pine forests, orchard, root crops
Resources/products	Timber, temperate vegetables, subsistence crops, water	Livestock, fruits and vegetables, rice	Timber, temperate vegetables, subsistence crops, rice, water	Timber, temperate vegetables, subsistence crops, water	Timber, temperate vegetables, subsistence crops	Medicinal plants, grasses, orchids, water
Issues	Land conversion to agricultural and residential use, depletion of soil nutrients, reduced yield, forest fires, stray animals, erosion	Depletion of soil nutrients, reduced yield	Land conversion from rice to commercial and residential use, depletion of soil nutrients, reduced yield, forest fires, stray animals, erosion	Land conversion to agricultural and residential use, depletion of soil nutrients, reduced yield, forest fires	Land conversion to agricultural and residential use, depletion of soil nutrients, reduced yield, forest fires	Conversion of land, decreasing biodiversity, depleted water resources, forest fires

Ankileng transect

Elevation	1,050 m	1,070 m	1,075 m	1,200 m	1,700 m	1,800 m
Land use	River, agricultural	Agricultural	Residential, institutional, agricultural	Agricultural, pine forests	Pine forests	Mossy forests
Agricultural system	Rotation of rice and vegetables	Swidden, agroforestry	Backyard garden	Swidden, agroforestry	Swidden	Mossy forests
Resources/products	Rice, vegetables, water from the river	Sweet potato, bananas and other swidden crops	Livestock, root crops, bananas and other swidden crops	Sweet potato, wood, sticks, grasses	Sweet potato, wood, sticks, grasses	Medicinal plants, grasses, mountain tea, orchids, water
Issues	Decreasing soil fertility, declining volume of yield, polluted river brought by chemical contamination from farmlands upriver	Decreasing soil fertility, excessive use of pesticides, erosion, land creep and slope failure, conversion of land to agricultural and residential use	Land creep and slope failure, erosion, water shortage for domestic use	Land creep and slope failure, erosion, conversion of land to agricultural and residential use	Erosion, forest fires, illegal cutting of trees, pine forest cover depletion	Conversion of land, decreasing biodiversity, depleted water resources, boundary disputes and unsettled common claims

Of the three villages we studied, the northernmost *ili* of Fidelisan is perhaps the most traditional. This is manifested in the strength and extent of traditional customs that people continue to practise as well as the social structures that remain in place. Community life still revolves around traditional activities like subsistence rice farming, swidden agriculture and gathering wild products from the forest, in addition to their auxiliary activities. Norms are still defined in customary ways as seen in the observance of the traditional rest day, called the *obaya*, which is declared by village elders. As well, traditionally ascribed statuses are still conferred on certain individuals. Therefore, the council of elders is still a force to reckon with in Fidelisan, responsible for much more than the performance of traditional religious rituals (San Luis, 2001).

In comparison, Demang is perhaps the least traditional. It is more open to the influences of modernization brought by tourism and agricultural commercialization. This is due primarily to its geographic location at the centre of Sagada. Nonetheless, Demang exhibits community solidarity amid economic and social change. Despite the fact that many traditional values are gradually being eroded, it remains a close-knit community. Traditional practices such as the rest day, exchange of labour and *begnas* (a community feast where the spirits are called home to bring protection and fertility) continue to be observed. As well, traditional sources of authority are respected.

Ankileng, our third site, lies between Demang and Fidelisan in terms of the extent to which tradition exerts influence over village life. In particular, rice production is guided by a traditional cropping calendar marked by community rituals that signal the different stages in the agricultural cycle. All farmers participate in community activities to repair and clean irrigation canals and people who refuse to participate are fined. Cooperative or exchange labour continues to be practised, specifically for house construction and during peak periods in farming. However, exchange labour is now limited to a more confined group, usually consisting of relatives, neighbours or ward members, and is not as commonly practised as in the past (Cabalfin, 2001).

The households in our three sites have access to individual, corporate and communal property. Rules regarding land access, use and control appear to be similar across all three. Typically, cultivation areas such as rice fields and vegetable gardens, as well as residential lands, are privately owned by individuals or households and passed on through inheritance. Among the indigenous people of Sagada, general primogeniture is practised, that is, parents' ancestral lands are given to the eldest son or daughter, with no gender discrimination. Land acquired during a couple's married life may also be given to lower-ranked siblings. Individual owners dictate how a particular piece of property will be used, by whom and at what price, if any. Rights and claims to these types of lands are clearly known, respected and sanctioned by community members.

Clashes between indigenous tenure systems and state law are most visible when rights to the forests are in question. By national law, Sagada's forests are publicly owned and fall directly under the management and control of the DENR. But day-to-day practice reveals that community members follow customary law in the utilization of the forest and its products. Communal forests can still be found in both Fidelisan and Ankileng villages, but not in Demang. In the former, the *barangay* council enforces the community rules on cutting limits, fines and penalties.

The *saguday* or clan forests are sometimes referred to as corporate forests to clarify that tenure is held collectively by a sub-*ili* group. *Saguday* are found in all three villages. Clan members designate the administrator, who is usually the oldest member. This admistrator supervises and manages the use of resources found in forests. The close-knit character of the community discourages abusive behaviour on the part of the administrator as well as among clan members. In many cases, they rely on customary practices in order to settle disputes. Cooperative behaviour is generally the norm and clan members follow communal rules with minimal monitoring and enforcement costs. *Saguday* owners generally observe cutting limits and prohibit logging for commercial purposes, and assist in fire control and prevention.

The formulation and implementation of the ADMP was an excellent opportunity for local residents to get involved in participatory development planning. The Local Government Code of 1991 (LGC or Republic Act No. 7160) proved crucial: it enabled the community-based planning process to take off. This law mandated the decentralization and devolution of government administrative functions in the Philippines. Local autonomy was encouraged through mechanisms that allowed local government officials and members of the municipality's different communities to join in order to implement their development plans and programmes. These include environment and natural resources in addition to other sectors. The local government is charged with enacting legislation, as well as implementing community development programmes and local resource management schemes (Colongon, 2001). The local government code provides an enabling framework for local government units and their constituent communities to exercise local autonomy. The extent to which any specific local government implements the provisions of this code indicates local groups' ability to exercise collective action.

In Sagada, environmental matters are addressed mostly at the *barangay* level. The *barangays* were established from new settlements growing out of the *ili* as the population grew. At the same time, the original settlement became established also as a distinct *barangay*. Hence, the *ili* could be a single *barangay* or a group of *barangays*. There are standing Barangay environmental committees. The ordinances at the *barangay* level indicate the institutionalization of the role of the *barangay* in addressing problems of the environment. In all three sites, there are reports of violations of community rules on forest use, that is, 'unauthorized logging'. In Barangay Demang, violations of forest rules are brought to the *barangay* officials for resolution. *Barangay* ordinances exacting fines from violators are enforced. In Barangay Ankileng, the Barangay assembly and the Lupon (adjudicators in the Barangay justice system) are involved in settling disputes. Several of the *barangay* officials are in fact the traditional elders of the *ili*. In both the *barangays* of Ankileng and Demang, the *barangay* captain is a traditional elder. These examples show how the state administrative unit (*barangay*) has been integrated in the traditional political processes of the *ili*.

Following are several of the activities the team undertook together with the community members in order to formulate their ADMP.

Participatory mapping to delineate the traditional ili settlement

Maps that can define the boundaries of ancestral domains are crucial to the process of their legal and political recognition that now extends beyond customary law. However, administrative maps usually do not show the spatial clustering of a community's social groups and customary settlements. Instead, they typically identify politico-administrative units such as provinces and municipalities. Maps produced by government agencies are woefully inadequate for reflecting both social and environmental parameters. Therefore, a participatory approach to mapping is a necessary and crucial component of ancestral domain delineation.

We undertook participatory mapping of the ancestral domain of Fidelisan, Demang and Ankileng in November 1998. The process continued through a series of community workshops in 1999 and 2000. Mapping activities were undertaken by *ili* members using extant base maps and technical support from a partner agency (Environmental Science for Social Change). In several community meetings, elders, *saguday* administrators and *barangay* officials along with other villagers confirmed and corrected these maps to identify the *ilis* They also enriched these maps by identifying cultural landmarks; locating resources such as forests, rivers and water sources; providing place names; and delineating traditional boundaries.

There was another very important outcome of the mapping. This was the identification of common areas located within the ancestral domain of *ilis* that were shared with other *ili* communities located in neighbouring municipalities and/or provinces.[7] In other words, these were common pasture grounds, hunting grounds and forests. Delineation would have meant drawing boundary lines between ancestral domains. On several occasions, the mapping exercises led to the recollection of old intervillage territorial conflicts that threatened the cooperative spirit that was slowly forming thanks to the project.

This situation prompted an early recommendation from the team. They thought that attention should be paid to enabling managers of neighbouring ancestral domains to discuss how to utilize the resources located in these common and shared areas. More specifically, the individual ADMPs of each of the neighbouring *ilis* were asked to identify and plan the use of the resources in such areas that are shared between *ilis*. In this way, the mapping exercise could be used as a tool not only for exclusion, but also for generating cooperation and reducing conflicts over resource use. The suggestion was passed on to the regional office of the newly formed National Commission on Indigenous Peoples (NCIP). With the passage of the Indigenous Peoples Rights Act (IPRA) in 1997,

NCIP took over from the DENR the mandate to oversee the implementation of government programmes to recognize ancestral domains and ancestral lands.

The *ili* maps were also important inputs in the preparation of the ADMP because they identified the traditional village settlement. In addition, they helped delineate areas of resource degradation and stakeholders' interests in resources.

Community-based land-use study

What resources do Sagada residents exploit? How and by whom are these resources utilized? To answer these questions, a community-based land-use study was conducted in the three project sites, led by a soil scientist and an economist. The goal was to assess the biophysical and sociocultural conditions affecting resource management practices in selected ecosystems in Sagada. Community-based land-use maps were generated through this exercise (see Figure 12.3).

The team used participatory procedures for biophysical and socio-economic assessments. An assessment of resources in the village was completed through a series of on-site visits, mapping exercises using geographic information system, soil and vegetative sampling, key informant interviews, community workshops and focus-group discussions. Since gender equality is largely upheld in these communities in matters of consultation and decision-making, participatory mapping and its related activities successfully incorporated women's views.

The activities of the research team served two functions. First, they legitimized customary rules and practices and enhanced the value of existing indigenous ecological knowledge by incorporating these into the community's plans, which were acknowledged by state agencies. Second, they informed community members about government programmes and policies which could affect them. The communities started to appreciate that new technologies could prove beneficial for use on agricultural land and forests, and for irrigation.

This participatory land-use study demonstrated concretely what a CBNRM approach could be. A close collaboration existed between the team's social and natural scientists during the study's design and implementation phases. Expert knowledge, in dialogue with indigenous and local knowledge, brought a better understanding of farming issues, problems and solutions for the community members.

Participatory mapping, resource assessment and land-use identification provided the inputs into the ADMP being prepared for the *ili* (Figure 12.4). These activities afforded a rare opportunity for dialogue. Discussions involved issues of customary and state law, scientific and local indigenous knowledge, as well as participatory and top-down approaches in the management of common resources. These may have contributed to the opening up of a line of communication between the people of Sagada and the DENR. Since the DENR had been the enforcer of the state's hardline stance against forest occupants and their use of forest resources, people approached DENR initiatives with suspicion and scepticism. This hindered dialogue and cooperation between the DENR and members of the local community.

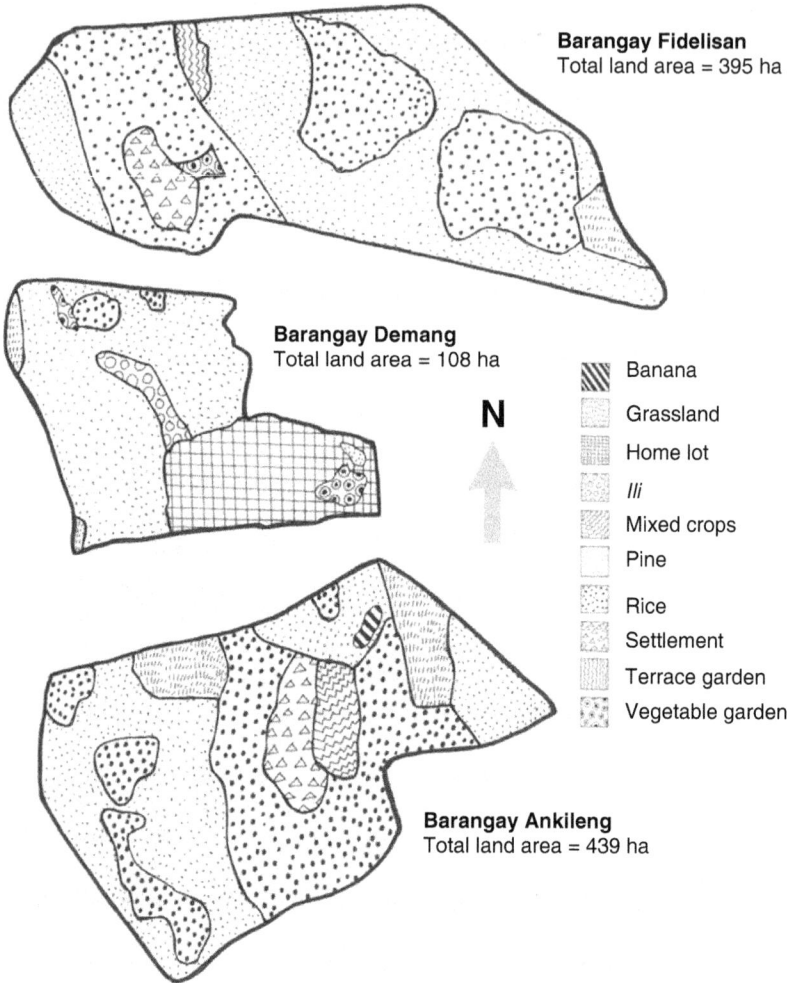

Figure 12.3 Community-based land-use maps

Community-based biodiversity assessment and identification of natural resources

Conducting a biodiversity assessment was among the first major activities completed in partnership with the communities. Its objective was to generate baseline data to identify the resources people used and how they managed them. Later on, results would allow us to consider options that could build on traditional practices. Community members were trained in scientific biodiversity assessment methods.

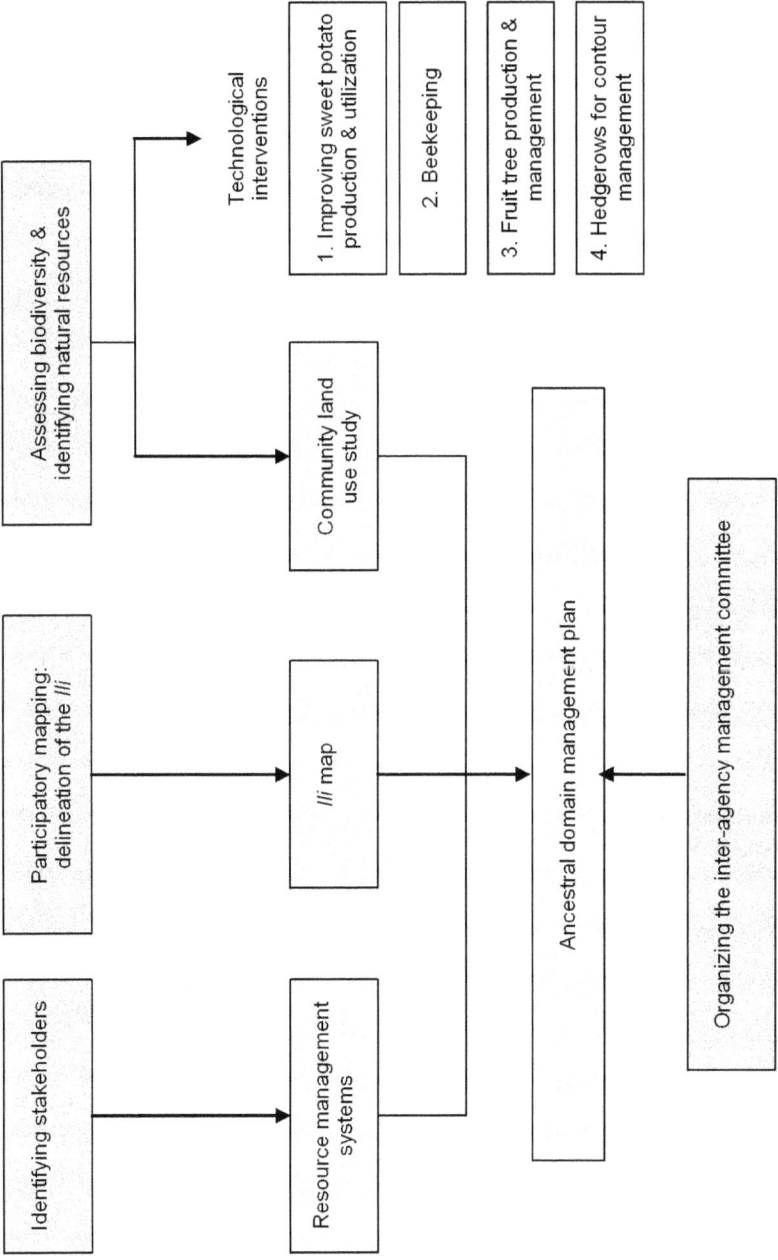

Figure 12.4 Project activities in formulating the ADMP

Guided by the study's leaders, research sites were selected and the selected community researchers helped us to understand their traditional use and management systems. Assessments included forests, *uma* (swidden plots) and rice fields, and involved *barangay* councils, elders, women, hunters and youth. It was not surprising that women were the most knowledgeable about the *uma* because swidden management is largely their responsibility. They also showed the most interest in new technologies that could benefit *uma* crops such as sweet potato. For example, women farmers proposed and collaborated actively with the study on rejuvenating traditional sweet potato varieties (described in more detail below).

Organizing the Inter-agency Committee for Natural Resource Management (1997–2000)

Besides the DENR, several government and non-government groups with activities or projects had designed projects for the sustainable management of natural resources by the local community. In the course of these agencies' work, duplication or overlapping activities and projects occurred. This situation is very frustrating to communities that are often visited by outsiders making various requests. Lack of coordination between such groups can sow confusion in the community because projects and researchers have different messages. These projects often place unwelcome demands on the same communities, to the detriment of well-intentioned agencies and their staff.

In July 1997, the research team hosted a consultation and dialogue for government and nongovernment agencies with projects in Sagada to address exactly this issue. As a result, an Inter-agency Committee for Natural Resource Management for the municipality of Sagada was created to share information and coordinate the actions of government and nongovernment agencies, as well as research institutions. The mayor of Sagada strongly supported this committee.

The committee agreed on:
- giving assistance to the institutional development of the municipality of Sagada to strengthen its ability to respond to issues and opportunities;
- approving joint implementation of training and other project activities; and
- making an inventory of resources and exchanging information and materials among agencies.

Of utmost importance was the agreement by all committee members to assist the municipality in creating its ADMP. The committee members included representatives of the DENR, Department of Agrarian Reform (DAR), National Irrigation Administration (NIA), Cordillera Highland Agricultural Resources Management Programme (CHARMP), as well as CONCORED (Consortium of Cordillera Organizations for Resource Equitability and Development), the NGO responsible for the CHARMP researchers, this project team and the municipality of Sagada.

After this initial agreement and dialogue, regular interagency committee meetings were held in Baguio City and in Sagada. The Baguio meetings were an occasion for agency representatives to share information on their current activities as well as report on the status of ongoing programmes in Sagada. In Sagada, consultations were held with the local legislative council and municipal representatives of different national agencies like the Department of Agriculture, DENR and DAR, both formally and informally. The most important outcome was a joint approach to the work.

The establishment of the inter-agency committee has contributed to the coordinated implementation of various projects by different agencies in the municipality. Duplication and overlap were significantly reduced and the waste of resources avoided. Moreover, the effort taken to complement and coordinate has improved working relations among the different government agencies as well as with the communities.

Other elements of the management plan

The role of the DENR and the municipality in the co-management of the ancestral domain within the *ili* structures still has to be clarified. Through dialogue, compromise, and negotiation among the stakeholders, a co-management strategy still needs to be produced. It ought to enable local resource users to obtain alternative livelihood activities that are consistent with sustainable resource use. In the case of the three *ili* where we worked, we think that good progress was made.

In addition, the project identified some outstanding issues. For example, the legal personality of the holders of the CADC remained to be clarified at the time of the research. The certificate was issued to the village elders or heads on behalf of a traditional community or *ili*. However, what authority do they have to enter into contracts regarding the use of resources in their ancestral domain? Can the certificate-holder accept or deny a proposal by a logging company to cut lumber from Sagada forests? Alternatively, is the DENR still the final arbiter and authority on this matter?

Fortunately, that issue has since been clarified by the procedures specified by the IPRA. This law made the NCIP the agency responsible for overseeing the titling procedures of ancestral domains and lands that were previously assigned to the DENR. Most importantly, a process for 'free and prior informed consent' is now required before any project can be implemented in an area covered by a CADC. The consent process requires that community members, through their village elders, come to an agreement to allow any proposal to utilize a resource found in their domain.

Land-use transitions

The village economy consists of livelihood systems that use household resources in three categories: on farm, off-farm and non-farm. To the household, the outputs of production provide direct subsistence and cash revenue from sales. Other engagements of resources yield benefits either in cash or kind. Typically, the extensions of the farming households are the members of the family who are absent from the household and the village. They include students enrolled in schools, workers employed outside Sagada and those who have moved permanently out of the municipality. Being extensions, they maintain their rightful claims over the village resources. Specifically, their claims come in the form of returns of the farmland, communally owned forests, grazing and mineral land, and water rights. In return, the farming household expects remittances to supplement its cash and assets.

The CBNRM framework is particularly applicable for research on indigenous people's land rights because of the emphasis it gives to the community as the locus of action, participation and decision-making. Defining community is always an issue. Collective action is defined as 'action taken by a group (either directly or on its behalf through an organization) in pursuit of members' perceived shared interests' (Meinzen-Dick et al., 2002).

However, what ensures that a group will share interests? What enables or constrains them to act collectively? After all, local communities are far from being homogenous. Groups or factions within a community face different stresses in their livelihoods, land-use systems and sociopolitical relations. They have competing interests over resources. Therefore, it is not enough that the community addresses its problems with external groups such as the state. It needs to resolve disputes internally over specific resources. However, what happens when traditional mechanisms of conflict resolution are slowly being eroded by a multitude of changes? Let us briefly recount some of these changes.

During the 1980s, US military bases in the Philippines created a high demand for locally produced salad tomatoes. In response, agricultural production shifted on Sagada farms. Farmers who originally planted only subsistence rice and practised swidden agriculture became engaged in commodity production for an external market. Market crops are now an important part of the local production system.

Tourism is a new and growing enterprise, and information technology is only the latest way in which the outside world has entered Sagada. On a popular website for international tourist travel, 13 entries gush about the charms of Sagada. In some seasons, all available local accommodation is fully booked.

But tourism is not the only application of the internet that has changed life in Sagada. A website designed for emigrants from the Cordillera allows expatriate Sagada residents throughout the world to log on and get news or send messages home. They can use the technology to maintain an active personal claim to common property and to its output. They do not lose their traditional rights just because they have moved away.

One of the most troublesome issues is lumber harvested from clan-owned forests and transported out of Sagada. The lumber that was traditionally a free but non-market good, used only for local consumption, has become an economic commodity with a market value. Such developments put a pressure on land and traditional rights and management agreements.

Communally-held forests are now subject to privatization and, thus, to a different set of tenure rules as a response to the rise of lumber prices. *Ili* forests have all but disappeared in the villages of Ankileng and Demang largely in response to population growth, which has led to their transformation into clan and family agricultural lands. Ankileng and Demang are closer than Fidelisan to roads that lead to urban centres.

Clan forests are also suffering from privatization pressures. Payments for tax declaration are made and filed in the name of the administrator of the clan forest. National law can interpret the resulting document as proof of the administrator's private ownership. However, from the point of view of customary procedure, the whole clan as a collective entity exercises ownership rights over the forests.

The potential loss of agricultural land is a widespread concern in Sagada. This anxiety appears to arise from two factors. First, the possibility of converting agricultural land to another use, such as residential construction or tourist accommodation, worries people. Second, concern is expressed over the choice between the subsistence rice crop with its perceived reliability to meet basic food requirements, and cash crops that are subject to the vagaries of the market but which offer much higher returns.

We noted above that emigration from Sagada did not sever an individual's claim to local resources: in fact, it actually augmented household resources because of remittance income. Therefore, the concept of household stretches geographically ever farther from the traditional home and village. As the land-use transitions in Sagada proceed in response to urban demand and market forces, the system of tenure shifts increasingly from open access and collective and common property tenure towards private tenure. These land-use transitions lead to new conflicts among land users, and it is possible that remote rights holders who have different interests from local residents could contribute to these. However, the sale of land and other property is still rare, particularly when it involves non-relatives and outsiders (Tapang, 2001). In order to prevent such land sales in future, customary law will have to be more strictly enforced.

The ADMP is a mechanism through which community members can control how new developments in agriculture and the economy will transform customary practices. As new crops and livelihood are adopted, rules governing their place in customary management practices can be negotiated in the consultative and consensual atmosphere of customary management.

Municipal and *barangay* officials may be thought of as formally representing state-created political structures. However, because of their ethnic affiliation with the communities in Sagada, local officials have always been advocates of the customary resource rights of their people in ancestral domain areas against the state's claim.

Adapting farming systems

One of the research objectives was to address some of these emerging issues in natural resources by developing and adapting farming systems and production methods that increase the sustainability of natural resource management. The following community-based interventions were undertaken (Follosco and Tacloy, 2001):

- improving the production and utilization of sweet potato, one of the most important crops in the region;
- establishing apiculture as a new activity;
- promoting fruit tree production as part of the home garden system; and
- testing new soil conservation measures.

These interventions were identified largely as a response to problems expressed by farmers. The sweet potato work involved the selection and introduction of new varieties and the rejuvenation of traditional varieties to address decreasing volume and diminishing quality of harvests. The project team arranged for a university-based sweet potato expert who is a widely respected fieldworker to undertake collaborative research with the women farmers (Follosco and Tacloy, 2001). The farmers were satisfied with the results of the experiment. However, researchers were frustrated with the limited data collected because of over-reliance on farmer participants for formal research protocols and monitoring (Ganga, 2001).

Another activity was the introduction of apiculture, an innovation suggested by the research team upon observation of the flora and fauna in the area. Thirty participants, mostly women, attended a short orientation course on beekeeping. Eventually, six of the participants established and managed bee colonies while undergoing a yearlong training programme. They also formed a producers' cooperative that was registered in 2002. One of the beekeepers has since set up demonstration colonies on the request of the Mountain province agricultural extension office. While this livelihood option was viable, it required specific skills and a strong interest to learn them, so it was adopted by only a few farmers.

There were two other less-successful interventions. One was a fruit-tree project. It failed because it required more motivation, skills and specialized inputs than people wanted to invest to manage the nursery and nurture seedlings in the field. Without the proper assignment of rights and responsibilities, the collective effort needed for maintenance of the tree nursery and newly-propagated seedlings dispersed into individual action.

The project also attempted to establish contour hedgerows for soil management. Seeds of various shrubs and trees were planted but some did not germinate, which resulted in gaps. Moreover, farmers did not prune the roots and shoots of the hedgerows, nor clear the site of weeds as part of the tasks of managing the plot. We learned that the labour requirements for hedgerows may be unacceptable to farmers even when they could prevent or reduce soil erosion, especially when compared with less labour-intensive traditional techniques. A tenure conflict in the community over the hedgerow test plot also demonstrated that it is crucial to resolve overlapping resource claims before investing in improved productivity.

In summary, the participatory technology development activities seemed to be successful if they addressed the community's immediate, high-priority concerns. Although requests came from the community, and meetings were held to discuss benefits and costs (for instance, inputs from the cooperators), it was impossible to ensure a continued collective engagement among participants. However, activities that met individual household needs were easily adopted and managed locally.

Despite such seemingly individual interests, a high level of community solidarity was also evident in the lending of land as test plots and in the cooperation of participants to address common issues. However, community solidarity is not sufficient for collective action to succeed. Organizational structures must be in place and responsibilities clearly defined so that benefits can be matched to specific activities. The greatest success occurred with technologies that offered additional income within the labour constraints of the household, using indigenous knowledge and expertise as much as possible, and where external experts responded directly to local feedback and initiative.

Impact and consequences: when communities take over

The recognition of native title received a boost with the passage of the IPRA, Republic Act No. 8371, which took effect on 22 November 1997, although its implementation was delayed by legal challenges.

The research results in Sagada became an important resource for implementing the IPRA in the Cordillera. The lessons and experiences documented in the research reports, *Tangguyob* (the project's newsletter) and the expertise of members of the research team from the centre were applied by the regional office of the NCIP. Not only did the office obtain copies of all research outputs, they selected the management plans for the villages of Fidelisan, Demang and Ankileng as prototypes for all communities intending to accomplish their own ADMP. Through a letter of agreement in September 2002, the CSC agreed to assist NCIP with their regional research and capability-building activities.

The formal management plan is called the Ancestral Domain Sustainable Development and Protection Plan (ADSDPP) under the IPRA of 1997. The processes that lead to the grant of the ancestral domain title under IPRA are similar to those previously specified by the DENR for the grant of the CADC. Hence, with the passage of the IPRA, all communities previously awarded with certificates can work towards converting their certificates into titles.

When Sagada was tasked to transform its plan into an ADSDPP under the provisions of the new legislation, community members formed a technical working group for this purpose with the help of the provincial officials of the Commission on Indigenous Peoples. The research team was subsequently invited to serve as advisers, ensuring that the participatory approaches of CBNRM could become institutionalized. The Sagada *ilis* are responsible for designing the new resource management plans. Although the formal ADSDPP will be approved for the entire municipality of Sagada, the plan will consist of sub-plans defined by each of the 11 *ilis*. At the time of writing (late 2004) the Sagada ADSDPP had not yet been approved.

Many of the research teams' and the community members' insights and lessons from this research were utilized by other Cordillera communities in their pursuit of legal recognition for their own ancestral domains. For example, two other municipalities in Mountain province have followed the *ili*-level planning exercises for their ancestral domain management plans. In addition, the ADSDPP planning exercises in Abra, a neighbouring province, has formally adopted the Sagada's ADMP model as a prototype. The participatory processes of CBNRM have been appreciated because they fit the consultative and consensual character of customary community decision-making. By using the traditional village elder structure, this project strengthened customary resource management practices. The plans now formally recognize customary decision-making mechanisms, which were previously ignored by government agencies.

Finally, the project demonstrated how local governments (the municipality and the *barangays*) can become facilitators and advocates of the customary rights of their people. When such partnerships are formed within communities, enduring examples are created that demonstrate how decentralization reforms were originally intended to work.

Conclusion

In conclusion, we can say CBNRM will work in practice when it builds the capacity of the community to decide for itself. In our case, the processes of participatory research empowered communities and built respect for local traditions and social structures, all of which encouraged and sustained participation. The existence of other groups working with and in the community can be helpful, but mutual awareness and coordination must be ensured to avoid project fatigue. The uniqueness (in social, political, economic and cultural aspects) of every community and its people is a third key element of a successful project. A CBNRM project or programme must be customized and modified from its prototypical form in order to suit local conditions.

The following section summarizes insights which the CSC shares with government agencies, other development and research projects and NGOs working on indigenous people's land rights.

Solid partnerships

Our research built upon a good working relationship with the municipality that had been nurtured through earlier CSC research projects. From its inception, our research project sought local support from both municipal and *barangay* governments, formal and indigenous social and political groups, and from both government and nongovernment organizations. The chief executive and members of the municipal council were informed of the objectives of the programme and were updated about activities undertaken in project sites. Both *barangay* officials and traditional elders provided us with assistance in various ways, from the identification of participants and key informants, to hosting meetings for planning or training.

Ownership of outputs

Because the project instituted a mechanism for ensuring that each activity was undertaken with community counterparts, community members readily accepted the outcomes of the research as their own, both successes and failures. This included the maps, community-based land-use studies for the three villages and the formal management plans.

Participatory technology development

Lessons come from both positive and negative outcomes. The improved production and utilization of sweet potato and beekeeping were successful projects. We learned that the probability of success appears to be higher if a project addresses immediate and priority concerns within the framework of household labour constraints. A significant factor contributing to the adoption of interventions was their indigenous nature, consciously minimizing external inputs by using local materials. Promising-sounding technologies alone are not sufficient to motivate their adoption.

Solidarity and local collective action

The community themselves generated proposals for activities and community meetings were held to discuss management aspects. However, this did and does not guarantee sustained interest or commitment. Community solidarity does not seem to be a sufficient condition for local collective action to succeed. It takes time for groups to achieve agreement on responsibilities. More importantly, benefits must match these responsibilities. Even customary law and traditional structures need to deal with the incentives and constraints of new conditions. We particularly learned not to make assumptions about customary and community solidarity. Deep rifts and suspicions remain and persist in any community. The challenge which this project met was how to work with these divisions in order to reach collective decisions and how to establish processes that enable communities to develop practical solutions.

Acknowledgements

The authors were members of the project Ancestral Domain and Natural Resource Management in Sagada, Mountain province, northern Philippines. This project was carried out under the auspices of the Cordillera Studies Centre (CSC), University of the Philippines Baguio, and it was funded by the IDRC, Canada. The authors gratefully acknowledge the cooperation of the following communities, organizations and people, in the successful implementation of this project between 1997 and 2002. We thank the communities of Fidelisan, Demang and Ankileng; the municipal government of Sagada, Mountain province, and particularly Mayor Thomas Killip; the Barangay councils of Aguid, Pide, Baangan, Fidelisan, Poblacion, Demang, Dagdag, Ankileng and Suyo; the Division of Natural Sciences (now the College of Science) and Division of Social Sciences (now the College of Social Sciences) of UP College Baguio (now the University of the Philippines Baguio); the College of Forestry and Department of Soil Science of Benguet State University; Northern Philippines Root Crops Research and Training Centre; Central Luzon State University; Environmental Science for Social Change; CONCORED, the NGO partner of the CHARMP for Sagada; and the Bureau of Plant Industry of Baguio City.

CHAPTER 13

Shaping the key to fit the lock: participatory action research and community forestry in the Philippines

Peter O'Hara

Abstract

This chapter highlights key lessons from a participatory action research (PAR) approach to community forestry in the Philippines. The main reason why community forestry initiatives in the Philippines are unsustainable is the lack of incentives for community members to invest in forest management. Interdependent issues such as corruption, policy instability and the lack of rights, as well as the absence of platforms for meaningful community participation and the blueprint nature of development projects, are all fundamental barriers that hinder such community investment. Despite this lack of incentives, donors, governments and NGOs remain focused on community capacity-building and organizing. This chapter questions the assumptions underlying such approaches. It emphasizes that the lack of opportunity for meaningful participation by community members is the most pressing barrier to community forestry. It argues that to tackle this barrier, it would be more effective to address the skills and practices of professionals in the forest sector, rather than those of community members. The chapter argues that today professionals should no longer be seen only as part of the solution in community forestry, but should be identified as a significant part of the problem.

In response to these insights, two new experimental initiatives were developed by the research team. They aimed to transform the role of professionals in the forest sector, and thus 'shape the key to better fit the lock'. These initiatives introduced new policy communications and advocacy tools to provide a fair platform for communities to address policy issues, and new training to provide skills for professionals to apply the principles of PAR to their work.

The learning context

This chapter explains how a research project which set out to support community forestry in three village sites on Luzon, the main northern island of the Philippines, led instead to a very different learning experience. The research team, the community members and various professional forestry officials were all engaged in learning. The research project became more like a journey of exploration and discovery than a predictable, carefully planned field study. Along the way, most of the actors found their basic assumptions about community forestry challenged and tested in unexpected ways. This learning journey is described below, by first explaining the methodological concerns which guided project researchers, and then describing early lessons and how these led to completely different interventions from those originally anticipated. The chapter provides a description of these interventions and how the participants responded to them, and draws some conclusions about the kinds of learning needed in community forestry in the Philippines.

The research project team is based at the International Institute for Rural Reconstruction (IIRR) in the Philippines. In responding to concerns raised about the difficulty of implementing community forest management, the research team proposed to undertake a participatory research project to explore community forestry implementation options with local forest user communities in the field. The team identified three different village sites, which varied in many respects: engaged or not in the national Community-Based Forest Management (CBFM) programme; assisted or not by local NGOs; having formal forest use rights or none. The identities of the villages will not be revealed in this chapter as part of an agreement with the community members who took part. The fieldwork was conducted over a two-year period.

A comprehensive historical analysis of the forest sector was undertaken early on in the learning journey as part of the conceptualization of community forestry issues in the Philippines It provides some insights into the origins of contemporary challenges to community forestry in the Philippines and also helps place the work in context.

Methodological concerns and early lessons

The fundamental methodological premise of this work was the value of experiential and participatory learning in addressing contested NRM issues at the community level. The PAR spiral in Figure 13.1 represents the approach of the research team along a shared learning journey that has so far lasted three years.

Assumptions were revisited after each cycle of experimentation and reflection, and were often changed and adapted. This process took the team in new directions involving varying actors at different times. Having some structure in such an organic process was important: this spiral provided clear process steps and milestones to help guide the team.

Box 13.1 Historical overview of community forestry in the Philippines

Pre-Spanish invasion The Philippines was composed politically of indigenous fiefdoms with their own traditions, cultures and languages. Custom-based, complex forest management systems were widespread, and in remote areas, remnants of these systems still survive today.

1521 Arrival of the Spaniard Ferdinand Magellan, who claimed the entire archipelago of the Philippines for the Spanish monarchy. This Regalian doctrine became the foundation of the colonial and then the modern land-tenure system. Land registration was only possible for individuals and legal corporations, customary and collective tenure rights were illegal, and land was appropriated by the Spanish or Spanish-Filipino elites.

1863 The first forestry bureau was established by Spanish administrators.

1894 The Maura Act required villagers and individual landowners to register their land holdings. Those who did not officially became squatters. The registration system was inappropriate for most rural dwellers: therefore, almost two-thirds of the Philippines territory remained unregistered. Unregistered lands legally belonged to the Spanish-governed state, not to those inhabitants who held customary rights.

1898 Beginning of American rule. The land classification system instituted by the Spanish was preserved by the American governors, including the recognition of land ownership based on the Maura Act. Forest cover was an estimated 70 per cent in 1900.

1946 Independence from the United States. The Philippine government adopted forestry policies in line with the colonial administrators. Nearly 60 per cent of the Philippines land area was state forest (much of it being lands unregistered under the Maura Act), and the government was deemed as the sole authority to allocate forestland uses and resource use rights.

1949–1960s A period of massive timber exploitation commenced, initiated by tropical hardwood companies who received concessions from the government. In 1949, forest products accounted for 1.5 per cent of the total value of Philippine exports, growing to 11 per cent by 1955, and reaching 33 per cent in the late 1960s. Deforestation proceeded at a rate of 172,000 ha per year at the end of this period.

1970s With dwindling forests, growing rural insurgency, and national and international concern about deforestation rates, people-oriented forestry programmes were undertaken. Their goal was reforestation. Various motives were involved in this initiative, including the improvement of public relations on the part of the government, which tried to appease the frustrations of the rural poor. The programmes were the Forest Occupancy Management, Communal Tree Farming and the Family Approach to Reforestation, which was adopted from the Burmese *taungya* system. In total, a mere 33,000 ha were reforested through these programmes.

1991 Massive floods on the island of Leyte killed nearly 5,000 people and deforestation of local watersheds was deemed to be the catalyst. The uproar over the disaster by NGOs and by the predominantly urban middle class put pressure on the government for quick and tangible action. A logging ban was introduced throughout the country, although a number of concessions were allowed to continue to term.

1995 All previous community forestry initiatives were brought under one umbrella, the Community-based Forest Management Programme (CBFMP). This programme focused on organizing communities and providing alternative livelihood strategies so that pressure would be taken off the natural forest. The Department of the Environment and Natural Resources (DENR) considered that a handful of community forests were sufficiently stocked, so the department granted utilization rights for wood products. However, utilization was often hindered through costly and complex procedural requirements set by the DENR.

1999 Forest cover 18.3 per cent.

2002–4 A review of the CBFMP is driven by reformers in the DENR. Revised CBFM guidelines were developed based on consultations by the DENR with numerous NGOs, academics and community members (including this project). Proposed revisions make the procedural requirements more appropriate for communities in terms of both complexity and cost. Revised guidelines were approved in late 2004.

2003–4 In response to widespread media coverage of the abuse of a single CBFM agreement that resulted in exploitation beyond the allowable cut, the newly assigned head of the DENR suspended the rights of all CBFM communities to utilize timber from their forests for commercial purposes.

Sources: Lindayati (2000), Kummer (1992), as well as personal communications with various forestry actors in the Philippines.

When it came to the 'P' in PAR, care was taken to define what kind of participation the team would employ. 'Participation' is a widely used term in development work and has many interpretations. Therefore, unless the degree of participation is qualified, its usefulness in defining an approach is questionable. The degree of participation and whose agenda is given the most weight can determine the entire direction and relevance of the action-learning journey. 'Whose reality counts?' This is a phrase that was coined by Robert Chambers (1997). It is a very appropriate question for any team of professionals to consider before embarking on a PAR learning journey. Figure 13.2 illustrates how the relationships between professionals and community members differ depending on the approach to participation in a research process. The team attempted to place its role within the lower section of this figure.

Great care and time were taken in building an appropriate relationship with community members as well as determining the most appropriate methodologies to guide the team away from a path of least resistance. We cannot overemphasize the importance of the time we spent in the village, including overnight stays and informal socializing with the villagers. At the outset of our fieldwork, no matter which tool we used, the kind of information villagers shared with us represented obvious fishing, on their part, for our material inputs. However, with time and continued interaction, these early shopping lists gave way to a

Appreciate multiple perspectives

Review/revise assumptions; re-conceptualize/re-plan

Experiment

Review/revise assumptions; re-conceptualize/re-plan

Reflect, critically analyse and document lessons, embrace failures

Experiment

Review/revise assumptions; re-conceptualize/re-plan

Reflect, critically analyse and document lessons, embrace failures

Experiment

State assumptions. Review all relevant existing information. Conceptualize/plan generally

Reflect, critically analyse and document lessons, embrace failures

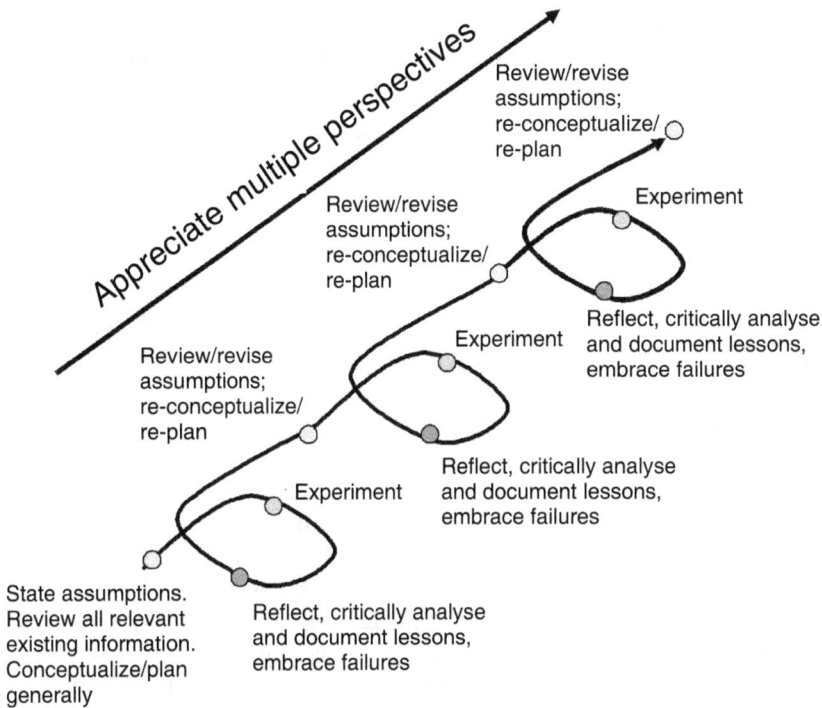

Figure 13.1 A PAR spiral, an iterative, experiential learning guide
Source: Adapted from King, 2000; Kolb, 1984.

more nuanced perspective, and when it became clear we were not providing them with the material inputs they requested, those individuals who had previously been most eager to engage with the research team lost interest.

A wide range of communications and analysis tools was used. Effort was made to match the purpose and context of tool use with the problem being analysed. Venn diagrams; ranking exercises; time lines; and strength, weakness, opportunity and threat (SWOT) analyses were all used on different occasions as well as focus-group discussions and chats with individuals. The team specifically attempted to procure feedback from as many individuals and groups as possible in the village, and from every geographical section of the community. In meetings, meta cards were used to capture written inputs and avoid the domination of oral discussions by the most articulate people (more than 90 per cent of villagers are literate). Confidential discussions with individuals were also conducted. Some of the quietest people seemed to open up and become at ease during long walks in the forest. Triangulation of information was carried out through formal and informal methods. All findings were reproduced and shared in every hamlet of the village, and feedback, adaptations or strong

	Role of development professional	Assumption by development professional	Role of community member
Participation	Sets agenda	Communities are the cause of their problems.	Participates
	Participates	Communities know the cause of their problems.	Sets agenda

Figure 13.2 Shades of participation

objections were solicited in confidence. Revised findings were then shared in group settings for discussion and verification.

Throughout the research process in the village, especially in the meetings where community members developed such procedures as problem analysis, there was often much debate, and at times discussions were heated. However, confrontation often produced the most insightful findings. What typically resulted (both in meetings and in individual feedback) was not what could be called consensus. Although sometimes there was compromise, sometimes it was a case of agreeing to disagree while the majority had their way. One such debate occurred when some villagers began to trust the research team enough to get beyond the standard handout requests and share more complex perspectives on forest management problems, while others remained wedded to problems that could be solved by convenient material inputs.

The use of questionnaires (even in semi-structured interviews) was dropped early in the research process, because this method seemed to stimulate biases. Although an easy method for the team, this tool was inappropriate in the Philippines' cultural context, where outsiders are unable to easily gain accurate feedback on sensitive issues. This situation became clear during triangulation with more open methods. When they responded to formalistic questions, respondents tended to downplay conflicts and concerns about the behaviour of other people. Reframing sensitive information using PRA methods where comments were written by the community members seemed a far more effective way to free up individual expression.

Breaking down false expectations regarding the purpose of the study became very important especially in the Philippines where externally funded, community-based development projects are common. Careful use of language is extremely important: many development words are value- and agenda-laden for community members, and can often take a learning process in the wrong direction. Considerations of semantics can affect the development of a suitable relationship. For example, the word 'study' rather than 'project' was used to describe the research team's work. Even more important to the interaction was using the words 'views' and 'opinions' rather than 'needs'. The word 'need' implies inherent assumptions about the roles of community members and researchers, assumptions with which the researchers were uncomfortable. Such terms play into a scenario where the professional is cast in the role of providing 'solutions' to community 'needs'. Using a needs-based terminology, we believe, would have directed the entire learning and action journey quite differently. The result could have been the development of alternative livelihood projects at the study sites. These might have provided temporary albeit tangible and photogenic benefits for a few hundred community members at most, and would not have led to the two initiatives described below.

During these initial months, the research team's initial plans were challenged by the perspectives of community members. Even when they were part of the CBFMP, the villagers were reluctant to become involved in forest management due to the policy environment. This contradicted one of the research team's initial assumptions: that the programme and policy environment was positive, but that examples of good practice of CBFM at community level were needed. As a result, the research plan shifted. Instead of building the forest management capacity of communities and developing tree nurseries, the focus became how to learn from communities while focusing on exploring and challenging those aspects of the policy environment that were problematic.

To assess whether the community's issues with policy were anomalies, the team spent a few days in villages in different parts of the Philippines. The team applied their methodological lessons from earlier work, and community members from the core study sites came along as 'assistants'. This strategy appeared to work reasonably well although care had to be taken that these community assistants would not influence what informants in other villages said. Perspectives we got were generally consistent with those in the core study sites but there was a spectrum of views between and within communities. For example, there were differences in perspectives about relationships with staff in the DENR. These differences seemed to be related to the different roles in which DENR staff had engaged community members. Some community members had encountered very helpful DENR staff, often involved in service delivery. Others had encountered staff who had a more regulatory or bureaucratic role.

The overall findings were also generally consistent with an independent study (Borlagdan et al., 2001) which was based on 27 communities who were all taking part in the CBFMP. This report concluded that the 'existing operational policies urgently need refinement, simplification, deregulation, and standardization. Higher transaction costs will mean lesser benefits to the communities.' It noted: 'Sustainable forest management practices will be sustained if and only if communities actually benefit from these resources ... (there should be a focus on) improvement of enabling policies, implementation of incentive systems, and assistance (to communities) in carrying out advocacy and collective action.'

Our research in the three village sites validated Borlagdan et al.'s (2001) findings in general, considering our interpretations were based on a smaller sample of communities. In the next section, we offer selected quotes from community members, because their personal comments illustrate the key issues in their own words, while preserving their anonymity. The quotes are representative of hundreds that we captured in interviews and meetings with villagers from different socio-economic groups and both genders. Care was taken to get broad representation from within communities, so that even so-called illegal loggers were involved.

Why communities do not invest in forest management

'We don't have rights over the forest, so why should we protect it?'

'When there is much restrictions in forest policy there is much corruption.'

'Cost of the permits/taxes is more than the value of the trees, it is best just to cut and bribe.'

'The reason there are rampant illegal activities is because we are forced into illegal activities because the forest policy is just so complicated.'

Lack of recognized resource tenure was the most common explanatory factor for communities' unwillingness to invest in forest management. From the handful of communities nationwide which had been granted limited rights to forest use (one of which was a research site), a common complaint was that fees for the required official papers were excessive. Documentation requirements were over-demanding. For example, community members argued that the DENR's obligatory requirements of environmental impact assessments and technical forest inventories were of such elevated scientific standards that they could only be undertaken by highly experienced professional foresters. Therefore, communities found them unaffordable unless external assistance was offered.

Although generally classified as illegal, the customary utilization of forests in the Philippines continues, as suggested by the statistical evidence (Kummer, 1992; FAO, 2001). The research team's observations echoed this; the ongoing cutting and transportation of lumber were also discussed by community members. At present, there is no legal option to allow the majority of community members to continue their customary utilization. Moreover, the few individuals who possess the legal right to harvest find that following an illegal route is less costly and more convenient than a legal one. This situation suits some individual officials. Villagers are critical of this situation, as these comments indicate.

'The government likes the log ban as there is much corruption then.'

'Forest guards do not guard the forest, they guard the road (so they can collect bribes to allow "illegal" wood products to be transported).'

'Restrictive policy only benefits government officials, forest guards and policemen on an unofficial, individual basis.'

'The law bans cutting hardwoods (but this has resulted in) lots of hardwoods being transported on the road.'

Community members currently involved in the (officially illegal) forest products trade were keen to see their commercial activities legalized, even if it meant paying reasonable taxes and fees. There is effectively a log ban throughout most of the country, which prevents legal utilization of natural forest, although limited exemptions can be obtained for plantation and private forestlands. According to one farmer who wanted to harvest trees he had planted on his private land, he had tried to follow procedures to obtain legal exemption, but became disillusioned with their complexity and decided it was easier to cut and bribe.

Another factor that discourages management investment by communities is the unpredictability of the regulatory environment for forestry and logging. Since forestry is a medium- to long-term investment, a reasonable measure of stability in the rules and regulations would appear to be an extremely important consideration with respect to investing in forest management. Unfortunately, according to community members, the frequent changes of leadership in the DENR seem to be partly responsible for the instability. One person noted, 'The changing of leadership at a national level has a big impact on (forest) policy.' It seems that every new senior official revises the policies of their predecessor as a matter of course.

Box 13.2 Community rights suspended

In early 2003, the incoming secretary of the DENR reacted to a single case that was widely publicized in a national newspaper. A particular CBFM cooperative was accused of 'abusing' its forest by suspending utilization rights for commercial purposes in all the CBFM areas throughout the Philippines. An affected community contacted the research team and invited it to investigate the impact of their resource utilization permit (RUP) suspension. (An RUP is the official document needed for legal harvesting and transporting of logs.)

With no other livelihood options, the community continued its customary harvesting of forest products from the CBFM area, despite the suspension of its RUP. At the DENR checkpoints (regular features along rural roads), in lieu of an RUP, villagers were asked for a bribe in an envelope. In addition, a fixed monthly allowance of about US$120 was demanded by the local Philippine National Police (PNP) to facilitate the continued transport. This had to be paid whether or not timber was being transported during that month.

Community members said that prior to the RUP suspension they had had to pay much lower bribes, usually to speed up the process. The relationship between the community members and the recipients of the bribes was also said to be more cordial at that time, with the communities often determining the size of the payment. Locals also noted that the RUP suspension had benefited buyers, because the black-market value of timber was lower than the legal rate. Community members explained that because of the heftier bribes coupled with their own reduced bargaining capacity with buyers, they were being forced to harvest more timber to cover their operating costs. They added that the communities and the forests were suffering from the suspension of the RUP, but that individuals in the DENR and the PNP were profiting.

Since the people power of the late 1980s overthrew President Marcos in a popular uprising, civil society (or, more accurately, vocal urban-based environmental NGOs and newspapers) has been able to exert considerable pressure on the government. However, populist reactions to high-profile incidents may ignore local realities, as in the log ban after the floods in Leyte in the early 1990s, or the suspension of formal community logging rights (see box).

The team notes from its experience in many workshop discussions that when the topic of community forest rights is mentioned, the question 'Can we trust communities?' is raised by government foresters. But when the issue of community forest rights is raised among community members, the question 'Can we trust forestry professionals/government?' is often raised. Even if legal rights to use the forest were handed over to communities today, community members say it may take many years for them to trust the government sufficiently to invest in forest management.

> 'Because of the past, how can we trust the government, we are being asked to plant trees but we do not know the future.'

> 'How can we be assured that in the future the government won't molest us?'

> 'Maybe the community will work hard (to restore the forest), but in the future, the rich will come and take the forest again. The forest was only given to communities after it was exploited by the rich.'

Ironically, professionals often cite the lack of management investment by communities or isolated cases of abuse after legal rights have been transferred. They use such instances to suggest communities cannot be trusted or lack capacity. Our research suggests that communities base their scepticism about long-term policy commitments on bitter experience. Lack of investment and overexploitation of forests are rational responses to such local insecurity as well as to frequent changes in policy or its implementation.

Why professionals contribute little to community forestry

Individuals from the research communities were vocal about injustices they perceived in forestry practices. A typical comment was, 'The "projectization" of community forestry is problematic. Projects come with solutions but don't understand the issues, how can you have a solution if you don't understand the issues?' Regarding CBFM projects, another community member said, 'What happens is that there is a consultation with us after they have been formulated, but they come with inputs so we say they are beautiful.'

> 'Yes there is 'slash and burn' here. Money from donors gets 'slashed and burned' before it reaches us the villagers.'

'There has been little success with forestry, because forestry takes time, (yet) projects come for two years- then after the project leaves there is no further implementation by us.'

There is a thin line between facilitating a process driven by community members for long-term positive change and 'facipulation' of a community to come up with a short-term, tangible success story for donor consumption. According to community members in the Philippines, this line is often crossed. As a result, temporary and site-specific projects rather than the fundamental issues of resource user rights have often driven the incentive for action, both for communities and development professionals. In fact, contrary to what the acronym would suggest, community members often perceive CBFM to be primarily focused upon alternative livelihood activities such as piggeries or pineapple production, rather than forest management. As far as our research team could see, separating communities from their forests as a way to promote forest recovery does not demonstrate any convincing evidence of success. Rather than promoting sustainable forest management, it seems to promote sustainable project funding.

'They (professionals) should learn from mistakes and our experiences.'

'It is important to deal with the truth to avoid duplication of mistakes.'

'As new acronyms (projects) were introduced there was no learning from the previous ones.'

According to community members, organizations and professionals involved in forest projects generally have preconceived plans and fixed assumptions. This seems to be true even though they do consult community members on the implementation of the projects. For instance, project promoters believe that providing alternative livelihoods projects will help the forest to recover. Community members also often report that these professionals do not learn enough from them beyond extracting supposed needs, and have a tendency to bury failure. This is part and parcel of the projectization phenomenon.

The key does not fit the lock

Figure 13.3 generalizes the apparent mismatches we have highlighted in the previous section between community perspectives on forest problems and the solutions provided by development professionals in the forest sector. The professional intervention 'key' does not fit the community forest management problem 'lock' identified by community members. Therefore, the parties are at cross-purposes.

We must emphasize here that our intent is not to blame specific individuals involved. We do not wish to blame community members who use forest resources but do not invest in management, government officials who take bribes to supplement their meagre salaries, local development professionals who are

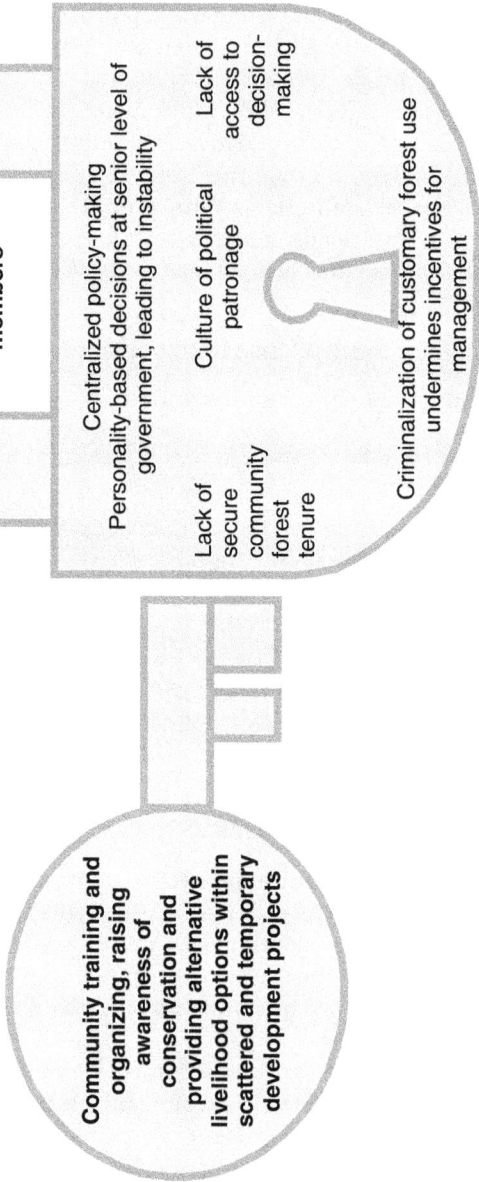

Conventional solutions proposed by development and forestry professionals

Community training and organizing, raising awareness of conservation and providing alternative livelihood options within scattered and temporary development projects

Origins of problems as expressed by community members

Centralized policy-making

Personality-based decisions at senior level of government, leading to instability

Lack of access to decision-making

Culture of political patronage

Lack of secure community forest tenure

Criminalization of customary forest use undermines incentives for management

Figure 13.3 Does the key fit the lock?

zealous about community organization and alternative livelihood projects, or well-paid foreign consultants engaged in training workshops, short site visits and recommendations. Rather, our critique is of the failing system that underpins the forest sector in which such individuals operate in the Philippines.

In this system, professionals receive inadequate information, are equipped with inappropriate skills and are misdirected by perverse incentives. These factors conspire to prompt them to take inappropriate actions. The questions communities and researchers are left with are: how do we move away from more of the same and challenge the current, failing system? How do we reshape the key to better fit the lock?

By starting our research in the field with community members, by using participatory methods to engage with their realities and by exploring the history and policy contradictions of the forestry sector, the research team members realized that their own preconceived notions for intervention to improve community forest management were inappropriate. This realization prompted a different kind of exploration for the team.

What kind of innovation made sense under this newly perceived set of constraints?

We found our inspiration in the opinions of community members. The team concluded that the most effective community forestry innovations would be those that attempted to help transform the roles of professionals and the relationships between them and community members in the forest sector. Two initiatives were primarily built on community perspectives to respond to these opportunities and to shape the key to better fit the lock.

Linking people to policy

It was noted in earlier consultation meetings concerning forest policy in the Philippines, that the consultation process was inappropriate for fostering community engagement, and as a result, there was limited participation. Realizing this, the team designed a more appropriate communication process that included substantial representation of community members. As far as possible, the strategy avoided constraints on the engagement of community members. The result of this communication design process was the workshop called Linking People to Policy, held for the first time in November 2002 at IIRR.

A year's preparation, engaging community members from the three research sites, was required for the workshop. Communities selected their own representatives using different criteria, sometimes local officials, sometimes geographical representation, and sometimes representatives were those who felt most strongly about the issues. All presented points of view that had been gathered from the communities they represented in a paper for presentation at the workshop. The research team facilitated the development of these papers through processes of local verification to ensure that there was a broad representation of local views.

Professional staff from key NGOs, the DENR and academic organizations from different regions of the country, of varying rank, were invited to submit papers based on editorial guidelines prepared by the research team. These guidelines were designed to ensure that participants had relevant interest and experience in forest policy issues, particularly related to the rights and responsibilities of community forest users. Eventually, 50 representatives from communities, NGOs, academics and the DENR were selected. Although they had been invited, no foreign development professionals or organizations active in the forest sector took part in the workshop.

The prospect of having the papers published in an internationally circulated book acted as a carrot to help attract some professionals. But community members did not need any encouragement because the idea was basically theirs.

'Well, I'm so eager! I'm so eager to meet them in order to give our ... you know, what we like and what we dislike to the government.'

'To link people to policy – this is rare for us. Meaning to say we don't have any opportunities in the past and probably not in the future, except this one.'

The workshop process was an adaptation of IIRR publication writeshops, which have been used to produce over 50 publications on technical issues and best practices in rural development using participatory editorial techniques. However, because Linking People to Policy was focused on potentially very contentious issues, the process needed a greater emphasis on appropriate communication strategies, rather than on editorial effort. In this case, the majority of the workshop was conducted in Tagalog, the local language.

The three basic steps in the five-day workshop were:
1. Enabling all to listen to each other first, before reacting. All groups of actors had an equal opportunity to present their perspectives through the presentation of their papers. Only written feedback was allowed. Each group was given time to digest the feedback before the next step of the process.
2. Facilitating multiperspective analysis. A debate was organized using a 'fishbowl' technique, which provided opportunity for all groups to state their position, justify it, receive and respond to comments, and identify issues of divergence.
3. Encouraging the development of joint recommendations. The final step was for small multistakeholder groups to develop practical, joint recommendations together to tackle issues of divergence in a constructive way.

Workshop actors reveal different views

The different actors in the forestry sector represented in this workshop expressed very different views, particularly about barriers to community forestry. The communities are the first to experience any negative consequences from decisions the professionals make concerning forest resource management. Yet they are often the last to have a say in these decisions. During the Linking

Box 13.3 Comments from the Linking People to Policy writeshop

Views of community members
'Projects for communities are thought up in air-conditioned rooms, that is why there are no successful community forestry projects in the Philippines.'

Regarding the DENR presentations, someone said: 'Many of the things that were explained are really good but in reality they are not true.'

Regarding an NGO presentation, one person said: '"lack of understanding" is rather on the part of external actors. Communities know their own dynamics. External actors sometimes bring problems instead of bringing solutions.' Someone else said: 'You have said that policy advocacy is very tiring but we hope you will continue your effort because NGOs are the only hope to help our concerns reach the national level.'

View of an NGO participant
'Not all the communities have the same level of social preparation, that is why community organizing is needed. It is not productive to say that community organizing is not needed because there are communities that need it and there are those that don't.'

Views of academic participants
From evidence presented in this workshop, someone said: 'It appears that there are two perceptions of CBFM. One is around conservation and the other around income generation. Maybe this is why there is misunderstanding and confusion in implementing the CBFM programme.'

Another academic commented on the DENR presentation: 'If utilization of timber is stopped, what incentives will the community have to protect the forest, will the DENR shoulder the cost of protecting (the forest)?'

View of a DENR participant
One person made this comment about the academic presentations: 'It is only the academe from books etc that insist that communities are the best managers. However, in reality many of our CBFM communities are the ones who exploit the resources.'

People to Policy workshop, the implications of current policy on community members were presented by those who are directly affected, to those who influence and implement such policies. Tears were shed by some DENR staff during some very direct and angry evidence-based arguments from community members. They spoke of the impact current policies and corruption have upon them and their forests.

What was very clear from communities was that they regard lack of use rights and the connected corruption as major barriers to community forestry. From their point of view, corruption not only involved professionals taking bribes, but also professionals taking more than their fair share of development assistance. They were openly cynical of forestry-related service provisions by the government and NGOs, saying that the service providers themselves were the biggest beneficiaries of the projects. Community members added that the projects were often not well thought out. Most, however, claimed they still welcomed projects and the assistance they brought.

One community group which had taken part in the CBFMP said they were worse off after a forest project was implemented in their village. After the project was completed and the alternative livelihood projects faded, they still had no rights to legally utilize wood from the forest and they had to deal with new problems in their community. This included feelings of jealousy and infighting because of the uneven distribution of project handouts. However, the community members acknowledged that because of the intervention, they felt more confident to speak to outsiders, and credited the DENR for this. Nonetheless, they added that what they now had the confidence to say, the DENR might not like to hear.

Participants from NGOs, the DENR and academia found it hard to talk about 'them', the community members, in the third person because the community members were present and speaking for themselves. When the professionals referred to deficient 'community capacities', they were often met by a strong reaction from community representatives.

The fish bowl debating tool proved very effective for handling contentious issues. Each group of participants had separately discussed and come up with five statements about community forestry that they thought had to be debated. Equal time was allocated for each group of actors to have their representative justify these points.

Workshop participants sat in a large circle of chairs, facing each other. At the centre of the circle, another small group of chairs were set facing each other. One of these central chairs was reserved for the proponent of a selected statement, while the others were for respondents. Only those in the centre could speak. The proponent first justified the statement, and then permitted respondents to enter the central circle and provide feedback. Once respondents had finished making their comments, they had to move to the outside ring to allow any other respondent to take part. The proponent had the right to remain in the centre throughout the debate, and could reply to any respondent's comments at any time. The maximum time that any person was allowed to speak was agreed in advance and managed strictly using time cards. This interactive process enabled all groups of actors to have an equal sense of control and provided space so everyone was able to take part. Heated debate took place in a controlled manner; therefore, this proved to be a constructive confrontation.

From observation among the professionals in the workshop, responses were divided. Some appeared willing to listen to perspectives that fell outside their own, and expressed genuine surprise and learning at the conclusion of the workshop. Others seemed less open and were more focused on getting their points of view across. However, it must not be forgotten that vested interests also came strongly into play.

There were challenges in managing the interactions. Perspectives of members within a group sometimes varied so much that some individuals within had more in common with another group. In such instances, sometimes groups asked for outside assistance.

In the final portion of the workshop, actors from each of the groups were brought together into think-tanks. They were challenged to find constructive steps for some of the issues in the debate where consensus was not reached. All groups found some forward steps that they could agree on, even if they did not reach consensus.

The workshop approach appeared to change both attitudes and behaviours, although these were difficult to measure. One method used to try and measure any changes in vision among participants was to ask participants at the beginning of the workshop to draw a picture of their vision of good community forestry, without using any words. Then, at the end, they were asked again to draw their vision of good community forestry. In particular, in the professionals' second drawing, people had generally become more prominent and trees less so.

Conclusions from the workshop

Beyond feedback from participants about learning and attitude change, it is difficult to identify direct impacts from the workshop. The innovation of this consultation process itself may represent the biggest outcome.

> 'As we have heard in the presentations there are experiences that are particular to a certain group. Like for example, the experiences of NGOs that are different from the experiences of the community members, the experiences of the academe are different to the experiences of the DENR ... In developing policy, I think we need to look at how this (process of bringing different perspectives together) could help to improve the policy.' Domingo Bacalla, Chief CBFM Division, DENR

Institutionalizing such communication platforms in policy development and review procedures may be a useful condition for programming, so that there is increased accountability and transparency in the forestry sector. Approaches such as this have the benefit of helping to democratize the forest sector by supporting reform efforts, and illuminating the contradictory perspectives and agendas in the sector.

Training learners

It was evident from the Linking People to Policy workshop that some forestry and rural development professionals required better learning and communication skills. Most training in these fields tends to be technical in nature, but this is inadequate to deal with the contemporary challenges facing community forestry. The dominance of blueprint planning and predetermined procedures seems to be a main cause of the mismatch between professionals' skills and community forestry challenges. Blueprint approaches to the forestry sector are characterized by a lack of respect, failure to incorporate multiple perspectives in decision-making, and a lack of systematic and experiential learning. Using this model, plans are built upon assumptions that are seldom tested in the field. In contrast, the strengths of PAR lie in an appreciation of multiple perspectives linked to a systematic framework for context-specific, experiential learning.

The IIRR research team, in partnership with the Regional Community Forestry Training Center for Asia and the Pacific (RECOFTC) and the IDRC, designed a new 'Training of Learners' initiative built around this gap. PAR principles were adopted to structure the training experience. As far as we know, this is the first time PAR principles have been used so explicitly in an international training course for professionals working with NRM. The PAR training initiative has been tested three times, under regional and national contexts, with a wide range of participants, building on participants' own experiences and a field programme that included exposure to multiple perspectives on NRM problems. Community members were the key resource persons and facilitators generally provided the process and methods.

Coming full circle

Between 2002 and 2003, reformers in the DENR conducted a consultation process with academics, NGOs and community members to try to improve the CBFMP. Just like communities, the DENR is not homogeneous, and strategic external support can be very helpful to internal reformers who are struggling for change, even if such changes are modest in scale. The Linking People to Policy workshop was designed as a part of this process.

The review process resulted in changes to programme guidelines, which now incorporate community perspectives. Many of the changes make it more difficult for corrupt government officials to receive bribes. For instance, endorsement of all the official papers required by communities in CBFM is now automatic if government officials do not act within a limited period after a community request. In addition, some of the excessive and costly prerequisites associated with communities seeking legal utilization rights have now been removed. Examples include the reduced requirements for environmental impact assessment; instead, a management plan that is prepared by the community now suffices. In addition, the required work plan now covers a five-year time frame rather than a one-year period, as suggested by community forest users.

In 2002, there were 4,956 CBFM sites in the Philippines covering 5,708,395 ha and including 496,164 households (Philippines Government,, 2002), so changes in the guidelines are potentially very significant. If initiatives such as the Linking People to Policy workshop have even a small impact on policy so that it becomes more supportive of community forestry, the benefits to community forest users could be immense.

Although these positive changes in the CBFM guidelines bring community investment in forest management a step closer, some obstacles remain. One is the requirement for a scientific inventory: this is a prerequisite to granting rights for the utilization of trees. The inventory still must be conducted by professionals and is based on requirements that have a technical sophistication, sample size and cost that are inconsistent with the reduced management plan procedures for CBFM. In the vast majority of CBFM areas, the inventory is impractical. Apart from reinforcing the control functions of professionals, its usefulness seems questionable. During the following two years, part of the challenge faced by the IIRR team at their study sites is to explore alternatives to this inventory that can be accepted by all parties.

The learning journey has now brought the research team full circle, to where it started back in the communities, albeit under a revised policy environment. Now the team plans to explore whether the changes in the CBFM guidelines are sufficient to merit local investment in forest management. If they are, the new guidelines will be tested in a learning-by-doing way in partnership with the communities and the DENR. It may be that policies and guidelines can be implemented on a trial basis to reduce barriers, for instance.

The research team's approach has now evolved into three components:
1. learning with and from community members in pilot implementation at study sites;
2. undertaking more 'Linking People to Policy' workshops; and
3. maximizing the impact of the Training of Learners initiative.

The three components are interlocking, with outputs from one structured to lead into the next. For example, lessons from the study sites will be incorporated into both the Linking People to Policy and the Training of Learners initiatives, thus magnifying their potential impact. Community members are involved in all three components and their participation anchors communications and training initiatives in local realities. The relationship between community members and professionals in all three components is unconventional. For example, in Training of Learners, community members are the teachers, while professionals are the learners. This reversal of roles and relationships may be crucial to advancing community forestry.

Reflections

Many professionals working on community-based initiatives profess to use participatory approaches. Yet they persist in planning projects whose outputs, outcomes and impacts five years down the road have already been determined at the proposal stage.

PAR challenges us to respond to local problems and local learning. In this case, the community perspectives explored by the IIRR research team led to a major change in the direction of the research project. Unfortunately, this level of responsiveness is a luxury that few development professionals have. As a research approach, we have found PAR may be most appropriate at a certain time and with certain participants. Sometimes it may be more effective at the community level, but at other times at the level of national government agencies.

Outcomes are very difficult to predict, particularly quantitative outcomes such as the numbers of trees planted. Switching to this kind of process planning and iterative learning requires great flexibility from individuals, organizations and funding agencies.

In particular, there are challenges involved with institutionalizing PAR approaches. These include devising operational planning systems that provide incentive and opportunity, yet offer sufficient guidance and structure for the iterative and interactive planning process that a PAR approach requires. PAR will not work as an add-on to existing systems. Instead, it is a different way of working that can produce better results.

In this case, it became clear that the key to advancing community forestry in the Philippines involves stepping into the shoes of community members to better understand their perspectives. Community forestry will not grow in the Philippines if there is no incentive for communities to invest time, effort and money in forest management.

Using an iterative PAR approach to shared learning within communities also made it clear that the skills, attitudes, and behaviour of forestry and development professionals were unsuited to the problems of community forestry implementation perceived by those who were responsible for its implementation. Therefore, the research team shifted its focus to understanding why the key does not fit the lock and how to reshape the role of professionals so that it fits better.

We conclude that there is a need for better professional training in listening and communication skills, a clear requirement for iterative and participatory learning processes rather than top-down blueprint planning and a need to transform the roles of all key actors.

The most exciting conclusion the team draws from its experience with PAR is its potential to challenge and change professional practice through shared learning. Professionals do not control the PAR agenda. This is a great opportunity for them to let go of their need to control outcomes, and allow community members to take more initiative and responsibility. The application of PAR also stimulated new critical questions about the roles of development professionals and their organizations. Often, this included critical self-analysis, which is always challenging. After all, development professionals, as well as community members, are motivated in part by self-interest. Therefore, it is important that we recognize and critically expose our self-interest in policy and project outcomes rather than hide behind claims of altruism.

There is nothing new about the concepts of participatory development, but it would be novel for them to be implemented in practice. The vested interests of powerful players in political and economic decision-making mitigate against meaningful participation, limiting what can be accomplished through new communications tools and training courses. This case has explored how the application of iterative PAR tools in a field-based learning and training environment can help expose these contradictions, provide forums for more balanced communication and challenge conventional professional assumptions and roles. These are essential measures to improving professional practice and public policy in CBNRM, and can serve as steps to broader reforms.

Acknowledgements

The author wrote this chapter on behalf of and in consultation with the IIRR staff members on the community forestry team, notably Amando Yambao, Adel Piso and Scott Killough.

Part IV

Poverty, community and policy impact in action research

CHAPTER 14

Creating options for the poor through participatory research

Julian Gonsalves and Lorelei C. Mendoza

Why should research be pro-poor?

Despite rapid economic growth, the magnitude of poverty in Asia remains daunting. In 1998, the population of the East Asia and Pacific region living on less than US$1 per day was 278 million or 15 per cent of the total. If we exclude China, this number dropped to 65 million or 11 per cent. For South Asia, the total was 522 million or 40 per cent of the total population. If we increase the threshold to $2 per day, the numbers become 892 million or 49 per cent of the total population in East Asia and the Pacific. And in South Asia, the total was 1,096 million or 84 per cent of the population (Smith and Jalal, 2000: 66). These figures pose an enormous challenge to the goal of poverty reduction. It is not surprising that the donor community and civil society clamour for more attention to poverty reduction.

The Millennium Development Goals mandate an eradication of extreme poverty and hunger. Goal No. 1 calls for halving the proportion of people who suffer from hunger between 1990 and 2015. Other goals endorse the need to promote gender equality and to empower women, and to integrate the principles of sustainable development into policies and programmes to reverse the loss of environmental resources (World Bank, 2001: 5). The emphasis of the Millennium Development Goals on poverty provides strong rationale for action which is informed by new knowledge from research. In fact, strategies and programmes for poverty reduction are better designed and implemented when based on pro-poor research. Consequently, there are three strategic roles for pro-poor research:

1. it ensures that the issues and concerns of the poor themselves are understood and given attention;
2. it promotes conditions in which the poor can use their own skills and talents to work their way out of poverty (IFAD, 2001); and
3. it empowers the poor to become agents of their own well-being (Moore, 1999).

An important first step for pro-poor research to meet the challenge of poverty reduction is to understand the constituents of poverty. Poverty must be dealt with not only in terms of changes in food supply and availability but also in terms of the complex social and economic factors that underpin it. Instead of proceeding from the conventional idea that poverty is about too little income, insufficient consumption or inadequate nutrition, it is necessary to accommodate more comprehensive notions of poverty such as vulnerability, insecurity and powerlessness. In addition, objective measures must be complemented with subjective ones that depart from the poor's descriptions of what poverty means to them.

From the poor's viewpoint, to be not poor means material well-being based on private consumption; access to common property resources; state-provided commodities and assets; physical well-being; a feeling of security and the ability to cope with emergencies; freedom of choice and action; autonomy and dignity. Corruption, conflict and violence, powerlessness and insecure livelihoods due to fewer economic opportunities are the poor's biggest problems. For the poor, security, dignity and autonomy are as important as income (Smith and Jalal, 2000: 67).

If poverty is multidimensional, it warrants no less than the comprehensive strategy proposed by the World Bank (2001: 6–7) to attack it. The strategy suggests three ways: promoting opportunity, facilitating empowerment and enhancing security. None is more important than the other because all three elements are complementary. Interventions as well as research that are pro-poor must not be judged only by their attention to income, but also by their focus on assets, rights and institutions, as these provide a structure for opportunities for the poor and reduce their vulnerability.

Over the last 10 years a consensus has developed that there is a need to move away from income or consumption alone as measures of poverty. Alongside these must be put broader measures that address qualitative measures such as rights, vulnerability, security and autonomy. In this regard, research into the qualitative elements of poverty by the World Bank's 'Voices of the Poor' study for the World Development Report 2000/1 leads the way. It is encouraging to see that many agencies are now more open to the qualitative assessment of poverty. Complementarities in qualitative and quantitative methods of poverty appraisal are being recognized and analysts and policy-makers are looking for a way forward in using the two approaches to effectively design poverty reduction strategies (Kanbur, 2001).

The failure of agricultural research establishments to sufficiently address issues that concern the poor are now well recognized. A significant part of past research has concentrated on high-input production systems in irrigated areas which have contributed to significant adverse environmental effects that further exacerbate the burden on the poor. But mountains, dry lands, forests and coastal areas have been largely ignored by agricultural research until only very recently, in spite of the fact that most residents of these areas are poor. Consequently, international agricultural research establishments have now become more focused on responding to the need for a pro-poor orientation.

Such organizations recognize the special role for research on NRM to complement their traditional emphasis on food crops, commodities and sectors.

This change in mandates has propelled research with a concern for the poor and provided researchers with crucial support. The real challenge for agricultural research organizations is how to translate the poverty emphasis into research processes and products. Strategies for enquiry and dissemination must change. For example, centralized research and development and extension that worked during the green revolution will not apply, because unlike research on commodities, research in resource management is extremely location-specific. While the green revolution was input-intensive, sustainable agriculture is highly knowledge-intensive. The extension system should be devolved away from the centre as much as possible, with the local governments in charge of the public system and the private sector (particularly NGOs) encouraged to participate (Smith and Jalal, 2000: 51).

However, what factors determine whether research in NRM is truly pro-poor? This is the question we will attempt to answer below.

How can research be pro-poor?

We first asked what it means to conduct NRM research that is pro-poor. One of the other contributors to this volume suggested to us that in order to be considered pro-poor, research would need to have had a 'demonstrable effect in bringing about empowerment of poor people, access to their rights and sustainable poverty reduction'.[1]

The authors do not disagree with the idea that the impact of research is an appropriate indicator of its being pro-poor. However, we propose that projects also be assessed in terms of their approach to the conduct of research, an activity that systematically produces and applies knowledge. We depart here from the concept of knowledge as a product or thing which exists outside us, which we possess and which is stored in finished form. We believe that the production of knowledge is a social activity relying upon linguistic, conceptual, cultural and material resources and that 'science is not a thing but a social activity' (Sayer, 1984: 19–20). Precisely because the poor are those who are excluded from social processes – falling through the cracks so to speak – we argue that research processes that ensure the meaningful participation of the poor are as important as research outcomes and impacts that can benefit them.

Research that intends to be pro-poor adopts a pragmatic research framework and employs participatory strategies and methods of enquiry in order to generate transformative knowledge that can then lead to social change. Armed with this research framework and imbued with its values and attitudes , all of this volume's CBNRM projects highlighted and applied these principles to the specific concerns of the communities with whom they worked. There was a deliberate choice about a problem-focused and people-centred research framework. Together with a participatory and interdisciplinary perspective, the project teams made a commitment to a collaborative undertaking with local research groups in government agencies, universities and NGO offices. In the following discussion, we focus on how the research framework,[2] – the study's approach to its subject matter, strategies and methods of enquiry – was implemented in order to consider the poor and their concerns.

Issues of NRM are a subject of vital importance and interest to the poor. Poor communities are particularly vulnerable to failed environmental governance, because they heavily rely on natural resources for subsistence and income.[3] In terms of site selection for their research, case study teams specifically targeted poor and marginalized communities. We can illustrate this deliberate emphasis in the following examples, although it applies to all the cases:

> In the mid-1990s, 70 per cent of the population in Ratanakiri was indigenous. But ethnic Khmer who are Buddhist and mainly paddy (wet rice) farmers are the dominant group in Cambodia, and 98 per cent of the government staff in Ratanakiri belong to this group. The Khmer culture regards shifting cultivation and the culture of indigenous communities with suspicion. (See Chapter 3.)

> Hong Ha and Huong Nguyen are two of the 16 poorest communes in the A Luoi district, and among the approximately 1,200 designated poorest communes in the country, according to national poverty criteria. (See Chapter 5.)

> Guizhou province is situated in the eastern part of the Yunnan-Guizhou plateau in southwest China, with mountains and hills accounting for about 90 per cent of the land, and minority people taking up 40 per cent of the population. It is one of the poorest provinces in China. The major socioeconomic indicators such as income per head, grain production and areas of arable land, are all among the lowest in China. Of the 34 million people in the province, 30 per cent are living below the poverty line and constituting over 10 per cent of the poor in China. (Deshou et al., 1997: 85; see also Chapter 9.)

The promotion of a community-based approach to NRM in these cases not only responded to the degradation of forest, water and land resources. At the same time it was an attack on poverty, because degradation affects livelihoods and destabilizes the natural resource base upon which the poor rely. Investments in NRM, aquaculture and livestock, agroforestry and other labour-intensive agricultural activities may be expected to have positive impacts on productivity and poverty (Hazell, Jagger and Knox, 2000). But payoffs in both production increases as well as poverty reduction result only if there is emphasis on the needs and productive possibilities of smallholders and the landless (Smith and Jalal, 2000: 51). These authors also noted that CBNRM finds allies in the poor because they 'have strong incentives to preserve natural capital as their only significant source of capital' (p. 55). Just as the Mongolia team observed, there was a keener interest from the poor herders in adopting CBNRM practices because these enabled them 'to improve their livelihoods, to secure pasture, to participate in decision making, and to reduce the costs of herding animals through economies of scale' (see Chapter 6).

Pragmatic framework

Poverty and the complexity of agricultural systems pose special research challenges. Less favoured areas where many of the poor live are characterized by a degree of heterogeneity that partly explains the failure of universal approaches to doing research. Cultures are astoundingly diverse. As well, social relations are a product of historical patterns and while they may share some characteristics from place to place, they are unique to specific locations. Similarly, nature represents a set of diverse ecosystems that have evolved and have been affected in many different ways from one location to the next (Smith and Jalal, 2000: 73). Therefore, pro-poor NRM research must successfully grapple with the high variability of ecological, technological, economic, political and cultural facets of the systems in which the poor live. To achieve this, the research must have a pragmatic framework[4] where knowledge claims arise from situation-based action and consequences. It must emphasize applications that work and solutions to problems. The most important factor is to identify the problem using pluralistic approaches (Creswell, 2003: 12).

Pro-poor NRM research is directed at the enrichment of people's practical knowledge, which constitutes the bulk of our social life and accounts for the everydayness of life. Such practical knowledge requires the notion of a knowledgeable human agent (including the poor). As Beck and Nesmith (2001: 120) argue, the prevailing bias against poor people's knowledge and agency in development studies and practice needs to be removed. The study of people doing the most ordinary things must rest on the presumption that most of what people do, they do intentionally. In addition, they probably know the reasons for their behaviour (Mendoza, 1999). Hence it will come as no surprise that participatory methods ought to be adopted.

The CBNRM cases presented in this volume faced the challenge of variability and complexity of local ecosystems because they concentrated on site-specific work. This enabled research teams to capture the wisdom of local knowledge of forests, water, fisheries and coasts. They faced the issues of resource and land tenure, including how local institutions framed people's NRM systems. This meant that even though research on the sustainable use of natural resources began with a strong focus on issues of the environment, eventually equal emphasis in the research analysis was placed on property rights and local institutional issues. In particular, there was an unwavering attention to security of resource access. The Ratanakiri project team (Chapter 3) facilitated the endorsement by the provincial governor of community maps and NRM plans for Somthom commune, which supported the villagers' customary land and forest rights. Rural transformation hinges upon the primary importance of pragmatic access to resources for the powerless and the recognition that access is the poor's most important resource.

Participatory strategies of enquiry

Participatory methods criticize conventional social science enquiry as reducing the subjects of research to objects of research. Practitioners of these methods argue that the subjects who will be affected by research should also be responsible for its design. Participatory methods uphold a worldview that sees human beings as co-creating their reality through participation: experience, imagination and intuition, reflection and action. The knowledge and experience of people, including those who are often marginalized or oppressed, is directly honoured and valued. PAR values the processes of genuine collaboration (Reason, 1998).

PAR goes by many names: action research (AR), practitioner research, participative enquiry, participatory learning and action (PLA), participatory research and action. It is widely recognized as a powerful way of facilitating changes in complex situations (Laws, 2003). The core process enables participants to share their perception of a problem, to find common ground and then to engage a variety of people in identifying and testing out some possible solution. This is a process of shared learning for everyone concerned.

What can the poor do through participatory research? They can set the research agenda instead of simply carrying out an agenda already designed for them. They can assist in the conduct of trials and experiments. However, they can do more than this. In the Guizhou Academy of Agricultural Sciences (see Chapter 9), the research team started to work with farmers. Together, they tested technological options on farmers' fields for fruit trees, mushrooms, and intercropping of maize and wheat, as well as rapeseed and maize. With exchange visits among farms, this project enabled farmers to share their experiences with one another. In another of the project sites, the village operates and maintains a drinking-water system through a set of rules the villagers drew up themselves. Community members also constructed the water system with the cooperation of male and female farmers who designed it and mobilized labour, materials and funds. This accomplishment is better appreciated if it is also noted that government technicians had previously told the villagers that the site did not have any adequate water source. It is worth emphasizing that in order to ensure that research results benefit the poor, researchers must ensure that the poor participate in the research processes.

In the Hue project, farmers in the rice production group developed their own criteria to monitor and evaluate results. They made decisions on which crop varieties to use, the amount of fertilizer to apply and which cultivation techniques are best (see Chapter 5). Through a special skills-building activity initiated in 1999, PM&E was introduced into the Chinese CBNRM projects, providing farmers and other learners with a powerful, systematic tool for directing further interventions. This experience is documented in Vernooy, Sun Qiu and Xu Jianchu (2003) and served as input towards the adoption of the methodology by other projects (Gonsalves and Mendoza, 2003).

During the PAR process, researchers typically worked with disadvantaged groups, serving as partners and facilitators, so that people had the opportunity to act effectively in their own interests. They were enabled to define their problems, define potential remedies and then take the lead in designing the research that was to help them realize their aims (Babbie, 2004: 296). The China team who worked with the villagers of Chaoshan successfully modified their agenda in order to adapt to the capacities of the poor. The team facilitated village participation in a government-supported biogas scheme, by negotiating more flexible qualification criteria and adapting the design to local conditions (see Chapter 9). In another case, the Hue project team adjusted their communications strategy in recognition of the difficulties of engaging the poorest members of the community and women. They helped form problem-oriented farmer groups and separate women's groups which could focus on innovations to suit their own needs. As a consequence, the research team was able to reach the very poor, including more women (see Chapter 5).

Even with participatory research methods, dominant members of the community still tend to monopolize the process. Therefore, researchers must devise innovative approaches for reaching and working with the poorest people if their specific needs are to be addressed. The Mongolia team used a wealth-ranking exercise to identify where the poorer herders were located among the project sites (see Chapter 6). Similarly, the Hue research team (see Chapter 5) also used a wealth-ranking analysis to successfully identify groups of poor farmers and, subsequently, to identify their concerns together. In the lagoon project (see Chapter 4), the team worked separately with each group of competing interests. They ensured that the mobile-gear fishers were able to raise their concerns about exclusion from the lagoon by the expansion of net-enclosures. The joint committee that negotiated and monitored community management of the lagoon consisted of representatives from different fisher groups, government offices and researchers.

Participatory methods enable flexible manoeuvring by local research teams while they explore, define and confront the challenges of context-specific environmental problems. An example is the experience of the PMMR team in Cambodia (see Chapter 8). The project team worked with a community that could be judged as culpable in the degradation of mangroves because many villagers deliberately migrated to the area in order to produce charcoal. Dissuaded by a significant government crackdown in 1999, the villagers switched to fishing. Through project activities the formation of village management committees was facilitated. When the resource management plan was drafted by these bodies, it included the community's affirmation of their own responsibility for stopping charcoal production and dynamite fishing.

NRM issues often involve multiple stakeholders, which include external groups, government agencies and different interest groups in the community. It can be difficult for researchers to nurture participation by the less influential groups such as the poor. Therefore, researchers must establish partnerships with local organizations and support groups (such as NGOs or farmers' networks), which are specifically linked with the poor, so that their interests and concerns can be effectively heard. This multiple-stakeholder approach enables dialogue among different groups within a community, between communities and between communities and external agencies. All the projects in this volume, in different degrees, faithfully carry out this crucial spirit of inclusion, dialogue and consensus-building. On the whole, teams indicate that this approach has many advantages. However, it is important that researchers periodically assess whether the poor's perspectives are being heard in such multi-stakeholder settings.

The adoption of participatory research methods by the project teams also enabled the introduction of a participatory mind-set among researchers and the personnel of partner agencies of the projects. It provided models of new practice which expanded the possibilities for both practitioners and communities. Nonetheless, engaging in PAR is insufficient to ensure that the poor benefit from CBNRM activities, because communities are differentiated and stratified. It is often easy for practitioners of PAR methods to forget that not all members of a group have equal access to the resources, rights and benefits of community life. Social and gender analysis provides occasions for critical reflection on PAR methods. Such analyses alert researchers to the fact that the poor and marginalized members of a group may not be involved and benefited (see Chapter 15).

Many CBNRM site-specific projects evolve over periods of at least three years if not longer, as in the China, Cambodia and Vietnam cases. This is to be expected because problem-solving for NRM issues in collaboration with poor communities requires time for participation, learning and action. Some may view this process as ineffective and costly. In addition to the arguments above, it is useful to emphasize the value of PAR in nurturing social capital in communities. The effectiveness of development efforts, particularly in rural communities, is closely linked to social capital that draws upon the mutual trust and understanding built and shared among individuals and households. This enables cooperation, reduces transaction costs and makes it possible to optimize solutions to many problems. Because of rapid change brought about by migration, urbanization and modern means of communication and transportation, social capital has declined in many communities. This is generally true, notwithstanding the rhetorical invocations of solidarity expressed by local people when questioned about the social relations in their communities. This weakening of social capital has important implications for the implementation of development strategies: efforts to decentralize resource management by returning control over assets to local communities are but one example. Indeed, decentralization may not be effective if social capital has dissipated (IFAD, 2004). In this light, PAR projects add value. They may contribute to a reawakening of a people's sense of community as they once again talk to each other, work together and act together to solve problems that beset them (see Chapter 16 for a more detailed discussion of community action and social capital).

Transformative knowledge

Undertaking research is not only a means of knowledge production. It is also a tool for the education and development of consciousness as well as mobilization for action. Vernooy and McDougall (2003: 116) define transformative learning as an approach whereby learners build a more integrated and inclusive perspective of the world together. Through the learning process, they jointly transform some part of their worldview. For advocates of PAR, access to information signifies access to power. It has been said that power over knowledge is held by members of the dominant class, sex, ethnicity or nation. When the poor and disadvantaged see themselves as researchers, as learners, they regain power over knowledge (Babbie, 2004).

The ability of poor households to utilize natural resources and enhance their livelihood strategies is influenced by scientific discoveries and technologies. Therefore, it is imperative that these are managed and directed with them in ongoing partnerships with research and scientific organizations. Otherwise, the benefits from innovative technologies leak to other groups and are not captured by poor and peripheral communities. The lessons from the green revolution of the early 1970s for increasing agricultural productivity are not to be forgotten. Not only was higher grain production not tackling poverty as quickly as presumed; the strategy was also not addressing the production needs of a vast number of the poorest farmers. On the whole, the research system was unable to address the needs of client groups (Hall et al., 2002). Therefore, the imperative is that agricultural researchers must work with communities on their problems. As Hall et al. propose, agricultural science must operate in a developmental framework rather than a scientific one if it is to make a contribution to poverty reduction.

These cases put a premium on learning by doing and accepted that the learning process in PAR was time-consuming and largely iterative (see Chapter 2 for an explanation, and Chapters 4, 6, 10, 11 and 13 for illustrations of this approach). They understood that such knowledge requires continuous learning and can lead to adaptive management. The CBNRM projects are a critical input into a broader advocacy effort towards the effective implementation of sustainable development projects by national, regional and local bureaucracies. These agencies need to learn to work with dedicated researchers and develop partnerships at the local, regional, national and international levels. CBNRM contributes to the overhauling of the perspectives of bureaucracies with reference to their role in working for the benefit of the poor. For example, in Chapter 10, the Bhutan team states:

> As the two case examples in water management and forestry illustrate, the RNRRC [Renewable Natural Resource Research Centre] reoriented its re-search agenda to reflect community priorities, rather than the interests of the researchers ... The project's integrated approach also altered the research planning process at the centre. Staff from all sectors and sub-sectors (crops, livestock, forest, Integrated Pest Management (IPM), socio-economics and

water) now discuss their plans together and explore opportunities for synergy. Hence, a more integrated planning and implementation of research occurs. More emphasis is placed on participatory technology development, participatory plant breeding and variety selection, and the need to build on farmers' knowledge and practices.

Other than enabling the poor to capture benefits from the results of the research, the empowerment of the poor also comes from their ability to exercise choices. Establishing linkages with policy-makers, policy formulation processes and networking with academics are main components of an empowering process resulting from pro-poor research. Once they find their voice, the poor enter into dialogues with the powerful. By organizing themselves in collective action, they can gain more control over their resources so that they continue to provide the foundation of their livelihoods and contribute to the formation of private and social assets. This empowerment of the poor to take active part in the decisions that affect them is what a participatory approach catalyses.

It is not unexpected that these projects provided a most appropriate policy complement to the decentralization initiatives that are rapidly taking place in Asia (see Chapter 17). The strategy to focus research effort on the transitional economies of Asia has provided an excellent opportunity to contribute to the democratization efforts in these countries. The research projects provided governments with occasion to learn how to be more responsive and accountable to their own people. CBNRM not only changes the power relations in local communities, it also transforms such relations between local groups and external agencies. For example, villagers of Somthom commune in Ratanakiri prohibited the military from entering their forests and even confiscated their chain saws to prevent their illegal logging (see Chapter 3). In Koh Sralao, the village management committee stopped a boat carrying mangrove logs cut without their permission. Although the boat-owner was related to the provincial police commander, the village management committee was able to negotiate with the former to pay a fine and sign a written commitment to stop his illegal activities in the area (see Chapter 8).

Transforming the lives of the poor requires that they be targeted. Pro-poor research must purposively identify and locate poor households in a community, as was done in the Hue project (Chapter 5) and the Mongolia project (Chapter 6). Local conditions contribute to poverty, yet they can also contribute to solutions. Long-lasting and workable strategies for poverty reduction are often those which are constructed by the poor themselves and managed by them rather than externally introduced. That being said, measures for poverty eradication cannot be left entirely to the poor, because their condition has excluded them from the normal operations of social and economic processes. They require the assistance and support of government agencies from the village, commune and district levels, as in Cambodia's community forestry project (see Chapter 11), or from commune to provincial governments as in the Ratanakiri project (see Chapter 3). Through networks, the poor may be provided with support by civil society groups at the local, national and international levels, as illustrated by the use of networking in Koh Kong, Cambodia (Chapter 8).

CBNRM is not just about technical improvements to resource productivity but also about governance and livelihoods. Natural resource governance and community-based approaches in particular, are all about process. And as a process, CBNRM changes power relations by strengthening capacities at the level of local communities. Choosing the participatory approach as its core strategy has concretized what a pro-poor policy or project requires. To choose to be participatory is not simply choosing one research method over another. It is declaring that this is the way to do development research, that is, research that is truly people-driven and democratic. The sciences, natural as well as social, must be at the service of communities and peoples. Development research is an enabling process for communities to find their way, their solutions, to live their lives, to make their own mistakes. But always it ought to be their project, with researchers acting as facilitators, midwives to the birth of empowering processes.

Strengthening pro-poor CBNRM research: methodological issues

We have shown above how the CBNRM research teams executed the PAR framework to promote opportunity, facilitate empowerment and enhance the security of the poor communities with whom they worked. Now we turn to a discussion of selected methodological issues that can enhance the ability of CBNRM research to be pro-poor. There is no hierarchy of importance implied in the order of presentation.

Utilizing local knowledge through site-specific studies

Research on marginal agricultural lands has been criticized for omitting important gaps (Jodha, 1991). Research work is not sufficiently oriented to local situations, it does not consider indigenous systems as sources of learning and it ignores locally specific research results. The CBNRM research teams have responded to these inadequacies by stressing the strategic importance of site-specific and context-driven research in NRM. The projects cover a diversity of sites from community forests, mangroves, rangelands, to freshwater and coastal fisheries, to upland watersheds. They engage farmers, fishers, livestock raisers and forest dwellers. They contribute to a wide range of learning opportunities grounded in local problems and solutions.

There are other uses of site-based action research. First, it demonstrates that alternatives exist to top-down or blueprint approaches to NRM. For example, the Ratanakiri project developed participatory land-use planning techniques which are now being scaled up across Cambodia with SIDA and UNDP support, as discussed in Chapter 3. Second, site-based findings provide a more credible basis for local communities to influence national policy-makers. The action research sites serve as opportunities for meaningful dialogue by villages with local officials towards establishing rules of NRM governance (see Cambodia community forestry, Chapter 11, or the Guizhou case, Chapter 9). Third, the local communities in the villages in Tam Giang lagoon and the uplands of Hue in Vietnam (Chapters 4 and 5, respectively), or in Koh Kong and Kampot, Cambodia (Chapters 8 and 11) have demonstrated the capacity of communities to manage natural resources effectively. More importantly, these cases also exemplify how communities can contribute to successful efforts at reversing environmental degradation (Gonsalves and Mendoza, 2003).

In addition, site-based projects act as focal points for multilevel networking, as illustrated by the PMMR team (see Chapter 8). They also serve as nodes that enable a range of actors to address changing sociopolitical contexts, as demonstrated by the Mongolia team (see Chapter 6), and as ground from which springs community-derived experiences influencing policy review and reformulation. Projects in Bhutan (Chapter 10), Cambodia (Chapters 8 and 11) and the Cordillera (Chapter 12) illustrate this. To ensure that the concerns of poor communities are neither neglected nor bypassed, pro-poor research in NRM must continue to be oriented to long-term, site-specific studies.

Addressing complex interactions in physical landscapes

Pro poor NRM research must address issues arising from the complex interaction between and across ecosystems. Within watersheds there are strong linkages between forests, uplands and the lowland areas. When watersheds degrade, crop and livestock production are at risk. Degradation at the landscape and ecosystem level is often linked with farm-level degradation. Furthermore, FAO data suggest that the biggest cause of deforestation is agriculture. We also know from the International Union for the Conservation of Nature (IUCN, now known as the World Conservation Union) that most protected areas in the world have people farming in them. Agriculture can also pollute collectively managed bodies of water such as lakes or lagoons. But farmers can also recapture some of these agricultural nutrient flows. In communities around the Tam Giang lagoon in Vietnam (Chapter 4), for instance, the fertilization of otherwise sandy soils is augmented by sea grass (macrophyte) found in the lagoon. There are also linkages between forests and agricultural lands. In Cambodia, forests are maintained by local communities partly because they believe it has improved yields in adjacent rice paddies (see Chapter 11).

In the Lingmutey Chu watershed, if food production has to be improved in the lower part of the watershed, the upper communities need to be assured that there is enough water early in the season which can be released to lowland communities without adversely affecting production in the upper parts. Such interconnectedness can only be handled by an integrated approach to resource management, one that includes crops, livestock, forests and water. Thus, the Bhutan team (Chapter 10) departed from their traditional research focus on specific agricultural commodities and farming systems so that they could adopt an integrated NRM approach to adequately handle the linkages among forests, water management and agriculture. Several of the CBNRM teams, for instance in Hue (see Chapter 5) and GAAS in Guizhou, China, (see Chapter 9), have had a strong historical engagement with traditional agricultural research, but have now shifted their research approach. Like the Bhutan team, they have adopted the more holistic and integrative approach of CBNRM.

Sustaining livelihoods

The poor rely on a variety of livelihoods which depend in turn on a wide range of natural resources. As the sustainable livelihoods framework proposes, a form of livelihood analysis is needed so as to assess the causes of poverty. During this analysis process, attention must be addressed to the poor's access to resources (be these financial, natural, human or social), as well as to livelihood opportunities. Relationships between and interactions with relevant factors at the micro, intermediate and macro levels need to be understood.. This form of livelihood analysis is used by an increasing number of organizations, including UNDP, the International Fund for Agricultural Development (IFAD) and the Department for International Development (DFID) of the UK.

The framework is primarily a tool to ensure that the diversity of economic activities in which poor people engage is fully understood. The process starts by analysing people's livelihoods, including their dynamic nature (how they change) as well as the multiple strategies they use to secure their livelihoods (Adato and Meinzen-Dick, 2002). Livelihoods provide the foci that enable an assessment of development interventions and can guide prioritization decisions. A key feature of sustainable livelihoods framework is that it recognizes the people themselves as actors with assets and capabilities who are capable of rational action in pursuit of their own livelihood goals. As discussed above, this resembles the premise of the research framework of the CBNRM teams. Now that the goals of agricultural research are broadening to include resource management and poverty reduction, such a framework – complex though it is – is an important tool for researchers in order to help improve the relevance of agriculture and NRM research for poor people, especially those living in less favoured areas.

The poor rely more on common resources than the non-poor (Beck and Nesmith, 2001). Higher productivity gains lead to commercialization, which may provide incentives to privatize common property resources and exclude the poor. Thus, pro-poor NRM research must concern itself with the changes in the allocation of resource rights over common resources. Researchers must pay attention to the processes that establish resource management structures in order to ensure that their design does not neglect the interests of the poor. Just as CBNRM research directs its attention towards the sustainable use of collectively managed resources, the same must also be done for privately managed ones. It is appropriate for the initial emphasis on resource management to shift gradually to livelihoods after new assets are built from the rehabilitation of highly degraded resources.

Engendering NRM research

Integral to the concern of pro-poor research is the concern for gender equality and the empowerment of women. Judging from some of the cases in this volume, capturing gender issues in NRM requires more attention. Procedures often equated with engendering research, such as enabling one or more women to attend meetings, participate in projects, or become part of decision-making bodies can address representation but do not by themselves solve inequities in NRM.

One must ask, what about a woman's right to own land, to inherit land, to sell and trade the output of her field, to negotiate her labour input in her plots as opposed to other family plots, to benefit from animals that she raises, or to choose which animals to raise? Are inequities present in these areas?

If CBNRM projects are to strengthen their pro-poor orientation and enhance their ability to deal with the internal inequity of poor communities, they need a better focus on such issues. Enhancing the opportunity of poor communities rather than external agencies or non-poor communities is an excellent starting point for pro-poor research. However, it cannot be its destination.

Of course, differences in the sociocultural context among countries need to be considered. Gender issues will vary among East Asian communities like China, South Asian communities like Bhutan and Southeast Asian communities like Cambodia and Vietnam. CBNRM teams need to ensure that their projects consider and respond to gender issues that surface in NRM practices. Even though the China and Hue teams began with some success to confront gender issues, more is required.

Engendering research concerns itself with changing perspectives. Gender relations are socially constructed, as are gender inequities. Like any social phenomenon, they are intrinsically meaningful and concept dependent (Sayer, 1984:31). The researcher and the 'researched' hold ideas, beliefs and concepts about gender relations and what constitutes gender inequities. Unlike non-social objects, social phenomena hold meanings which are intrinsic and are not merely externally applied descriptions. In studying gender, status, politics or ethnicity, the social scientist must interpret what these actually mean to those who are affected or involved. This is not the case when studying atoms, cells, rock formations or black holes. Therefore, the distinction between social science, the humanities and everyday social knowledge on one hand, and (natural) scientific knowledge on the other, is fundamental. Ideas and meanings are not only in society but also about society. Therefore, researchers may adapt gender-sensitive procedures but may still fail to account for gender relations and, in fact, remain insensitive to gender inequities.

Two possible research 'blinders' can exist. One occurs when researchers from a different cultural background become conscious of gender inequities and seek to impose these concepts of gender relations on another community. What they see are inequities they have become sensitized to from their own social and cultural world; ones which may be completely misplaced for the new situation. The other blinder occurs with someone born and raised in the same community, but who is unable to escape his/her own gender ideology. This happens to many researchers in CBNRM projects. Engendering research will have to confront these blinders and enable researchers to change their perspectives. In this regard, more capacity-building initiatives in gender and social analysis for the research teams are welcome.

Embedding social scientific analysis in multidisciplinary NRM research

Project interventions often result in inequalities and unanticipated negative consequences. There is a growing awareness that the manner in which projects can reduce these inequalities and adverse impacts depends upon the integration of strong social criteria in the project design. This requires the contribution of the social sciences in research design and implementation andnot merely in evaluation. NRM research today not only must deal with issues of degradation and management of natural resources. It also has to take account of livelihoods, asset-building and gender inequities. For example, gender equity means giving women access and control over fundamental assets. This is increasingly perceived both as an objective of, and as an effective instrument for, poverty reduction. These considerations justify the strategic if not central role of social scientists working together with natural scientists in agricultural research teams of the future. The research teams profiled in these cases are already multidisciplinary teams. However, some of the cases point to ways in which the social science capabilities of the research teams continue to need strengthening, despite the efforts already made in this regard (also Gonsalves and Mendoza, 2003).

In research into biophysical conditions related to social processes, current research has done good work on farming systems. Among the identified inadequacies are the disregard for indigenous systems as sources of learning and the disregard of traditional systems and their adaptation to limitations as well as opportunities in marginal lands. Jodha (1991) traces these problems to the subsidiary role of social sciences in agricultural research. This leads researchers to give inadequate attention to social relations and rural power structures. Therefore, appropriate methods must be derived and developed to foster opportunities for multidisciplinary work in NRM, first among natural scientists and then with social scientists. Specifically, social scientists must be brought into the beginning phases of NRM projects so that they can work with natural scientists in research design, technology development and the evaluation process. Logistical implications and transaction costs of such a strategy should be viewed as essential and strategic investments that need to be made. Invariably, a menu of options should be developed for each agro-ecological niche.

Social scientific inputs are required not only at the level of projects but also at the level of organizations. Analytical skills in the social sciences must be introduced, strengthened or rebuilt. Organizational environments need to be re-crafted to nurture a change in attitudes and behaviour in the agricultural research community. Without a substantially enhanced social scientific perspective in research institutions, the goal of reaching larger numbers of poor could well be missed. It is fortunate for the CBNRM projects in this book that there was an early recognition of the necessity of balancing social and natural sciences as inputs in a research framework. Through this process, an interdisciplinary perspective is brought to bear on the problems at the community and landscape levels. Many of the CBNRM teams from Bhutan (Chapter 10), Cambodia (Chapter 8) and Vietnam (Chapters 4 and 5) have already internalized substantial sensitivity and analytical capacity in social sciences. However, more work must be done in this respect as researchers with natural scientific training learn and master social scientific skills, and as both natural and social scientists develop more integrative ways of working together. These challenges are difficult, even for experienced researchers.

Highlighting the need for conflict resolution and facilitation skills

Whether in watersheds, forests or mangrove coastal areas, CBNRM projects witness growing competition and conflicts over the control of natural resources. When assets are depleting, conflicts arise. As a result of the regeneration and restoration of resources, new assets are created and conflicts arise here as well. Conflicts also arise when existing resources are made available to local communities as a result of the decentralization of the management of natural resources. Conflicts occur all too often between upstream and downstream communities over water (Chapter 10), between aquaculture and fisheries (Chapter 4), between governments' objectives for protected areas and indigenous peoples' livelihoods (Chapter 12), and between local forest users and agencies of the state (Chapter 13).

Skills are needed to anticipate and resolve conflicts. CBNRM researchers and practitioners are often called on to contribute to the settlement of conflicts. However, they are not always properly trained for the task of conflict resolution in NRM. It is suggested that more explicit attention be given to this concern. The Tam Giang lagoon case relates how difficult it was for the researchers to address these issues of conflict (Chapter 4). Researchers are aware of the conflicts; however, they lack the knowledge, skill and experiences required to build awareness of the conflicts and change people's attitudes and behaviours. The IIRR case (Chapter 13) demonstrates how the recognition of fundamental conflict reoriented the entire research effort, leading to creative interventions directed specifically at improving conflict management.

The cases have amply demonstrated how important facilitation skills are for CBNRM researchers. The teams dealt with conflicts in many interesting ways. For instance, conflict resolution processes helped build trust, brought parties together and, in the case of Bhutan, employed role-playing exercises to build mutual understanding. Researchers helped build external policy support that resolved conflicts over water in Bhutan and reduced conflicts over pasture in Mongolia. Failures and successes were both evident while resolving conflicts over the use of the lagoon in Vietnam; intercommunity conflicts in resource claims in the Cordillera; and conflicts caused by the CBNRM interventions themselves in Laos.

Facilitation skills are also needed to discern to which issues the participatory methods apply. Some public issues require the reconciliation of stakeholders' priorities with agency priorities so that policy formulation can be tackled through participatory methods. This is because such methods are more suitable to the investigation of issues which are already shared by the community members. However, these methods may not be as successful in the investigation of issues that divide community members, such as inequalities in the family over control of land and other resources, or violence against women or children. A high level of community participation is likely to make it more difficult, rather than less, for those with less power in the community to raise issues which may be seen as private (Laws, 2003: 65).

Reforming research organizations

Research organizations are transformed by implementing CBNRM projects. Researchers engaged in PAR undertaken within a broad context need mandates from their own organizations that will not only allow – but also actually encourage – the forging of partnerships with a range of stakeholders. In addition to the reinforcement of teamwork, this requires the adoption of an interdisciplinary orientation as boundaries of various disciplines become diffused, and as research projects opt to address problems within a more complex and perplexing institutional and socio-economic environment. Institutional mandates need broadening in order to address a wider range of issues through new mechanisms and modalities of research. Reward systems that feature incentives and compensations in the organization, as well as methods of evaluation that favour a concern for the poor, are also important.

The new orientation has important implications in terms of organizational structure and environment, processes and staffing, not to mention the attitude and behavioural changes in research administrators and scientists. Some of the difficulties that the researchers experienced in these cases include the following.

- University instructors and professors in Hue were challenged not only to prepare scientific studies and technical analysis, but also to organize information-sharing and multistakeholder negotiations for lagoon planning (Chapter 4).
- The Bhutan research team struggled to introduce social science perspectives to their natural science backgrounds, and to integrate across sectoral studies and issues (Chapter 10).
- The GAAS researchers in China were not accustomed to public speaking or advocacy, yet had to develop diplomatic and negotiating skills when dealing with government officials. These were areas in which they felt they needed more training (Chapter 9).

Agricultural research organizations were originally designed to deal exclusively with the enhancement of productivity and commodity-oriented scientific research. Simply revising their mandates, refocusing conceptual frameworks and adding a new interest in poverty might not suffice. These CBNRM cases show how donors, international and regional research establishments can play critical roles in testing, developing and scaling up institutional approaches that have a clear focus on pro-poor issues. Local research organizations and researchers require assistance in institutionalizing CBNRM research. This is not limited to methods and tools, but includes strategies of scaling up research outputs, and improving the impact of research results on policy and uptake among local policy-makers in addition to interorganizational networking. The expanding skill set demanded for effective pro-poor research requires ongoing attention to research capacity-building. This means building on work which has started in some of the cases, such as the development of communications tools, gender and social analysis, as well as PM&E.

Conclusion

These CBNRM research cases demonstrate that research can respond to the issues and concerns of the poor, even as they seek solutions to the problems caused by the continuing degradation of natural resources. The teams profiled in these cases adopted and executed PAR as their core strategy, choosing project sites in marginal areas and equipping themselves with a problem-oriented and people-centred perspective. Through PAR, the project teams facilitated the ability of poor communities to act effectively in their own interests, whether this was defining a research agenda, undertaking trials and experiments or evaluating research results. Poor communities were assisted to contribute to changes in policies and procedures of natural resource governance at the local as well as national levels. They have been enabled to enter into dialogue with government officials and other user groups in multistakeholder negotiations over appropriate arrangements for the management and use of resources on which their survival depends.

To be more effectively pro-poor, research in CBNRM must sustain its site-specific work, and continue to apply holistic and integrative perspectives that enlighten our understanding of the complex linkages among ecosystems and social relations. Pro-poor research in NRM cannot be limited to confronting issues of external equity that arise from the relationship of poor communities in marginal and less favoured areas to external agencies and groups. It must also consciously seek the poor and disadvantaged groups in the community and ensure that their specific needs are brought forward and addressed. The concern for the sustainable management of resources must include giving importance to the poor's livelihoods; ensuring the poor's access to forests, waters, fisheries and pastures; and protecting the village's resource rights, both individually and collectively.

Working for the interest of poor communities as well as with the poorer groups within them demands that individual researchers and research organizations acquire new attitudes and skills. This includes the recognition that people are subjects – not objects – of research and that the poor are their own main resources in their quest to overcome poverty. Researchers and research organizations must become facilitators, mediators and partners in an empowering process of learning and transformation.

Acknowledgements

We gratefully acknowledge the comments and suggestions of Stephen R. Tyler, Tony Beck, Liz Fajber, John Graham, Peter Vandergeest and Hein Mallee. All interpretations and errors are ours.

CHAPTER 15

Exclusive, moi? Natural resource management, poverty, inequality and gender in Asia

Tony Beck and Liz Fajber

Introduction

Writing about CBNRM these days brings to mind the musician Van Morrison's comments on love: 'There are no more words to say about it.' Yet plenty of poets and singers keep writing about love. So what else can be said about CBNRM?

A lot is known about the dynamics of CBNRM. However, this chapter takes the discussion one step further by analysing exclusion and inclusion across the countries whose case studies are included in this book. We have focused on the case study findings, which are supported by a literature review. First of all, this chapter illustrates some broad trends in Asia related to poverty and social differentiation, in order to contextualize challenges faced by practitioners and action researchers working on CBNRM. Then it succinctly covers relevant theories that attempt to explain issues of exclusion, poverty and inequality in relation to CBNRM. Our purpose is to analyse how far current theorizing explains the dynamics of local resource management.

The main section of the chapter ties this theory to findings at the field level and asks what these action research cases tell us about intra-community relations, poverty and inequality. After this, implications for future research, policy and practice are considered. The chapter focuses specifically on intra-community issues of social and gender equity and inequity. We recognize that inequities between different geographical communities and conflicts between communities and external actors have been driving forces in the creation of CBNRM, and continue to be significant elements of its dynamics. However, we deliberately set these latter elements aside for the purposes of this chapter.

Why did we decide to focus on socio-economic dynamics as well as exclusion and inclusion? Primarily because there are several gaps in the current understanding of what happens when CBNRM is introduced by external actors. First, much collective action literature and many cases (see 'Conceptual issues' below) which dominate the CBNRM field deal with these areas sporadically at best. Second, many government policies at least implicitly support fair societies and explicitly support poverty reduction. As well, many donor programmes, including those of the IDRC, consider the promotion of equity as central to their mandate and vision (Ford Foundation, 2004; Gonsalves and Mendoza, 2003). But there has been little analysis of what this means in practice. Third, issues related to poverty and gender must take a higher profile in CBNRM planning and practice. We argue that even a well-intentioned emphasis on participation and collective action that fails to adopt specifically proactive measures towards gender and poverty is likely to exacerbate local inequities.

Attempting to take a pan-Asian perspective is impractical in a short chapter such as this, so here are our disclaimers. Our attention to theory is not intended to provide any new frameworks or concepts, but rather to examine what has been written about inclusion and exclusion. We have focused on the countries whose case studies are mentioned in this book, but we have included India because it has generated a substantial literature. However, we do not pretend to have anything comprehensive to say about CBNRM in these countries. Nor do we attempt to summarize significant social processes across several diverse Asian countries. What we have done is ask a number of questions about the cases as far as inclusion and exclusion are concerned, in order to provide some pointers to key areas which need to be systematically tracked.

As we note in 'Conceptual issues' below, most authors display a normative bias towards a particular perspective on CBNRM. The most common is one which goes beyond treating CBNRM as merely the decentralization of management of natural resources, such as forests and water, towards an approach which links community-based management to tenure, rights and poverty reduction. Our own perspective has been moulded by the belief that CBNRM advocates and practitioners should ensure that their interventions promote equality and reduce poverty. This means it is crucial that these people possess an adequate understanding of the society in which they intervene. We discuss some of the implications of this perspective below.

Trends in poverty, inequality and governance in Asia

What has been the broad socio-economic context for the introduction of CBNRM? Here we describe some relevant trends that have affected how these interventions have played out, although there is limited scope for a detailed analysis of causes and consequences of these trends.

Although macro-level figures always need to be read cautiously, key trends are fairly clear. Quality of life as defined by the UNDP Human Development Index (HDI) has improved, albeit slowly, across most of Asia over the last 10 years (UNDP, 1995; 2004). Poverty as defined by narrower measures such as the head-count ratio[1] has also declined through the 1990s, albeit unevenly, in most of the region and in some cases quite dramatically. The head-count poverty ratio in East Asia and the Pacific declined from approximately 27 per cent in 1987 to roughly 15 per cent in 1998, and in South Asia from 45 per cent to 40 per cent in the same period (ESCAP, 2003; IFAD, 2002). The poor in Asia can be described as being predominantly female, often part of female-headed households, landless, indigenous and internally displaced, socially excluded as in the case of scheduled castes in India, victims of land mines, and both pastoralists and coastal fishers (IFAD, 2002). Throughout Asia they are also disproportionately dependent on the natural resource base to sustain and improve their livelihoods.

We are seeing overall decreases in head-count ratio measures of poverty. However, existing intra-country inequalities, which were already quite high in comparison with the global situation, have remained the same or increased. For example, as measured by the Gini coefficient,[2] inequality has increased in Laos from 0.29 to 0.36 and in China from 0.26 to 0.38 between 1982 and 2002 (World Bank, 2004; ESCAP, 2003). This partly reflects widening urban and rural

Table 15.1 Gender-related Development Index (GDI), with ranking in brackets (out of 130 countries in 1995 and 144 in 2004)

Country	1995	2004	Change in %[a]
Bhutan	–	–	
Cambodia	–	0.557 (105)	
China	0.578 (71)	0.741 (71)	28.2
India	0.401 (99)	0.572 (103)	42.6
Laos	0.405 (96)	0.528 (107)	30.4
Mongolia	0.596 (67)	0.664 (94)	11.4
Philippines	0.625 (64)	0.751 (66)	20.2
Vietnam	0.537 (74)	0.689 (87)	28.3

Note: a. Calculation: (2004 figure – 1995 figure) / 1995 figure.
Sources: UNDP, 1998, 2004.

Table 15.2 Human Development Index (HDI), with ranking in brackets (out of 174 countries in 1995 and 177 in 2004)

Country	1992[a]	1995[b]	2004	Change in %[c]
Bhutan	0.305 (160)	0.347 (155)	0.536 (134)	54.5
Cambodia	0.337 (153)	0.422 (140)	0.568 (130)	34.6
China	0.594 (111)	0.650 (106)	0.745 (94)	14.6
India	0.439 (134)	0.451 (139)	0.595 (127)	31.9
Laos	0.421 (138)	0.465 (136)	0.534 (135)	14.8
Mongolia	0.604 (110)	0.669 (101)	0.668 (117)	−0.1
Philippines	0.677 (100)	0.677 (98)	0.753 (83)	11.2
Vietnam	0.539 (120)	0.560 (122)	0.691 (112)	23.4

Notes
a. The UNDP 1995 *Human Development Report* features the HDI figures from 1992.
b. 1995 figures as featured in the UNDP 1998 *Human Development Report*.
c. Calculation as in Table 15.1, based on the 1995 figures in the 1998 UNDP *Human Development Report*.
Sources: UNDP, 1995, 1998, 2004

disparities, an effect of marketization in Asia. At the same time, as measured by the UNDP Gender and Development Index, between 1995 and 2004 gender equality improved in all the countries studied in this book. In some cases, improvement has been quite substantial and occurred at a higher rate than the HDI for all study countries

However, significant gender inequality persists in all case study countries and has been a major factor related to CBNRM, as discussed below. Although gender equality has improved, it has done so at a slower rate than in other regions.

Geographical and ethnic inequalities are also common, in particular between lowlands on the one hand, and uplands and coastal regions, on the other. For example, while countrywide poverty in Vietnam decreased from 58 per cent in 1993 to about 29 per cent in 2002, poverty in the Central Highlands remained the highest, at about 52 per cent, with ethnic minorities displaying a poverty rate as high as 69 per cent (ADB, 2004). IFAD (2002: vii) comments that:

> The indigenous populations who live in the uplands – the hills and mountainous areas which cover almost half the total area of Asia – have perhaps been hit hardest by this process of de facto (at times de jure) exclusion and marginalization ... Policies for indigenous peoples have, so far, been framed mainly with a view to the benefits that can be extracted for outside economies. Whether it is for irrigation or power supply, whenever it is deemed necessary for the national interest, indigenous peoples have been displaced – with most of them losing their livelihoods – to make way for dams. What the states covet from the hill-forest areas are also their resources, like the timber and minerals that they extract from local economies. In most cases, the indigenous peoples do not own the forest and mineral resources of their economies. As a result, revenues from mines and forests accrue to the economies of the lowlands.

Conflicts arising from what has been called an economy of pillage are perhaps most vividly described in this volume in the cases depicting struggles between logging companies and ethnic minorities in Cambodia (Chapters 3 and 11).

Another key contextual feature related to CBNRM is the rollback of the state in all the case study countries, complemented by the interlocking processes of marketization, privatization and decentralization. As Agrawal and Gibson (2001: 1) comment: 'The poor conservation outcomes that followed decades of intrusive resource management strategies and planned development have forced policymakers and scholars to reconsider the role of community in resource use and conservation.' CBNRM has been part of extensive privatization and decentralization of management and in some cases control of natural resources throughout Asia. But as IFAD (2002: 52) argues: 'The emphasis of such devolution has been the sustainability of resources used by all, rather than poverty reduction through securing livelihoods for the poor.' And in several countries policy interventions leading to marketization, decentralization and privatization have led to the exclusion of the poor and increasing inequality.

To provide some examples from the case study countries, Fujita and Phanvilay (2004) discuss how the Laos land and forest allocation policy exacerbated inequities between rich and poor, and the landed and landless. Poorer households, in particular those that practise shifting cultivation and depend on forest resources to support their livelihoods, became further marginalized. This occurred after the state imposed new boundaries that differed from customary resource use practices. These restricted their access to swidden and forest resources, a pattern which has become common in other parts of Asia (Li, 1999). In Cambodia, the privatization and enclosure of state-owned but communally managed fisheries is reported to have led to increased social differentiation and conflict. When the colonial system of fishery lots was reintroduced in the 1990s, enclosure of the most productive fisheries by an elite group significantly reduced poor people's access to fish. The lots were protected by heavily armed guards and violent conflict with local resource users became common. The more unproductive fishing areas that had remained accessible experienced increased pressure because more fishers depended on them. The poorest sectors of society were most affected, including women, ethnic minorities and displaced people. After the 1997 riots around Tonle Sap Lake and heavy flooding in 2000, donor pressure forced the government to return half the fishing lots to the communities for management by the village fishery communities themselves (Tarr, 2003).

Similarly, in Vietnam, land titling has meant the problem of concentrated land ownership and landless agricultural labourers has re-emerged. In addition, customary and proprietary rights to the gathering and use of certain plants, which were often held by women, are usually not reflected in land titles registered in the name of one individual (Razavi, 2002). The Tam Giang lagoon case in Vietnam (Chapter 4), which is also highlighted in this chapter, provides an important example of how increasing privatization of lagoon resources and changes in production systems led to exclusion of the most marginalized groups, which in turn led to conflict.

Evidence from South Asia indicates that the poor's access to CPRs is being eroded by several factors. These include privatization, encroachment from the rich, government and corporate schemes such as plantations, and the commoditization of CPRs. All shift access to men and the better-off (Beck and Ghosh, 2000; Beck and Nesmith, 2001). Agricultural intensification has led to the reclamation of wastelands, pastures and marshes, the privatization or enclosure of common areas and the degradation of forests followed by stricter access controls. These authors note there is also evidence suggesting that the decentralization of NRM in South Asia has often complemented rather than halted or reversed these processes.

Less is known about the relations between exclusion, inequality and decentralization of forest management in South-East Asia, China, Bhutan and Mongolia. In part this is because decentralization has come to these areas later than in South Asia, with the possible exception of the Philippines. Social and community structures also differ. Therefore, it is uncertain if South Asian processes will be repeated elsewhere in Asia.

Initial research suggests that exclusive processes in India are being repeated in some Asian countries as a result of the decentralization of NRM. For example, IFAD (2002: 51) notes:

> IFAD provided funding to CIFOR [Centre for International Forestry Research] for an analysis of various Asian experiences with the devolution of forest management. The conclusion was that the decentralization of forest management in China, India and The Philippines, has been dominated by the agenda of either the forest departments and/or local elites. The forest departments emphasized timber production; and the participation of the local elites led either to low priority – or no space at all – for the livelihood needs of poorer categories including women.

Barr et al. (2002) and McCarthy (2001) report similar findings from Indonesia; as do Resurreccion, Real and Pantana (2004) in relation to water resources in Thailand. The picture which consistently emerges is that interventions such as decentralization and privatization have exacerbated rural inequity instead of ameliorating it.

New forms of resource management are being introduced across Asia as poverty is slowly decreasing, while privatization and inequality grow, and while poor people – and particularly poor women – are being increasingly excluded from customary access to natural resources. This is the overall context in which we must examine the local impacts on poverty and inequality and the stories from these cases.

However, it would be wrong to suggest that poor resource users are merely pawns in a globalization game whose main aim is to provide resources for an elite of global gluttons. Both historical and current studies show these users display remarkable wherewithal particularly given the odds they face (Thompson, 1975; Scott, 1985). Therefore, these macro-level figures hide many local situations where the micro level does not match the macro; where against all odds, poor ethnic women have managed to achieve significant improvements in their livelihoods, or where communities in marginalized regions have organized themselves to work their way out of poverty.

Simultaneously, a sense of balance is required so as not to romanticize the resilience of poor resource users. Chances are that if you are a poor, ethnic, landless woman in an Asian coastal or mountain region, you may have experienced some improvements in your quality of life. However, you are more likely to have seen the gap between yourself and your better-off neighbours grow. In addition, you probably have the same difficulties making ends meet as you did 20 years ago, as well as being increasingly alienated from the natural resource base.

Conceptual issues

In this section we examine hypotheses provided by recent theory in relation to conflict, inequality, exclusion and poverty. Much CBNRM theory is marked by three characteristics: it is directed at other theorists; it is couched in somewhat obscure language (e.g. 'articulated space'); and it is earnest in tone. Despite our reservations, we think theory can be very helpful to practitioners if it provides an explanation why things happen at a local level. By 'local' we mean the actual location of the village, commune, or even district and region.

Most theorists agree that inequality, exclusion, conflict, gender and ethnicity are important to CBNRM. Johnson (2004) has divided common property theorists into two schools. One consists of 'collective action' scholars, such as Ostrom, Baland and Platteau, and Agrawal. Their primary interest is in rules, regulations, incentives and management structures supporting collective action for NRM. They have also been called new institutionalists, because of their focus on how institutions that can sustainably manage natural resources are formed and maintained. Agency, as viewed by collective action scholars, mainly concerns group formation and dynamics (Ostrom, 1992).

The other consists of 'entitlement' theorists, including Ribot, Agarwal and Peluso (Johnson, 2004: 415), who are 'centrally concerned with the problem of inequality, and with the ways in which formal and informal rules create and reinforce unequal access to common pool resources (or CPR). Implicit (and often explicit) in the entitlement literature is the normative assertion that socio-economic equality or, at least, a reduction in poverty, is desirable.' Agency for entitlement theorists mainly concerns ways in which the resource-poor are excluded from or include themselves in access to resources (Ribot and Peluso, 2003).

Johnson argues that there is limited intellectual interchange between these two schools. However, we suggest there is a middle ground between them currently being occupied by research such as that of the Collective Action and Property Rights Initiative (Meinzen-Dick and Di Gregorio, 2004).

There are two main areas of disagreement between these theorists that are relevant to this chapter. The first relates to how conflict over natural resources is understood. Johnson notes (2004: 418): 'Conflict, of course, does play a role in the collective action literature, but it is most commonly understood in terms of a bargaining scenario, in which individuals and groups negotiate and pursue strategies that will best meet their individual and collective interests.' Incentives for collective action, the effects of heterogeneity of groups and, increasingly, market and technological influences are all analysed in detail (Baland and Platteau, 1999; Varughese and Ostrom, 2001; Ostrom et al., 2002).

In the entitlement literature, conflict and bargaining between classes, men and women, and different ethnic groups are central elements related to individual and group identity as well as the control of natural resources. From this perspective, power relations heavily influence access to and control over resources and benefits, and are essential to understanding how institutions govern the use of natural resources. However, Ostrom et al. (2002: 471) note that we do not know enough about CBNRM and conflict. 'The need for least-cost methods of conflict management has long been recognized in the resource management context ... but little research has been given to this aspect of institutional design.'

Understanding intra-community conflict, which we examine below in the section entitled 'Inequality, poverty and gender: evidence from the field', and how it is or is not resolved, is important. It allows us to understand why certain groups are excluded from resource management and use and to design action research, policy and local interventions. If we conceptualize conflict mainly in terms of incentives or class struggle, then our solutions to natural resource issues are likely to differ quite dramatically. But what is often missing is how those involved in CBNRM view conflict. Their perspectives might differ radically from an outsider's viewpoint; which is why research such as that carried out by Tuyen et al., Ykhanbhai and Bulgan, Tubtim, and Nong and Marschke (Chapters 4, 6, 7 and 8 respectively), as discussed in the next section, is important in terms of understanding how to design policies and programmes that fit with local realities.

The second area of disagreement among theorists is whether CBNRM leads to greater or less inequality, and related to this, an increase or reduction in poverty. Collective action scholars tend to think that collective action structures support equality. However, for the most part, in their work they appear to be referring to customary, or pre-CBNRM initiatives. Two quotes illustrate this point (emphasis added).

> With detailed historical and contemporary evidence, scholarship on the commons has shown that resource users often create institutional arrangements and management regimes that help them allocate **benefits equitably**, over long time periods, and with only limited efficiency losses. (Agrawal, 2001: 1649).

> Most [collective action studies of the commons] have an implicit sense of successful institutions as those that last over time, constrain users to safeguard the resource, **and produce fair outcomes** ... Their focus on local institutions and resources is understandable in light of their objective: to show that common property arrangements can result in efficient use, **equitable allocation**, and sustainable conservation. (Agrawal, 2001: 1650).

Several important examples tell us that egalitarian access to village CPR can exist in differentiated societies. When irrigation allows land to be cultivated, communities that have a highly asymmetrical social structure sometimes ensure that new land is distributed to all members (Baland and Platteau, 1996: 310).

Equally, Guha (1989) argues that historical and relatively equitable forms of resource management existed in the Garhwal and Kumuan regions of the western Himalayas in India. Agarwal (2001) stresses that historical forms of communal resource management in India typically recognized the rights of all villagers.

Entitlement scholars focus on inequality and exclusion, but mainly with reference to recent state or donor agency supported CBNRM initiatives, such as the joint forest management in India:

The literature is replete with cases of groups using the state and other forms of authority to recognize and enforce their claim over natural resources. (Johnson, 2004: 418).

> **Our evidence ... suggests that unless management regimes are specifically designed to include poor people, and particularly poor women, then 'community'-based natural resource management may be externally supported control by elites.** (Beck and Nesmith, 2001: 130, emphasis added)

There is a growing body of evidence illustrating that participatory approaches included in CBNRM lead to exclusion for some groups (Menzies, 2006; Agarwal, 2001; Cornwall, 2002; Sarin, 2001; Sundar, 2000; but for alternative views see Johnson, 2001; Foster and Rosenzweig, 2001). Such evidence suggests that the development of formal institutions for CBNRM such as user groups often does not support meaningful participation by women, poor and marginalized groups. Most of the evidence on either side of the argument, however, comes from a limited number of cases; for example collective action scholars are fond of McKean's (1986) research on Japan. Entitlement theorists have relied heavily on studies from India. Much research has been carried out in those locations which prove that CBNRM leads to greater exclusion of the poor, in particular poor women, who are most dependent on natural resources (Kumar, 2002; Agarwal, 2001; Beck and Nesmith, 2001; Leach, Mearns and Scoones, 1999; Sarin, 2001; Sundar, 2000; but see the section above for studies from elsewhere in Asia which arrive at similar conclusions).

The relation between CBNRM and poverty reduction is not well covered by scholars from either school. Reasons remain unclear, although it may be that NRM is still often defined as a technical sphere, which excludes detailed attention to socio-economic dynamics. We define poverty reduction broadly here to mean not only an increase in incomes but also an improvement in a household's asset base and in livelihoods in general.[3] First, we need to understand the impact of devolution in general on poverty reduction. Ribot (2002: 17) argues:

> Central governments tend to be more generous toward the poor than local governments. In decentralizations concerning natural resources, inequitable local decision making and benefit distribution is frequently observed. Local elites may be more prejudiced against the poor than those at higher levels. Dominant ethnic groups can use their new powers to take advantage of weaker ones. Yet, poverty alleviation is often assumed to be one of the positive outcomes of decentralized governance. On the contrary, a very important comparative study of decentralization and poverty alleviation concludes that 'responsiveness to the poor is quite a rare outcome,' and 'positive outcomes are mainly associated with strong commitment by a national government or party to promoting the interests of the poor at the local level.

A review of evidence from 19 case study countries (OECD, 2004: 7) also found that:

> an unambiguous link between decentralisation and poverty reduction cannot be established. In some of the poorest countries characterised by weak institutions and political conflicts, decentralisation could actually make matters worse. Interestingly, the poverty impact of decentralisation would appear to depend less on the physical country setting, for example a country's size or quality of infrastructure, than on the capacity and willingness of policy makers to ensure a pro-poor devolution process.

This points to the need for strong central policy direction, as discussed in the conclusions to this chapter.

There has been some recent attention to this issue from a theoretical perspective. Thorp, Steward and Heyer (2003) hypothesized that the chronic poor participate less in groups because of a lack of assets (education, capital, social status); a lack of access to markets and networks; a lack of rights (citizenship, territorial claims), and because 'the chronically poor are disadvantaged in group formation, and this may form a significant part of the vicious circle and dynamics of chronic poverty' (p. 1).

Di Gregorio et al. (2004: 3–4) comment on the lack of research in this area. This is surprising given the attention of governments and international agencies to poverty reduction. The authors note:

> Much recent work on property rights and collective action focus on their roles in natural resource management (NRM), rather than on how they can contribute to poverty reduction ... Despite the importance of property rights and collective action for poverty reduction, there is still a knowledge gap regarding exactly how the poor are affected by changes in the property rights regime. Further research is required to directly address the question of how poverty shapes men's and women's incentives and abilities to engage in collective action ... and maintain claims to resources on the one hand, and how different property rights and collective action institutions affect the poor, women, and marginalized groups on the other.'

From what we currently know, we must ask whether CBNRM processes are likely to lead to more or less poverty reduction. This question is especially pertinent when we broadly define poverty reduction as an improvement in livelihoods of poor women and men. For instance, what happens over a five- or 10-year period when a new form of resource management is adopted? Do everyone's incomes rise while inequality stays the same? Or is there some other shift in income patterns? And perhaps more importantly to some poor people (or so some of them have said when asked what they think is important): do their relative bargaining power and respect improve within the household or between households?

Clearly these are not arcane intellectual questions but are central to the daily experience of the inclusion and exclusion of poor resource users across Asia. If, as many entitlement theorists have suggested, the introduction of CBNRM leads to the exclusion of the poor and in particular poor women from participation and decision-making, CBNRM presumably also excludes them from benefits. And given the importance of CPR to poor women across Asia (Chapter 7; IFAD, 2002; Beck and Nesmith, 2001; Ireson-Doolittle and Ireson, 1999), this must contribute to decreased income and depleted livelihoods.

Therefore, more action research is required that analyses who has an influence on decisions and who benefits from resource use, so that interventions can be designed better to support gender equality and improvements in the livelihoods of the poor.

Inequality, poverty and gender: evidence from the field[4]

Poverty, exclusion and intra-community conflict

IDRC's research programme selected project sites in marginal environments, in particular, coastal and upland zones, in order to work with poorer communities reliant upon the natural resource base, and whose access to it was probably declining. Research sites were specifically chosen from among the poorest regions of the countries. A key aim was to help poor communities improve their livelihoods by ensuring they have a stronger role in planning and decision-making regarding the natural resources on which they depend.

However, it is important to remember that geographical targeting does not necessarily mean that the livelihoods of the most marginalized in specific communities are being supported. The case studies suggest that in some cases IDRC partners recognized that intra-community equity issues were important, but that such efforts were not universal and were generally at an early stage of execution. These partners were able to present only limited evidence.

Although not always obvious in these case studies, in order to support local capacity during their action research several project teams took what might be termed a livelihoods approach to their work. In addition to supporting local user groups for the management of natural resources, project teams also responded to local needs and requests by taking a holistic view of their action research. In several cases the local resource base was overexploited. Because of this, either alternative sources of livelihoods had to be developed or innovative technologies adopted to increase productivity. The researchers' approach to CBNRM rapidly spread beyond strictly resource-based activities to a range of other collective initiatives that were often conducted in a participatory fashion. Some of these initiatives were specifically targeted to support poorer households.

Examples discussed in the cases that supported the livelihoods of the poor included: women's income-generating groups in Mongolia; pig production and home gardening in Hong Ha in the Vietnam uplands; peach and strawberry production in China; and mangrove replanting in the PMMR case in Cambodia. Three cases noted improvement or development of a drinking-water system as a key intervention. This will probably be of considerable benefit to poor women who usually have to carry water, as long as they retain access to the resource. It will be important for researchers to track and further document the impacts of these livelihood interventions to relate how they, in association with the development of user groups, affect the marginalized over the longer term.

One of the strengths of the case studies in this volume is how they bring to light the complex interactions between people and their environment. Exclusion, inclusion and conflict and its resolution are central to this. Unless an attempt is made to understand this complexity, outsiders will usually misinterpret issues when trying to intervene. These cases bridge the chasm between the complexities of rural life and the need for policy and programme planning that is capable of following these communities' unique internal and often much simpler logic.

In this section, drawing on the case studies, we highlight some of the main intra-community issues arising from the action research. In the next section, we discuss gender and participation, bringing in the wider literature where appropriate. The case studies reveal contradictory findings in terms of who gains and who loses from the introduction of CBNRM. This is not surprising given the range of countries, cultures and resources involved.

Tubtim's Laos case (Chapter 7) delineates some of the subtleties of the trade-offs villagers must make when resource management regimes change and CBNRM is introduced. In the Nong Bua wetland, villages that were excluded from what was previously an open-access resource were willing to accept exclusion. This was in part because Kaengpho village used the enclosed resource for collective purposes and redistributed benefits to poor people. As we noted above, it is relatively rare for case studies to examine the poverty reduction effects of CBNRM, but in this case Tubtim concludes:

> In fact, some of the village's poor gained a larger proportion of the benefit, especially the women. After Nong Bua was exclusively fished by Kaengpho people, these women could catch some shrimp and buy fish from the other fishers in the village for trading. The women were able to sell them to Kaengpho families who did not often fish and to outside communities without any competition from the excluded villages ... At the same time, according to the village head, he and other wealthier members of the village gave up benefits because the new rules prohibited the use of their gill nets. These decisions added to the village committee's good reputation and their claim demonstrated their commitment to collective benefit.

We discussed in the previous section Baland and Platteau's (1996) point that egalitarian access to village CPR can exist in differentiated societies. While Tubtim does not argue egalitarian access, she analyses a kind of patron–client relationship that involves the redistribution of resources. The inequities of such a relationship are another matter. But Tubtim ties the success of the redistribution to the culture of socialism in which collective benefits have become normative social values. Powerful local elites may accept new and more equal institutional structures if the outcomes are consistent with such values.

Similarly, in their case on Cambodian community forestry (Chapter 11), Kamnap and Ramony found that one community forestry committee organized a pool of finances and supplies to allow the poorest five families to construct housing. As well, in recognizing the importance of forest resources to the poor, one owner of a private forest allowed poorer households access to this resource. Perhaps this is a case of what Beck and Nesmith (2001: 120) mean when defining CPR as: 'an indigenous system which works through unequal power structures to provide significant benefits to the poor'.

In studying access to resources, training and technologies by different social and gender groups in Hong Ha commune, the researchers found that it is usually richer farmers and those who have higher or better social status in a community who participate more in, and have better access to, donor or government extension projects (Sen and An, 2006). There were similar findings from parts of the Tam Giang lagoon in Vietnam, discussed below.

A further theme from the case studies is intra-community tension and its resolution. Entitlement theorists tend to conceptualize natural resources as a central axis of class, gender and ethnic conflict. This is particularly true in the context of rapidly industrializing societies. While we feel there is much truth in this conceptualization, the case studies point to a complex situation where communities must come to terms with changing resource regimes either among themselves, or with outsiders' support. Findings from three of the case studies discussed below suggest that external facilitation, which has the specific purpose of reducing inequalities and resolving conflicts, will be required to ensure that changes in resource regimes do not lead to the further marginalization of poorer groups.

Central to assessing inclusion and exclusion processes is the determination of who actually participates in resource management committees or user groups, including who participates over time. Throughout Asia, governments may sign co-management agreements with the community or decentralize the management of resources. However, often there is no analysis of who controls the governing committee, and hence, who has the formal power to decide on rights governing the access and use of resources (Agrawal, 2001). Members of such committees are often those more politically powerful, wealthier, of the dominant ethnic group or caste, and often men (Ribot, 2002). Membership rights, in the case of forest management and water user committees, often require land ownership and are limited to heads of households who are permanent residents (Sundar, 2000; Zwarteveen and Meinzen-Dick, 2001). This effectively excludes other resource users, particularly the poorest, from having any voice or decision-making power in the management of the resource. Those people who are excluded may be pastoralists and shifting cultivators, poorer residents who do not own land, or women who are not usually either heads of households or owners of land titles (Sundar, 2000).

Consequently, participation in local institutions and decision-making concerning resources are heavily influenced by and embedded within community social and power relations. Supporting community processes for collective action does not automatically address issues of equality and inclusion, and may or may not exacerbate inequities. Hence, it is important 'not to romanticize the concept of collective action, but rather to understand group formation, group dynamics and power relations, and to examine how decisions are made in terms of participation, making, monitoring and enforcing agreements, and who benefits and loses from these processes' (Di Gregorio et al., 2004: 23). In the following case studies, the model that has been promoted by IDRC and partners involves bringing together as many stakeholders as possible for participatory discussion in order to overcome some of the more common problems with CBNRM.

A detailed account of intra-community tensions is given in the case of the Tam Giang lagoon in central Vietnam, as analysed by Tuyen et al. (Chapter 4). Covering two quite distinct ecologies in the same lagoon, this case illustrates that privatization of common property resources hurts the poor. It also shows how external intervention aimed at conflict resolution may be central to enabling all groups to participate, and thus at least ameliorate the effects of privatization and decentralization. Most households around the Tam Giang lagoon rely on aquaculture and fishing for their main livelihoods. However, approximately 1,500 households live on boats and rely on fishing using mobile gear, rather than fixed nets or traps in the lagoon. These people comprise the poorest of the poor and are heavily dependent on aquatic resources for food and income. This supports our hypothesis, noted above, that it is usually the poorest who are most dependent on the natural resource base to support their livelihoods. Moreover, this is the group most likely to be affected by changes in resource regimes.

Doi moi reforms in Viet Nam did not include policy direction for lagoons; instead these were privatized in an ad hoc fashion. In the middle lagoon at Tam Giang, new technologies and policy support led to an increase in net-enclosure aquaculture. In addition, the numbers of households participating in aquaculture increased and the numbers of net-enclosures and fish pens rapidly expanded. One consequence was the exclusion of poor mobile fishers from their customary fishing grounds when resources came under the direct control of wealthier users. Although smaller-capacity fishers had to compete for lagoon resources in the past, the intensity of competition and conflict now increased, with mobile fishers relying on the narrow waterways between net-enclosures. Government attempts at conflict resolution only exacerbated the situation. Without third-party intervention specifically aimed at managing this conflict, the livelihoods of mobile fishers were in decline and conflict increased.

However, in the northern lagoon, the research team played a central role in supporting interventions aimed at conflict resolution. The case argues against much of the literature cited in this chapter, demonstrating that CBNRM may indeed promote greater equality and the shared control of resources.

In Quang Thai, one of the poorest communities in the northern lagoon, the researchers supported a targeted pro-poor programme, providing training and technical advice in cage aquaculture and subsidies for the poorest households.

With trust having been developed after a history of working in the village, the researchers were able to promote participatory planning processes. A new user organization, a Fishing Coalition, was created for the management of the lagoon, and included all members of the fishing and aquaculture households, both fixed- and mobile-gear, rich and poor.

The research team then facilitated a consensus among the key stakeholders, including respected villagers, the Fishing Coalition, village leadership, the commune government, and representatives of district and provincial departments who were in charge of lagoon management. User groups were formed and helped refine, govern and enforce access and fishing practices, which met many of the resource planning purposes. Ninety per cent of village households participated in these user groups. Members of these user groups, including the mobile-gear and most marginalized fishers, were able to play a role in identifying and discussing problems, planning solutions and monitoring results on a more equal footing. The case concludes that the research team has been successful in engaging very poor households in the planning process and securing their access to lagoon resources. However, as we note below, including women and marginalized groups remains an ongoing challenge.

As part of their case study, Nong and Marschke (Chapter 8) relate a particular instance of conflict and its resolution during their research of in-migrant fishing villages located in and around Peam Krasaop Wildlife Sanctuary (PKWS) in Cambodia. They raise the important issue of the relationship between CBNRM and local politics, which, while rarely assessed in CBNRM studies, often play a major role in determining if new resource management regimes work for the poor or not. In addition, most of the case study countries are newly democratizing. That is, all are promoting local democratization in one way or another, even if several remain one-party states. In this sense, democratization has opened space for new village institutions. However, the CBNRM literature rarely addresses the implications of poverty reduction and inequities in establishing new resource management institutions parallel to political reforms.

Nong and Marschke discuss how conflict arose around distribution of water from holding tanks established by the village management committee (VMC) with support from the research team in one village located on a mangrove island. Two poorer households, active in the VMC, were selected as caretakers of the holding tanks. Several people complained to the research team that one of the female caretakers only sold water to members of a particular political party. Resolving this conflict involved the active facilitation of the research team. The team was obliged to remind all villagers publicly that resource management decisions were intended to benefit all users, and not be instruments of partisan political activity on either side.

Authors Nong and Marschke (Chapter 8, p. 165) reach an important conclusion concerning local politics and the likely impact of political bias on CBNRM:

> In Cambodia at least, community-based management work often ignores the influence of local politics. It is important that CBNRM initiatives are seen as

politically neutral so that all villagers can feel comfortable to participate. It is equally important that government facilitators do not spread their political beliefs to influence who participates in resource management at the local level. What needs to be fostered is the notion that technical departments have a role in supporting local resource management institutions.

While we might argue with the need for neutrality, given our bias towards the idea that CBNRM initiatives should actively promote the interests of the poor, the authors raise a key point for consideration by practitioners who must deal with local political interests if they are to establish successful resource management institutions. This raises a conundrum for CBNRM practitioners and action researchers: in order to be respected by all parties as facilitators of conflict-ridden community processes, they need to appear neutral, something that was also found in the Hue and Bhutan cases in this volume (Chapters 5 and 10). But how does this fit with our notion that CBNRM needs to be pro-poor and pro-gender equality? This points strongly to the need for a pro-poor policy, to which we return in the concluding section.

The case of co-management of Mongolian pasturelands, analysed by Ykhanbai and Bulgan (Chapter 6), provides further counter-evidence to the view that CBNRM management committees will necessarily be controlled by the rich and powerful. In this case study, they comment:

> Both rich and poor herders were interested in reducing environmental deg-radation and increasing economic benefits. But there were also some differ-ences between rich and poor. The latter were the most interested in being involved in CBNRM. This is because they needed to improve their liveli-hoods, secure pasture, participate in decision-making, and reduce the costs of herding animals through cooperation with others.

In the Mongolian case study, the main challenge was to involve the rich and powerful who already had preferential access to the resource in engaging in dialogue with the poor. Better-off herders may have feared CBNRM initiatives would affect them negatively by reducing their access to resources. This group also might have felt they did not want to engage in dialogue because of their social status. In Mongolia, the authors tell us, the rich herders initially were unwilling to join in the community organizations and co-management system. In other words, by boycotting CBNRM proceedings, rich herders hoped for the maintenance of the status quo. After repeated discussions with rich herders, the team persuaded them of the value of engagement. They became interested in addressing the problems of degraded grazing lands. As well, they were interested in maintaining positive social relations and ensuring that they had access to hired labour for agricultural production. The researchers report a high level of community cohesion after one or two years of co-management that involves continued external facilitation.

Similar issues were found in the Bhutan case (Chapter 10) where there was conflict between the upper and lower communities of the watershed when customary practice was highly inequitable. Communities in the upper watershed with unlimited access to the water supply did not want to jeopardize the status quo that benefited them. The research team took a normative position on the issue of equitable water rights as opposed to the narrow legalistic court rulings in favour of traditional practice. The signal of impending policy reforms, along with role-playing simulations and shared analysis of water volumes to ensure sufficiency, provided the impetus necessary to convince upstream users to relinquish some of their traditional rights.

We have highlighted four cases where action researchers have proactively attempted to engage and include diverse members of the community in new forms of NRM. Such cases demonstrate that a more equitable sharing of benefits probably will be continued, and that models of effective conflict resolution will be established. The role of researchers has been to not only guide, but, more importantly, to also increase dialogue between different factions in communities. It is important to monitor how far CBNRM groups can continue to be inclusive. As well, ongoing studies must be conducted to reveal whether CBNRM groups successfully redirect resources to the poor and marginalized, or whether even with external intervention such initiatives repeat many of the mistakes made in South Asia, as discussed in 'Conceptual issues', above. An additional question is whether this type of action research can develop models that are sustainable once researchers withdraw (see Chapter 16).

CBNRM, gender equality and participation

Communities are typically differentiated, divided, segregated, opposed, conflicting and split in many ways, and when it comes to CBNRM, perhaps no more so than by gender. As external interventions aim (and claim) to involve all stakeholders, more questions are now being raised as to who participates and who benefits, as well as how and when. Which stakeholders are involved? Are the poor included? Marginalized peoples? Women? How are they participating, in identifying problems, in planning, in designing and testing interventions, in implementing management plans, in evaluation?

These and related questions raise critical perspectives about who actually participates, but they also raise a challenge. How can participatory approaches to research and development enable these marginalized groups, including women, be more active participants and decision-makers in these programmes, in CBNRM and ultimately in the evolution of their societies? In this section, we explore these questions in relation to gender equality. While many stakeholders are increasingly aware of gender issues, patterns of gender exclusion persist, even among CBNRM interventions.

The copious literature on gender relations in Asia[5] highlights the region's widespread gender inequities, which are similar for issues of power, decision-making and control over natural resources. Women's participation is often limited by historic, social, cultural and political norms, which govern relations between women and men, including who should attend and speak at meetings, and how women and men should behave in public (Razavi, 2002; Agarwal, 2001). For example, in the case of water management, governments, donors and other stakeholders often view irrigation for agriculture as a male domain, although women are active agriculturists relying on these water resources. Men are often involved in constructing and maintaining the irrigation canals; women are not seen to be involved' or to have stakes in irrigation. As a result, development interventions limit women's participation in water user groups and resource management decision-making (Zwarteveen and Meinzen-Dick 2001; Resurreccion, Real and Pantana, 2004). In this collection of cases, the research teams all faced the challenges associated with addressing the issues of exclusion affecting women.

Even where there is participation of marginalized groups, including women, is it meaningful? Agarwal differentiates between nominal participation, essentially membership in a community group for representation, and active participation, where the powerless and marginalized actually have a voice in decision-making, thus leading to equality and empowerment. On the basis of research in India and Nepal on community forestry groups and water user groups, Agarwal (2001), Ahmed (2001) and Mohanty (2004) all argue that women's participation is generally nominal. This leads to few changes being made in gender resource-related roles, as well as responsibilities and rights at the household level.

This was also the case in the Tam Giang lagoon (Chapter 4) where group membership was defined at the household level and members were primarily men. The research team faced a real challenge in supporting the meaningful participation of women and very poor households in planning processes. In some cases, women from the better-off households did participate. Generally, these are in a better position to participate in community activities since they may have more financial security and spare time. However, even if women participated in the planning discussions, they were not very active and men dominated decision-making (Chapter 5). Promoting fuller participation of women is much more difficult because of complex field conditions than is typically represented in project documents.

The case studies illustrate how difficult it is to work towards gender equality or even to discuss strategies to promote more meaningful and equal participation of women. Even if they are included as members of a user group, women can find it difficult to participate. Many reasons exist for this: meetings may be held at inopportune times when they also have household, farm and family care responsibilities, or at locations that are socially awkward for women. This was a challenge noted in the Mongolia case study (Chapter 6) where meetings among nomadic herding households were held at distances of up to 15 km from the households' camps during the winter season. In the Vietnam uplands study, many women said they were not comfortable attending meetings in the community centre. The researchers noted:

The centre is usually too far from their homes and is mainly used by commu-nity leaders, not by women. They stated that they were uncomfortable in this setting. Organizing meetings near their hamlets facilitated higher attend-ance and more active engagement.

As a strategy to increase women's participation, some projects supported the establishment of separate groups for women. This provided a space for them to meet and voice their thoughts and concerns on problems related to resource degradation and discuss strategies to address them. As noted by the female secretary of a community group in the Mongolia case (Chapter 6, p. 116): 'Women have clear roles in natural resource management. By establishing a women's group, they can join and share opinions, make joint decisions, and help each other.' Such meetings have a much wider importance for women because they derive social support and opportunities for learning. The authors note: 'During community meetings, people could meet with each other and chat, get community help when someone was sick or needed money, or learn the best practices of herding, farming, and livelihood improvements from each other.' (p. 115)

In these ways, strategies supporting separate women's groups moved beyond the direct agenda of finding space for a voice in the management of the specific resource. Processes such as these can strengthen women's self-confidence and leadership skills, and build a collective identity. Such awareness helps transform some of the social and cultural norms that limit women's participation in the public sphere (Agarwal, 2001; Cornwall, 2003; Mohanty, 2004). In this volume's Guiyang case study (Chapter 9), women joined men farmers in the planning, decision-making, design and mobilization of resources in the resource management groups. The authors noted:

Increased numbers of community groups, especially women's groups, be-came organized and so women's voices became more prominent. As well, self-learning groups grew in importance. Meetings became more lively com-munity events whereby issues could be discussed. This broke with the past, when everyone simply had to listen to government officials deliver instruc-tions, and the villagers rarely met to develop a new activity.

There were similar findings in Vietnam and Mongolia:

Women's interest groups make women feel comfortable and confident so they can explain their problems, and plan and implement solutions by them-selves (Sen and An, 2006).

After one year, all initial co-management agreements were revised and re-approved in the communities taking into consideration the recommenda-tions of the women's groups. The ideas and perceptions of women were included so as to promote gender equity. As women defined their views on co-management agreements, they started to become more actively and mean-ingfully involved in the community decision-making around NRM (Chap-ter 6, p. 118).

In these cases, women now are recognized as initiators and active participants in making decisions regarding NRM. It is important to note that through these processes, it is not only those who have been marginalized who change their attitudes and actions. As the cases show, community leaders, government actors and extension agents are now more aware of the needs and priorities of these disadvantaged groups and are changing programmes accordingly to support their needs and participation (see, for example, Sen and An, 2006). The rich are also now more willing to listen to and engage in dialogue with the poor.

One characteristic of the literature on gender exclusion is that it has tended to deal with participation in formal user groups. Yet there may be other means of participation outside user groups that are sometimes invisible to the outside researcher – in other words tacit as opposed to explicit participation. This may involve men and women in a household making joint decisions on the use of natural resources (Shah and Shah, 1995), decisions made outside actual user group meetings, or formal decisions being subverted and undermined. While patriarchal and other political and cultural norms are powerful and widespread, there are many examples of these being challenged by marginalized groups (Scott, 1990; Sarin, 2001). As Agarwal notes (2001: 1643): 'Left to themselves, women typically rely on covert and individual forms of protest (their "everyday forms of resistance"), ranging from simply ignoring the [forest] closure rules or challenging the authority of the male guard, to persistent complaining.' However, researchers often take the view that women and men have conflicting interests rather than being involved in a form of cooperative conflict where roles and responsibilities are negotiated (Sen, 1990). Therefore, researchers can miss less formal types of participation.

In the case of the Tam Giang lagoon in Vietnam, Le, Nguyen and Nguyen (2002) describe an interesting case where gender roles have been used by poor women to their advantage. In Tan Duong commune, male and female mobile-gear fishers have customarily shared fishing activities. However, after enclosure many households had to find alternative employment because they lost their claims to the fishing grounds. In those households which maintained fishing activities, women became the main fishers in narrow waterways between net-enclosures. In Tan Duong, mobile-gear fisherwomen were able to acquire better access to fishing grounds than men. Aquaculturists allowed women to fish in the waterways between net-enclosures, but denied the same right to men. They said that men might be more likely to use more powerful and destructive fishing practices, such as motorized dragnets. Female mobile fishers were able to capitalize on assumptions about the more trustworthy nature of their gender to negotiate rights where male family members were unable to do so.

While this case may appear unusual on the surface, there are very likely other unexplored examples in CBNRM of disadvantaged groups using the characteristics that marginalize them to their advantage.

Conclusions

Action researchers and practitioners working on CBNRM are faced with a number of difficult questions: How can the poor and marginalized be included in CBNRM when they already face highly exploitive and unequal social structures? How can this be done without alienating those, including the wealthy, whose support is usually needed for user groups to work? Should interventions be politically neutral, or specifically proactive towards the most marginalized? Should separate women's groups be established, or does this work against gender mainstreaming? How long can action researchers realistically be involved in facilitating participatory processes? When is the time to withdraw? What are the indications that, in the future, CBNRM can support the rights of the poor without external interventions? How much research time and effort needs to be put into understanding social processes in order to be able to intervene?

We certainly do not have clear answers to many of these questions. Nonetheless, after drawing on the experience of the cases, we can suggest some ways of progressing towards an actively pro-poor agenda. While noting that they interlock, we cover implications for three areas: research, policy and practice.

Implications for research

What are the research implications? We know that without external intervention CBNRM may support marginalization of the poor, and in particular poor women who are most dependent on the natural resource base. These represent processes already promoted by marketization and privatization in most Asian countries. This reality, combined with the many questions mentioned above, suggest that there is a need for greater action research capacity to understand social dynamics in Asia and to feed CBNRM policies and practice. It is challenging for researchers to generate field-based evidence of the equity implications of CBNRM in practice, because these can be subtle. As well, attention can be easily diverted to broad resource conservation concerns.

This section identifies some examples from the cases in this volume which illustrate how researchers can start down this path, so that they can provide analytical guidance and generate best practices which pay specific attention to questions of gender, poverty and inequality.

In many development arenas in Asia, issues of social and gender equality in CBNRM institutions are colloquially termed as second-generation problems. That is, in countries such as Nepal and India where there have been over two decades of community forestry, joint forest management or water users' associations, the development focus has been on the overall community. It is only recently that issues of inequality within communities have been given more attention. One government actor in a country newer to such decentralization noted: 'First we are worrying about decentralizing governance to the community. Equity issues are "second generation" and we can deal with those later down the road.'

Postponing issues of equality as well as inclusion and exclusion to a next generation of development interventions is dangerous. In countries which are new to these processes of devolution of NRM, there are an opportunity and a necessity to learn from the bad experiences elsewhere in Asia and actively address these critical issues at the outset as first-generation.

Here, action research can play the crucial role of highlighting issues of poverty and gender equality. Explicit attention must be given to this analysis because it affects different contexts of precisely how CBNRM can strengthen the agency, rights and livelihoods of the poorest, of women, ethnic minorities and other marginalized peoples. Several of the cases in this volume provide useful examples of ways in which researchers have tailored their fieldwork, their participatory processes and their analysis to direct attention to these questions. They have made efforts to ensure that the structure of interventions addresses the priorities and constraints of these groups, and their facilitation has helped build the confidence and negotiating skills of society's weakest. Such interventions are critical because they strengthen participatory research and ensure that it generates the kinds of insights which are needed in order to expand beyond the localized level of a project, to become an integral part of policies and implementation programmes.

Successfully targeting the poor in hierarchical societies has proved extremely difficult. Most development strategies do not meet the expectations placed upon them, and very often programmes benefit the non-poor instead. However, ensuring environmental sustainability while further marginalizing the poorest sections of the population is an unacceptable development strategy. Experience in the field of CBNRM shows that unless it is proactively pro-poor, pro-gender equality and pro-ethnic equality, it will harm the very groups it aims to assist. In other words, 'If we are not for them, then we are against them.'

Implications for policy

It is critical to examine the central importance of policy. We want to emphasize that policies must consider explicitly issues of equality and inclusion at all levels of governance, and must place greater emphasis on implementation strategies that support and enable the rights of the poor and marginalized. Participatory research on CBNRM can play a crucial role in guiding and informing the development and implementation of policies which are more relevant to local realities and needs. As well, such research can strengthen the equality, rights and decision-making power of women, the poor and ethnic minorities.

One of the first questions to ask is how policies which are typically aimed at environment and natural resource management specifically address issues of poverty reduction and social or gender equality. We discussed above how policies that decentralize NRM, as well as marketization and privatization, can exacerbate inequality in a community. More needs to be understood about the role and potential of policies to support and strengthen the rights and livelihoods of the poor and marginalized in the context of CBNRM (see Larson, 2004, for a review of 20 countries from the global south). As Di Gregorio et al. (2004: 4) argue:

> Demand for research on the links between poverty and the institutions governing property rights and collective action is widespread and growing ... A wide range of policymakers (those guiding local and national government officials, non-governmental organization decisions, donor representatives) require relevant research findings that can be transformed into policies on property rights and collective action to improve the livelihoods of the poor.

In order for natural resource policies to be effective, they must draw on experiences in the field, so that they can address the diversity of local realities and situations. In several case study countries, these policies are relatively new or currently being developed. Research from the case studies is timely, enabling research results to influence policy (see Chapter 17). In addition, field-based results sometimes illustrate important equity outcomes from devolution, rights transfers and resource management policies.

Many unknowns remain regarding how such new policies and their implementation can help strengthen the livelihoods of the poor. In many cases, involvement of indigenous or marginalized groups in the official co-management of resources is new. Even for policies that aim to be equitable, little is known about their implementation and how they may play out on the ground. Research and development actors must also address the very real possibility that CBNRM policies may inadvertently perpetuate or exacerbate exclusion. Such policies must be informed by iterative research and analysis that can monitor the implementation of policy reforms and reveal gender-and poverty-differentiated impacts within communities.

Implications for practice

We must also consider implications for practice. What can realistically be expected of CBNRM in terms of promoting equality and poverty reduction? Given the range of contexts in Asia, we cannot hope to be prescriptive here, but only suggest some ways forward.

Four of the case studies discussed above suggest that external facilitation is required to ensure that changes in resource regimes do not lead to the increased marginalization of poorer groups. The research teams in these cases have taken a multistakeholder, participatory approach to CBNRM. Despite constraints that limit the inclusion of some groups, these researchers attempted to create space for discussion and include all villagers, including women. This demonstrates how facilitators of CBNRM must be able to see the perspectives of different village interest groups, possess strong negotiation skills and proactively support NRM that provides sustainable benefits to the poor. These are not easy tasks. However, a multistakeholder, participatory approach is a key strategy for achieving these goals. Experience from these cases adds much to the knowledge base. Practitioners need to strengthen their familiarity with multistakeholder tools and processes, with a particular view to ensuring that poorer groups are playing a more equal role in planning and decision-making on livelihood development and resource access. This has to include meaningful participation in village meetings, as well as representations to local and higher levels of government.

In terms of what is feasible in order to promote gender equality successfully, several of the cases (for example, in China, Mongolia, Cambodia and Vietnam) demonstrate steps towards the more meaningful participation of women. This includes incorporating women in village committees, holding meetings in places convenient for women, or setting up separate women's groups for resource management or income generation. These tentative first moves towards promoting gender equality are appropriate given the patriarchal nature of most Asian societies, and the need to build confidence and avoid any backlash. Over time, projects can work towards further inclusion of women in village committees, through quotas if necessary, in positions of power, such as the chair or secretary, and as active participants in meetings. Capacity development and training may be necessary for this.

Action researchers and practitioners need to pay particular attention to the missing voices of the marginalized. If poor people do not come to researchers and practitioners, then researchers and practitioners must go to the poor. Ongoing reassessment of the impacts on poverty, inequity and gender equality in any intervention must be conducted through planning workshops of project teams and in the villages themselves. After all, we are dealing with the most intractable of development problems.

Researchers, practitioners and policy-makers also need to consider carefully how effective CBNRM interventions actually are, from the standpoint of poverty and gender equality. The most obvious indicator of a CBNRM project which successfully addresses these questions is equitable and sustainable resource use, that is, providing more resources that will be available in the future for those who are the most dependent on them; typically, poor women comprise this segment of the population. A litmus test of whether CBNRM is effective might be to talk to poor women and see what the results have been for them. If they do not believe they are benefiting, there may be a problem.

Although this type of research is not easy, the goals emphasize that research must be directed for the most disadvantaged groups. We must be 'for them', and we must endeavour to support ways that CBNRM can strengthen the rights and livelihoods of the poor and the marginalized.

Acknowledgements

The authors would like to thank Silke Reichrath for background research on a parallel literature review paper, as well as helpful comments on earlier drafts from fellow authors in this volume, in particular Stephen R. Tyler; and inspiration from Luis Figo and Thierry Henry.

CHAPTER 16

CBNRM communities in action

Peter Vandergeest

Introduction

CBNRM advocates often take the concept of community for granted (Agarwal and Gibson, 2001: 8; Mansuri and Rao, 2004: 13) as the basic form of social organization in the countryside in regions like Asia (Lynch, Talbott and Berdan, 1995; Vandergeest, 2004). At the same time, however, some of the more convincing criticisms of CBNRM, those based on detailed fieldwork, argue that one of the most serious practical problems inherent in CBNRM practice revolves around unexamined assumptions about the nature of rural communities (Li, 1996, 2002; McDermott, 2001). These critiques have had some impact in policy circles and among development practitioners (Mansuri and Rao, 2004), calling into question the value of community-based approaches to natural resource management and development.

The effectiveness of the projects described in this volume and the continued importance of the concept of community in more people-centred development work, however, point to a need to go beyond the critiques, so as to develop a more robust and realistic concept of community than what currently circulates among uncritical advocates of CBNRM. A more robust notion could better highlight its potential as an approach that is not just about micro-level intervention, but which also contributes to restructuring broader development practices, power relations and the distribution of economic benefits. This stronger and nuanced concept of community is, therefore, an essential element of more effective practice in development work.

In this chapter, I examine the concept of community as it emerges from the case studies in this volume. I will pay particular attention to how these communities were made, how they were structured and what they did. The accounts of community contained in this volume on CBNRM in practice can be compared and contrasted with how community is typically understood in the academic and practitioner literatures on CBNRM.

I will show that that the studies described in this volume may not give much self-conscious attention to the concept of community (with a few exceptions). Nonetheless, they present a complex notion of how communities are made, what they do, and how they facilitate collective action. I will highlight three aspects of these complex communities:

1. these projects brought together both local and trans-local networks of actors to make communities;
2. the communities can be usefully understood as ways of mobilizing collective action around common projects; and
3. by doing this, communities become collective actors, active both locally and in broader networks.

My analysis points to how CBNRM can do much more than simply organize interventions for the management of natural resources. Understood broadly, CBNRM can also make a substantial contribution to a broader rethinking of sustainable development, one that takes account of ways that rural people can act collectively. This broad perspective also points to the way that the communities described in this volume were the product of hard work by rural people, project teams and government actors. Because of this, they represent fragile accomplishments that need continued effort to be sustained.

I will use the term 'CBNRM community' to highlight how the communities discussed in these case studies were the product of CBNRM research projects. I should be clear that I am not arguing that there was a vacuum before organizers came in and made a new community. The point is that the projects remade or transformed existing institutions and networks into what I call CBNRM communities, based on a combination of trans-local methods and local practice. In other words, the studies described in this volume produced specific kinds of communities, whose characteristics I will attempt to summarize.

Critical perspectives

CBNRM and participatory development are often framed as alternatives to top-down development planning. Over time, this vision has been undermined somewhat as large development institutions have mainstreamed community-based development (Cooke and Kothari, 2001; Mansuri and Rao, 2004). Proponents of alternative approaches link development based at the local level with sustainability, social justice and resistance to top-down, mainstream development. These views are often expressed as the prioritizing of local communities in development practice. That is, alternative development is often based on the notion of the community as a social group bound by locality, with the idea that localities should be the starting point for development.

CBNRM programmes can have many different motivations, too many to review here. If we limit our attention to alternative development, however, at its core CBNRM means finding ways of increasing the participation of rural communities in resource management, especially in environments where many resources are claimed as state property by government resource agencies: forestry, water, fisheries. The argument is that rural communities have a more intimate knowledge of their localities than state resource agencies. They also have a greater stake in managing resources sustainably, because their livelihoods depend on it. These arguments complement ethical arguments about the rights of communities to use resources in places where they may have lived for many generations. CBNRM, along with the protection of common property institutions, is promoted as a way of helping the poor and vulnerable in society to gain more secure access to livelihood resources (Johnson, 2004). In a broader economic and political context in which both socialist collectivization and centralized state NRM have been largely discredited, CBNRM also promises to address a need for finding ways of managing resources through decentralized collective action (see Chapter 2).

What is notable in all this is the way that advocates of CBNRM and common property often frame local communities as existing outside state and market institutions. The more political scholar activists often go further and argue that states and markets are the main threat to local communities and common property management (Li, 2001; Vandergeest, 2004). However, even among those whose views about market integration and joint forest management with state agencies are more positive, the basic assumption still tends to be that local communities are outside these institutions.

Many elements of alternative development theory and practice have been subjected to critical examination (Li, 1996, 2002; Brosius, Tsing and Zerner, 1998; Bebbington, 2000; Agarwal and Gibson, 2001; Hart, 2001). The most useful critiques acknowledge that simplifications are necessary for effective policy advocacy on behalf of rural people whose access to resources may be threatened by state claims or private interests, but go on to cast doubt on whether the particular simplifications associated with CBNRM and common property advocacy might not cause more harm than good for many rural people (Li, 1996, 2002). The critics present evidence that rural people such as migrants to upland areas who do not fit into the kinds of stable local communities assumed by this approach can be marginalized or erased from consideration. They argue that this approach is often characterized by a lack of attention to gender, class, caste or racial differences in rural areas, and that CBNRM can have the effect of diverting resources to local male elites (Beck and Nesmith, 2001). And they point out that advocates of local development often ignore evidence that many rural people desire greater access to both markets and the state (Li 1996; Brosius, Tsing and Zerner, 1998; Vandergeest 2004). Some of the critics suggest that the older language of agrarian reform might be a better approach to policy advocacy for the rural poor. In particular, the problems of rural people might be better addressed through land reform and enhanced citizenship rights than community rights.

As I will outline in detail below, the chapters in this volume suggest that the practitioners who prepared these case studies have developed a better practical understanding of rural communities than that found in much of the literature on CBNRM or in advocacy circles. The critique outlined above, moreover, has been around now for close to 10 years, and a good part of the practitioner network has responded with increased attention to the issues it raises. As I describe below, rural difference is now addressed through gender analysis, wealth rankings and projects targeting the poor. These methods have become part of the repertoire of CBNRM projects that try to address inequalities, although there is cause for some scepticism about the impact of these exercises in countering entrenched local inequities (Chapter 15).

The considerable efforts put into increasing community capacity, building confidence and enhancing social cohesion suggest that in practice the projects in this volume do not take local communities for granted as pre-existing their projects. The case studies also demonstrate that community-based approaches can be effective ways of addressing some of the key problems facing rural people. For example, in situations where entire communities or villages do not have secure property rights, these insecurities are better resolved through community-based collective action than land reform. This does not take away from the relevance of inequality in property rights within communities, but does suggest that programmes to resolve these inequalities need to be undertaken within a broader understanding of the marginalized position of many rural communities vis-a-vis state and other claims on land and resources.

At the same time, the tension between simplifications that seem necessary for effective policy advocacy for the resource rights of local people on one hand, and the inherent dangers posed by ignoring the complexity of rural communities on the other, is not going to go away. The basic issues emerge over and over again. Thus it is not enough to simply expose and criticize the romanticization of the local that is inherent in alternative development arguments. It is also important to find ways of advocating for local or community rights in the face of state claims or private development that are not so susceptible to the problems outlined by the critique. What these studies demonstrate is that the agendas of agrarian reform that focus on rural inequalities and complexity on one hand, and community-based development efforts on the other, are not necessarily incompatible. It depends what is meant by community, what these communities do and how inequalities within communities are addressed.

Constructing communities

Some reflection and a brief review of literatures on communities and community activists show that there are many different ways of understanding community. Some of these include the following.

- People who live together in a specific locality or territory such as in rural villages and urban neighbourhoods (Agrawal and Gibson, 2001: 8–9).
- The existence of dense or frequent forms of social interaction, a concept now often linked among development practitioners to the notion of social capital (Meinzen-Dick and Di Gregorio, 2004). More recently, this approach has given considerable attention to social networks that can stretch across localities. For example, trans-local migrants often organize their lives across borders; and electronic communications facilitate the formation and main-tenance of diverse networks across space.
- Shared norms, linked to locally made institutions for organizing collective action to enforce these norms (Agrawal and Gibson, 2001: 10–12). Examples

include prohibitions on the use of spirit or conservation forests, or collective institutions for distributing access to land for swidden farming.
- Local administrative institutions created by the state, in particular, administrative villages.
- Collective imaginaries, or the way that certain collectives imagine themselves having commonalities or collective identities. Examples include national communities, ethnic groups, indigenous peoples and peoples affected by dams.

This list indicates that there is a wide range of ways of understanding community. All have some relevance to the case studies in this volume, and in practice there is considerable overlap. But for the purposes of this chapter, it is worth thinking through the contrast between what might be called the locality-based versus network approaches to understanding communities.

Locality-based approaches to community

Locality-based approaches begin by asking if people living in close proximity for a long period of time can develop shared norms and collective institutions for managing resources. This understanding often allows for the incorporation of the concept of locality into community through the term 'local community'. It can also be tied into territorial definitions of local communities. In other words, a community consists of the people living in a given territory. Finally, it is often linked to the concept of tradition through the assumption that many local communities in rural areas have developed stable norms and institutions by virtue of living with each other and facing collective challenges over a long period of time. At a smaller scale this approach has led to many community studies in the disciplines of anthropology and sociology,[1] although it can be scaled up to the idea of homogeneous national communities and traditions.

Community-based development often draws on this tradition of community when studies assume the persistence of stable and relatively homogeneous rural communities. It can be argued that these traditional communities are capable of undertaking development initiatives for the common good. Many proponents of alternative community-based development add that community stability depends on maintaining some kind of boundary or separation between local communities on one hand, and institutions external to the community, especially states and markets, on the other hand. Boundaries and exclusion are also tenets of common property theory (Chapter 7).

Network approaches to community

The second approach to communities is currently gaining influence in academic research. The focus is less on the boundaries separating local communities from external institutions or other communities, and more on how these are connected and how they construct each other through these connections. Or, put differently, the focus is less on the attributes of communities that emerge out of local interaction, and more on social relationships emerging from networks that span localities (Massey, 1993; Raffles, 1999; Li, 2001). Although such networks are located in space, they are not necessarily contained by spatial boundaries, nor are they located in just one locality. For example, research on transnational migration now pays a lot of attention to how communities can be made across localities that are often separated by national or other borders. The term 'trans-local' is becoming popular as a way of pointing to how these networks cannot escape locality, while simultaneously underlining how they are also not contained by just one locality.

In practice, these case studies suggest that both of these approaches are relevant for CBNRM. Most authors do not discuss whether they understand community in terms of bounded territory or social networks. However, all the studies described in this book began with the assumption that communities were at least partly defined by geography. Most often, community was understood in terms of territorially based administrative units like villages or communes. This is reinforced by the way that the collective NRM practices that give CBNRM its name usually rely on clear and exclusive definitions both of the community and the resources to be managed. The idea that CBNRM is in part about creating boundaries around localities in order to exclude resource users who are not community members comes through clearly in a number of papers in this volume. The most explicit statement was made by Ykhanbai and Bulgan, in their chapter (Chapter 6) on the co-management of pastureland in Mongolia. They write that for their paper 'community refers to a geographical area containing a number of herder households'. A key issue this project had to grapple with was when and how to exclude herders who were not community members. Tubtim's chapter (7) on community fisheries in Laos points out that the idea of collective benefits is widely accepted in rural Laos, but refers exclusively to a single village. In this situation, 'when a particular resource becomes scarce or valuable in the market, village boundaries can be easily brought into play to claim exclusive rights'.

At the same time, the case studies give considerable attention to the way that the projects were implemented through social networks of various kinds, some of them local, but often trans-local. Many of the case studies in this volume emphasize the importance of networking, with NGOs, neighbouring communities, state actors and so on. Even the territorial boundaries of communities can often be understood as the product of social networks, so that the second approach can encompass the first. In other words, administrative villages, herder groups and other territorially defined resource user communities are defined through social interactions with states, or with external donor projects.

My reading of the case studies in this volume suggests another definition of community that might be particularly useful for CBNRM, one that offers a way of incorporating both approaches to communities. All these case studies mention community not only in terms of networks and territories, but also as collective action. The cases outline how the projects facilitated 'voluntary action taken by a group to achieve common interests' (Meinzen-Dick and Di Gregorio, 2004). More specifically, these case studies all describe instances of people acting collectively to manage resources and to achieve a series of other collective goals related to NRM. I should immediately add, however, that interests in practice need not be common for this kind of collective action to occur (Chapter 7), and that this does not imply that all members of a community participate in or benefit from collective action in the same way (Chapter 15).

I am not trying to suggest that the notion of community as collective action is the correct one; only that it is a particularly useful one when thinking about CBNRM communities. Nor does it imply abandoning other ways of understanding community. Rather, we can work them into this way of understanding community by paying attention to the ways that collective action can be facilitated and structured both by the spatial arrangement of people and by social networks. In other words, the focus on collective action resolves the tension between geographical and network approaches by directing attention to a community-building process that can exhibit both network and geographical characteristics. It is also more dynamic and helpful to practitioners, because it draws attention to what people actually can do collectively. It focuses our attention on the ways that collective action can be mobilized to intervene in managing common pool resources (CPR), or secure better access rights to resources that are important for livelihoods. It thus fits well with an approach that thinks about community in terms of networks of actors. Collective action undertaken by communities can be understood in terms of both the local networks comprising the group and their specific roles, and how communities become one actor in a broader network of actors that include state agencies, private interests, development agencies, NGOs and others.

It is through collective action that groups of people become community-based actors. In the section below, I review in more detail what communities do when they become actors. If we take this approach, the relevant questions become reformulated into questions around the specific ways that people get organized to act collectively. For example, how is collective action facilitated by spatial arrangements, local histories and existing institutions for collective action? What is the role of the outsider in collective action? How does external financial support facilitate collective action? How do the links between a rural community and broader networks of actors facilitate or structure collective action? How might these interactions with broader networks affect policy formation and implementation (Chapter 17)? How might collective action be institutionalized and routine? How does it reflect power and inequality within community (Chapter 15)? How might it change these inequalities? How might collective action address broader inequities between communities and other powerful actors?

This approach also helps link CBNRM to practitioners and scholars concerned with identity. When a group of people becomes an actor, these people are creating a shared identity. Usually, identity is framed in terms of community, but collective identities can also emerge from other identities and roles: women's groups, indigenous peoples, the village poor, and farmers. It is worth briefly highlighting one of these broadly speaking ethnic (or racial) identities. Only a few of the case studies in this volume discuss ethnic identities explicitly as having an impact on resource management and property rights (examples include the Philippine Cordillera in Chapter 12; the two Cambodian community forestry cases, Chapters 3 and 11; and upland Vietnam, Chapter 5). Diverse ethnic identifications are a fundamental feature of rural life in Asia, and they are often linked to resource management and property rights. This is especially true in the upland and coastal zones where CBNRM projects are usually located.

In the rest of this section, before I move to what community actors do, I will elaborate upon some of the lessons that can be drawn from the case studies which describe how we think about community. I will discuss a series of characteristics of these communities, some of which overlap, but each of which is worth highlighting as important to developing a more realistic and robust concept of community in CBNRM practice.

Diverse actors

I have already mentioned that critics point to how CBNRM programmes and advocacy often assume that rural areas are comprised of stable communities, and that they often overlook or fail to address gender, class, caste or racial differences in rural areas. With respect to stability, for example, many if not most rural people in Asia have been mobile in the recent past, due to war, economic changes and state policies. It is usually the migrant communities which are blamed for resource degradation, have the most tenuous property rights and are poorest.

Nevertheless, this book suggests that CBNRM can work effectively in communities that have settled in their locations relatively recently. Nong and Marschke (Chapter 8) note that in coastal Cambodia it was the in-migrant fishing villages, consisting of households displaced from other provinces, who were initially most interested in participating in the CBNRM activities. Because they were new to the coast, they had not developed strong local institutions for managing resources. Their prevailing livelihoods (charcoal production) were insecure because they were illegal, and the project offered them a way of gaining legitimacy. The project in Hong Ha commune in Vietnam also worked with recently resettled communities, which similarly expressed a need for improved livelihood and resource management practices in their new environment.

When we think of communities in ways that do not rely on the assumption of the long-term stability of a homogeneous set of people, then we open CBNRM to a much broader range of practice. Now we can include communities that may not exhibit the sorts of characteristics associated with classic conceptions of stable social interaction and collective institutions. In particular, we can incorporate ways of doing CBNRM that target those who often need these activities the most, as Nong and Marschke's case suggests.

In cases where there were community-based institutions for managing resources prior to the research projects, the projects have had varied relations with the prior institutions. Communities were often self-consciously built on existing institutions (China, Bhutan). But it is also possible for government or NGO-led programmes in support of community resource rights to undermine existing community institutions, replacing them with less effective administrative institutions (Agrawal, 2001). In this book, Mendoza et al. describe how the community definitions created by certificates of ancestral domain in the Cordillera existed in tension with the *ili*, the traditional community. The certificates were awarded to a municipality, a territorially defined administrative community, but the municipality in turn consisted of several *ilis*. As indicated by the title of the chapter, their project was concerned with harmonizing the actions of these two communities. This chapter makes perhaps the clearest case for paying careful attention to diverse and changing expressions of community, because it was the definition of community that was built into the ancestral domain policy that produced the problems that the CBNRM project needed to resolve.

Similarly, in the Tam Giang lagoon project in Vietnam, the government was forced to think about how to constitute the collective entity that could hold collective resource rights. None of the existing legally recognized collective institutions (Farmers' Union, Women's Union and so on) were appropriate, and eventually one of the project's pilot activities was to form a user group-based community, the Fishing Coalition. These cases illustrate why writers of laws and policies need to work with legal definitions of community that allow for considerable leeway in how communities can be made at the local level. Sometimes they are best based in local government institutions, but sometimes they are not.

There is another sense in which CBNRM involves diverse kinds of communities and other actors. Most of the projects in this book began with administrative villages or communes as the unit around which people organize collective projects. But they very quickly became much more specific about who comprised the collective actors, and how they built on collective actions that preceded the project interventions. For example, the most common actors are committees organized around a particular task, which create management plans or build infrastructure. Sometimes actors are groups involved with many different kinds of activities and goals, such as marketing, crop improvement, credit or management of a specific resource, such as mobile-gear fishers in the Tam Giang lagoon in Vietnam.

This does not mean that such committees or groups actually comprise the community. Instead, committees typically act on behalf of some broader group of people that they call the community. Nonetheless, this focuses our attention on the way that many community-based activities are not the collective action of everyone living in a given area. Not everyone participates equally or in the same way in community actions. As Beck and Fajber make clear in Chapter 15, forms of inequality represented by economics, power, gender and other social relations are part of community. Therefore, careful examination of the local as well as trans-local networks of actors who are involved in collective action takes us beyond assumptions that communities are simply everyone living in a geographic area, although that assumption can remain a useful starting point.

In some countries, CBNRM activities have become so popular that village committees for mobilizing collective action are proliferating, creating problems with coordination, duplication, and organizational fatigue (Marschke, 2004; Mendoza et al., Chapter 12). The Cordillera project addressed this problem through the formation of yet another collective institution, an interagency committee for NRM. Below I discuss how making CBNRM communities requires work and effort. This suggests that it is important for practitioners and policy-makers to pay careful attention to the demand placed on rural people by community-based initiatives that rely on local participation or work. Heavy demands on time, the scheduling of meetings and difficult logistics all represent complicating factors in the effort to include women and the poor in community-based work. For instance, Mongolian women were unable to leave their domestic duties to make 15-km trips in midwinter to attend meetings.

Cooperation and conflict

Some chapters go further, and discuss conflicts among the resource user groups or among individuals who comprise rural communities. The chapter on coastal Vietnam is exemplary in highlighting the diversity of actors and violent conflicts over resource access among different user groups. In these cases, the kinds of collective action that defined community became highly contentious. Other chapters that address conflicts or disputes over resource access within or among communities include those on Laos, Cambodia, Mongolia and Bhutan. These chapters demonstrate that the assumption of harmonious communities is not essential for CBNRM to be effective. Indeed, the most effective projects in terms of facilitating collective action to manage resources, secure tenure access and enhance livelihoods are those that aim to understand how conflicts among rural people can be based on inequalities. Such discrepancies can be in access to resources, or in the ways that economic and political changes may threaten the resource access of some groups while promising benefits to others. We can go so far as to say that collective action does not need to be based on shared interests at all. Instead, as Tubtim explains in her case study in Laos (Chapter 7), CBNRM can be a platform allowing for a single process involving actors with diverse interests and worldviews. In this sense, CBNRM can be a way for diverse groups to find ways of working through conflicts of interest and worldviews, to achieve multiple goals.

Power relations and inequality

If we pay attention to the way that communities are not necessarily based on common interests, but may also be multiple collectives that reflect economic and power differences among rural people, then we are taking an important step towards addressing many of the possible problems identified by critics of CBNRM. Many more mainstream CBNRM projects give this only superficial attention. However, an examination of this volume's case studies demonstrates how the CBNRM repertoire includes methods allowing practitioners to address the need to work differently with various groups in communities. Attention to the gendering of livelihood practices and resource access was common to many of these projects. Sensitivity to differences in wealth was expressed through the wealth-ranking exercises that have become a standard feature of this approach, one used in most of the projects described in this volume, although not always mentioned in the case study chapters.[2] In other words, the template for doing CBNRM at the village level does not ignore differences within communities. The studies in Bhutan and Mongolia mention that the project formed groups based on relative wealth in order to address the specific needs of each group and as a way of targeting the poor. Both projects in Vietnam devoted considerable effort to identifying and working with poorer people, while the Lao fisheries project also highlighted different impacts the project had on wealthy and poor villagers.

Identifying, organizing and working with the rural poor is one thing, but projects that aim to actually change how inequality can be based on unequal access to resources are another. In the next section on what communities do, I discuss the question of whether CBNRM activities can or do address the causes of inequality in the context of understanding CBNRM communities. Beck and Fajber discuss this more fully in Chapter 15.

The cases paid less explicit attention to issues of power in rural communities. To my knowledge, an assessment of power relations has not yet been worked into standard field repertoires for CBNRM more generally. Therefore, it is not surprising that these cases did not apply standardized techniques to trace and address power differentials, in a manner similar to those addressing inequalities of wealth. But at the same time, the cases in this volume demonstrate it is difficult to avoid engaging with local power relations if researchers aim to target poorer villagers and inequitable gender relations. Case studies that address power relations in CBNRM include those on Laos, coastal Vietnam and coastal Cambodia. Other chapters mention local power indirectly, for example, in discussions of how collective institutions are organized, and most often, in struggles that occurred in communities over specific projects. Tuyen et al.'s chapter (Chapter 4) makes explicit how CBNRM practices in the coastal lagoon involved finding ways of mediating struggles among different user groups. Tubtim (Chapter 7) mentions how in Laos it was normally the village committees that were influential in making decisions, and that not all villagers were fully active in village meetings. In Bhutan (Chapter 10), upstream water users benefited from their advantaged location to gain preferential access to water, and resisted attempts to find more equitable ways of allocating water supplies.

Articulation with government institutions

Many of the studies described in this volume are concerned with local resource rights, often in opposition to the claims of state resource agencies. This should not be taken to mean that rural communities are created in opposition to the state and market. To the contrary, the projects address these sorts of conflicts not by keeping the state out of the community, but rather by inviting the state into them. The goals usually include finding ways of convincing state actors to provide formal recognition of informal management and access rights.

Along the way, community-based institutions for organizing collective action often broaden to incorporate non-community-based collective actors to negotiate conflicts, allocate resources or draw up management plans. The coalition of actors involved typically includes village authorities, village-based user groups, project staff and local governments. For example, in coastal Vietnam, planning for allocating resource access began with a workshop that brought together project staff, fishing user groups, the village leadership, the commune government and representatives of district and provincial departments. As Tuyen et al. write, the 'new participatory planning process ... emerged from interaction among resource users and other concerned stakeholders'. Other chapters also describe how community resource access and management are organized through institutions that bring together CBNRM teams, government authorities and rural people. These cases include those on the Cordillera project, Mongolia, Laos, China and all the Cambodia cases.

The ties between rural communities and the state that characterized most of the projects described in this book were reinforced by the way most projects worked with the village or commune administrations. These institutions are the lowest level of government civil administration, and although they are usually comprised of elected villagers, they nevertheless represent the state in the village, as Tubtim notes in her Lao case study (Chapter 7). In this way, the projects accepted that these hybrid state-village institutions were an important part of how communities organized collective action.

State institutions affected the formation of community in other ways as well. For example, resource management plans were often based on what forestry departments or other government authorities consider legitimate. Although relations between local government officials and village/user groups described in these chapters were sometimes difficult, the cases capture many examples of how villagers, village authorities and government officials worked together to achieve collective ends, or worked together on common projects even when they had different interests.

One reason for the spread of CBNRM is that practitioners have worked out a repertoire of practices and institutions that can make sense both to villagers and to government officials, enabling cooperation even where objectives may differ. Nonetheless, tensions exist. For villagers, for example, enlisting government assistance requires reconciliation with official definitions of community, technocratic criteria for resource management, and in some cases accepting a government role in managing what villagers might previously have considered their own resources. Government officials must recognize that villagers have knowledge and skills that can be helpful in meeting some of their objectives, although other objectives may be compromised. But overall, the close interaction between state administration and rural people described in this volume belies images of rural communities that are separate from – or in simple opposition to – local government (Chapter 17).

A concept of community that allows for conflict also allows us to see that in part, rural communities are made through interaction with state institutions, even when that interaction includes conflict. Without exception, CBNRM communities described in this volume were constructed through complex relationships between government agencies and rural institutions, instead of outside government.

Engagement with markets

The other kind of opposition that sometimes characterizes CBNRM advocacy is one between rural communities and common property on one hand, and private actors and markets on the other. Are local communities opposed to markets? Is common property incompatible with private property? It is true that in many of the cases in this book, communities acted to curtail the expansion of private property rights at the expense of common property resources. For example, one of the goals of the Cambodian community forestry project was to create and formalize community forests so as to stop timber poachers and agrofood entrepreneurs from privatizing and destroying forests. The lagoon project in Vietnam worked to maintain community access in the face of the enclosure of lagoon resources. In Mongolia, community control of pasture was strengthened to help solve problems caused by unregulated private use.

A single-minded focus on these apparent oppositions, however, would misrepresent the way that communities often form around ways of regulating or improving market access. There is no inherent contradiction between market engagement and the strengthening of community control over common property.

Many of the cases in this book describe projects designed to increase the productivity of common property or privately held resources so that villagers can get more income by having more products to sell in local markets. What made the work specifically CBNRM was the application of collective sustainability objectives to activities aimed at increasing market integration. Projects in upland Vietnam, Mongolia, China and the Philippines worked to enhance commodity production and monetary income. Their efforts included the improvement of specific commercial crops, better pasture management, rotating credit schemes and collective marketing. For example, in Laos, the government and village authorities involved in the communal fish pond understood the project represented an investment in increased productivity. Fish caught through communal fishing was sold in the market and the income used to fund a primary school, while privately caught fish were also sold, especially by poor women.

In summary, the projects described in this volume aimed to find collective ways of controlling unregulated market activities and stopping unsustainable use of common property resources. This is not the same as saying that common property and local communities are opposed to markets. On the contrary, it is impossible to understand the formation of communities without addressing the way in which rural people are already integrated into markets and usually want to increase their engagement with appropriate community-based regulations. This implies that advocates and practitioners of CBNRM should devote increased attention to the way that power and benefits are distributed in market processes. It also suggests that a community-based approach to market engagement might include facilitating the collective regulation of commodity production, for example, through community involvement in certification. In particular, practitioners might give more attention not only to ensuring that market processes do not undermine resource access among the poor through privatization of common property, but also to exploring ways of instituting markets in ways that allow for the increased capture of benefits by the poor (Ribot, 1995; Watkins and Fowler, 2003).

Articulation with CBNRM networks

In this chapter, my basic argument is that CBNRM communities are made through CBNRM projects, which are in turn part of broader networks that research, practise and promote CBNRM. Practitioners in these networks develop new techniques and analyses, which then move across sites, to be appropriated and further refined in new sites. All of this produces a repertoire for practice: how to facilitate the collective action that characterizes a CBNRM community. This does not mean that there were no communities before the projects, but simply that the projects draw on models that circulate through CBNRM networks to remake existing institutions for collective action, or in some cases build new institutions. Every case study in this volume, with the possible exception of the policy-oriented writeshops presented by O'Hara (Chapter 13), describes how project teams worked with rural people to build institutions, increase their confidence, plan NRM and so on. What made these projects more than simply another way of imposing new institutions on rural people was the commitment to meaningful participation and local leadership. Participation was organized by the CBNRM project teams, but was also a way for villagers to work with project members to identify forms of collective action appropriate to their circumstances.

This idea can be illustrated by the case studies located in transitional economies. In these sites, the communities created by the research projects often filled voids left by the dissolution of collectivization. Although collectivization was often resisted or failed to take hold, especially in Laos and Vietnam, in other cases it superseded local institutions for managing resources.

For example, according to Ykanbai and Bulgan (Chapter 6), in Mongolia customary management institutions that had been in the control of feudal officials, clans and tribal groups were dissolved in 1921 and replaced with state ownership and centralized management. In 1992, when the government moved to a more market-oriented system, herders were left with very little collective management. In this situation, herders needed the research project's outside intervention to introduce CBNRM as a form of co-management. Similarly in Guizhou, China, the end of the rural commune system in which farmers were organized to work and manage resources collectively left villagers with few incentives and few formal institutions for this purpose. Again, CBNRM project activities helped fill this gap, in part by building on informal collective institutions.

In some mainstreamed approaches, CBNRM networks can affect local action by rigidly imposing a formal model without regard for local context. While this may often be the case when CBNRM ideas are applied broadly by government agencies or larger institutions (Vandergeest, 2003), the case studies in this volume demonstrate how a flexible model can be applied sensitively in response to varying local circumstances. When applied like this, projects often adopt new or unexpected meanings and opportunities. One important dimension of this flexibility involves the many ways that local communities can be made or remade through participatory research and collective action.

Outcomes of hard work

A striking feature of the chapters in this volume is just how hard the project teams, rural people, programme officers, NGO staff and sometimes even government officials worked to achieve the many results described by the authors. CBNRM project staff spent much time traveling to and staying in rural areas. As well, rural people travelled to and attended meetings, did resource assessments and mapping, planned resource management, enforced rules and regulations, performed trials of specific crops, visited government offices and accomplished many more tasks. In the case of Mongolia, community members sometimes had to travel 15 km on horseback in winter temperatures that even most Canadian participants in this collective effort had never experienced. The point is that communities described in this book do not just exist naturally; rather, they are the product of considerable effort or work.

This observation is important not only because the project teams participating in this book should be recognized for their hard work and dedication. It also points to a fundamental characteristic of CBNRM communities: if communities are the outcome of ongoing work, it must be recognized that when people stop working, these communities can disappear. This does not mean that the memories or multilayered institutional legacies of these communities disappear or that they cannot be recovered. What it does mean is that communities are often fragile and unstable. As the kinds of work people put into making communities changes, the characteristics of the communities also change. When projects lose their funding, or when rural people lose their commitment, communities may decline. When the work involved in making communities becomes institutionalized, routine or supported by ritual practices, as described by Tubtim regarding Laos, communities can be stabilized or even become inflexible.

A central concern of many of these projects, which was discussed at length in several cases, is exactly how to stabilize communities so that they endure even without the input of project funding. According to O'Hara (Chapter 13), the projectization of community forest management in the Philippines is more about sustainable development assistance than sustainable forests. These projects are kept going by the incentives created by external funding, and they disappear when the funding ends because the larger problems based on disincentives in the policy environment are never addressed. Even when community-making work becomes institutionalized, routine or turned into ritual, it is easy to overestimate the stability of these practices, as earlier CBNRM advocates tended to do. Thus, the crucial characteristic of the communities described in this volume is that they are almost always the tenuous accomplishment of considerable effort, and because of this, they are unstable and in constant transformation.

CBNRM communities in action

I mentioned above that what CBNRM does more than anything else is facilitate collective action. This raised several questions. What kinds of collective action? What is specific about the collective action that defines it as being CBNRM? Since the emphasis in this chapter is on conceptualizing community, I will keep this discussion short as it is intended primarily to illustrate the broad range of collective activities in which CBNRM communities have engaged in these examples. In fact, CBNRM communities are actors both in relation to local issues and to trans-local networks, which include markets, government and so on. I will stress the latter because that is what is emphasized in many of the chapters, and it helps to counter the idea that the impacts of CBNRM work are limited to micro or local levels.

Although the activities covered in these case studies vary too widely for me to describe them all, some of the more important actions include:

1. managing resources;
2. holding and exercising property rights;
3. becoming a vehicle for multiple development activities and other types of collective action;
4. changing power relations and inequalities; and
5. becoming a voice for local villagers so that they can communicate to project staff, government and other actors.

Managing resources

All the projects described in this book were part of a broader programme to promote CBNRM; therefore, NRM was usually a core activity. Because the project was about community-based management, projects were oriented toward managing those resources where it made sense to take a collective approach. These included forests in, for example, the Philippines, Bhutan, Cambodia, Vietnam and China; water supplies for irrigation or household use in China and Bhutan; grazing lands in Mongolia; and fisheries in Vietnam, Laos and Cambodia.

The approach to the collective management of resources taken by these projects emerged in part from what we might call a kind of CBNRM methodological template. It circulates through the programming of the IDRC and, more generally, through community and common property advocacy circles (see Chapter 2). Usually this involves creating formal management plans, as well as doing wealth rankings, gender analysis and so on. But the methodological template also emphasizes the importance of local participatory processes to involve communities and work from local priorities. In some cases, management plans hardly involved project staff at all, for example, in the management plan for the fisheries project described by Tubtim. Resource management plans were also oriented towards doing what was necessary to obtain government recognition and thus formal legitimacy for community resource rights, as in Cambodia, Mongolia and the Philippines.

In the chapter (Chapter 11) on Cambodian community forestry, for example, Kamnap and Ramony detail the process leading to the creation of a management plan. They mention electing a community management committee, doing a forest assessment, creating a management plan with rules and restrictions regarding forest use and obtaining recognition from the provincial government. Plans were usually based on existing forest management and use, which were transformed into the kinds of territorialized zones and regulations required by the CBNRM management plan. However, the creative use of the CBNRM methodological template is indicated by the way communities frequently added many regulations to reflect new forest uses. For instance, in the case of lagoon management in Vietnam, the development of a fisheries management plan meant finding ways of resolving conflicts among different user groups, and involved government officials as well as community members.

The CBNRM template should not be considered only as an imposed form. In many cases the community used its formalization of resource management to address problems or conflicts that had emerged, for example, as forests became more oriented towards commercial use. One element of the management plans I have discussed is the inclusion of mapping the resource's territorial boundaries where very often there had been overlapping uses among different communities. In other words, the creation of a formal management plan often has the effect of defining exclusive community rights to some resources, while excluding other communities and reinforcing territorial definitions of community. In this way,

CBNRM contributes to redefining communities in a way that brings out territorial characteristics and, arguably, produces enclosures (Tubtim, Chapter 7; see also Tubtim and Hirsch, 2005).

Claiming and exercising property rights

This activity is closely related to the creation of management plans in two ways. First, property rights, including collective or common property, necessarily imply both exclusions and finding ways of distributing rights, obligations and benefits. I have already described how community-based property claims means excluding neighbouring communities. However, in other cases, it has enabled communities to exclude more powerful claimants – loggers, palm oil companies or the military – as illustrated by the two Cambodian case studies on community forestry.

Powerful actors making claims on community resources not only include extractive businesses, but also resource agencies in governments that have historically claimed jurisdiction and ownership of specific resources. The case studies in this volume mention forestry departments (Vietnam, Bhutan, Cambodia and the Philippines), irrigation departments, fisheries departments (Cambodia), conservation departments, watershed management authorities (Vietnam) and mineral departments (Cambodia). Many of these resource agencies are closely linked to private companies that hold concessions to extract resources or to NGOs and other international actors that provide resources and legitimacy to these agencies. The latter are especially important in the case of conservation and watershed protection. CBNRM emerged in part as a programme to defend community access to crucial resources over which they had weak or non-existent formal property rights. One strategy was to exploit differences within governments, specifically, to approach local authorities (or provincial governments) as a way of getting leverage on centralized government resource agencies.

Inherent in the exercise of establishing collective property rights is the allocation of responsibilities and benefits among community members. Most case studies did not describe these processes in detail, the exceptions being those cases that also paid more attention to inequality within communities, for example, Bhutan, China, Laos and coastal Vietnam. The way that this activity is organized is central to the way that CBNRM either reduces inequality or is captured by local elites for their own benefit.

Property rights require both legitimacy and enforcement. It is because of these requirements that government officials were brought into a project's activities. As the two case studies on community forestry in Cambodia make clear, government authorities are often reluctant to accept community claims to resources unless the community involved can demonstrate that the resources can be managed in ways that satisfy what they understand to be scientific criteria. For example, forestry management plans need to use zoning categories and regulations that are recognizable to professional foresters, or they will not be accepted as legitimate. This is especially clear in the cases of Bhutan, Cambodia and the Philippines.

Few of the case studies describe in much detail how property rights were enforced in communities. Nonetheless, as the case studies in China and coastal Vietnam and Cambodia show, the lasting impacts or failures of the CBNRM research projects often followed from the community's ability to enforce rules and regulations among its members. Enforcement became more difficult when the resources were of potential value to powerful actors outside the communities. In such cases, government recognition was crucial though not necessarily sufficient. For instance, a central goal of the two Cambodian community forestry cases was to give the communities a better chance of enlisting government support for their claims to resources.

Transforming power relations and some inequality

Beck and Fajber's chapter (Chapter 15) examines the question of CBNRM and equity in depth, but I include some brief comments here because of this subject's importance in the critique of community in CBNRM. Critics have argued not only that CBNRM often fails to recognize inequality and difference within a community, but also that interventions can exacerbate these inequalities. In practice, any project that changes people's livelihoods and reorganizes their access to resources must also have an impact on inequality. How has community collective action changed wealth, gender and other forms of inequality? Do the projects described here proactively seek to improve livelihood security for the most disadvantaged? Do they ensure that projects do not increase inequality? It is one thing to identify inequality and to devise projects that address the needs of the poor as well as the wealthy. It is another thing altogether to address and change the actual causes of the inequity.

In the agrarian studies approach, rural inequality was often identified with inequality in access to productive resources, especially land. If land was a key cause of inequality, the solution was either land reform or collectivization. With its broader attention to all natural resources, CBNRM has the advantage of potentially offering a more contextually sensitive assessment of the sources of inequality. These include not only a disparity in access to land, but also differential access to a variety of other natural resources such as fish, water and forests. Because of the emphasis on participatory approaches to identifying differences in wealth and livelihoods, CBNRM research can also potentially account for inequalities not directly linked to natural resource access. These include a variety of ways to access labour markets, migration and education.

At the same time, it could be argued that with its emphasis on the community, CBNRM often diverts attention from efforts to reduce intra-community inequalities in access to resources, or postpones them as problems to be addressed after community control has been secured (Chapter 15). Even projects that identify differences within communities might nevertheless take these as given and simply make sure that the specific needs of the different wealth groups are on their agenda, without specifically addressing the causes, or attempting to reduce inequalities. As described more fully by Beck and Fajber in Chapter 15, most of the case studies in this volume did recognize inequality. Some devoted considerable effort to working with the poorer strata in rural communities, and a few – such as those in Bhutan and coastal Vietnam – went beyond this and attempted to reduce local inequities in resource access.

It is important to recognize that attempts to reduce intra-community inequalities through CBNRM do have some significant limits. Even if the rural poor derive a large part of their livelihoods from common property resources, inequality is multidimensional. These CBNRM case studies do not make any attempt to address inequalities that are not based on access to common property. Other sources of inequality could include differential access to private land, labour markets, education and migration opportunities. These inequalities are often shaped by gender and ethnicity. None of the projects described in this volume suggests redistributing private property like land, or cattle as in the case of Mongolia. The focus is on the implications of these private asset allocations for common property resource management.

CBNRM can have a significant impact on inequalities between rural people and other actors such as logging firms and powerful government resource agencies. In fact, a significant goal of CBNRM is to strengthen communities' claims to resources. Those cases which gave less attention to intra-community inequalities and differences were those that directed their primary attention to relationships between rural people and powerful actors, including state resource agencies, logging enterprises or agribusinesses. Examples include the case studies on community forestry in Cambodia (Chapters 3 and 11) and the one on policy incentives for community forestry in the Philippines (Chapter 13). The explicit reduction of diverse positions for the term 'community perspectives' in Chapter 13 can be understood as a simplification useful for effective external policy advocacy. However, readers must be cautioned that these sorts of simplifications should not be extended into arenas of local CBNRM practice. There is plenty of evidence that intra-community difference can be crucial for CBNRM practice even in the Philippines (McDermott, 2001; Mendoza et al., Chapter 12).

Becoming a voice for local villagers

If we base our understanding of collective action on what Meinzen-Dick and Di Gregorio (2004) call 'voluntary action taken by a group to achieve common interests', then one of the most important actions undertaken by the communities described in this volume was to speak for their own communities to other actors, with respect to interests held by some or all community members. Many of the techniques of PAR are to create a voice for communities, or more often, specific groups in rural communities. The cases are particularly self-conscious about community voice in relation to government. As this is addressed more thoroughly in Chapter 17, I will restrict myself to a few brief comments on the implications for understanding the concept of community.

In some ways it is through the question of voice that we might achieve the best understanding of community. This is because a group of people become a community when they are able to speak with a collective voice. It is around questions of voice that the importance of participation emerges as crucial, and it was the research that mobilized the active participation of community members that enabled communities to speak collectively.

There are three, perhaps four, cases in this volume where research projects were organized primarily around helping communities to establish a collective and effective voice with respect to government policy and practice. The project described by O'Hara (Chapter 13) found innovative ways of enabling community members to express their views to government officials, CBNRM practitioners and academics. Members emphasized that the broader policy context served to disable community forestry management. O'Hara's chapter shows that communities are not necessarily bound by locality, but that when they engage in broader networks they can contribute to changing the views and actions of other actors, including policy-makers.

The two community forestry papers on Cambodia also focus on the ways in which communities can convince governments to recognize collective rights to access, manage and use community forests. In other projects, while the collective voice to government was not the central activity, it appeared nonetheless. For example, Le Van An (Chapter 5) describes how residents in both of the upland communes in which the teams worked in Central Vietnam had lost access to significant livelihood resources. The research project prepared villagers to go to government officials to ask for expanded resource rights.

My observations so far, however, also point to a need for care in understanding community voice. The voices created through these studies are not the authentic voices of a pre-existing community, previously silent but encouraged to speak out through the project. Instead, like the communities themselves, voice is a product of interaction between communities and other actors. The most obvious interaction is that between research team members and community members, but more generally voice needs to be seen in the context of networks of actors. The ubiquitous resource management plans are an example: they are never simply the representation of pre-existing community strategies and intentions, but always need to be framed in terms that make sense to government officials. The case study set in Laos (Chapter 7) illustrates this well: Tubtim writes that she thought that prohibitions on fishing linked to the widow spirit represented a form of management; however, government officials did not consider this to be management. The new exclusive management regime was understandable to government officials, and emerged through interactions between the research project, government officials, residents in neighbouring villages and various groups in the community. However, the villagers were uncomfortable with the scheme until the widow spirit endorsed it.

Tubtim's chapter also points to an important qualification regarding the assumption of common interests in the articulation of community voice. She avoids ascribing voice to the entire community. Instead, she shows that the project had different meanings and outcomes for different members in the community, and indicates that not everyone was equally involved with respect to decisions and voice. In particular, as Tubtim notes, the village committee was in an ambiguous position because it represented the state to the village, but also the village to the state. Not all groups in communities may be present in the same way when a community speaks collectively. Inevitably, voice is also an outcome of power relations in communities.

As I noted above, the chapters (Chapters 3, 11 and 13) that are primarily focused on how communities can represent their collective interests to other actors pay the least attention to power relations and inequality in the community. Indeed, having an active community voice tends to put aside questions of power and inequality in communities. One way that power relationships in the community could be emphasized more in this kind of action research might be to systematically explore the networks traced by informal communication practices in a community, and see how these can coalesce into a community voice.

Becoming vehicles for other types of collective action

The projects described in this volume relate innovations in collective resource management as part of a CBNRM research programme. However, one of the striking features is how many different kinds of activities were undertaken in the name of CBNRM. Once the work to create collective action has been accomplished to achieve one purpose, those collective practices can become vehicles for achieving other goals. Although most of the activities reported in these chapters involved direct improvements to livelihoods (for example, crop improvement and credit schemes), the kinds of activities varied widely. One suspects there may also be related activities that were not mentioned because they seemed irrelevant to a volume on CBNRM. Ykhanbai and Bulgan's chapter on Mongolia (Chapter 6) provides some examples, in part because the opportunities for spin-off activities created more support for the research project. They point to how women supported co-management in part because it filled an unmet need to be involved in community social activities and services. 'During community meetings, people could meet each other and chat, get community help when someone was sick or needed money, or learn the best practices of herding, farming and livelihood improvements from each other.'

All this points to the ways that collective action and institutions can have multiple goals and unpredictable results, and can be sustained for reasons that do not fit entirely into a CBNRM framework but are nevertheless an important support for CBNRM. Although these case studies do not provide a lot of evidence for this, it seems that the motivation for the hard work necessary to sustain these communities was not just the promise of better resource management.

The opportunities such activities provided for socializing and organizing other unrelated activities were also crucial. Finally, there are hints in many chapters that CBNRM communities can easily transform into other types of collective action and communities: marketing collectives, service provisions, political actions demanding citizenships rights and so on.

Evaluation and new directions

Over the past couple of decades much has changed in development research and development policy. In academic work, questions of agency, actor-oriented development theory and actor-network theory have helped broaden ideas of who or what can be an actor in development. In development politics, revolutionary movements have been displaced by a plethora of social movements and NGOs, and class analysis has been displaced by community-based development work. This does not mean abandoning the notion of class-based agents. But it does mean contextualizing class-based agents in the broader realm of networks of actors including corporations, NGOs, communities, farmers, wage workers, consumers, academics, development agencies and others. In the case of communities, an approach concerned with collective action and networks of actors points to the recognition that local communities will never be idealized expressions of some kind of collective local action. Nevertheless, communities can be important actors in many fields of development practice.

One of the weak points of the broader field of CBNRM, including both advocates of community rights and mainstream development institutions, has been its concept of community. Practitioners, researchers and policy-makers often assumed that rural communities were stable and relatively homogeneous. Some proponents also argued that most rural communities have over time developed collective institutions for managing resources, and that these livelihood-based institutions were threatened by state intrusions and market integration. An examination of the case studies in this volume suggests a more nuanced approach, which understands community rather differently. With respect to the case studies in this book I have argued as follows.

Communities are best understood as being made through project activities. The projects remade existing communities or made new ones based partly on models for doing CBNRM that circulated in the IDRC and other networks involved with doing CBNRM. Such models were adapted according to local priorities as identified through participatory research.

The CBNRM communities did not just exist ready to be mobilized, but were the contingent and often tenuous outcome of considerable effort and hard work.

CBNRM activities were often welcomed and were appropriate to diverse kinds of situations, not just the idealized stable community with strong pre-existing collective institutions for managing resources. CBNRM activities are particularly important among migrant groups in coastal and upland areas, as they are often among the poorest and have the least secure resource rights.

More broadly speaking, the communities described in this volume are the result of trans-local networks communicating with local networks (or communities). The term 'trans-local' allows us to talk about institutions or networks stretching outside the localities in which these projects are working, but without necessarily falling into the idea that they are external to these localities. In particular, the communities mentioned in this book often sought to strengthen their relationships with states and markets, and were created partly through these interactions, not outside them.

Not everyone participated in the communities in the same way. Differences were based partially on relative wealth and poverty, gender, ethnicity, status (government official or villager) and so on. This is a way of emphasizing that the case studies recognize that communities are internally composed of diverse networks, and that this diversity affects community participation.

The communities in these cases almost always became important collective actors in local and trans-local networks. Because the CBNRM communities participated in and thus influenced these networks, they could affect macro- as well as micro-development practices.

Rethinking community based on these studies of CBNRM in practice is useful not just for academic purposes, but also for policy and practice. I conclude with a few comments on the implications of this analysis for further research and practice.

If we understand the community in CBNRM as the product of articulation between local and trans-local networks, and as a collective actor in non-local networks, it becomes apparent that CBNRM is much more than simply a way of increasing community participation in NRM at the local level. The most optimistic scenario is that CBNRM can challenge the premise of 'trusteeship' that arguably underlies much development practice (Cowen and Shenton, 1996). In other words, communities can become rights-bearing agents in the practice of development, rather than simply trustees of agencies that act on their behalf. In this sense, CBNRM can make a substantial contribution to rethinking development policies more broadly. Nonetheless, much caution is warranted in relation to the widespread application of CBNRM, as there are many potential pitfalls that could undermine both local rights and anti-poverty work. In particular, a rigid or formulaic CBNRM could undermine existing informal community practice, undermine the livelihoods of the poor and empower local elites.

These are some of the implications for the broader academic analysis of development policies. What of the more practical insights for CBNRM research, practice and policy? I offer a few suggestions here, suggesting key arguments from my analysis of the cases.

When practitioners and researchers abandon unrealistic images of stable rural communities, they pay more attention to people who have been mobile, displaced and who often have the weakest property rights. A specific implication regards collective rights to hold and manage resources that may be created for people who can frame their identities as indigenous (not an obvious category in most parts of Asia). Where appropriate, these sorts of rights might also be extended to peoples who cannot frame themselves as indigenous, including people who have been mobile or who are described as migrants.

Practitioners need to pay careful attention to the way that creating CBNRM communities also creates territorial and social exclusion. Who is being excluded? How is it justified? For example, do programmes allocate resource rights to indigenous peoples at the expense of displaced or more mobile communities?

CBNRM research and practice need to come to terms with the way in which rural communities are integrated into markets. Research might explore ways that more of the benefits of market integration can be captured by the poor, as well as find ways of protecting collective rights and resource quality in the face of marketization.

Policy-makers need to recognize diversity and multiple forms of community in administrative villages or local government units. Enabling legislation for CBNRM must accommodate flexible definitions of community, to allow for adaptation to local circumstances.

Practitioners might want to acknowledge the limits on community-based collective action as a strategy to reduce inequality, although CBNRM is well placed to target and work with the poorest groups in rural areas. These kinds of efforts can be important for reducing poverty, but are not well suited to reducing inequality based on differential access to private property, labour markets, education and so on. Moreover, CBNRM is not the only kind of collective action that rural people can engage in, and other kinds of collective mobilizations (from social movements to electoral politics) might be more appropriate for addressing these kinds of inequalities. However, CBNRM is well suited to protecting important resource rights for entire communities that are threatened by powerful external actors such as state resource agencies or private enterprise.

CBNRM practice needs to develop more systematic methods for understanding and working with power in rural areas. For example, tracing informal communication networks might reveal power relations in the same way that wealth-ranking exercises trace economic inequities. This becomes important especially when we think of CBNRM as a means for creating collective actors who can speak for rural people. In turn, this suggests that we need to understand how the resultant collective voice is the product of power relations both locally and trans-locally.

Understanding that CBNRM communities are the product of hard work, and not naturally existing before a project's interventions, directs our attention more to the demands made on rural people to contribute their effort to this objective. The nature of these demands can filter the choice of participants. Women and the poor may not find it as easy to participate, which can lead to elite domination by simple selection.

If CBNRM communities are the unstable products of ongoing effort and work, then sustainability becomes an important issue. How can the effort made to create these communities be sustained through institutionalization? How can institutionalization happen in a way that maintains the flexibility necessary for institutions to continue to address new problems while they emerge?

CHAPTER 17
Shaping policy from the field

Stephen R. Tyler and Hein Mallee

Introduction

The research projects underlying this series of cases proceeded from the supposition that the meaningful participation of poor farmers or fishers might produce more effective and sustainable innovations than technical interventions driven by outside experts. The common framework underlying this action research approach is outlined in Chapter 2. In light of this starting point and the common framework, what is surprising about the cases is how much the authors have come to emphasize engagement with policy. Their starting point was the understanding of local resource degradation trends and management problems, with the emphasis on improving productivity and sustainability through the meaningful participation of local actors. Yet this local engagement in understanding and testing collective action for resource management has generated a much greater sensitivity to and engagement with NRM policies. In some cases, research effort in the field became specifically oriented to informing policy.[1]

In this chapter we explore how that happened, and assess successful strategies for policy influence. We adopt a broad view of policy, which recognizes not only its important content character, but also its procedural and contested character. This perspective includes both the discursive nature of policy (underlying concepts, principles and values) as well as its practical implementation. The process offers considerable opportunity for influence and interpretation.[2] This view of policy allows us to engage a perspective which is missing from most policy studies: what does policy look like through the lens of local experience? The collection of cases in this volume illustrates in a number of important ways how field-level views of policy can be influential in reforming policy substance, discourse and implementation.

Policy-making everywhere is somewhat of a black box: very few people really understand how it happens.[3] Most researchers, even those directly engaged in policy-relevant work, have rather naive expectations about policy influence and how research results connect to policy systems (Lindquist, 2001). Yet we conclude here that these participatory research projects have had a substantial degree of policy impact.

There is a broad literature on participatory approaches to the study and design of rural development interventions. The work of Robert Chambers has figured prominently in it during the past 20 years (Chambers, 1983, 1997; Chambers, Pacey and Thrupp, 1989; Pound et al., 2003). Efforts to link these participatory methods to policy have demonstrated the value of the tools in generating policy-relevant information, but have also concluded that this information is seldom applied successfully to policy change (Holland, Blackburn and Chambers, 1998). The rhetoric of participatory development can also be appropriated, more perversely, by the state itself as a means to implement policies which actually may undermine the empowerment and learning intentions of participatory methods (Sarin et al., 2003). For example, Vandergeest (2003) describes how a national programme of land reform in Laos used participatory local planning and formalized collective forms of resource tenure, yet arguably resulted in greater centralization of control and dispossession of local communities.

In most of the cases in this volume, technological innovations to improve resource productivity are introduced and then implemented by households for resources they control. As the cases demonstrate, the more challenging innovations were those directed at the development of functional local institutions for collective action and management of common-pool resources (or CPR). This is not only a difficult research problem, which requires attention to ecological, indigenous and scientific knowledge, power relations and social differentiation in the community. It is also an area which lacks good policy guidelines.

There has been widespread experience with the devolution of forest management throughout Asia. However, reviews of this experience reveal little evidence that such policies have led to improved equity or local economic benefit (Edmunds and Wollenberg, 2003). As a result, there is little consensus on what constitutes an effective policy regime for CBNRM. As these cases continue to demonstrate, meaningful devolution or co-management of CPR remains elusive despite the rhetoric of many governments in Asia.

By starting, not with arguments for policy reform, but with the situation of local resource users, these cases shed light on to what is working and what can work at the field level. They provide insights into the failings of good policy in implementation, as well as point to workable mechanisms in the field. These can serve both as models to challenge assumptions and transform policy discourse, and as examples from which to design policy reforms. By looking at policy issues from the field and from the perspective of the resource users most directly affected, these participatory research cases demonstrate ways in which the strategic interaction of resource users, local governments and researchers can influence policies of decentralization and NRM. This chapter explores the factors from the case experiences which enabled such a policy impact. We conclude that both context and research approaches have an important bearing on the policy effects of participatory local NRM research.

The chapter proceeds by exploring what policy is about, and proceeds to discuss how policies are typically shaped by a variety of influences both in their design and implementation at different levels of government. We present the experience of the cases in two ways: first, we link the opportunities for CBNRM to the national decentralization policy framework of several of the countries represented here. Next, we demonstrate the types of policy influence demonstrated by the cases in this volume, and illustrate the strategies the participants adopted to exploit opportunities for policy influence. We then show how these strategies and influences arose from the context and methods applied. These comparative assessments demonstrate the importance of social learning, and the transformative effects of local initiative and innovation on policy change. Finally, we examine the new roles which researchers have adopted through these experiences, and the ways in which these roles have been instrumental in the policy change outcomes.

What is policy?

It is common to conceive of policy as being the explicit statement of government priorities as interpreted in action and reflected in laws, operational directives and regulations. The local impact of policy, however, is as much related to the way it is put into practice (or perhaps filters down) as to the letter of the central government documents (Shankland, 2000). Policy also often changes during the process of its implementation. Therefore, we will be interested in the formulation and formal content of policy as well as its implementation and local administration. This perspective brings out the process nature of policy: it is formulated and implemented, but also modified, deflected, interpreted, contested and resisted. This also draws attention towards the various actors involved in policy at different levels, the roles they play, the ways they relate to each other, and their networks of information exchange and learning.

In this chapter, we focus on the role in the policy process of researchers who are engaged in community-level PAR. In this role of considering researchers as actors, sometimes unexpectedly the researchers became part of the policy community (Lindquist, 2001; Lindayati, 2002). This type of community consists not only of one or more government departments, legislators and/or state leaders. Depending on the national context, such a community also includes journalists and commentators, political parties and donors, as well as other international organizations, consultants and lobbyists, and various interest groups. A policy community can be small, closed and opaque, as in China. There, major recent NRM initiatives such as the logging ban and the upland conversion policy were initiated by key central and provincial leaders. They were subsequently worked out in central government agencies and implemented top-down through the associated line departments. In contrast, Cambodia is characterized by a much more open and diverse policy community, even if key decision-making power is concentrated in few hands. Here we find major multilateral and bilateral donors, international environmental (NGOs, domestic NGOs, foreign and domestic corporations, and researchers who are all playing key roles alongside government agencies.[4]

Policy communities are not static. Lindayati (2002) shows how in Indonesia, during the period of Suharto's New Order, the forestry policy community was small and dominated by the bureaucracy. The political upheaval of the late 1990s brought a major change, particularly with respect to parliament, local governments and NGO-based societal interest groups, which all began to play a larger role in the policy process. However, the extent and type of linkages researchers can make with policy processes depends on the kind of policy community in the country and its dynamics.

The ways in which the various actors interact in the policy process has been extensively analysed in terms of policy networks, advocacy coalitions and other kinds of groupings.[5] In the wider policy community, different actors can rally around certain issues or promote certain directions of change. They do not necessarily share the same interests or values, however, and may come from different backgrounds and play different roles in the network. Often more than one policy network is active in a policy community, working to maintain or change certain policy directions. As we will see below, many of the research teams became part of or helped initiate specific policy networks. With the authority that came from international support and the credibility provided by field-based research evidence, the teams were able to enrol senior policy-makers and others into their networks through a variety of mechanisms, which we discuss below. Straddling local community and decision-making levels, research projects uniquely brought the voices of local men and women into the policy networks in diverse ways.

Focusing on policy as a process and on the role of different actors within it also illustrates how policy-making is multidirectional. In other words, policy does not simply come down. It is constructed in practice and the bureaucracy and other organized stakeholders as well as local people all play a role in its construction. In this chapter, therefore, we are not only concerned with the ways in which researchers and local people managed (or failed) to influence policy (in the sense of its formulation and implementation), but also with how they used policy in the local context for a variety of purposes. Seen in this way, the policy process is also intimately intertwined with politics and power.

Finally, policy can be regarded as a discourse or narrative: a story about issues, their causes and solutions, as well as basic assumptions underlying them.[6] Such policy discourses can be quite powerful and pervasive, with people being hardly aware that their actions are guided by them. In the context of the case studies in this volume, most research teams faced entrenched policy narratives about environmental degradation (caused by local and indigenous people's NRM practices), about the need for state control over natural resources and about the inability of communities to conserve these resources.

In practice, the basic assumptions of mainstream policy discourse often blind actors from different groups to realities that do not conform to the model. In the process, certain groups become marginalized. For example, in many settings, NRM policies are based on the experiences of lowland, irrigated, smallholder agriculture. However, policies become extended without further consideration or adjustment, and applied to upland areas which have radically differing systems of land use and access rights (see the Ratanakiri case study, Chapter 3).

Different discourses also mean that certain kinds of knowledge become privileged. For example, narratives associated with Western modern and scientific forestry are still dominant throughout most of the world and explicitly legitimize the knowledge of technically trained foresters over that of the forest dwellers. We will see this type of legitimacy repeated time and time again in the scientific forest inventories and management plans that are required before communities can be granted management rights. One key role that the CBNRM research teams in these cases have played is to provide alternative policy ideas and narratives. Like the mainstream discourse, these consisted of a story about issues, causes and solutions, but instead, these policies emerged from and were substantiated with contextual field evidence.

Policy positions and narratives often show a remarkable tenacity, even after changed circumstances or an evident lack of effectiveness. This is primarily because policy discourses become embedded in the routines and practices of organizations and are internalized by their staff through training (Shankland, 2000).[7] Therefore, promoting policy change in practice often means a struggle with the bureaucracy. However, despite its stickiness, policy does change. Such change can be brought about by officials in government agencies who after learning more become champions for change. Learning can also be more broadly shared social learning within the institution in which they work (Korten and Sy, 1988). In some countries like the Philippines, changes in departmental leadership as a result of elections can be an important factor in uprooting entrenched perspectives. Sometimes, shock events trigger policy change, with environmental crises like major floods being a common and prominent factor in NRM policy changes. Whatever the specific drivers of change, it is clear that policy is more responsive to external influences in certain situations and at certain times than others. This phenomenon of important coincident factors, sometimes referred to as windows of opportunity (Lindquist, 2001), leads us first to examine the substantial policy context in which the case studies took place. We discovered all of these cases are characterized by windows of opportunity that were vital to enabling the eventual policy impacts.

Governance reform and decentralization

In this section, we will examine the policy context in which the case studies are situated. We will show how broad processes of national policy reform around decentralization provided opportunities to which the researchers responded adroitly. The types of impact and strategies they deployed in these windows of opportunity are analysed in the next section. Most of the research teams soon realized that certain policies were obstacles to CBNRM, or that certain policy processes could help push along local change. This change towards policy orientation was most pronounced and explicit in the case of the IIRR. Chapter 13 describes how their learning process quickly took the research team away from a focus on community capacity-building towards policy issues. They realized that the main bottleneck to community forest management was not the community's capacity, but the disincentives inherent in the wider political economy.

Decentralization of NRM is occurring in many countries around the world (Larson, 2003), including most of the countries covered in the case studies. This trend has been under way for some years in Asia, with mixed results (Tyler, 1995; Dupar and Badenoch, 2002; Edmunds and Wollenberg, 2003). Most experiences have been sectoral. In particular, there have been extensive government programmes in the forestry sector to engage communities in forest management, from the very widespread adoption of forest user groups in Nepal (Kanel, 2003) to the much less comprehensive results in Southeast Asia (Fisher, 2003). In the Philippines and, more recently, in Vietnam there has been some devolution of coastal fisheries management to local government authorities (Ferrer, Polotan de la Cruz and Domingo, 1996; Tuyen et al., Chapter 4). To the extent that these experiences have been reviewed critically, the main conclusions have been that despite many years (sometimes decades) of formal policy implementation, they remain contested because of the difficulty of wresting significant management authority from the state to better serve the interests of the local poor. It should also, however, be noted that most of these policy reforms were introduced centrally as a response to internal or external political pressure, but not in response to specific local NRM initiatives or examples.

Such programmes of governance reform sometimes involve the decentralization of functions and responsibilities to local governments in general, or reforms specifically related to natural resources, or both. Although the situation of Cambodia in many ways is unique and anomalous, it well illustrates these trends and the responses of researchers.

In the Cambodian context, researchers responded to take advantage of this fluid context and shifted the focus of their work in response to policy opportunities. Detailed illustrations are provided in the section below. However, the community forestry research project (Chapter 11) also provided inputs to the formulation of the community forestry sub-decree and organized consultations with communities around constructing a draft language for this document. The CFRP team has presented experiences with field processes such as participatory inventories and management plans to the FA to assist it in formulating guidelines for such processes.

Although the specific historical context in Cambodia is unique, many elements of this picture of decentralization as well as the responses of researchers in Cambodia are common to the other case studies as well. First and most important, the countries covered in the case studies are all undertaking decentralization reforms. In the Philippines, this also involves general decentralization to local government units and special provisions related to indigenous peoples and community forestry. In Mongolia, Laos and Vietnam (and in China, considerably earlier), user rights over natural resources were also devolved away from collectives or state entities, to households and local communities.

Box 17.1   Governance reform and decentralization in Cambodia

Cambodia suffered decades of turmoil before it gradually began to restore some degree of normalcy in the early 1990s. As conflict subsided and security improved, society and the economy struggled to overcome the results of the country's traumatic past. With the entire administrative class wiped out, and with all records and structure systematically destroyed, the government realized it needed to (re-)create much of the administrative infrastructure in order to be able to govern. Since the Paris peace accord of 1991, Cambodia has been heavily influenced by international donors, who fund a substantial part of the government budget and play a key role in the structuring of the country's governance arrangements. Part of this process has entailed a simultaneous deconcentration and decentralization initiative. A programme of administrative reforms started in the late 1990s aimed to enhance the position of the provinces, which were given responsibility for the provision of basic public goods (if not entirely the financial powers to raise funds for this). The role of the provincial governors as main coordinators and promoters of provincial development was strengthened (Royal Government of Cambodia, 2000). Deconcentration also affects the sectoral NRM line agencies including, for example, the Forestry Administration (FA), which emerged as a separate independent bureaucracy extending below the provincial level.

Decentralization focused on the role of elected commune councils (CCs), seen as the primary agents of local development and democracy, with local elections taking place for the first time in 2002. Assisted by village development committees, the CCs follow a detailed participatory process to produce commune development plans. They receive funds from higher levels to put such plans into practice (Royal Government of Cambodia, 2002). Much of the decentralization reforms were pioneered and funded by the Seila/PLG programme, coordinated by UNDP. The mandate of the CCs is now being extended from the oversight of health and education service delivery, to management and allocation of natural resources to users. This shift originally was not part of the decentralization plans developed by the Seila/PLG programme. The experience of the research programme in Ratanakiri and the recognition of the importance of land and resource planning were instrumental in modifying the national Seila/PLG programme to include PLUP as a key task of local governments.

At the same time, sectoral initiatives to reform tenure rights over different resources were introduced. Some elements of these reforms involved the devolution to communities of certain, limited management rights over natural resources such as forests and fisheries. The land law of 2001 introduced the recognition of customary collective tenure of cultivated and forested lands in ethnic minority areas. A new forestry law was adopted in 2002, which recognizes aspects of the community rights of indigenous communities. Alongside several other policy documents that regulate forest use, a sub-decree specifically dealing with community forestry was issued.

In principle, the sub-decree allows communities to manage officially recognized community forests, based on a management plan approved by the FA. Such technical requirements, which are often difficult for communities to meet, allow central government agencies to retain control over resource use and are common in other countries as well. Although hundreds of community forestry experiments are going on in Cambodia, none was officially recognized as of late 2004.

New legislation for community fisheries management is under development, with analogous issues of defining local rights and formalizing management and approval requirements through sub-decrees to be prepared by the sectoral agency responsible.

Second, policy-making is often in a state of considerable flux throughout the period covered by the case study. In Cambodia, both policies and institutions were being created from scratch or were being recreated. While the extent of such policy fluidity may differ, it is also found in most of the other countries. Often, promulgation of legislation is not the end of policy-making but the beginning of complex processes of policy exploration and negotiation. We see this, for example, with the new land law in Mongolia, with legislation on indigenous peoples' land rights in the Philippines and with the formalization of a water policy in Bhutan. Policies must find the right fit with reality on the ground, and CBNRM research projects have been instrumental in facilitating exactly such processes.

A third commonality suggested by the Cambodian cases is that the CBNRM teams pursued local research objectives that were broadly consistent with the government's policy goals under the decentralization programme. Rather than taking an oppositional approach to government policies, research teams contributed to their improvement and implementation. However, while broad government policy initiatives pointed in certain directions, sectoral agencies and local governments usually had little guidance and few ideas on how to implement them. But with their CBNRM outlook and extensive field experience, the researchers had concrete ideas on how to translate broad policies into practice on the ground. They were able to frame interventions to benefit local communities in the context of these policy opportunities.

In one sense, this is not surprising. Decentralization transfers authority and responsibilities to the local level, which is exactly where the CBNRM projects were active. But the connection between the field research and decentralization in practice was conditioned by the nature of the resources which are at the core of CBNRM work (see Chapter 2). Water, forests, grassland and swidden land are all CPRs. They have multiple users and some degree of collective action is required to prevent overuse and degradation. For this reason, as well as their economic and strategic value (such as national security or biodiversity conservation), governments usually assume responsibility for their management. This combination of local use and state authority directs CBNRM projects to activities that combine rearrangement of local tenure and roles with policy advocacy. As such, this is in contrast with agriculture, for example, where land rights are already at least quasi-private, and where management is universally acknowledged to be at the household level. For example, the Hong Ha commune project in central Vietnam includes work related to agriculture and to forestry (Chapter 5). In contrast to the forestry work, which almost immediately drew the project into questions of national policy in relation to forest access rights, the agricultural component has been quite successful without needing to concern itself with policy at all.

Where these research cases merged with decentralization policies, they worked to establish or strengthen community claims to resources. This usually involves the delineation of boundaries and the definition or change of access and management rights by different user groups. For rights and claims to be secure, they need to be officially recognized and supported by the state. Therefore, a considerable amount of researcher advocacy relates to such state recognition (see the discussion of legitimacy below).

However, state legislation of resource rights often ignores the complexity of local property relations and access arrangements. Perhaps the clearest example of this is the Ratanakiri case, where the indigenous people practise swidden agriculture. Here, land use patterns cannot be easily classified in terms of agriculture and forestry. Customary land use rights consist of a complex mix of private and collective arrangements. When the national government initiated a land titling drive based on PLUP, the Ratanakiri experience influenced it to develop special procedures for indigenous areas. In other cases, state policy on resource rights may lead to deliberate or inadvertent enclosure of CPR, resulting in the selective exclusions documented in the Laos and Tam Giang lagoon cases (Chapters 7 and 4 respectively). In the Philippines, the ancestral domain case (Chapter 12) illustrates how the hasty conferment of indigenous land rights on local administrative units led to a mismatch between the authority responsible and the customary organizational forms for managing these rights. The matching of local institutions and rights to resource use and management are at the core of what the research cases do, but such reforms are also central to the effective expression of decentralization policies.

What does policy look like from the field?

As demonstrated in these cases, participatory research provides insights which allow the characterization of policy alternatives or policy implementation more starkly in the lived experience and quality of life of local men and women. This provides an immediacy that is more arresting than quantitative analysis, and is more likely to reveal contradictions in underlying assumptions than detailed analyses that take such assumptions as a starting point. Indeed, conventional policy research often fails to take account of local realities. Priorities and measures of success for policy-makers (as well as standards of evidence, assumptions and systems of belief) are not necessarily the same as those of community members.

In these cases we see that local resource users, community leaders and researchers, once engaged in the action research enterprise, display a broad range of explicit or implicit strategies by which they engage, manipulate and make use of policy opportunities to strengthen the legitimacy, power and effectiveness of new CBNRM schemes. The actions of the various local actors are motivated by a keen desire to improve conditions for local men and women.

It is the local perception of policy which is most important in guiding and motivating interventions for change. What does policy look like from the field? In many of the projects, it was the contradictions between the stated intent of the policy and its actual implementation (or unintended side-effects), which were key to shaping the project innovations. So, in the IIRR case (Chapter 13), an experimental approach to shared learning was developed to address the conflict between the stated intent of the community forestry policy and the systemic barriers to implementation which were revealed in preliminary field investigations. In the Tam Giang lagoon in Vietnam (Chapter 4), national policies to foster aquaculture development led to unexpected transfers of resource rights and to the exclusion of poor resource users, which the project tried to address. And in Mongolia, the dismantling of traditional forms of community pasture management under state socialism, followed by the introduction of economic reforms which encouraged the growth of private animal herds in the 1990s, led to serious degradation of grazing land (Chapter 6). In all these cases, the local view of policy change was decidedly different from what had been intended by the drafters of the original policies. In recognizing this contradiction, the research teams began to act strategically to influence policy.

Recent studies of how research influences policy suggest that while there are no universal guidelines, some generalizations can be drawn about factors which strengthen or weaken the potential for such influence (IDRC, 2004). One of the most important elements in policy influence from research was the relationship between governmental needs for knowledge and researcher interests and capability in providing it. This relationship can be characterized along a spectrum where, at one end, policy-makers and analysts in government know that they need knowledge about a particular policy issue and are faced with a need for urgent action. In this situation they are actively seeking knowledge and insight. At the opposite end of this contextual spectrum, governments may be hostile to addressing an issue which is in the public domain, leading them to not only ignore, but also to bury research on that issue. Most of the research cases in this volume can be situated in the middle of this spectrum, where the government is at least nominally committed to addressing the issues (e.g. decentralization, poverty, environment and resource degradation) and has only a limited sense of how policies should be framed, or what specifically could be done to implement them. In this context, researchers must act strategically to assure policy attention to and impact from their work.

The kind of knowledge which is provided through PAR, such as the cases presented in this volume is rich, but often perplexing to policy analysts. Participatory research generates messy evidence: local interactions between resource users and the environment are shown to be complex and shaded by culture, history, social relations, the ways power is used, by ecological context and by external forces. This picture contradicts the simplifying assumptions about behaviour, incentives and causation made by policy-makers who necessarily operate at a high degree of generalization. Such studies also reveal that local interests in resource use overlap and conflict. New, hitherto unrecognized interests are frequently exposed, to further complicate situations in which power and political trade-offs are often central. None of this makes policy decision-making easier. It also tends to make policy-makers respond defensively to the conclusions of such exercises, or to dismiss them entirely (Freudenberger, 1998). Despite the apparent mismatch between the methodology and policy impact potential, these cases demonstrate how researchers can highlight key elements of this complex field reality and successfully link field learning to focused policy change.

The success of delivering policy impacts from participatory research depends crucially on the skills and initiative of the researcher. We have seen how those cases which engage most directly with policy reforms took place in a context of policy fluidity and under national policy trends of decentralization coupled with the devolution of NRM. However, this context merely structured the opportunity: it was up to the researchers and their colleagues in government and other agencies to identify and seize such opportunities. They proceeded from local research insights to policy influence in a variety of ways.

Direct research input to policy formulation

The most obvious way in which the participatory research affected policy in these cases was when the research results provided direct input into the formulation of new policies on resource tenure or resource management. In a number of cases, the research team has been in a position to draft or influence the framing of policy reforms associated with the decentralization of natural resource governance. In such instances, important provisions of the new policies are based on the results of the participatory local research work. These are cases in which the research is led by staff from a key national government agency. In the Mongolian case, the research project leader is a senior policy adviser in the Ministry of Nature and the Environment. But this is an unusual situation: research project management and policy advisory units are normally separate, and in the cases presented, the research may even be undertaken in a completely different agency from that charged with direct policy responsibility for management of the natural resources in question.

Two of the Cambodian cases in this volume demonstrate a direct influence on national policy formulation. The community forestry case (Chapter 11) demonstrates how participatory research in multiple field sites was specifically structured to provide evidence to support policy reform. In this case, the evidence was intended to show the feasibility of participatory local demarcation and control of forest utilization to a sceptical forestry agency. This was effected by developing practical tools for local forest planning and management, by demonstrating congruence with other government policies (particularly local government reforms), and by demonstrating the potential for improving local livelihoods. The research was led by the Ministry of Environment, not the Ministry of Agriculture, Forestry and Fisheries, which controls policy jurisdiction. This situation made the policy linkage particularly delicate, in order to avoid jurisdictional rivalries. We discuss relevant strategies below.

In the Ratanakiri case (Chapter 3), the early research work of the project influenced the process of framing new national land tenure legislation. The legislation was guided under the influence of various donors and with multiple objectives in mind. However, the research project provided the critical evidence needed to justify the creation of a new category of collective land and resource tenure which was appropriate to the customary practices of upland ethnic communities in Ratanakiri and other provinces. The significant aspect of this example was that the project was based in a provincial not national government office. The office had no policy responsibilities and was only responsible for implementing a large donor-funded programme throughout the province. With careful strategic effort, the research work done by the provincial office was used to leverage national policy change (Muny, 2001).

In the case of Bhutan, the team worked in a national policy context favouring decentralization. However, during the course of their fieldwork the team uncovered evidence proving that customary water allocation principles were inequitable. The research helped explain and overcome these problems, and helped form the structure and content of a new national water policy. This occurred even though the research group was not part of the line department responsible for water resources management.

These examples suggest that one way for the participatory research to provide direct input to policy formulation is for government agencies that have access and policy credibility to be involved in the research itself. Local NRM issues create conflicts, and government is not a neutral player (Tyler, 1999). For these reasons, it may be difficult if not ill advised to engage the line agencies with direct administrative jurisdiction over the resource base in participatory learning at the community level. Nonetheless, these examples also show that the researchers do not have to come from the responsible resource management agencies in order to be effective in influencing the policies adopted by those agencies. This is a delicate situation because jurisdictional issues and inter-agency rivalries frequently hinder relations between the different groups.

To overcome frictions, it is important that government researchers do not attempt to claim jurisdiction or to provide specific policy recommendations, because such strategies would inevitably be interpreted as interference. Researchers' influence stems from being able to provide unique knowledge and insight from within the government system. We can see in the inter-agency dynamics of these cases (particularly in Cambodia) that research partners who are in the government system are better able to attract the attention of senior political figures, convene formal or informal inter-agency working groups and assign staff across departmental boundaries for special projects.

It is also significant to note that policy insights which arose from research were not due solely to the technical expertise of the researchers. Technical expertise and authority reside in the line agencies whose staff are trained in forestry, fisheries or water resources. While the natural science background of most of the researchers was an important element in their work, policy insights came from their use of innovative participatory methodologies. It was the unique knowledge and insights generated from these participatory learning processes, rather than special technical qualifications, which gave legitimacy to the researchers, enabling them to provide advice on policy formulation. Such insights were not available to the technical specialists in line agencies, although once engaged they were often able to validate conclusions from their own field experience.

Framing policy implementation

An even more widespread mechanism by which these cases influenced policy was through the shaping of policy implementation at the local level. This kind of policy influence is very important to successful policy reform. The experience of failed development programmes throughout the world illustrates that while policy is crucial to effective change, it is not sufficient. Carefully designed policy and programmes aimed at reducing poverty frequently fail to meet expectations at the implementation stage (Pritchett and Woolcock, 2004). It is the intersection between policy and practice which forms the locus of the work described in these cases. By identifying specific interfaces between policy and field innovations, the research teams went beyond policy recommendations to testing policy in field experiments.

For example, the ancestral domain case in the Philippines (Chapter 12) defined one of its goals as demonstrating and persuading the government of the utility of using the indigenous *ili* as the unit for ancestral domain titles. This project also facilitated the development of ADMPs, which formed a focus for work on the interface of policy and practice. On the one hand, they entailed a series of concrete activities in the field, in which communities analyse, plan, devise rules and finally develop a specific management plan that also guides their future behaviour. On the other hand, such participatory management plans provide examples of how policy could be implemented. This is because they are the objects of formal recognition by state agencies charged with implementing the new ancestral domain policies.

The cases illustrate many similar kinds of examples, where the research practice in the field provided concrete illustrations of how policies could be implemented to better achieve their stated aims (typically related to poverty reduction, equity and resource conservation): PLUP protocols developed by researchers in Ratanakiri (Chapter 3); the rearrangement of waterways and net-enclosures facilitated by researchers in the Tam Giang lagoon (Chapter 4); the forest management plans developed in Cambodia for the community forestry case (Chapter 11) and the villagers' NTFP cultivation activities which required legalizing access to forest resources in Hong Ha commune (Chapter 5). The Mongolian pasture management project has been involved both in the drafting of national legislation as well as in the local details of how it might be implemented (structuring leases, developing participatory management plans, providing for oversight and approval mechanisms and so on). In the Lao case study (Chapter 7) research reveals how policies can be implemented in unexpected ways, as community and government staff framed exclusionary interventions in terms of the new policy orthodoxy.

The practice of participatory research addresses local policy conflicts and contradictions between intentions and outcomes, by building shared insight and trust between men and women resource users and local government. This is a fundamental element of improving governance and policy. It allowed the local people and researchers to move beyond typical complaints ('there needs to be more participation') to jointly developing the mechanisms that embody solutions (participatory planning, consultation processes, resource user groups). This changes the way that policy is implemented, and allows opportunities for local interests to be better served under existing policy, through more sensitive and appropriate implementation strategies.

It can also help overcome resistance to policy change which is already under way. In China's Guizhou province, researchers found that despite supportive policies on poverty reduction and local participation in extension and resource management, intermediate levels of government are locked in narrow technocratic approaches and are unable to take advantage of higher-level policy reforms. Implementing agencies are frequently resistant to policy change, even when mandated by new legislation. PAR can help to build common understandings and move away from irreconcilable conflicts.

In most of these cases, the participatory research process involved engaging local governments in experiencing learning with local men, women and researchers. Typically, rights over and use of natural resources were disputed. These represent important sources of local conflict and sensitive elements of policy. A frequent criticism of decentralization policy reforms in NRM and other sectors is that local officials are not provided with the training and resources necessary to implement the policies effectively (Cheema and Rondinelli, 1983; Tyler, 1995). Several of the cases specifically refer to the confusion of local officials who had little idea how to implement new policy guidelines for local resource management. Because their research offered new insight into problems, new ways for local people to communicate with governments and new approaches for responding to and engaging local people, these participatory action research projects were able to overcome policy implementation pitfalls.

The cases report a wide range of innovations which improved the ways that policy could be delivered. Most of these were achieved by transforming perceptions and possibilities. In the Philippines, despite the comprehensive reforms recognizing indigenous peoples' rights, government agencies had not considered ways to implement the legislative requirements through indigenous management institutions. Similarly, forestry officials had not paid attention to communities' management competence and people's frustration with official intransigence. In Cambodia, Vietnam and Mongolia, the cases show how research is providing officials with evidence of plural, rather than homogenous, local interests, pointing to the need for more inclusive consultation and decision processes. In all the cases, the research helped to transform assumptions by allowing local participants (farmers, government officials and researchers) to experiment with new roles and build common platforms of shared information. As a basis for making policy (and governance in general) more effective, these represent significant mechanisms of change.

Introducing new concepts through provisional legitimacy

Without changing policy, researchers can help foster new ways of looking at rural development by demonstrating successful local interventions and seeking formal government sanction for the innovative processes which generated them. Even if it is provisional, such formal recognition and sanction changes the nature of policy discourse by introducing new concepts and gaining commitment from policy actors to testing them. This also serves to build political interest in the outcomes of the research.

The situation is that when local resource users develop innovative responses to resource management problems which are not yet sanctioned by official policies and precedents, it is often crucial for them to seek political support and legitimacy using ad hoc mechanisms. Ratanakiri researchers introduced and tested a wide range of new local planning processes with the support of the provincial governor, before the framing of the Seila programme procedures. It was their experience with these provisional processes which led to the definition of more formal and widely applied processes in the national programme.

In some cases, because the work on the ground was ahead of formal policy formulation, it operated in a kind of policy vacuum. This happened in the PMMR project (Chapter 8), partially due to the remote location of Koh Kong province. It was only in 2003, after the local commune council elections, that the Seila programme began to be implemented in this coastal area. Formal national regulations for community fisheries have not yet been developed. In this context, the team was able to mobilize key politicians such as the provincial governor to support and authorize the CBNRM experiments. The team (Marschke and Nong, 2003) observes that the policy vacuum in which the project activities took place may have been an advantage, because the work was not constrained by particular models of resource management. Therefore a lot of experimentation could be done. They also argue, however, that over the longer term formal legal recognition of a community's right to manage resources is needed.

In conditions of policy fluidity and with appropriate facilitative support, this kind of contingent support for local cases can have a strong influence on national policies, both by allowing the development of local experience with innovative alternatives, and by providing policy actors with new concepts, tools and vocabulary for them to use in policy negotiations and debates. There is some interplay here with the politics of decentralization. CBNRM offers a practical tool for local political leaders to demonstrate their capacity for more independent action, in the context of dynamic tension between local and national authorities over the details of decentralization processes. When there is no policy in place, sometimes it is easier to lead locally by experimentation.

Learning from failures

Authors of the cases mostly highlight the success of their attempts to influence policy and government programme implementation. However, there are some examples of how researchers have also learned from their failures and the failures of others to effectively influence policy. In the case of Guizhou province in China, for example, the research team expresses their frustration with the unwillingness of county-level officials to reform programme management and field guidelines. This occurred despite supportive policies for poverty reduction and participatory rural extension, the encouragement of senior (provincial) government agencies and positive reports from local field officers. Although their vertical scaling approach had limited success, the researchers found much better results from horizontal efforts to scale up lessons and influence government programming through farmer-to-farmer and local government agents in adjoining jurisdictions.

In Vietnam, the Tam Giang lagoon research team learned from the failure of conflict management efforts in Phu Tan commune. When the government imposed a solution to contested fishing rights, violence ensued after it had failed to consult all the parties affected. Such a failure was instructive to both the research team and the government, and helped convince authorities to try participatory multistakeholder co-management processes which gave much more attention to marginalized fisher groups.

Researchers have recognized the need for persistence in these efforts. Some initiatives have been successful, others have not. In particular, researchers struggle to gain recognition and support of line agencies with formal jurisdiction over the resources. Even under favourable policy regimes, as in Bhutan and Philippines, the problems facing CBNRM continue. This is partly because of the challenges associated with interpreting and implementing a supportive policy, once a regime is approved, and partly due to the contingent nature of all policy change. Legislative reform can change the relative power of different actors, and can address certain issues. However, this action frequently just shifts the focus to other issues. Therefore, the need for research effort and the continued refinement of policy is evident. The impact of effective action learning in the field can be substantial.

Strategies for achieving policy influence

The participatory research cases in this volume influenced policy formulation, implementation and discourse. Researchers found ways to legitimize local innovations even without the existence of formal enabling policy. It is worth examining the strategies used by the researchers and their local research partners (village leaders, farmers, local government) to achieve policy influence in these ways. These strategies are rooted in the PAR framework adopted by the researchers. Therefore, they provide insights for researchers and practitioners in other contexts on how they can better shape enabling policy conditions for CBNRM.

Opportunity and initiative

Policy influence is born from both preparation and opportunity. Opportunity cannot always be planned into a long-term, site-based, complex research project. And participatory research is unpredictable because local men and women play an active role, not only in contributing information, but in setting priorities for learning and innovation as the project unfolds. Successful cases of policy impact were those in which researchers were prepared to respond to dynamic opportunities in the policy system. Good examples of this include opportunities created while new legislation is being proposed; when there is uncertainty associated with large-scale projects; or when conflicts or deadlocks are difficult to resolve under old policies. Because these opportunities often arise unexpectedly, researchers need to use accumulated experience from long-term research, together with strategic preparation, in a flexible and responsive way.[8]

For example, in the Ratanakiri case (Chapter 3), research evidence was applied to the development of new legislation (the land law), the formalization of local governance reforms (with the Seila programme) and the development of new forest management approaches. Each of these influences required project responses to emerging opportunities, the timing and structure of which could not be predicted in detail. Their success also relied on the cultivation of networks of information sharing and exchange. In the case of ancestral domain in the Cordillera region (Chapter 12), researchers were familiar with the customary social and governance structures of indigenous societies because of their earlier extensive fieldwork. They were able to respond to the changing policy context by developing a participatory local planning process. It brought together customary and statutory governance bodies to address resource management planning. These and other successful cases demonstrate two important prerequisites for policy influence. One is that the research teams, or their close collaborators, need to identify the emerging policy opportunity; and the other is that the teams need to be able to respond in a timely fashion based on accumulated evidence at hand.

In most policy opportunities, timing is crucial. In conditions of fluidity, widespread debate or contested policy implementation, early examples of successful solutions are influential. These projects demonstrate how innovations in CBNRM, such as examples of the first innovative leasehold rights or the first participatory community forestry management plans, can provide compelling models for change.

Communication of credible results

The impact of the local participatory research projects on policy design or implementation also depends on the strength of their evidence, analysis and the presentation of results. The research had to generate new ideas and concepts in action, not merely tell a story about complicated local conditions. It is not the complexity of local conditions which is helpful in policy decision-making;

instead it is the practicality of precisely how innovations can respond to such complexity at various levels. Good documentation, of the process as well as the analysis and outcomes of the research, is essential for research to influence policy. But documentation alone is insufficient.

Policy influence requires timely and effective communication. It is important for research insights and lessons to be communicated using language and tools appropriate to the local culture. The research cases reported here all built on extensive international work in related fields (including such aspects as participatory research, agricultural extension, common property and tenure). However, because research teams were able to engage local participants in the local language and produce documentation that local officials could read, they were able to have a much greater impact. Many of the cases also make use of direct farmer-to-farmer and local-government exchange visits (particularly the Hong Ha and Guizhou cases, Chapters 5 and 9). In addition, the PMMR, CFRP and Ratanakiri projects went to great lengths to ensure that senior national politicians had an opportunity to visit the field site. These are particularly effective mechanisms for communicating outcomes because they put practical men and women with analogous problems together to critically assess proposed solutions. First-hand experience to verify outcomes is vital to overcoming scepticism when most policy actors are continually subject to promotional hyperbole from various advocates.

Government officials learning with researchers

In several of the cases, government staff from the responsible agencies have been strategically engaged in the project as researchers or advisers from the outset. This has been particularly significant as a tool for building trust between local people and government officials, and for transforming commonly held assumptions of government officials about causes of local problems. However, this strategy also has risks (Freudenberger, 1998). Government staff typically have very little time to devote to project work, particularly when it involves lengthy field visits, and their attention is continually drawn away by the interventions of their superiors. Reorganization or reassignment of staff is common and can result in the loss of key project supporters, so that the research team has to start all over again with new (and perhaps less sympathetic) personnel. It is also frequently difficult to overcome the deeply embedded assumptions and behavioural models of government staff (see above section on governance reform and decentralization). Initial responses are likely to be defensive, particularly by line-agency officials charged with NRM and policy implementation.

The research teams in these cases adopted a variety of strategies for enrolling government officials with direct responsibility for resource management in their projects. In the case of the community forestry project in Cambodia, for example, FA officials responsible for community forestry were invited to serve on the project advisory committee, and through this role became involved in fieldwork and became familiar with site-based research success. The PMMR project in Cambodia (Chapter 8) was led by national government staff. However, to implement the project they had to fully engage provincial level staff, not only in the Department of the Environment, but also other line agencies. These officials have become key supporters of the innovations introduced by the project. This strategy has perhaps been most clearly applied in the case of the Tam Giang lagoon project. Here, the provincial Department of Fisheries officials served as members of the research team in the project's early phases. As well, the department's director is strongly supportive of the new participatory planning approach to lagoon management (see Chapter 4).

Note that in a number of cases, the researchers themselves were government staff in the line agencies responsible for introducing innovations (Mongolia, Bhutan). However, even in these cases, the research work was clearly separate from the agency's regular policy responsibilities and was normally carried out by different staff in separate groups. The Bhutan RNRRCs, for example, did not have line responsibilities for resource management. And in the Cambodia cases, both the community forestry and PMMR projects were led by staff from the Ministry of the Environment, which has line responsibility only for protected areas, not forestry or fisheries. Similar approaches were employed in the Mongolia case. So even when the research was led by government staff, a deliberate strategy of inclusion and building line agency buy-in was needed.

In all cases, the benefits of this strategy arise from social learning: the transformation of perceptions and understanding through interaction with other people and the shared interpretation of evidence. Such interaction went beyond formal field engagement to social interaction in the field after working hours, which helped break down formal inter-agency divisions and barriers. Research team members did not merely undertake independent studies and write analytical reports. They also shared field experiences and interpreted and debated what they saw.[9] Research planning, fieldwork, communications with villagers, strategies for engaging government, reviewing and analysing data, interpreting outcomes and reporting were all shared through interactive experience. The participation of government staff in many of these elements helped them to buy in to the conclusions of the research work and to recognize how those conclusions had been reached. The experience of the researchers engaging government staff has shown them new ways of collaboration to ensure the relevance and impact of applied research.

Networking and alliance-building

The literature on policy-making refers extensively to the importance of networks of influence and information exchange, through which policy agendas take shape (see reviews in Lindquist, 2001; Neilson, 2001). Many of the projects have been quite deliberate and strategic in both enrolling in such networks and in recruiting influential network members. This point has already been explained, for example, in relation to the credibility and communication of research results, and the engagement of government officials in the projects.

This strategy has been presented most clearly in the PMMR case study (Chapter 8). It focuses on the networking element of the project and demonstrates the attention paid by project leaders and members in engaging a variety of local, national and international networks.

Part of this strategy is also the construction of alliances with sympathetic individuals inside or outside government. Even large organizations which might be inimical to policy change are seldom monolithic, and different individuals or groups in the government or donor agencies can approach policy issues from diverse perspectives and strategic interests. This kind of alliance-building is not limited to government officials. Indeed, international NGOs and donors can form important strategic partners to introduce and support new ideas with local governments. Once convinced of the efficacy of local research results, large international donors have many channels for coordinated influence on policy which are not available even to well-placed government officials. This strategy has been employed by the Ratanakiri research team, including an early decision to locate the research project as part of a large, donor-funded governance reform programme (Muny, 2001).

Overall, networking has been adopted by almost all the projects represented in these cases, often with a high degree of sophistication. Research teams have contributed to alliances and coordinating groups, sometimes even creating these where they did not exist but where the need was evident. For example, development coordinating committees in the Philippine Cordillera region were designed to implement ancestral domain claims. Another set of examples where research has helped to build alliances and networks for change is the linking of local resource users to local government structures. This example merits discussion in its own right.

Linking resource user groups to local government

An inherent element of the PAR framework applied in these cases is the simultaneous strengthening of local resource user groups and the linking of them to local government structures. This is strategically important in policy influence, particularly in the fluid environment of policy change which characterizes many of these cases. CBNRM processes and local resource user groups rely on the sanction of senior government officials to enforce local planning and resource decisions (as well as technical support and inter-agency coordination). Therefore, they interface directly with reforms to fundamental processes of governance. One aspect of this, the learning on the side of communities, is borne out by a quote from the Mongolia chapter: 'CBNRM is a process where herders learned how to represent themselves to the local governors, and learned about democratic procedures by participating in decision-making on pasture and NRM.'

CBNRM projects have been criticized for the way in which, under the sanction of powerful external donors and NGOs, they have created parallel institutional structures which can disempower local government authorities (Ribot, 2002).

However, most of the cases reported in this volume appear to have unfolded somewhat differently.

The CBNRM action research projects in these cases created platforms or mechanisms for cooperation and dialogue of communities with the institutions of local government, as for example the *sum*-level co-management teams in Mongolia, and the combined project-line agency activities of GAAS in Chapters 6 and 9 respectively. In other cases, non-formalized channels for functional relations between communities and local government are fostered in the resource planning and delivery of services such as extension, credit or infrastructure. The Cordillera, Ratanakiri and Tam Giang lagoon cases are all good examples of this.

Operating in legal and policy vacuums, in many cases the projects create new structures, particularly at the lowest level. Instead of disregarding existing or evolving local governance bodies, however, these projects interact intensively with those bodies. Rather than being set up as alternatives to the formal institutions of government, they operate in a complementary and collaborative way. Researchers are keenly aware of fostering such relationships and inclusive arrangements:

> The field research team helped the community to form their own organizational structure. A community forestry management committee was formed with local participation, including local authorities like the village, commune and district chiefs, through free election. *The new community forest management structure has to stay under the existing Village Development Committee, in which community forestry planning can be integrated in the commune development plan.* Doing this can address the issue of overlapping roles and responsibilities among commune council members and provides the community forestry committee and Village Development Committee with an opportunity to build relationships and work together with the other fields of the development program. (Royal Government of Cambodia, 2004: 19; italics added)

Of particular note here are those few cases in which the interaction of user groups and local government gave prominence to gender-based differences in needs and interests. In Mongolia, women's interests in pasture management and livelihoods were represented explicitly through women's discussion groups. In the Tam Giang lagoon, researchers made special efforts to recruit women to the lagoon management committees. In Guizhou, women emphasized to village leaders the importance of water supply as a local resource management priority. The research projects provided entry points for identifying gender-differentiated development needs in local government processes.

Instead of simply being standalone new creations, CBNRM institutions become part of local political decision-making, and in some cases report to accountable policy-making bodies. This is one key aspect of the decentralization context exploited by these cases. Specifically, instead of paralleling existing governance structures, CBNRM institutions mesh with them, renegotiating roles and rights. This is possible because of the fluidity entailed in the ongoing decentralization initiatives. Where governance structures are well established and policy flux less pronounced, as in Guizhou province in China, the integration of CBNRM processes and structures with those of the government is considerably more difficult.

Strengthening local voices

Participatory research which builds local NRM institutions strengthens community organization and leadership and gives local resource users voice in their dealings with policy decision-makers. Researchers can create opportunities for local men and women to engage with decision-makers indirectly through the profile of their projects or contacts. However, experience suggests that the message is far more powerful if it comes directly from the people, stated in their own terms. By building the capacity of local actors to understand, integrate and articulate the policy implications of local NRM alternatives, PAR builds essential policy feedback opportunities in governance systems.

As Holland, Blackburn and Chambers note (1998: 85), 'it is difficult for decision-makers to challenge the views of the poor'. This is particularly true when the poor are in the same room, when their views are presented in an articulate and confident way, and when their opinions are substantiated with local evidence.

This is especially important in the case of marginalized groups which otherwise would not have any reasonable opportunity to communicate their experiences to policy-makers. As explained in the Ratanakiri case:

> Direct meetings of the indigenous people with policy-makers were found to be more effective than contacts mediated by NGO representatives or through other official channels. Policy-makers at all levels seemed to appreciate this, probably because it was clear that the indigenous people were speaking for themselves rather than telling the government what they had been primed to say by development organizations. These direct discussions also resulted in breaking down negative stereotypes about minority peoples which were widely-held by national authorities (John and Phalla, Chapter 3, p. 42).

Through such processes, community members were also able to review draft policies and provide feedback on how these might affect them. As noted in the Mongolia case (Chapter 6): 'Discussions with herder groups on the drafts of national level policy and legal documents was another way to promote feedback on strengths and weaknesses. Changes were made in drafts because of local inputs.'

Several other cases in this volume demonstrate this effect explicitly. For example, the PMMR project made a point of engaging policy-makers directly with local people. Because of their position, even though project team members could not assume public positions on controversial issues, they could identify and connect powerful decision-makers to opportunities for personal inspection and familiarization with the field situation. They could make introductions to local leaders, and turn up the volume of local voices quite a bit. The whole intent of the IIRR policy linkage workshop (Chapter 13) was to provide a forum for village voices to be heard effectively by government officials. Even in the Tam Giang lagoon case (Chapter 4) an important role of government officials in the participatory local planning scheme was to validate and approve local lagoon reallocation schemes, thus demonstrating that they had heard local concerns and endorsed their priorities. These opportunities for direct communication of local concerns in NRM are vital elements of effective governance when natural resources form such an important part of local livelihoods.

New roles in policy reform

Through most of these policy-influencing strategies, the cases also demonstrate how conventional roles for the key actors in resource management policy are changing. Researchers, for example, have conventionally been considered as objective analysts of empirical evidence, publishing results to foster greater discussion which build on existing disciplinary frameworks. However, in these cases researchers served a variety of roles in building local awareness and the capacity to respond to, or even initiate, policy reform. By applying new models of learning which engage local men, women and government officials in generating shared insights, researchers are connecting local practice to national policy. They are facilitating multistakeholder exchanges and negotiation through social learning.

For example, the Cambodia community forestry project (Chapter 11) structured its research teams, site selection and field interventions in ways which facilitated policy-relevant learning for forestry officials, partner NGOs, newly constituted commune councils and village development committees. Local forest user groups and village development councils are experimenting with their new roles as resource managers. Commune councils are experimenting with new roles which allow them to sanction village resource planning and enforcement. FA officials are learning how they can be technical resources and guides rather than focus on regulatory enforcement. Researchers are learning facilitative, rather than analytical, roles from field experience and from interaction with policy stakeholders at multiple levels.

Other cases provide similar evidence. In Bhutan, researchers confronted their traditional roles and practices in the face of learning from participatory research experiences. In the Guizhou case, researchers are explicit about the challenges of encouraging government officials to adopt new roles. The IIRR case is concerned with how to help government officials rethink their conventional resource management roles. In Mongolia, the participatory research is defining new individual and collective roles for pastoralists as resource managers.

However, the case which most clearly demonstrates the ways in which multiple actors have adopted new roles through participatory research is probably the Tam Giang lagoon case (Chapter 4). The authors elaborate how each set of actors has adopted unconventional roles in lagoon resource management as a result of their positive experience with PAR on CBNRM.

Challenges

The successes which a number of the cases report in strengthening the voices of local resource users in communications with policy decision-makers will evolve further. Some reforms have been introduced; new processes are beginning to institutionalize consultation and accountability mechanisms. But while these reforms may have strengthened democratic mechanisms, there remain many governance issues to be addressed. Even strong democracies with a long tradition of open public access and complaint to decision-makers (e.g. India, Philippines) have failed to effectively devolve resource rights and management responsibilities to the benefit of local communities (Sarin et al., 2003).

The successes reported here belie the complexity and non-linearity of the project experiences. A close reading of the cases demonstrates that most of these successes were several years in the making. For example, the Tam Giang lagoon research team had five years of research experience, which enabled them to diagnose the inequitable impacts of aquaculture policy. But it was only after the enabling co-management policies were introduced that their participatory research experience provided a platform for a robust community response and a new model for implementing this policy. Most of the other cases similarly tried many ways of consulting and sharing their research lessons, often with limited success, before they identified the key policy issues or the appropriate linkages and mechanisms to leverage policy impacts in their own context. Through more systematic analysis and comparison of these lessons, field practices can be strengthened, experiences shared and project efforts directed more effectively.

Many of the research teams are also only beginning to explore the latitude for using decentralized NRM to better respond to the needs of women resource users. While resource decentralization policies of one form or another were widespread and attracted considerable attention, policies which linked resource management to gender and equity concerns were not, and hence provided less opportunity for interpretation and implementation. Few of the projects identified barriers to the security of women's resource assets and rights which might be strengthened through policy reforms. However, several cases built women's awareness, knowledge, skills and confidence, as well as their capacity to articulate such interests.

Conclusions

The essential argument of this chapter is that the research cases presented in this volume have had a surprising degree of influence on policy formulation and implementation. In part, this points to the growing recognition by the project research teams that local innovations required enabling policy changes, and that local innovations alone would not be sufficient to address the problems communities face in NRM. But it also appears that many of their strategies for policy influence were successful precisely because they started with local PAR. These cases provide examples of how PAR was able to generate local successes and thereby to influence policy reforms.

It is helpful for CBNRM practitioners to understand the potential and mechanisms by which field experience can shape policy, as a guide to strengthening their own practice and building a more supportive context for sustainable and equitable resource use. We argue that there are several important reasons for the outcomes reported here, and that CBNRM practitioners can use these lessons to better diagnose and intervene in policy contexts. One of the factors is the extent of contextual policy flux, particularly around decentralization initiatives. These are ubiquitous, but they offer contexts for CBNRM experimentation of varying potential. Local practice which engages resource users and government officials in social learning about innovative solutions to essential livelihood problems or conflicts will challenge the assumptions of many of the actors involved. Innovative local practice can have a striking influence on decentralizing policies in three situations in particular: when policy is still taking shape; when the local evidence demonstrates that policy commitments are not being fulfilled; or when local government is interested but lacks the capacity to implement policy effectively.

The connection between local participatory innovations and policy change is not a simple cause–effect relationship. Policy processes and the influences which feed into them are complex, idiosyncratic, opportunity-driven and non-linear. Yet the introduction of new information, especially when it challenges fundamental assumptions or contradicts long-standing simplifications, can open doors to new perspectives.

These cases influence policy in several ways. While the most obvious is that, in some cases, the research provides direct inputs to policy formulation, perhaps the most important influence is on the actual implementation of policy. Here, participatory local research which engages government officials and local resource users in social learning offers potential for improving governance and increasing the effectiveness of policy reforms. These research cases illustrate strategies which respond to contextual opportunity, relying on astute leadership and documented insight from local learning more than careful planning or analysis.

However, some strategies can be fairly widely transferred, such as the engagement of government officials in the learning process, and the strengthening of connections between the research (learning) team and networks of policy influence. Effective participatory research also builds both the confidence and the voice of local resource users in their own interactions with government agencies. An important element of facilitating policy change through participatory research in these cases is in the adoption of novel roles by key actors in the process. By exploring and practising these new roles, development actors are redefining conventional relationships which constrain policy options and are thereby opening doors for innovative alternatives.

These cases demonstrate the difference between investing in research as a product (that is, as analytical conclusions and reports) and investing in research as part of a process of action and change. As others have also concluded, it is the process, and the strengthening of specific actors within that process, which leads to policy influence, more than the product itself (Holland, Blackburn and Chambers, 1998).

These cases provide evidence to policy-makers, inform strategy for advocates and direct policy implementation by government agents. Indeed, it is likely that effective policies fostering the emergence of CBNRM can be designed only through evidence from PAR. This approach provides a unique set of tools for small-scale policy experimentation and for social learning of participants around issues of contradiction and conflict. PAR provides practical examples that can stimulate enabling policy reforms and transform the roles of researchers, officials in line agencies and local government, and men and women who rely on the resources. This combination of impacts allows new collaborative resource management processes to take root and grow in diverse contexts.

CHAPTER 18

Conclusions: community-based natural resource management in action

Stephen R. Tyler

Learning from the cases

The significance of the case narratives in this volume is that they all demonstrate – in different ways, under different contexts, and across a wide range of resources – the potential of practical action to address both poverty reduction and resource degradation. Many rural poverty reduction schemes have had unexpected impacts on natural resource degradation. Economic policy reforms, which ease market access and boost commercial production, have encouraged the use of farming technologies which further degrade the resource base. Tenure reforms that provide incentives for sustainable exploitation practices and allow access to credit and input markets can result in further exclusion and impoverishment of the poorest rural people. Much of the prolific literature optimistically linking rural poverty reduction and environmental objectives in the past 15 years remains either wishful thinking or elaborate justification. These cases provide signposts for positive practice.

The case stories also show how research can lead to development and social change. The authors reveal the complexity of the historical and social web within which local action must be set, and the results of diagnostic analysis of community resource problems. But they also describe joint learning processes which led to the creation of new livelihood approaches; the development of new institutions for resource rights, planning and governance; the increased engagement of marginalized local groups in the political discourse of NRM; and the evolution of research paradigms towards more interdisciplinary and holistic methods and frameworks. The insights from these CBNRM research experiences come less from generalized analytical conclusions than from testing and modelling innovative development practice.

Rural development practitioners are trained in social or natural science so as to interpret the phenomena they observe, and also in technical application so as to design changes or interventions. In addition, they learn through the practical application of skills and by confronting complex, non-formulaic problems. The notion of learning through practice is fundamental to how we expect effective professionals to work (Schon, 1983), yet it is seldom made explicit. These cases provide helpful models for both researchers and practitioners-as-learners, demonstrating how informed action can serve both to reveal new knowledge as well as to direct good practice.

Case narratives like these have a particular value in learning for practice. The reality that professionals face is always ambiguous. Social science theory, which provides a useful basis for structuring observations, has a relatively low predictive value when it comes to the complexities of human affairs. The acquisition of practical knowledge for real expertise is always based on experience from cases (Flyvbjerg, 2001). We do not learn from cases because the solutions from one can be generalized to many others, but because the case experience provides an example which illustrates broader insights, demonstrates how complex relationships play out and provides clues to practitioners about how they can respond in their own unique context-dependent situations.

This concluding chapter will focus on interpreting what these action-learning studies accomplished. We are primarily concerned here with the application of research in development practice and change. For that reason, the discussion will be oriented towards practitioners-as-learners, and draws insights for rural poverty and NRM practice.

What happened?

In Chapter 2, I explained how the projects came to have a common starting point and a shared conceptual framework. Despite a wide range of political contexts and focus on different resources, there are also many consistencies in how they unfolded and what the main outcomes were. Across widely divergent settings, research teams struggled with novel PAR methods. They focused on the collaborative design of positive interventions to address local poverty. They worked with community groups to strategically build consensus and present a common political position in dealings with more powerful external agents; or they sought to differentiate local interests in order to assess how resource benefits were distributed. They helped to build capacity for NRM analysis and decision-making among resource user communities, government officials and researchers. They developed new institutions and processes for resource planning and decision-making, and they used field-level insights and experience to influence policy change and policy implementation.

The case chapters relate diverse paths through which the projects' CBNRM focus emerged. Sometimes this evolved from a starting point of on-farm productivity enhancement; sometimes from exploring a novel integrated resource management perspective (such as watersheds); sometimes from a crisis in a key common property resource system (such as fishery or pasture); and sometimes from a policy change opportunity (such as recognition of community resource rights). The learning value of the research projects was enhanced by results which were often unexpected.

Capacity building and learning were fundamental outcomes of the cases. Importantly, the learners were not only the researchers but also local men and women, farmers and fishers, government extension agents, local government officials and senior policy-makers. In the early stages of some of these CBNRM projects, capacity-building for the researchers themselves was a crucial objective. Many of the cases relate examples of how natural science research teams struggled at the outset to interpret and apply participatory methods in the field. As their experience reveals, participatory research skills are best learned in the field, through practice and reflection (Blackburn and Holland, 1998 draw similar conclusions). Throughout even the long-term research cases, it is instructive to see how research teams continued to identify capacity-building as an important rationale for the work, as they focused on new challenges such as conflict management, policy influence, communications and networking. Of course, they also applied and extended the conclusions from their own fieldwork as they built these additional skills.

In these cases, farmers and fishers also learned from the research. They demonstrated an increased general awareness and perception of natural resource systems and degradation issues. However, they also adapted new production technologies, gained experience with new marketing arrangements, as well as new forms of organization for the production, conservation and management of shared resources. Farmers and fishers are practical above all, so the value of experience as a teaching tool is hard to beat. Several of the cases report on the effectiveness of farmer-to-farmer learning, which became increasingly systematized. This experience was analogous to successful 'farmer field schools' organized elsewhere (CIP-UPWARD, 2003). As discussed in Chapter 9, these means may be most effective when government bureaucracies are especially resistant to change. Local resource users also started to recognize their political voice by acquiring skills in collective action, organization, innovation and advocacy, so as to demonstrate and argue for changes to government policy and implementation.

In many of the cases, government officials proved to be another important category of learners. The lessons they learned may have been slightly different from those of the researchers or of the farmers. For example, district-level extension staff realized that by providing opportunities for meaningful local participation, they could be more effective in improving productivity and reducing poverty (this is referred to in each of Chapters 4–11). Local government leaders who were engaged in the projects recognized the value of new processes for planning and managing natural resources. They endorsed or adapted new institutions which helped them meet their devolved authorities for resource management. In local pilot projects, senior-level officials recognized the strength of arguments for policy change and the evidence for feasible alternatives (Chapter 17).

Researchers also learned to adapt methods and tools, and even to develop new tools which crossed disciplinary boundaries on their problem-solving, interdisciplinary teams. This resulted, for example, in the modification of participatory appraisal tools to specific contexts.[1] The cases refer frequently not only to using and adapting PRA methods in the local context, but also to the refinement of wholly novel approaches. For example, most of the research teams had to learn, modify and apply methods of conflict management in order to proceed with institutional interventions. In Hong Ha and Ratanakiri, the researchers developed formal participatory communications strategies (Bessette, 2003). In China, research teams were able to strengthen the roles of local farmers and resource user groups by developing PM&E tools for them to use in evaluating the research work themselves (Vernooy, Qiu and Jianchu, 2003). Through experience and networking with peers, many of the teams learned strategies for policy influence and networking. This increased the effectiveness of their community-level interventions and the likelihood that local innovations could be more widely disseminated (see Chapter 17 for examples). Thus an important outcome of these CBNRM projects was the development of new methods and tools for effective PAR.

During the course of their research work, most of the teams generated interdisciplinary and participatory problem diagnoses. These built on the scientific knowledge and studies of the researchers, as well as the indigenous and informal knowledge of local resource users. They were validated with different groups in the community and with government officials. Having developed and validated priority problems with members of the community and government officials, the researchers were more or less obliged to follow up if they wished to maintain their credibility. Community priorities that could not be framed as researchable questions, or to which the researchers could not respond directly (such as school or road construction, seed funding for new activities), were often addressed by obtaining resources from other organizations or existing government programmes. But even when research was feasible, responding to community priorities sometimes stretched the researchers' usual disciplinary comfort zones.

Participatory diagnoses led to action, which was the core of the learning experience in these research cases. CBNRM action was, in the first instance, local in scale and context-specific. Local actions proved to be essential for learning and impact. This is the proof of concept: if the CBNRM process cannot generate local change, it has to be regarded as ineffective from a development standpoint. This is one of the areas that differentiate CBNRM from policy-oriented research. Many of the cases point to the importance of policy in shaping local possibilities for change. But the cases also show that without the tools and processes for implementing changes to local practice, policy reforms are insufficient.

As originally intended in the conceptual framework for the research, the project teams selected research sites where the population was relatively poor. The research developed interventions to address this poverty through resource management. But even though these were very low-income rural households, over time the researchers came to broaden their concept of poverty. Appropriately enough, in most cases the initial actions addressed rapid improvements to food production, water supply or basic income. But through socially differentiated analyses, some of the teams came to take actions on the problems of marginalized sub-groups in the community. Others recognized the importance of building diverse assets, such as social capital, access to credit, political influence, and human-resource skills in leadership, communication or organizational management. These asset-building activities by the research teams became important elements of the experimental community-level actions to reduce poverty.

Both production technologies and resource management institutions were the subject of innovation and testing in the research cases. Most of the cases revolved around issues in which these factors interact: the benefits of improved production systems and management practices for common property resources can only be realized if institutional reforms also ensure access to poor users (Leach, Mearns and Scoones, 1999). The cases document new awareness of social exclusion and community heterogeneity among the researchers, and often even among community members themselves. New processes for resource-planning and decision-making reinforced governance reforms by strengthening transparency, accountability and representation. Together with communities and resource users, researchers and local officials reflected on how well such new institutions were working and devised ways in which they could be improved. This obliged them to deal publicly with issues of governance, an experience which sometimes reflected poorly on the performance of the conventional administrative mechanisms of the state (Vernooy, Qiu and Jianchu, 2003).

Given these awareness-expanding lessons, and the importance of resource tenure and rights in these cases, the field lessons often led researchers and communities to policy engagement. Chapter 17 documents ways in which both the analysis of researchers and the novel experience in the field affected policy. Such impacts took the form of new resource tenure systems, legislated collective resource rights and the introduction of formal participatory planning processes, as well as extensive local reinterpretation of decentralizing policy implementation. All these policy innovations helped broaden the scope for local initiatives on resource management.

Finally, a crucial element of these case experiences is that they were transformative for the actors involved. Most cases document transformational recognition of processes and causal links, the exposure of power relations and the adoption of new roles by key actors. The research did not merely generate new data, it generated new perceptions of the problems.

The cases document examples where government staff adopted more facilitative, rather than regulatory and enforcement, roles. Researchers guided the enquiries of other learners. Farmers became researchers, agreeing on criteria and evaluating experiments. As well, women assumed new roles in resource-planning and decision-making. Finally, resource users demanded more responsiveness and accountability from local governments. These kinds of transformational changes opened up new avenues for creative endeavour which the actors would not have considered previously. Such changes demonstrate shifts in fundamental operating assumptions. These are not marginal or incremental changes.

None of the cases concludes that the problems are solved. Despite the strong desire of most of the research teams to solve problems, and despite the concrete accomplishments of the cases, each successful innovation generates a new set of challenges. The point is that technical innovations and new institutions can enable resource users, both individually and collectively, to adapt from a stronger platform of resource access, knowledge, experience and confidence. The cases document how CBNRM researchers have moved from an approach of designing optimal solutions to strengthening the capacity of poor communities for adaptive learning and collective action.

In the most advanced cases, despite continuing political tensions and dynamic ecological conditions, adaptive learning is becoming institutionalized. In Koh Kong province, for example, the new VMCs are becoming adaptive learners who are experimenting with new techniques and management interventions, and seeking technical advice to frame their options and interpret outcomes (Chapter 8). In the Tam Giang lagoon, members of the new Fishing Coalition are responsible for monitoring changes in resource conditions, in order to adjust plans as required (Chapter 4). In Cambodia, successful community forestry groups have developed their own outreach activities to share lessons with other organizations (Chapter 11). In Hong Ha, Vietnam, and in Changshun county, Guizhou, district officials are integrating new participatory diagnosis and extension tools developed by the research teams because they work better than previous practices (Chapters 5 and 9). There will continue to be changes in these situations, some for the better and some for the worse. But the status quo ante is no longer an option.

Explaining what happened

The research outcomes and actions described above can be characterized in terms of three qualities that can be linked to the ways in which the researchers combined science, participation and action.

1. The research was effective, in the sense that it posed questions which were relevant to the key actors and was able to develop innovations to address them.
2. The research results were adopted by resource users, local government organizations and development professionals such as extension agents or project staff.
3. The research was empowering and transformative in its effect on the actors who were involved.

One reason for the effectiveness of these CBNRM action-research projects was that they embraced the complexity of their cases, rather than seeking ideological or reductionist simplifications. As they gained experience, the research teams increasingly recognized the contradictions and anomalies, as well as the heterogeneity and dynamism, in CBNRM. They adopted pragmatic approaches to the specific histories of their different sites. For example, they recognized that indigenous environmental knowledge was of limited value in migrant communities (Chapter 8). As well, they recognized that although the concept of collective resource management had deep cultural roots, traditional practices could not be revived in contemporary contexts (Chapter 6). They identified divergent interests in the community, and in some cases exposed awkward inequities that otherwise might have remained buried to both community members and governments (Chapter 4, Chapter 10). They helped build transparency and accountability into new governance processes for CBNRM, while tying these to existing structures of local government (Chapters 3, 4, 8, 12). In these respects, the researchers succeeded because they did not dodge difficult questions.

But it was their characteristics as PAR projects which played the most important role. Both the 'participatory' and the 'action' in PAR crucially affected the outcomes described above. This is because participation and action were much more than methodological approaches or techniques of research. They conditioned the attitudes of the researchers and those of the other actors involved in the projects. They framed the interaction of the various parties and reinforced the learning processes that were essential to social change.

The participatory nature of the research work went far beyond engaging resource users in data collection or in testing interventions. Men and women in the affected communities became involved in defining the problems and setting research objectives, in identifying criteria for success, and in monitoring and evaluating changes. Researchers gave up some of their control in exchange for more effective outcomes. A number of the cases recount ways in which the research objectives and agenda changed after engagement with resource users who identified problems and priorities that the researchers had not seen. This strongly participatory nature of the research processes was challenging for the researchers. They have been trained and socialized for many years to understand legitimate scientific research as an elitist and reductionist activity, which demands specialized technical, as opposed to relational, skills (see a discussion of African experience in Opondo et al., 2003).

But it is only through participation that life and meaning are given to any phenomenon. This is partly related to the pedagogical maxim that most of us do not recall new information, even if told repeatedly, unless we actually process it by applying it in practice. The vital connection of neural synapses in the human brain which comes from acting on new information is obviously an important element of learning. Without processes of engagement and participation, any organized intervention is reduced to words on paper, or seeds, or fertilizer, or other material inputs. That is, the full comprehension of any phenomenon can only be grasped through personal engagement. To design an innovation which is likely to be widely and quickly adopted requires the participation of the users.

Participation is how people build confidence, trust and essential communication skills. These skills are all empowering, so the processes themselves are important elements of social change and poverty reduction. Participatory approaches recognize and respect the agency of individuals: their ability to assess situations, make choices and change their behaviour in the face of constraints. Of course, participatory processes expose participants to politically charged and confrontational situations. Those in a vulnerable position can suffer from this exposure. That is why participatory processes need to be managed thoughtfully and respectfully. The research project context can help to level the playing field and provide judicious facilitation.

Sayer and Campbell (2004) argue that participatory approaches to resource management and livelihood issues are essential for effective research. Without them, scientists will miss key explanatory elements of a complex situation, will fail to unlearn erroneous assumptions and will continue to use their conclusions to promote interventions which are either inappropriate or unpopular.

Building trust, confidence and relationships may have little to do with the science, but it has a great deal to do with the process of adopting innovations. Intervention must start from where people are. The process of ongoing research, learning and adoption will not proceed without the required credibility and confidence in relations between community users of new knowledge and the generators of this knowledge.

Participation was not only important in the enquiry stage of the research, but also in the analysis and sharing of lessons. Most of the learning outcomes described in the previous section occurred through participation in the research effort, and through discussion of the meaning of these outcomes together, rather than through transmission of knowledge by reports, formal presentations or publications. This applies not only to the participation of farmers and resource users, but also to government officials and other external actors. It was the first-hand experience of field conditions, the inevitable modification of simplifying assumptions when confronted by complex realities and the practical adaptation of innovations by users interacting with each other that led to the most powerful insights.[2]

Research directed towards behavioural change is most effective when it engages the parties who are intrinsically implicated in such change. The research process can remain rigorous and analytical, but it responds to complex local conditions and priorities. In such cases, the insights from PAR have been followed by actions undertaken by resource users themselves, along with support from researchers or extensionists. Implementation, which is often left to other players, here became the central aspect of CBNRM research.

Taking action is messier than merely reporting on analytical conclusions. But it has a catalytic effect on the commitment of participatory agents and on the quality of the lessons learned. Because the researchers were not merely producing another academic or extension publication, they had to learn how to motivate people to make changes, to test new production systems or to organize so that they could implement new institutions. This kind of action depended on the accumulated goodwill of relationships between researchers and the communities. It required high levels of awareness and trust on both sides which could only be built over time. It was supported by the responsiveness of researchers and by the motivation and enthusiasm of resource users and community leaders.

The explicit social dimension of learning from participation and action in these CBNRM cases was important. Lessons were derived from theory, observation, analysis and testing – but also through interaction. The cases recount numerous different forums for local interaction around the research process. These included: identifying and validating problems with resource user groups where they existed already or facilitating their development where they did not; exploring gender-differentiated perspectives with individuals and women's groups; presenting conclusions to local government; sharing crop performance assessments between farmers; developing collective regulations for resource use; and interpreting outcomes to those inside and outside the community. These interactive processes stimulated discussion and challenged conclusions. They built consensus among different actors on problems, interpretation and results. They created opportunities for mutual exposure to participants in the research process who had very different worldviews and experience, such as local fishers and senior government officials. And in many cases, these processes created new opportunities for local people to interact among themselves. Indeed, as Vandergeest argues in Chapter 16, the research processes essentially redefined the community in ways that were consistent with its learning and action functions under CBNRM.

The roles of the researchers became altered by these processes. They remained community outsiders. But their role in facilitating the processes of learning and change was an important element in accomplishing the outcomes documented above. At different times in most of the projects, researchers were called upon to provide coaching and problem-solving for other learners. They also assisted with conflict management, awareness-raising, capacity-building, networking and policy support, as well as more conventional analysis and training.

An actor-oriented approach to development emphasizes the capacity of the poor and marginalized to assess options and take the initiative in their own self-interest. This approach is contrasted with an expert-oriented approach, which relies on specialized expertise to provide solutions to complex problems. These cases marry both approaches. Specialized expertise across multiple disciplines is essential in CBNRM research in order to diagnose complex social and natural system problems, to apply a broad menu of potential solutions and to integrate these in order to address multiple dimensions of these problems simultaneously. However, action is the true measure of the viability and effectiveness of conclusions and innovations. At the same time, it is the most effective way to ensure learning and continued adaptation. Only through action can innovations be institutionalized. This requires more than knowledge; it requires changes in behaviour, roles, attitudes, skills and capacities. In short, institutionalization requires transformation.

Combining science, participation and action generates strong learning outcomes and builds the capacity of organizations, in the ways described above. Many of the cases describe the process they followed as iterative cycles of investigation / reflection / planning / action / investigation / reflection / planning / action ... The research teams themselves emphasize this research process and framework as being crucial to the successes they achieved. For a diagrammatic illustration of this process of participatory action research, see Figure 13.1 (or similar diagrams in Chapters 4, 5 and 11). Overall, we can think of this iterative process of participatory action as a model of adaptive social learning. It combines enquiry with interaction and learning by doing.

Reflecting on challenges and implications

None of the various elements here are new in themselves. In particular, it is worth pointing out that the strongly interactive and participatory research strategy employed in these cases often owed much of its initial success to the application of new production technologies and systems which were originally developed using much more reductionist agricultural research frameworks. As the authors of the Bhutan case note in Chapter 10, the participatory field research methods led to new insights which could guide on-station agricultural experimentation, but did not eliminate the need for these entirely. The research project teams managed to put familiar elements together in new ways.

But CBNRM researchers and practitioners still face many challenges. One of the most difficult aspects of their work so far has been addressing social exclusion and inequity in communities. Researchers can be confronted with an apparent dilemma here. Not only can these be issues that communities would rather not deal with, but by highlighting power relations, researchers risk exacerbating resource conflicts. They may feel forced to choose between a socially targeted approach to collective action for resource management (as recommended by Beck and Fajber in Chapter 15), or an explicitly neutral position to avoid annoying elites whose support will be essential to reforms.

In the long term, this issue becomes more tactical than strategic. If power relations and other forms of social marginalization are strongly prejudiced against specific social groups in the community, then poverty reduction, resource governance and sustainable resource use will remain out of reach. If CBNRM processes are functioning, it may be more effective to capture social conflict within them, empowering disadvantaged players to engage more effectively in the inevitable political struggles. Eventually, the issues of exclusion and power relations have to be addressed in order for the fundamental objectives of poverty reduction and resource degradation to be achieved.

Another challenge which frequently arises in the field is dealing with government staff. The cases reveal how government officials have become engaged in the research projects, and how their learning has been helpful for the success of site-based work and the spread of lessons to other sites. But, except for Chapters 9 and 13 which specifically address this problem, the case studies mostly gloss over the frustrations involved. Despite formal policies which may be supportive, many government officials are antagonistic towards the devolution of NRM to communities. It threatens their power, and they may not trust the capacity of local decision-making to protect the resource base. There is no incentive for officials to move from the enforcement and approval of local actions to the facilitation of local management decision-making. Paternalistic attitudes and punitive relations towards community resource users are deeply ingrained in many government resource management agencies. Staff rotate through field positions quickly, never gaining much appreciation for local knowledge or context.

These issues can be very difficult to overcome. Little can be accomplished without meaningful support from senior levels of the bureaucracy, but even that may not be sufficient. The fundamental inconsistency between participatory, actor-oriented and learning-driven field methods on one hand and the hierarchical, structure-oriented and power-driven behavioural rules of bureaucracies, on the other, complicate efforts towards change. It is impossible to create effective participatory field interventions just by grafting the rhetoric into programme documents or training manuals. Nor is there much point in introducing participatory techniques if the underlying philosophy, practices and assumptions about power and agency in the organization remain unchanged. Policy goals can sometimes be invoked to build incentives for behavioural change, but these must penetrate an often impervious organizational culture. But despite their monolithic external images, most large organizations are heterogeneous. It is often possible to find committed, entrepreneurial innovators within the ranks. It may also be possible to generate some enthusiasm or recognition for new professional roles more consistent with support to CBNRM, especially among younger staff.

The CBNRM action-learning processes described in these cases were time-consuming and required substantial external resources and community effort. The researchers, different groups in the communities, government staff and other external groups all had different interests, assumptions and agendas. Initial responses by the communities were frequently superficial and dismissive. It was only after research teams had made a demonstrable commitment to learning from and change with the communities that they could gain respect, trust and shared commitment to innovation.

The research teams found that their initial efforts rapidly built procedural experience, and their own skills in managing participatory research and group dynamics improved with practice. As a result, they could expand their work to new communities with much less investment and effort than was required for the pilots (see examples in Chapters 4, 5, 9, 10). Their early successes also created a reputation for their work among nearby jurisdictions: this reduced the challenges of establishing their initial credibility. However, it remains important to emphasize that the case experiences suggest that scaling up CBNRM innovations relies first on scaling down. That is, it is important to get the pilot experiments right. This can be achieved by concentrating on mechanisms for meaningful participation, enhancing learning on the part of key change agents, and building sustainability of new institutions and processes before devoting a lot of resources to trying to repeat the experience elsewhere.

Given the effort put into building CBNRM institutions and collective action for resource management at the local level, how sustainable are these innovations? Some of the cases describe ongoing long-term research projects, while others are indeed already winding down or have terminated completely. There is no doubt that the engagement of an international donor, as in these cases, generates legitimacy for innovation and change which may disappear once funding and donor interest decline. However, all these cases document the embedding (sometimes still contingent or contested) of new resource rights, new planning and consultation processes, and production systems in the regular practices of farmers, the regular interactions of community members and the administrative mechanisms of government agencies. The innovations developed by each research team are no longer merely artefacts of a discrete donor-funded project. Naturally, without the patronage of an external donor, innovations such as these are vulnerable to political change and to the attrition of key personnel. Ironically, the more successful and widely applicable these innovative CBNRM pilots are, the more likely that their leaders will be diverted by other offers and career opportunities. This is surely a positive outcome, although it may pose challenges to local leadership succession.

In the cases presented in this volume, there is varied evidence of how communities will likely respond to diminished project engagement. In Cambodia, the VMCs in the coastal communities of Koh Kong are already taking initiatives to continue adaptive learning for resource management without project support. Occasionally, they need to be reminded of the main principles of CBNRM, as described in Chapter 8 when researchers emphasized that the process should be non-partisan. Like the Fishing Coalition in the Tam Giang lagoon or the herder organizations in Mongolia, they have gained legitimacy and recognition from the government through the project experience. As a result, now they are able to call on public agencies for technical support and other resources. In the case of ancestral domain in the Philippines, the new participatory planning processes and collaborative institutions for local resource governance developed by the research project have served as models for other municipal governments since the project's completion in 2001 (Chapter 12). The participatory learning framework developed by the IIRR to support community NRM processes has become a regular training programme offered by the institute, and has been modified, elaborated and offered commercially numerous times in different countries (Chapter 13). The reduction or termination of research support from the donor has not led to the erosion of these innovations.

Several kinds of support would be helpful to sustain nascent CBNRM initiatives as described in these cases. Researchers played a key role in participatory diagnosis, and the extension and facilitation of the community interactions with governments or other agencies. Now that the research teams have a greater understanding of the processes and tools, these roles are being taught and transferred to practitioners. Support is needed for the development of curricula, strengthening the field experience of teachers, as well as training and practice for both students and adult learners. These efforts can build on related skills in participatory development among other organizations and on the strengths of existing research groups.[3]

Communities which have already established new institutions for collective action and resource management will face less need for technical support or facilitation in planning and gaining government approvals. But the cases show that even after gaining support from government and establishing successful processes for resource planning and management, local organizations occasionally need external facilitation for dealing with difficult conflicts, and for addressing new challenges in dynamic ecosystems and economies. This suggests the need for new kinds of extension services, or service providers. Such services are not tied to site-specific projects or outcomes nor to sectors or technologies. They could be funded from government poverty-reduction programmes, which are typically targeted at regions in which CBNRM initiatives would be appropriate.

The cases also demonstrate the importance of enabling policies for CBNRM. The specific characteristics of local institutions for the adaptive management of common property and collective action will vary widely, and can really only emerge from the dynamic interaction of complex socio-economic and ecological systems (Ruitenbeek and Cartier, 2001). Prescriptive policies specifying the form and structure of CBNRM institutions would not only be inappropriate given the wide range of local conditions, but they would also fail to accommodate the adjustments needed to adapt to system changes. However, most of the cases clearly benefited from national policies that support decentralized resource management and representative, accountable governance at the local level. They also benefit from strong policy support for poverty reduction and social equity. In the case of Cambodia, participatory resource management plans designed to meet the specific conditions of ethnic-minority communities in Ratanakiri province proved so significant to local politics and planning that they were adopted in the national Seila programme of governance reform (Chapter 3). In Bhutan, new national CBNRM policies were informed by project research results. The new policies helped spread the PAR model and provided national resources for local implementation. These kinds of policy frameworks provide the flexible recognition and support needed to help sustain adaptive learning by CBNRM communities.

As a result of these research projects, new roles and expectations have been adopted by the key players associated with local resource management. Community resource management organizations created through the research projects will face difficult challenges, and in some cases may fail. However, in many instances, the precedents they have set are already being institutionalized. Data needs for resource management will continue, and may even grow as management interventions or resource conflicts become more complex. The need for action research in these communities will decline as they become adaptive learners themselves. It is important to remember that the sustainability of CBNRM does not mean entrenching permanent structures, but rather enabling the appropriate evolution of adaptive management responses over time. Persistence is a less useful criterion of sustainable institutional structures than is adaptability.

Another reason for optimism for the future of CBNRM in Asia is that, despite the modest scale of the early efforts, many of the researchers and the community organizations themselves are well connected to networks of information-sharing and exchange throughout the region. Local efforts are magnified and reflected through these networks, which are increasingly oriented to local-language users and to decentralized memberships of activists and, through them, community organizations. Small-scale, low-profile initiatives which meet the common needs of many marginalized rural communities may gain disproportionate recognition and influence.

In transferring CBNRM experiences, however, it will be difficult to reduce them to standardized guidelines or checklists that can be easily conveyed in new contexts or made routine for large-scale replication. CBNRM practice does not work like that. Initially, many researchers and practitioners sought simple rules and blueprints for their research fieldwork. But once they became comfortable with the approach, they recognized that such short cuts tend to circumvent the fundamental premises of CBNRM, which are meaningful participation, responsiveness, context and adaptation. Methodological pluralism, multiple and flexible tools, and supportive attitudes are all approaches which can be fostered through practice to build and spread CBNRM expertise.

Sharing knowledge in this field will be challenging. The most powerful and difficult lessons from the cases were lessons which probably had to be gained through experience. On the one hand, this demonstrates the importance of practice in learning. But on the other hand, for problems that are widespread, it would be helpful to strengthen alternative methods of learning which might be able to reach a larger audience more quickly. A wide range of teaching and communications approaches is probably needed to strengthen the dissemination of outcomes.

The path to sustainability then is to build a body of skilled CBNRM practitioners through training and experience; support continued networking and information-sharing among resource user groups and with government to share that experience; and build enabling policies for CBNRM consistent with decentralization, poverty reduction and local governance reform. All of these measures are easily supportable by governments or by international donors, and involve only modest expense.

Still, even with the insights from these case studies, the task of building effective CBNRM practice appears daunting. The process is complex, idiosyncratic and generally inconsistent with the capacities and structures of existing government organizations. While the challenges are significant, the key lessons from the cases are that despite challenging situations it is possible to take sensitive and practical action towards CBNRM. Although such action is not always successful, it is a good way to gain support and recognition. Sometimes it is the immobilizing effect of daunting challenges that is the biggest barrier to change.

Directions for practice

The main lessons of this volume for practitioners point to practical processes for adaptive social learning. Local resource-management contexts are always complex, because they involve not only dynamic and poorly understood ecosystems, but also implicit social institutions and inequitable power relations. However, responsive action does not have to address all this complexity at the same time.

The simple foundations of effective CBNRM practice lie in values of mutual respect, trust and learning, rather than power. Because existing relations between the various actors are generally based on power, this change takes time to develop. Actions to build awareness, share knowledge, validate knowledge claims and pilot interventions are undertaken to strengthen these values, using participatory methods which themselves help to change attitudes.

Conventional training for field practice encourages the separation of discrete elements of complex systems, reducing them for specialized analysis and solution. However, these cases suggest that practitioners should embrace complexity without needing to analyse every aspect of complex local systems. The crucial elements of the system demand urgent analysis and intervention. But after this, researchers should be prepared for surprises and will need to act, learn and adapt. Authors of these case studies and their teams encouraged learning by all the partners, not just the researchers. Iterative social learning can help integrate complex and dynamic interdisciplinary problems across space and time.

Learning itself is often less of a barrier than expected, if learning opportunities are built on these foundation values. Most people like to learn, and the different actors involved in CBNRM have many incentives to do so: income enhancement, risk reduction, political power, increased confidence, career recognition and opportunity. Behavioural or role change can be harder than learning, and requires practice. Here, processes which build on shared intention, collaboration, consistency, observation and reflection in collective action seem helpful. These are some of the central elements of management, and in cases where these local management elements can take root, they helped to solidify learning and change.

Note that control of these processes was not particularly significant in affecting outcomes. Learning processes moved at different paces and in response to different pressures. Contention was inherent in the political dynamics of decentralized resource management. Sometimes, learning processes were driven by farmers, sometimes by researchers, sometimes by government agencies. However, the successful innovations in each case depended on details which had to evolve with the projects in the field. These considerations included who was engaged, how conflicts could be addressed, production systems preferred by male or female farmers and the nature of political support for tenure change. Such detailed strategic choices, crucial to the research outcomes, arose from creative exploration, from interaction and from opportunity, not from the carefully planned predetermined objectives of either the researchers or the farmers.

While CBNRM is mainly concerned with managing common property resources through collective action, practitioners have to pay attention to productivity issues on private lands. This is not only because initial income gains are important to strengthen precarious local livelihoods, but because the common and private resource holdings interact ecologically. Specific constraints which the poor face in terms of access to and use of resources have to be addressed. Attention should be given to disentangling symptoms from causes and effects with those people who are most involved. Suggested improvements need to be subject to technical validation and joint investigation, while recognizing that criteria for success may be different for different actors.

Building successful innovations from a small number of sites to much broader applications can involve both horizontal scaling (outward diffusion to adjacent or comparable sites) and vertical scaling (gaining support from senior levels of government). Either strategy can be effective. But programmatic approaches to these efforts, driven by external government or donor targets, can actually frustrate the local process of participatory learning and systemic co-evolution which is essential to success. Scaling up has to be driven by the same factors that lead to local success: supportive attitudes modelled through practice, capacity-building and leadership (see also Blackburn and Holland, 1998).

Building policy influence from field lessons is an important enabling and scaling factor. Practitioners need to recognize opportunity in policy flux, develop networks and allies, and test new ideas in the field. In addition, they must provide evidence, and engage government staff and policy-makers in project learning in various ways. Participatory methods build local voice and confidence, but practitioners can play an important role in giving direction and focus to this voice. Implementing policies to decentralize NRM does not mean that senior governments have no role. Instead, as the case experiences demonstrate, technical support, data management, legitimacy, oversight and sanction are all important roles for senior governments in their dealings with community resource managers.

Directions for research

These cases have demonstrated new and effective ways to connect science, participation and action. They illustrate how researchers can play facilitative roles in helping other actors to learn from interdisciplinary innovations. They point to processes which build confidence and creativity in integrated NRM at the local level, while also dealing with the challenges of political conflict. Beneficiaries of these research projects were, in the first instance, poor local farmers and fishers who were able to capitalize from more secure individual or collective tenure, improved productivity and better resource management to improve incomes.

But there were many public goods generated from this research as well. Reducing natural resource degradation generates benefits far beyond the local level. Watersheds are stabilized, erosion declines, and the quality of water and other resources increases. The protection of the coastal habitat such as mangroves encourages marine biodiversity and strengthens stocks of commercially valuable fisheries. Social and gender analysis focuses community and political attention on marginalized members of society to address fundamental issues of human rights and equity. Local governance reforms build capacity, transparency and accountability, as well as strengthen the delivery of a variety of services. Participatory processes build citizenship and social engagement. These are all examples of public goods that are both essential to development and outcomes of the research cases presented here.

The task of action research shifts as CBNRM takes root in a policy context of decentralization and local governance capacity-building. From the introduction of basic awareness and baseline information, coupled with the challenge of introducing and gaining support for innovations, researchers must now devote more attention to monitoring outcomes. Development of criteria and indicators for resource management and for local livelihood outcomes offer important opportunities for extending participatory research methods. An important element of monitoring outcomes is to focus research attention on groups that are not benefiting from the resource management changes. By continuing to examine the nature and allocation of benefits after the introduction of CBNRM reforms, researchers can contribute to maintaining open and adaptive governance processes and verify that targeted interventions have the intended effects.

A particularly challenging area of CBNRM practice is the transformation of the role of government officials. They evolve from being leading actors and enforcers of natural resources and rural development decision-making, to becoming technical consultants, facilitators and guides to local planning and management. The difficult area of sorting out performance expectations between local and senior levels of government will need research attention. Another aspect of this is the clarification and elaboration of new roles and opportunities for government agencies at various levels as CBNRM practices gain strength. These might include roles in strengthening collaborative learning processes, managing and sharing information for local decision-making, enforcing sanctions to support local resource management practices and continuing to build a broader public awareness of outcomes. All of these are areas to which applied research can contribute.

Most of the cases in this volume concentrate on the learning that must accompany a broader awareness of resource management problems and the implementation of novel institutional solutions, at both the local and higher levels of governance. These exercises have only begun to explore some of the linkages between the ways local communities used their natural resources and external forces for change. For example, the influence of international markets for high-value commercial products was a key factor in driving the enclosure of common property in several cases.

However, other external factors create constraints and opportunity for local resource management action. Global climate change may increase the severity and frequency of extreme climatic events such as floods, droughts or storms, which force communities to introduce changes to their conventional resource management strategies to adapt to higher risks. Opportunities for new products and markets will affect potential returns to collective management, or else change the balance of investment between collective and household-managed resource assets. Changes in national and international economies affect opportunities for migration and off-farm income generation. These, in turn, affect available household labour and capital for local agricultural production or investment in resource management.

Conflicts in resource management regarding claims of tenure and jurisdiction, as well as in development goals, will continue to be prominent features of rural development. In some respects, the decentralization of management decision-making creates even greater potential for local conflicts. The development and institutionalization of conflict management processes to accommodate collective and household resource management, and to adapt to dynamic external conditions, will provide researchers with important opportunities to contribute to high-priority governance issues. This is an area of work that will benefit from the participatory action methods and social learning processes recounted by the cases in this volume.

These CBNRM experiences demonstrate that applied research which engages local actors respectfully as partners in an iterative process of social learning can have transformative outcomes far beyond drawing scientific conclusions. Poor farmers and fishers in the most marginal parts of rural Asia have been able to improve their livelihoods, reduce risk and halt or even reverse environmental degradation. But they have also introduced new institutions of resource management which reinforce local government reforms and challenge national policies of resource management.

These experiences demonstrate the potential of applied research to deliver a wide range of productivity and public-goods benefits. However, outcomes are not guaranteed. The form and function of local resource management institutions are neither universal nor fixed. The political and economic gains of the poor are contingent and vulnerable. These research cases are particularly valuable because they demonstrate how applied research can build the capacity for adaptive learning by local resource users, as individuals and groups, to meet the continued challenges of dynamic change in their environment.

Notes

1 Introduction: poverty and environment in practice

1 For additional information about the centre and its programmes see: www.idrc.ca
2 For an independent review and assessment of the CBNRM programme, see Gonsalves and Mendoza (2003).

2 Community-based natural resource management: a research approach to rural poverty and environmental degradation

1 An example is the editing and distribution of a nine-volume compendium of key readings and bibliographies on topics related to social science concepts, as well as methods of agriculture and NRM (IDRC, 1999).

3 Community-based natural resource management and decentralized governance in Ratanakiri, Cambodia

1 Activities in Yeak Loam focused on community-based protected area management, using tourism to generate income for protection.

4 Participatory local planning for resource governance in the Tam Giang lagoon, Vietnam

1 The researchers were from Hue University of Sciences, Hue University of Agriculture and Forestry and the Department of Fisheries of Thua Thien-Hue province. Phase 1 of the project (1995–7) was funded by CIDA/IDRC/VISED. Phase 2 (1998–2001) was funded by CIDA/IDRC/VEEM.
2 The national average poverty rate in rural areas was 35.6 per cent. The poverty line is defined as the per-person per-day expenditure of buying a local food basket equivalent to 2,100 calories (definition used by World Bank).
3 It was approved by the National Assembly on 26 November 2003, effective 1 July 2004.
4 Core villagers are the key village informants and/or influential people who are representatives to community groups, and who are the most experienced farmers and fishers.

5   Decree 130 (April 2003) by People's Committee of Quang Dien district on reorder-
      ing the fish-trap corrals.

6   Co-management of Pastureland in Mongolia

1   For more information on gender issues, see H. Ykhanbai et al., 2003.

7   Exclusion, accommodation and community-based natural resource management: legitimizing the enclosure of a community fishery in southern Laos

1   Small-scale Wetland Indigenous Fisheries Management Project, Provincial Live-
      stock and Fisheries Office, Champassak Province and Living Aquatic Resource
      Research Centre, Ministry of Agriculture and Forestry, Laos. This paper is based on
      research for an MA in Sustainable Development, Chiang Mai University, Thailand
      (Tubtim, 2001).
2   I refer to these small wetlands as 'backswamps', an idiomatic English term which
      is both descriptive of their origin and analogous to Lao terminology.
3   The prohibited fishing activities are: scooping or draining water from the
      backswamp; blocking off areas for fishing; and using two-person bait nets, *mung*
      (fine mesh nets), or *khaa* (basket traps), *jan* (drop-door traps) or *soum* (conical
      basket traps). It is also forbidden to fell or cut roots of trees that are close to the
      edge of the backswamp. The main fishing gear employed include hook and line,
      floating hook, cast nets, gill nets, one-person bait nets and handled scoop nets.

8   Building networks of support for community-based coastal resource management in Cambodia

1   Cambodian social relations take place within authoritarian, hierarchical constructs
      (see Meas and O'Leary, 2001). According to Buddhist thinking, merit accumulated
      in previous lives helps to explain one's current social position; therefore, those
      with power are thought to belong in power and it is an accepted social concept
      that one's fate should be in the hands of others (Chandler, 1991).

11 Strengthening local voices to inform national policy: community forestry in Cambodia

1   See McKenney and Prom Tola (2002) for a review and analysis of forest concession
      experiences in Cambodia.
2   This is an international NGO that later took on the role of independent monitor of
      forest crimes for the government.
3   In mid-2002, the FA reported that 14 companies held contracts for 19 concessions
      covering approximately 3.9 million ha; 15 concessions covering approximately
      3.0 million ha had been cancelled (Cambodia Government, 2002). However,
      deconcessioned forests were reportedly logged out and no longer of commercial
      timber value, so the disposition of these forests remained unclear.
4   Department of Nature, Conservation and Protection.

5   Within the Department of Forestry and Wildlife (DFW) under the Ministry of Agriculture, Forestry and Fisheries.

6   Such as the FAO-supported community forestry project in Siem Reap and CARERE/ PLG support for commmunity forestry in Ratanakiri.

12 Harmonizing ancestral domain with local governance in the Cordillera of the northern Philippines

1   See Rood and Casambre (1994) and Prill-Brett (1994, 2001) for a discussion of the legal context for the change in the Philippine state's attitude towards indigenous people's land rights.

2   See Prill-Brett (1988, 1992, 1994); Mendoza (1992); Rood and Casambre (1994); and Rood (1994).

3   Common property refers to those situations where there are multiple users of a resource who hold divided title but undivided shares in the resource (Appell, 1991). According to Appell, a divided title may either be a parallel right, a right held by multiple title holders, or a stratified right. The latter is divided by type, such as residual or use rights, and is vested in jural persons.

4   This is the smallest unit of the Philippine government system, roughly corresponding in scale with a neighbourhood or small rural community, which is responsible for the organization of many community development and public service functions based on budgets allocated by senior governments. The *barangay* captain is the senior administrative official at this level.

5   The municipality is a political unit of the government that has political jurisdiction over several distinct communities, or *barangays*, but which may not correctly represent the unique geographical or cultural characteristics of the traditional *ili*.

6   Philippines Government (1997). Our copy has no date, but the signatory was supposed to be the DENR Secretary, Victor Ramos. Hence, we surmise that this may be a document drafted in 1997 or 1998.

7   The province is a politico-administrative unit composed of municipalities and cities.

14 Creating options for the poor through participatory research

1   Workshop comment by Tony Beck, May 2004.

2   A research framework makes assumptions about what constitutes knowledge, that is, how and what researchers will learn during their enquiry, and adopts procedures for data collection, analysis and writing (Creswell, 2003).

3   Dr Kristalina Georgieva, Director of the Environment Department of the World Bank, cited in Gonsalves and Mendoza, 2003: 60.

4   The pragmatic approach that framed the CBNRM projects finds agreement with the conclusion of the August 2000 meeting of scientists from 13 of the 16 CGIAR centres in Penang, Malaysia. Discussing the role of integrated natural resource management (INRM), they concluded it was a way of doing development-oriented research that often must deal with the effects of agricultural advances that resonate across the landscape. They agreed on a number of essential characteristics in undertaking such research: a systems approach is required; work must be process-oriented at multiple scales involving multiple stakeholders; it must be capable of scaling up and out; and it is crucial to employ new tools and methods.

Most importantly, the group recognized the need for a problem analysis phase that primarily has to be a participatory process.

15 Exclusive, moi? Natural resource management, poverty, inequality and gender in Asia

1   Numbers below a poverty line, usually constructed by income level. For discussion of conceptual issues with different poverty measures, see Beck (1994).
2   The Gini coefficient is the standard measure of income distribution across the entire population of a country, where 0 = absolute equality (all incomes equal), 1 = absolute inequality (one person captures all income).
3   In much of Asia the head-count ratio remains the main measure of poverty. While politicians and administrators may claim that poverty is being reduced because the head-count ratio is decreasing, this ignores the complex patterns of changes in livelihoods that occur during the processes of privatization and marketization.
4   The authors have relied on the self-reporting of IDRC partners in much of this chapter, and findings have not in most cases been independently verified.
5   There is an extensive literature on gender relations in Asia which we do not have the scope to review here; some of this literature has also touched on CBNRM and gender relations; see Reichrath (2005).

16 Community-based natural resource management communities in action

1   In the social sciences, bounded notions of community were particularly strong in the fields of social and cultural ecology (Goldenberg and Haines, 2000). In turn, these schools were the basis of many anthropological studies of community-environment interactions in Southeast Asia from the 1950s through the 1970s (Peluso, Vandergeest and Potter, 1995). These studies and their assumptions about community and ecological stability have had a strong influence on CBNRM advocates who also emphasize the idea that stable rural communities have lived in balance with their environments for a long time.
2   Personal communication, John Graham, Senior Program Officer, IDRC.

17 Shaping policy from the field

1   The IDRC research programme supporting the various projects reported here included policy innovation as one of its objectives (IDRC, 2000). Therefore, as researchers began to speculate on what should be done about the institutional problems uncovered through their participatory research projects, IDRC staff encouraged them to explore the policy dimensions of their work further. Of course, the support and encouragement of the funding agency is an important preequisite to reorienting any long-term research project.
2   For a useful review of policy implementation literature, see Najam (1995), who concludes there is broad agreement that the rational distinction between political and administrative decision-making breaks down in practice. The author cites Majone and Wildavsky (1978), who wrote: 'To implement a policy is to change it.'

3   Those who are familiar with policy-making processes generally recognize that while they may be well organized, they are seldom predictable, linear or strictly analytical in nature. Policy systems are driven by time and information constraints, opportunity, surprise, political tactics, and communications just as much as analysis. (Neilson, 2001; Wildavsky, 1979; Gyawali, 2001)

4   For example, see the recent review of the forestry sector in Cambodia headed by a donor representative and the head of the FA. See: www.bigpond.com.kh/users/dfwjica/Forest-Sector-Review.pdf (accessed December 2004).

5   The differences between these various concepts need not concern us in this chapter, because we do not adopt a particular definition here. See Neilson, 2001 for an overview of the literature on the various concepts used. Also see Lindayati, 2002; Keeley and Scoones, 2003; Lindquist, 2001.

5   See Keeley and Scoones, 2003: 21; Wrangham, 2002; Neilson, 2001: 21–3. They make a distinction between policy narrative and discourse, which refers to a wider set of values and way of thinking.

7   To the extent that policy narratives justify arrangements that favour certain interests, their continued existence may also be explained by underlying interests and power relationships. This does not, however, mean that discourses as such do not play an important role. Ideas do matter (also see Lindayati, 2002).

8   Note that other organizations whose main objective is policy advocacy and influence may adopt different strategies for longer-term leverage. Here we focus on the links between participatory research and policy.

9   This section draws on the authors' experiences in monitoring these projects, and on the insights of IDRC colleagues, frequently documented in their trip reports from project visits.

18 Conclusions: community-based natural resource management in action

1   For example, methods and tools for CBCRM were collected, reviewed and assembled in a sourcebook format (IIRR, 1998), subsequently also translated into Vietnamese.

2   This is consistent with the conclusions of Douthwaite (2002) on user roles in innovation.

3   A number of the research organizations represented in this collection are collaborating on CBNRM curriculum development already.

References

Adato, M. and Meinzen-Dick, R. (2002) 'Assessing the impact of agricultural research on poverty using the sustainable livelihood framework', Environment and Production Technology Division Discussion Paper No. 89, IFPRI (March), Washington, DC.

Agarwal, B. (2001) 'Participatory exclusions, community forestry, and gender: an analysis for South Asia and a conceptual framework', *World Development*, **29** (10), pp. 1623–48.

Agrawal, A. (2001) 'State formation in community spaces? Decentralization of control over forests in the Kumaon Himalaya, India', *Journal of Asian Studies*, **60** (1), pp. 9–41.

Agrawal, A. (2001) 'Common property institutions and sustainable governance of resources', *World Development*, **29** (10), pp. 1649–72.

Agrawal, A. and Gibson, C., eds (2001) *Communities and the Environment: Ethnicity, gender and the state in community-based conservation*, Rutgers University Press, New Brunswick, NJ.

Agrawal, A. and Ostrom, E. (2001) 'Collective action, property rights, and devolution of forest and protected area management', available online at: http://www.capri.cgiar.org/pdf/agrawal.pdf

Ahmed, S.(2001) 'Empowering rural women? Policies, institutions, and gendered outcomes in natural resources management', *Development in Practice*, **11** (4), pp. 535–7.

An, Le Van (2002) 'Review on methodology, contents and results of CBNRM', in Le Van An, ed., *Community-based Upland Natural Resource Management 1998–2001*, Agricultural Publishing House, Hanoi, Vietnam.

Appell, G.N. (1991) 'Resource management regimes among the swidden agriculturists of Borneo: does the concept of common property adequately map indigenous system ownership?', paper presented at the International Association for the Study of Common Property Conference (26–29 September), University of Manitoba, Winnipeg.

Arnstein, S. (1969) 'A ladder of citizen participation', *Journal of the American Institute of Planners*, **35**, pp. 216–24.

Ashby, J. (2003) 'Introduction: uniting science and participation in the process of innovation – research *for* development', in B. Pound, S. Snapp, C. McDougall and A. Braun, eds, *Managing Natural Resources for Sustainable Livelihoods: Uniting science and participation*, pp. 1–19, Earthscan Publications, London.

Asian Development Bank (ADB) (2004) *Asian Development Outlook 2004*, Asian Development Bank, Manila.

Babbie, E. (2004) *The Practice of Social Research*, 10th edn, Wadsworth, Thomson Learning, Belmont, CA.

Baland, J. and Platteau, J.P. (1996) *Halting the Degradation of Natural Resources*, Clarendon Press, Oxford.

Baland, J. and Platteau, J.P. (1999) 'The ambiguous impact of inequality on local resource management', *World Development*, **27** (4), pp. 773–88.

Bao, Le Quang (1999) 'Management of forest resources in Hong Ha: existing situation, dynamics, and paths towards sustainability', in Le Van An, ed., *Community-based Natural Resource Management in Hong Ha*, Annual Report 1999, Hue University of Agriculture and Forestry.

Bao, Le Quang (2002) 'The system of land tenure and the forest tree and land use in Hong Ha', in Le Van An, ed., *Community-based Upland Natural Resource Management 1998–2001*, Agricultural Publishing House, Hanoi, Vietnam.

Barr, C., Wollenberg, E., Limberg, G., Anau, N., Iwan, R., Sudana, I., Moeliono, M. and Djogo, T. (2002) 'The impacts of decentralisation on forests and forest-dependent communities in Malinau District, East Kalimantan', Centre for International Forestry Research, Bogor, Indonesia.

Bebbington, A. (2000) 'Reencountering development: livelihood transitions and place', *Annals of the Association of American Geographers*, **9** (3), pp. 495–520.

Beck, T. (1994) *The Experience of Poverty: Fighting for respect and resources in rural India*, Intermediate Technology Publications, London.

Beck, T. and Ghosh, M. (2000) 'Common property resources and the poor in seven villages of West Bengal', *Economic and Political Weekly*, **35** (3), pp. 147–53.

Beck, T. and Nesmith, C. (2001) 'Building on poor people's capacities: the case of common property resources in India and West Africa', *World Development*, **29** (1), pp. 119–33.

Béné, C. (2003) 'When fishery rhymes with poverty: a first step beyond the old paradigm on poverty in small-scale fisheries', *World Development*, **31** (6), pp. 949–75.

Berger, P.L. and Luckman, T. (1966) *The Social Construction of Reality: A treatise on the sociology of knowledge*, Anchor Books, Garden City, NJ.

Berkes, F. (1993) 'Traditional ecological knowledge in perspective', in J.T. Inglis, ed., *Traditional Ecological Knowledge: Concepts and cases*, pp. 1–9, Canadian Museum of Nature and IDRC, Ottawa.

Berkes, F., ed. (1989) *Common Property Resources: Ecology and community-based sustainable development*, Belhaven Press, London.

Berkes, F., Feeny, D., McCay, B.J. and Acheson, J.M. (1989) 'The benefits of the commons', *Nature*, **340** (6229), pp. 91–3.

Bessette, G. (2003) 'Isang Bagsak: a capacity-building and networking program in participatory development communication', IDRC, Ottawa.

Bessette, G. (2004) *Involving the Community – A guide to participatory development communication*, IDRC, Canada.

Bhutan, Royal Government of (1999) 'Bhutan 2020: a vision for peace, prosperity and happiness', Planning Commission, Thimphu, Bhutan.

Bhutan, Royal Government of (2002) 'Community-based natural resources management in Bhutan: a framework', Department of Research and Development Services, Ministry of Agriculture, Thimphu, Bhutan.

Bhutan, Royal Government of (2003) 'Mandates and functions of the Ministry of Agriculture', Ministry of Agriculture, Thimphu, Bhutan.

Biggs, S. and Farrington, J. (1991) 'Agricultural research and the rural poor: a review of social science analysis', IDRC, Ottawa.

Blackburn, J. and Holland, J., eds (1998) *Who Changes? Institutionalizing participation in development*, Intermediate Technology Publications, London.

Borlagdan, S.B. (2001) *Community-Based Forest Management in the Philippines: A preliminary assessment*, Institute of Philippine Culture, Ateneo de Manila University, Philippines.

Bottomley, R. (2000) 'Structural analysis of deforestation in Cambodia (with a focus on Ratanakiri Province, Northeast Cambodia', Mekong Watch and Institute for Global Environmental Strategies, Japan (March/April).

Brand, L. van den and Jamtsho, K. (2000) 'Water management in small farmer managed irrigation schemes in the Lingmutey Chu watershed in Bhutan', paper presented at 'Water Policy and Politics – Approaches to Watershed Management' seminar series, Department of Environmental Sciences, Wageningen University, The Netherlands.

Brosius, J.P., Tsing, A.L. and Zerner, C. (1998) 'Representing communities: histories and politics of community-based natural resource management', *Society and Natural Resources*, **11** (2), pp. 157–68.

Brundtland, G.H., ed. (1987) *Our Common Future: the report of the World Commission on Environment and Development*, Oxford University Press, Oxford.

Brzeski, V.J. and Newkirk, G.F., eds (2000) *Lessons from the Lagoon: Research towards community-based coastal resource management in Tam Giang Lagoon*, Vietnam, CoRR/CIDA/IDRC, Dalhousie University, Halifax, Canada.

Brzeski, V.J. and Newkirk, G.F., eds (2002) *Lessons in Resource Management from the Tam Giang Lagoon*, CoRR/CIDA/IDRC, Dalhousie University, Halifax, Canada.

Buckles, D., ed. (1999) *Cultivating Peace: Conflict and collaboration in natural resource management*, IDRC, Ottawa.

Cabalfin, M.R. (2001) 'An analysis of the social arrangements for the management of natural resources: the case of Ankileng, Sagada', in Research Report No. 2, *Community Studies in Resource Management*, pp. 2–32, Cordillera Studies Center (CSC), University of the Philippines Baguio, Philippines.

Cairns, M., ed. (2005) *Voices from the Forest: Integrating indigenous knowledge into sustainable farming*, Resources for the Future Press, Washington, DC.

Cambodia, Royal Government of (2000) 'Seila Programme Document 2001–2005', Seila Taskforce, Phnom Penh, Cambodia.

Cambodia, Royal Government of (2002) 'National Poverty Reduction Strategy 2003–2005', available online at: www.imf.org/External/NP/prsp/2002/khm/01/

Cambodia, Royal Government of (2004) *Community Forestry Research Project. Annual report April 2003–March 2004*, Ministry of the Environment, Phnom Penh, Cambodia.

Cambodia Royal Government of, Department of Forestry and Wildlife (DFW) (2002) 'Progress report on forest policy reform to the sixth consultative group meeeting with donor', Phnom Penh, Cambodia.

Cambodia, Royal Government of, Ministry of the Environment, Participatory Management of Mangrove Resources (PMMR) (2002) 'PMMR annual progress report for IDRC, July 2001–June 2002', Phnom Penh, Cambodia.

Cambodian Area Regeneration and Rehabilitation Project (CARERE) (1997) '1997 review – workplan 1998', unpublished, Ratanakiri, Cambodia.

Chambers, R. (1983) *Rural Development: Putting the last first*, Longman, London.

Chambers, R. (1995) 'Paradigm shifts and the practice of participatory research and development', in N. Nelson and S. Wright, eds, *Power and Participatory Development: Theory and practice*, pp. 30–42, Intermediate Technology Publications, London.

Chambers, R. (1997) *Whose Reality Counts? Putting the first last*, Intermediate Technology Publications, London.

Chambers, R., Pacey, A. and Thrupp, L.A., eds (1989) *Farmer First: Farmer innovation and agricultural research*, Intermediate Technology Publications, London.

Chandler, D. (1993) *The Tragedy of Cambodian History: Politics, war and revolution since 1945*, Yale University Press, New Haven, CT.

Chapin, M. (2004) 'A challenge to conservationists', *World Watch*, **17** (6), pp. 17–31.

Cheema, G.S. and Rondinelli, D.A. (1983) *Decentralization and Development: Policy implementation in developing countries*, Sage, Beverly Hills, CA.

Chen Deshou, Zhou Pidong, Pan Jiawen, Sun Qiu, Xia Yuan, Yuan Juanwen, Li Zhinan and Zhao Zeyin (2002) 'Community-based natural management in mountainous areas of Guizhou province', Final Technical Report, Phase 2, Guizhou Academy of Agricultural Sciences (GAAS), Guiyang.

CIP-UPWARD (2003) 'Farmer field schools: from IPM to platforms for learning and empowerment', International Potato Center (CIP) – Users' Perspectives with Agricultural Research and Development (UPWARD), Los Banos, Philippines.

Colm, S. (1996) 'Effects of oil palm plantation development on indigenous communities', Natural Resource Management Project, Ratanakiri Province, Cambodia.

Colongon, A.A., Jr (2001) 'Key policy issues in implementing a community-based natural resource management program in Sagada, Mountain province', in Research Report No. 1, *Perspectives on Resource Management in the Cordillera Region*, pp. 23–47, CSC, University of the Philippines Baguio, Philippines..

Cooke, B. and Kothari, U., eds (2001) *Participation: The new tyranny*, Zed Books, London.

Cornwall, A. (2002) 'Making a difference? Gender and participatory development', in S. Razavi, ed., *Gender and Agrarian Change under Neoliberalism*, pp. 197–232, Kumarian Press, Bloomfield, CT.

Cornwall, A. (2003) 'Whose voices? Whose choices? Reflections on gender and participatory development', *World Development*, **31** (8), pp. 1325–42.

Cowen, M.P. and Shenton, R.W. (1996) *Doctrines of Development*, Routledge, London.

Creswell, J.W. (2003) *Research Design: Qualitative, quantitative and mixed methods approaches*, 2nd edn, Sage Publications, Thousand Oaks, CA.,

de Koninck, R. (1997) 'Le Recul de la forêt au Viet Nam', IDRC, Ottawa.

Deshou, C., Yuan, X., Yuanlong, H., Jianwen, P., Peidong, Z. and S. Qiou (1997) 'Practices and realizations on community-based natural resource management in the mountainous area of Guizhou province, China', paper presented at CBNRM Workshop (12–16 May), Hue University of Agriculture and Forestry, Hue, Vietnam, IDRC, Ottawa, available online at: http://web.idrc.ca/en/ev-80508-201-100828-1-IDRC_ADM_INFO.html

DeWalt, B.R. (1994) 'Using indigenous knowledge to improve agriculture and natural resource management', *Human Organization*, **53** (2), pp. 123–31.

Di Gregorio, M., Hagedorn, K., Kirk, M., Korf, B., McCarthy, N., Meinzen-Dick, R. and Swallow Brent, M. (2004) 'Property rights, collective action and poverty: the role of institutions for poverty reduction', paper presented at 10th Biennial Conference of the International Association for the Study of Common Property (IASCP), Oaxaca, Mexico (9–13 August).

Douthwaite, B. (2002) *Enabling Innovation: A practical guide to understanding and fostering technological change*, Zed Books, London.

Dove, M.R. (1993) 'A revisionist view of tropical deforestation and development', *Environmental Conservation*, **20** (1), pp. 17–24.

Du, Vo Van (2003) 'Current situation and strategy for forest management in Thua Thien Hue', in Le Van An, ed., *Community-based Upland Natural Resource Management in Hong Ha*, Annual Report 2003, Hue University of Agriculture and Forestry.

Dupar, M. and Badenoch, N. (2002) *Environment, Livelihoods and Local Institutions: Decentralization in mainland Southeast Asia*, World Resources Institute, Washington, DC.

Economic and Social Commission for Asia and the Pacific (ESCAP) (2003) *Promoting the Millennium Development Goals in Asia and the Pacific. Meeting the challenges of poverty reduction*, ESCAP and UNDP, New York.

Edmunds, D. and Wollenberg, E., eds (2003) *Local Forest Management: The impacts of devolution policies*, Earthscan Publications, London.

Ellis, F. and Biggs, S. (2001) 'Evolving themes in rural development 1950s–2000s', *Development Policy Review*, **19** (4), pp. 437–48.

Enkchimegee, P. and Tsendsuren, B.B. (2003) 'Co-management questionnaire', *Report of Independent Survey in the Communities of SUMCNR Project Study Sites*, Ministry of Nature and the Environment, Ulaanbaatar, Mongolia.

Evans, G. (1995) *Lao Peasants under Socialism and Post-socialism*, Yale University Press, New Haven, CT.

Evans, P. (2002) 'Fishing disarmed: community fisheries in Cambodia', *Samudra* (March), pp. 6–12.

Ferrer, E., de la Cruz, T. and Newkirk, G.F., eds (2001) *Hope Takes Root*, CBCRM Resource Centre, University of the Philippines, Diliman, Philippines.

Ferrer, E.M., Polotan de la Cruz, L. and Domingo, M.A., eds (1996) *Seeds of Hope: A collection of case studies on community-based coastal resources management in the Philippines*, College of Social Work and Community Development, University of the Philippines, Quezon City, Philippines.

Fisher, R.J. (2000) *Decentralisation and Devolution of Forest Management in Asia and the Pacific*, Regional Community Forestry Training Centre for Asia and the Pacific (RECOFTC), Bangkok, Thailand.

Fisher, R.J. (2003) 'Controlling the forests: community forestry in the Mekong region', *Mekong Update and Dialogue*, **6** (2), pp. 2–3.

Flyvbjerg, B. (2001) *Making Social Science Matter: Why social inquiry fails and how it can succeed again*, Cambridge University Press, Cambridge.

Follosco, A. and Tacloy, J.G. (2001) 'Community-based interventions in Sagada', in Research Report No. 4, *Community-based Technological Interventions*, pp. 35–53, CSC, University of the Philippines in Baguio, Philippines.

Food and Agriculture Organization (FAO (2001) *State of the World's Forests*, FAO, Rome, also available online at: http://www.fao.org/documents/show_cdr.asp?url_file=/DOCREP/003/Y0900E/Y0900E00.HTM (accessed 3 January 2005).

Ford Foundation (2002) *Building Assets to Reduce Poverty and Injustice*, Ford Foundation, Los Angeles, CA.

Ford Foundation (2004) *Asset Building for Social Change: Pathways for large-scale impact*, Ford Foundation, New York.

Foster, A.and Rosenzweig, M. (2001) 'Democratization, decentralization and the distribution of local public goods in a poor rural economy', mimeo, Department of Economics, University of Pennsylvania, Philadelphia, PA.

Fox, J. (1996) 'Customary land use of Kreung ethnic minorities', IDRC/NTFP/East-West Center.

Freudenberger, K.S. (1998) 'The use of RRA to inform policy: tenure issues in Madagascar and Guinea. Whose voice?', in J. Holland, J. Blackburn and R. Chambers, eds, *Whose Voice? Participatory research and policy change*, pp. 67–79, Intermediate Technology Publications, London.

Fujita, Y. and Phanvilay, K. (2004) 'Land and forest allocation and its implication on forest management and household livelihoods: comparison of case studies from CBNRM research in central Laos', paper presented at 10th Biennial Conference of the International Association for the Study of Common Property (IASCP), Oaxaca, Mexico (9–13 August).

Ganga, Z.N. (2001) 'Improving sweet potato production and utilization in Sagada, Mt. Province', in Research Report No. 4, 'Community-based *technological interventions*, pp. 1–13, CSC, University of the Philippines Baguio, Philippines.

Goldenberg, S. and Haines, V.A. (2000) 'Social networks and institutional completeness: from territory to ties', in M.A. Kalbach and W.E. Kalbach, eds, *Perspectives on Ethnicity in Canada*, pp. 35–54, Harcourt Canada, Toronto.

Gonsalves, J. and Mendoza, L. (2003) 'Final report: external review of IDRC's community-based natural resource management (CBNRM) program initiative (PI) in Asia', pp. 1–97, Report prepared for the Evaluation Unit, IDRC (7 November).

Grenier, L. (1998) *Working with Indigenous Knowledge: A guide for researchers*, IDRC, Ottawa.

Guha, R. (1989) *The Unquiet Woods. Ecological change and peasant resistance in the Himalaya,* Oxford University Press, Delhi.

Gurung, T.R. (2003) 'Companion modeling to improve water sharing among villages at rice transplanting in upper Lingmutey Chu watershed of central-west Bhutan', Council of RNR Research of Bhutan (CoRRB), Ministry of Agriculture, Thimphu, Bhutan.

Gyawali, D. (2001) *Water in Nepal*, Himal Books, Kathmandu, Nepal.

Hall, A., Rasheed Sulaiman, V., Sivamohan, M.V.K. and Yoganand, B. (2002) 'Public-private sector interaction in the Indian agricultural research system: an innovation systems perspective on institutional reform', in D. Byerlee and R.G. Echeverria, eds, *Agricultural Research Policy in an Era of Privatization*, CAB International, London.

Hardin, G. (1968) 'The tragedy of the commons', *Science*, **162**, pp. 1243–8.

Hart, G. (2001) 'Development critiques in the 1990s: culs de sac and promising paths', *Progress in Human Geography*, **25** (4), pp. 649–58.

Hazell, P., Jagger, P. and Knox, A. (2000) 'Technology, natural resources management and the poor', paper prepared for the International Fund for Agricultural Development (IFAD) by IFPRI (9 January), Rome.

Helmers, K. (2003) 'Summary of main findings from the rural sources of income and livelihood strategies study', Cambodia Development Resource Institute, Phnom Penh, Cambodia.

Henderson, D. (2003) 'Progress and recommendations for the operational plan for CBNRM', Consultancy report submitted to the Ministry of Agriculture, Thimphu, Bhutan.

International Development Research Centre (IDRC) (1999) 'RPE social science resource kit: a guide for researchers', available online at: http://www.idrc.ca/en/ev-85758-201-1-DO_TOPIC.html

IDRC (2000) 'CBNRM Prospectus Phase II', available online at: http://web.idrc.ca/en/ev-32916-201-1-DO_TOPIC.html (accessed 8 February 2005).

IDRC (2004) *Annual Report of Evaluation Findings 2004*, IDRC, Evaluation Unit, Ottawa.

International Fund for Agriculture and Development (IFAD) (2001) 'Enabling the rural poor to overcome their poverty: Strategic Framework for IFAD 2002–2006' (December).

IFAD (2002) *Assessment of Rural Poverty. Asia and the Pacific*, IFAD, Rome.

International Institute for Rural Reconstruction (IIRR) (1998) *Participatory Methods in Community-based Coastal Resource Management*, 3 vols, IIRR, Silang, Cavite, Philippines.

Ireson-Doolittle, C. and Ireson, W.R. (1999) 'Cultivating the forest: gendered land use among the Tay in Northern Vietnam', in I. Tinker and G. Summerfield, *Women's Rights to House and Land: China, Laos, Vietnam*, pp. 115–30, Lynne Rienner, Boulder, CO.

Ironside, J. and Nhem, S. (1998) 'Right to invent their own future: the development of community-based natural resource management, Ratanakiri', Report on CARERE/IDRC Project (CBNRM) July 1997–August 1998, unpublished, Cambodia.

Jentoft, S. (1989) 'Fisheries co-management: delegating government responsibility to fishermen's organizations', *Marine Policy*, **13** (2), pp. 137–54.

Jodha, N.S. (1991) 'Sustainable agriculture in fragile resource zones: technological imperatives', *Economic and Political Weekly*, **26**, p. 13.

Johnson, C. (2001) 'Local democracy, democratic decentralisation and rural development: theories, challenges and options for policy', *Development Policy Review*, **19** (4), pp. 521–32.

Johnson, C. (2004) 'Uncommon ground: the "poverty of history" in common property discourse', *Development and Change*, **35** (3), pp. 407–33.

Kanbur, R., ed. (2001) 'Contributions to a workshop on qualitative and quantitative poverty appraisal: complementarities, tensions and the way forward' (15–16 March), Cornell University, Ithaca, NY.

Kanel, K.R. (2003) 'Revisiting community forestry in Nepal: Achievements and challenges', paper presented at Regional Workshop on Community Based Natural Resource Management, Ministry of Agriculture, Lobeysa, Bhutan.

Keeley, J. and Scoones, I. (2003) *Understanding Environmental Policy Processes, Cases from Africa*, Intermediate Technology Publications, London.

King, C.A. (2000) *Systemic Processes for Facilitating Social Learning – Challenging the Legacy*, Swedish University of Agricultural Sciences, Uppsala, Sweden.

Knox, A., Meinzen-Dick, R. and Hazell, P. (1998) 'Property rights, collective action and technologies for natural resource management: a conceptual framework', Collective Action and Property Rights (CAPRi) Working Paper No. 1, International Food Policy Research Institute (IFPRI), Washington, DC.

Kolb, D.A. (1984) *Experiential Learning: Experience as the source of learning and development*. Prentice-Hall, Englewood Cliffs, NJ.

Korten, F.F. and Siy, Robert Y., Jr, eds (1988) *Transforming a Bureaucracy: The Experience of the Philippine national irrigation administration*, Kumarian Press, West Hartford, CT.

Kuhn, T. (1962) *The Structure of Scientific Revolutions*, University of Chicago Press, Chicago, IL.

Kumar, S. (2002) 'Does "participation" in common pool resource management help the poor? A social cost-benefit analysis of joint forest management in Jharkhand, India', *World Development*, **30** (5), pp. 763–82.

Kummer, D.M. (1992) *Deforestation in the Postwar Philippines*, Ateneo de Manila University Press, Manila, Philippines.

Larson, A. (2004) 'Democratic decentralization in the forestry sector: lessons learned from Africa, Asia and Latin America', Centre for International Forestry Research, Jakarta.

Larson, A.M. (2003) 'Democratic decentralisation in the forestry sector: lessons learned from Africa, Asia and Latin America', paper presented at CIFOR International Conference on Rural Livelihoods, Forest and Biodiversity, Bonn, Germany.

Laws, S. with Harper, C. and Marcus, R. (2003) *Research for Development: A practical guide*, Sage Publications, London.

Le, Thi Kim Lan, Nguyen, Thi Tuyet Suong and Nguyen, Thi Thanh (2002) 'Some gender aspects of communities in Tam Giang lagoon', in V.J. Brzeski and G.F. Newkirk, eds, *Halifax Lessons in Resource Management from the Tam Giang Lagoon*, pp. 69–84, Coastal Resources Research Network, Dalhousie University, Halifax, Canada.

Leach, M., Mearns, R. and Scoones, I. (1999) 'Environmental entitlements: dynamics and institutions in community-based natural resource management', *World Development*, **27** (2), pp. 225–47.

Leeuwis, C. and Pyburn, R., eds (2002) *Wheelbarrows Full of Frogs: Social learning in rural resource management*, Koninklijke Van Gorcum, Assen, Netherlands.

Li, T. (1999) *Transforming the Indonesian Uplands. Marginality, power and production*, Harwood Academic Publishers, Amsterdam.

Li, T.M. (1996) 'Images of community: discourse and strategy in property relations', *Development and Change*, **27** (3), pp. 501–27.

Li, T.M. (2001) 'Boundary work: community, market, and state reconsidered', in A. Agrawal and C.C. Gibson, eds, *Communities and the Environment*, pp. 157–79, Rutgers University Press, New Brunswick, NJ.

Li, T.M. (2002) 'Engaging simplifications: community-based resource management, market processes and state agendas in upland Southeast Asia', *World Development*, **30** (2), pp. 265-83.

Lindayati, R. (2000) 'Community forestry policies in selected Southeast Asian countries', IDRC working paper, IDRC, Ottawa.

Lindayati, R. (2002) 'Ideas and institutions in social forestry policy', in C.J. Pierce Colfer and I.A.P. Resosudarmo, eds, *Which Way Forward? People, forests, and policymaking in Indonesia*, pp. 36–59, Resources for the Future, Washington, DC.

Lindquist, E.A. (2001) 'Discerning policy influence: framework for a strategic evaluation of IDRC-supported research', unpublished paper, IDRC, Ottawa.

Long, N. and van der Ploeg, J.D. (1994) 'Heterogeneity, actor and structure: towards a reconstitution of the concept of structure', in D. Booth, ed., *Rethinking Social Development*, pp. 62–89, Longman Scientific, Harlow.

Lynch, O.J., Talbott, K. and Berdan, M.S. (1995) *Balancing Acts: Community-based forest management and national law in Asia and the Pacific*, World Resources Institute, Washington, DC.

McCarthy, J. (2001) 'Decentralisation, local communities and forest management in Barito Selatan District, Central Kalimantan', Centre for International Forestry Research, Jakarta.

McCay, B. (1999) 'Property rights and regimes', in K.L. Dougherty, ed., *Collective Action under the Articles of Confederation: State support of the federal government*, Cambridge University Press, Cambridge.

McDermott, M.H. (2001)' Invoking community: indigenous people and ancestral domain in Palawan, the Philippines', in A. Agrawal and C. Gibson, eds, *Communities and the Environment*, pp. 32–62, Rutgers University Press, New Brunswick, NJ.

McKean, M.A. (1986) 'Management of traditional common lands (*iriaichi*) in Japan', in National Research Council, *Proceedings of the Conference on Common Property Resource Management*, pp. 533–89, National Academy Press, Washington, DC.

McKenney, B. and Prom Tola (2002) 'Natural resources and rural livelihood in Cambodia', Working Paper No. 23, Cambodia Development Resource Institute, Phnom Penh, Cambodia.

Majone, G. and Wildavsky, A. (1978) 'Implementation as evolution', *Policy Studies Review*, **12**, pp. 103–17.

Mansuri, G. and Rao, V. (2004) 'Community-based and -driven development: a critical review', World Bank Policy Research Working Paper No. 3209, World Bank, Washington, DC.

Marschke, M. (2003) 'From planning to action: what can resources management committees do "on the ground"?', *Cambodia Development Review*, **7** (3), pp. 7–10, 12.

Marschke, M. (2004) 'Analysis: mainstreaming NREM into commune councils and PLUP tools', Technical Report for Seila, Cambodia Development Resource Institute, Phnom Penh, Cambodia.

Marschke, M. (2004) 'Planning is only one step', *Cambodian Development Review*, **8** (3), pp. 7–12.

Marschke, M. and Nong, K. (2003) 'Adaptive co-management: lessons from coastal Cambodia', *Canadian Journal of Development Studies*, **24** (3), pp. 369–83.

Massey, D. (1993) 'Power-geometry and a progressive sense of place', in J. Bird, ed., *Mapping the Futures: Local cultures, global change*, pp. 59–69, Routledge, London.

Meinzen-Dick, R. and Di Gregorio, M. (2004) 'Collective action and property rights for sustainable development: overview', in R. Meinzen-Dick and M. Di Gregorio, eds, *Collective Action and Property Rights for Sustainable Development*, IFPRI, Washington, DC.

Meinzen-Dick, R. and Di Gregorio, M., eds (2004) *Collective Action and Property Rights for Sustainable Development*, IFPRI, Washington, DC.

Meinzen-Dick, R., Knox, A., Place, F. and Swallow, B., eds (2002) *Innovation in Natural Resource Management: The role of property rights and collective action in developing countries*, Johns Hopkins University Press, Baltimore, MD.

Mendoza, J.D. (1999) 'Structuration theory and the nature of social science', University of the Philippines at Baguio, Philippines.

Mendoza, L.C., ed. (1992) *Building Local Administrative Capability for Regional Autonomy in the Cordillera*, Cordillera Studies Center (CSC) (Philippines), University of the Philippines Baguio, and Friedrich Ebert Stiftung, Manila.

Menzies, N. (2006) *Our Forest, Your Ecosystem, Their Wood. Communities, conservation and the state in community based forest management*, Columbia University Press, New York.

Mohanty, J. (2004) 'Institutional dynamics and participatory spaces: the making and unmaking of participation in local forest management in India', *IDS Bulletin*, **35** (2), pp. 26–32.

Mongolia, Government of, Ministry of Nature and the Environment (MNE) (2003) *State of the Environment, 2002*, Ulaanbaatar, Mongolia.

Mongolia, National Statistical Office (2003) *Mongolian Statistical Yearbook*, Ulaanbaatar, Mongolia.

Moore, B.H. (1999) 'The integrated planning and management of land resources: a framework to empower the rural poor', presentation by the Popular Coalition to Eradicate Hunger and Poverty Secretariat (IFAD) at the Conference on Cultivating Our Futures (September), at Maastricht, Netherlands. FAO, Rome.

Muny, M. (2001) 'Connecting local research to public policy in Cambodia', IDRC Workshop on Linking Local Research and NRM Policy, unpublished paper, Chiang Mai, Thailand.

Najam, A. (1995) 'Learning from the literature on policy implementation: a synthesis perspective', working paper, International Institute for Applied Systems Analysis (IIASA), IIASA, Laxenburg.

Neilson, S. (2001) 'Knowledge utilization and public policy processes: a literature review', Evaluation Unit, IDRC, Ottawa.

Nelson, N.and Wright, S., eds (1995) *Power and Participatory Development: Theory and practice*, Intermediate Technology Publications, London.

Odgerel, T. and Naranchimeg, B. (2004) 'Integrating social and gender analysis (SA/GA) in natural resource management', unpublished case study report on SA/GA, SUMCNR project.

Opondo, C., Stroud A., German, L. and Hagmann, J. (2003) 'Institutionalizing participation in Eastern Africa research institutes', *PLA Notes*, **48**, pp. 58–62.

Organization for Economic Co-operation and Development (OECD) (2004) 'Decentralisation and poverty in developing countries: exploring the impact', OECD Development Centre Working Paper No. 236, OECD, Paris.

Ostrom, E. (1990) *Governing the Commons: The evolution of institutions for collective action*, Cambridge University Press, Cambridge.

Ostrom, E. (1992) *Crafting Institutions for Self-governing Irrigation Systems*, Institute for Contemporary Studies, San Francisco, CA.

Ostrom, E. (1994) 'Institutional analysis, design principles and threats to sustainable community governance and management of commons', in R.S. Pomeroy, ed., *Community Management and Common Property of Coastal Fisheries in Asia and the Pacific: Concepts, methods and experiences*, pp. 34–50, International Centre for Living Aquatic Resources Management (ICLARM), Manila, Philippines.

Ostrom, E., Dietz, T., Dolsak, N., Stern, P., Stonich, S. and Weber, E., eds (2002) *The Drama of the Commons*, National Academy Press, Washington, DC.

Peluso, N.L., Vandergeest, P. and Potter, L. (1995) 'Social aspects of forestry in Southeast Asia', *Journal of Southeast Asian Studies* (special anniversary issue), **26** (1), pp. 196–216.

Pender, J., Hazell, P.B.R. and Garrett, J.L. (2001) 'Reducing poverty and protecting the environment: the overlooked potential of less-favoured lands', in P. Pinstrup-Andersen and R. Pandya-Lorch, eds, *The Unfinished Agenda: Perspectives on overcoming hunger, poverty and environmental degradation*, IFPRI, Washington, DC.

Phap, Ton That (2002) 'Co-management in the planning for a waterway system for aquaculture', in V.J. Brzeski and G.F. Newkirk, eds, *Lessons in Resource Management from the Tam Giang Lagoon*, pp. 85–99, CoRR/CIDA/IDRC, Dalhousie University, Halifax, Canada.

Philippines Government, Department of Environment and Natural Resources (DENR) (n.d., but possibly 1997 or 1998) 'Prescribing guidelines on the management of the indigenous 'Batangan' forests of mountain province', unpublished draft memorandum circular, DENR Headquarters, Manila.

Philippines Government, Department of the Environment and Natural Resources (DENR) (2002) 'Philippine forestry statistics, Table 1.05 Community-based forest management projects', DENR, Manila.

Pinkerton, E., ed. (1989) *Co-operative Management of Local Fisheries: New directions for improved management and community development*, University of British Columbia Press, Vancouver, BC.

Pound, B., Snapp, S., McDougall, C. and Braun, A., eds (2003) *Managing Natural Resources for Sustainable Development: Uniting science and participation*, Earthscan Publications, London.

Pretty, J.N. and Scoones, I. (1995) 'Institutionalizing adaptive planning and local-level concerns: looking to the future', in N. Nelson and S. Wright, eds, *Power and Participatory Development: Theory and practice*, pp. 157–69, Intermediate Technology Publications, London.

Prill-Brett, J. (1988) 'Preliminary perspectives on local territorial boundaries and resource control', CSC Working Paper no. 06, p. 15, CSC, UP College Baguio (August).

Prill-Brett, J. (1992) 'Ibaloy customary law on land resources. CSC Working Paper No.19, p. 31, CSC, University of the Philippines Baguio (January).

Prill-Brett, J. (1994) 'Indigenous land rights and legal pluralism among Philippine highlanders', *Law and Society Review*, **28**, 3, pp. 687–97.

Prill-Brett, J. (1995) 'State vs. indigenous tenurial security', in *Law and Society Conference Proceedings, Indigenous Law vs. National Law on Land Resources*, pp. 92–105, CSC, UP College Baguio, Philippines.

Prill-Brett, J. (2001) 'Concepts of ancestral domain in the Cordillera region from indigenous perspectives', in Research Report No. 1, *Perspectives on Resource Management in the Cordillera Region*, pp. 1–22, CSC, University of the Philippines Baguio, Philippines.

Pritchett, L. and Woolcock, M. (2004) 'Solutions when the solution is the problem: arraying the disarray in development', *World Development*, **32** (2), pp. 191–212.

Quy, Chu Huu (1995) 'Overview of highland development in Viet Nam: general characteristics, socioeconomic situation and development challenges', in A. T. Rambo, Le Trong Cuc and M.R. Digregorio, eds, *The Challenges of Highland Development in Viet Nam*, East-West Center, Honolulu, Hawaii, HI.

Raffles, H. (1999) 'Local theory: nature and the making of an Amazonian place', *Cultural Anthropology*, **14** (3), pp. 323–60.

Rambo, A.T. (1995) 'Perspectives on defining highland development challenges in Viet Nam: new frontier', in A.T. Rambo, Le Trong Cuc and M.R. Digregorio, eds, *The Challenges of Highland Development in Viet Nam*, East-West Center, Honolulu, Hawaii, HI.

Razavi, S. (2002) *Gender and Agrarian Change under Neoliberalism*, Kumarian Press, Bloomfield, CT.

Reason, P. (1998) 'Three approaches to participative inquiry', in N.K. Denzin and Y.S. Lincoln, eds, *Strategies of Qualitative Inquiry*, Vol. II, pp. 261–91, Sage Publications, Thousand Oaks, CA.

Reibe, K. (1999) 'Policy making for sustainable development and the Yeak Loam commune protected area', unpublished consultancy report, IDRC and CARERE, Ratanakiri, Cambodia.

Reichrath, S. (2005) 'Overcoming inequities in access to natural resources', IDRC, Ottawa.

Renewable Natural Resource Research Centre (RNRRC) Bajo (1995) 'Wetland production systems research in Bhutan: A project proposal', unpublished, Ministry of Agriculture, Thimphu, Bhutan.

Resurreccion, B., Real, M. and Pantana, P. (2004) 'Officialising strategies: participatory processes and gender in Thailand's water resources sector', *Development in Practice*, **14** (4), pp. 521–33.

Ribot, J. (1995) 'From exclusion to participation: turning Senegal's forest policy around?', *World Development*, **23** (9), pp. 1587–99.

Ribot, J. (2002) *Democratic Decentralization of Natural Resources: Institutionalizing popular participation*, World Resources Institute, Washington, DC.

Ribot, J. (2003) 'Democratic decentralisation of natural resources: institutional choice and discretionary power transfers in sub-Saharan Africa', *Public Administration and Development*, **23**, pp. 53–65.

Ribot, J. and Peluso, N. (2003) 'A theory of access', *Rural Sociology*, **68** (2), pp. 153–81.

RNRRC Bajo (1997) 'CBNRM research in Lingmutey Chu watershed: characteristics of Lingmutey Chu, problem diagnosis and major research themes', Ministry of Agriculture, Thimphu, Bhutan.

RNRRC Bajo (1998) 'Participatory forest management for local use: a survey report', Ministry of Agriculture, Thimphu, Bhutan.

RNRRC Bajo (2000a) 'Community based natural resources management research in the Lingmutey Chu watershed: a process documentation', Ministry of Agriculture, Thimphu, Bhutan.

RNRRC Bajo (2000b) 'Community based natural resources management research in the Lingmutey Chu watershed: technical reports 1997–2000', Ministry of Agriculture, Thimphu, Bhutan.

RNRRC Bajo (2000c) 'Farm household categorisation in the Lingmutey Chu watershed', Ministry of Agriculture, Thimphu, Bhutan.

RNRRC Bajo (2000d) 'enhancing productivity through integrated natural resources management in Bhutan: a project proposal', Ministry of Agriculture, Thimphu, Bhutan.

RNRRC Bajo (2001) 'Management and use of FYM in the Lingmutey Chu watershed: results from a household survey', Ministry of Agriculture, Thimphu, Bhutan.

Rood, S. (1994) *Protecting Ancestral Land Rights in the Cordillera. Peace, conflict resolution and human rights*, Research Report No. 94–001, p. 39, University of the Philippines Press, Quezon City, and the Centre for Integrative and Development Studies, University of the Philippines.

Rood, S. and Casambre, A.L. (1994) 'State policy, indigenous community practice, and sustainability in the Cordillera, Northern Philippines', CSC Working Paper No. 23, p. 23, CSC, University of the Philippines Baguio, Philippines (March).

Ruitenbeek, J. and Cartier, C. (2001) 'The invisible wand: adaptive co-management as an emergent strategy in complex bio-economic systems', Centre for International Forestry Research Occasional Paper No. 34, Bogor, Indonesia.

San Luis, M.C.R. (2001) 'The social relations in natural resource management: co-management of common property resources (the case of Fidelisan, Sagada, Mt. Province)', in Research Report No. 2, *Community Studies in Resource Management*, pp. 53–80, CSC, University of the Philippines Baguio, Philippines.

Sarin, M. (2001) 'Empowerment and disempowerment of forest women in Uttarakhand, India', *Gender, Technology and Development*, **5** (3), pp. 342–63.

Sarin, M., Singh, N.M., Sundar, N. and Bhogal, R.K. (2003) 'Devolution as a threat to democratic decision-making in forestry? Findings from three states in India', in D. Edmunds and E. Wollenberg, eds, *Local Forest Management: The impacts of devolution policies*, pp. 55–126, Earthscan Publications, London.

Savet, E. and Sokhun, T. (2002) 'Cambodian forest policy review', country report to the 19th session of the Asia-Pacific Forestry Commission held in Ulaanbaatar, Mongolia, (26–30 August), DFW, Phnom Penh, Cambodia.

Sayer, A. (1984) *Method in Social Science: A realist approach*, pp. 16–46, Hutchinson, London.

Sayer, J. and Campbell, B. (2004) *The Science of Sustainable Development: Local livelihoods and the global environment*, Cambridge University Press, Cambridge.

Schon, D.A. (1983) *The Reflective Practitioner: How professionals think in action*, Basic Books, New York.

Scott, J. (1985) *Weapons of the Weak: Everyday forms of peasant resistance in Southeast Asia*, Yale University Press, New Haven, CT.

Scott, J. (1990) *Domination and the Arts of Resistance. Hidden transcripts*, Yale University Press, New Haven, CT.

Scott, J.C. (1998) *Seeing Like a State: How certain schemes to improve the human condition have failed*, Yale University Press, New Haven, CT.

Sen, A. (1990) 'Gender and cooperative conflict', in I. Tinker, ed., *Persistent Inequalities*, Oxford University Press, New York.

Sen, Hoang Thi and An, Le Van (2006) 'Creating opportunities for change: a case study of strengthening the social capital of the poor and of women in upland communities in Hue, Vietnam', in R. Vernooy, Linxiu Zhang and E. Fajber, eds, *Integrating Social and Gender Analysis in Natural Resource Management Research: Learning studies from Asia*, IDRC, Ottawa.

Sen, Hoang Thi, Nguyen Xuan Hong and Nguyen Thi Thanh (2003) 'Practical situation of the access to the land/forest management and community forestry development programs/policies in Hong Ha', in Le Van An, ed., *Community-based Upland Natural Resource Management in Hong Ha*, Annual Report 2003, Hue University of Agriculture and Forestry.

Shah, M. and Shah, P. (1995) 'Gender, environment and livelihood security: an alternative viewpoint from India', *IDS Bulletin*, **26** (1), pp. 75–82.

Shankland, A. (2000) *Analysing Policy for Sustainable Livelihoods*, Institute of Development Studies (IDS) Research Report No. 49, IDS, Brighton.

Shi Xingrong and Shi Xiangzhou (2003) 'Guizhou poverty alleviation practice: empowerment is better than giving money', *Outlook Weekly*, Xinhua News Agency, Beijing.

Sick, D. (2002) 'Managing environmental processes across boundaries: a review of the literature on institutions and resource management', available online at: http://web.idrc.ca/uploads/user-S/10378201220MEPfinal_Nov_-2002.pdf (accessed 30 April 2004).

Smith, D.V. and Jalal, K.F. (2000). *Sustainable Development in Asia*, pp. 53–112, Asian Development Bank, Manila, Philippines.

Sun Qiu (2001) 'Promotion of sustainable rural development by scaling up CBNRM approach in Guizhou province', Project Proposal, GAAS, Guiyang.

Sun Qiu (2004) 'Development of community-based institutions for sustainable natural resource management in rural Guizhou, China', Wageningen University and Research Centre (WUR), Wageningen, Netherlands.

Sundar, N. (2000) 'Unpacking the "joint" in joint forest management', *Development and Change*, **31** (1), pp. 255–79.

Sustainable Management of Common Natural Resources (SUMCNR) (2003) 'SUMCNR Project Phase II', unpublished second-year project technical report (June), Ulaanbaatar, Mongolia.

Tapang, B.P. (2001) 'Economic transaction flows in a typical Cordillera village', in Research Report No. 1, *Perspectives on Resource Management in the Cordillera Region*, pp. 49–71, Cordillera Studies Center (CSC), University of the Philippines in Baguio, Philippines.

Tarr, C.M. (2003) 'Fishing lots and people in Cambodia', in M. Kaosa-ard and J. Dore, *Social Challenges for the Mekong Region*, pp. 347–69, Chiang Mai University Press, Chiang Mai, Thailand.

Thompson, E.P. (1975) *Whigs and Hunters. The origins of the black act*, Allen Lane, London.

Thorp, R., Steward, F. and Heyer, A. (2003) 'When and how far is group formation a route out of chronic poverty?', paper presented at conference on 'Staying Poor: Chronic Poverty and Development Policy', University of Manchester, Manchester.

Toan, Ngo Huu (2003) 'Pig production – an approach to work with the poor and women in uplands to build human and social capital and to improve income', in Le Van An, ed., *Community-based Upland Natural Resource Management*, Annual Report 2003, Hue University of Agriculture and Forestry.

Tserenbaljir, T. (2003) 'Livelihood analysis of herders' communities, *Report of Household Income Survey in the Communities of SUMCNR Project Study Sites, Ulaanbaatar*, Ministry of Nature and the Environment, Ulaanbaatar, Mongolia.

Tubtim, N. and Hirsch, P. (2005) 'Common property as enclosure: a case study of a backswamp in southern Laos', *Society and Natural Resources*, **18** (1), pp. 41–60.

Tuyen, Truong Van (2002) 'Dynamics of property rights in the Tam Giang lagoon', in V.J. Brzeski and G.F. Newkirk, eds, *Lessons in Resource Management from the Tam Giang Lagoon*, pp. 39–54, CoRR/CIDA/IDRC, Dalhousie University, Halifax, Canada.

Tuyen, Truong Van and Brzeski, V.J. (1998) 'Property right issues in Tam Giang lagoon, Vietnam', paper presented at 1998 Conference of the International Association for the Study of Common Property (IASCP), Vancouver, Canada.

Tuyen, Truong Van and the research team (2002) 'A review of participatory research methodology', in V.J. Brzeski and G.F. Newkirk, eds (2002) *Lessons in Resource Management from the Tam Giang Lagoon*, pp. 17–26, CoRR/CIDA/IDRC, Dalhousie University, Halifax, Canada.

Tyler, S. (1995) 'The state, local government and resource management in Southeast Asia: recent trends in the Philippines, Vietnam and Thailand', *Journal of Business Administration*, **22/23**, pp. 51–68.

Tyler, S. (1999) 'Policy implications of natural resource conflict management', in D. Buckles, ed., *Cultivating Peace: Conflict and collaboration in natural resource management*, pp. 263–80, IDRC, Ottawa.

United Nations Department of Economic and Social Development (1992) 'Agenda 21. UN Conference on Environment and Development', available online at: http://www.un.org/esa/sustdev/documents/agenda21/english/agenda21toc.htm (accessed 8 November 2004).

United Nations Development Programme (UNDP) (1995) *Human Development Report*, UNDP, New York.

UNDP (1998) *Human Development Report*, UNDP, New York.

UNDP (2000) 'Decentralisation: bringing governance closer to the people', discussion paper, UNDP, Bhutan, available online at: http://www.undp.org.bt/discussion_papers/Decentralization.pdf

UNDP (2004) *Human Development Report*, UNDP, New York.

United Nations Millennium Project (2005) 'Investing in development: a practical plan to achieve the millennium development goals. Overview', United Nations Development Programme, New York.

Vandergeest, P. (1996) 'Mapping nature: territorialisation of forest rights in Thailand', *Society and Natural Resources*, **9**, pp. 159–75.

Vandergeest, P. (1997) 'Rethinking property', *Common Property Resource Digest*, **41**, pp. 4–6.

Vandergeest, P. (2003) 'Land to some tillers: development-induced displacement in Laos', *International Social Science Journal*, **175**, pp. 47–56.

Vandergeest, P. (2004) 'Common and uncommon themes in the politics of the commons', *Mekong Update and Dialogue*, **7** (1), pp. 2–3.

Varughese, G. and Ostrom, E. (2001) 'The contested role of heterogeneity in collective action: some evidence from community forestry in Nepal', *World Development*, **29** (5), pp. 747–65.

Vernooy, R. and McDougall, C. (2003) 'Principles for good practice in participatory research: reflecting on lessons from the field', in B. Pound, S. Snapp, C. McDougall and A. Braun, eds, *Managing Natural Resources for Sustainable Livelihoods: Uniting science and participation*, pp. 113–37, Earthscan Publications, London, and IDRC.

Vernooy, Ronnie, Sun Qiu and Xu Jianchu, eds (2003) *Voices for Change: Participatory monitoring and evaluation in China*, Yunnan Science and Technology Press, Kunming, China, and IDRC, Ottawa.

Vietnam Development Report (2004) 'Poverty. Joint donor report to the Vietnam Consultative Group Meeting', Hanoi, Vietnam (2–3 December 2003), available online at: http://www.worldbank.org.vn/news/VDR04%20Poverty.pdf (accessed 6 March 2005).

Vietnam, Socialist Republic of (1999) *Vietnam Living Standards Survey 1997–98*, General Statistics Office, Hanoi, Vietnam.

Vietnam, Socialist Republic of, Department of Fisheries of Thua Thien Hue Province (2003) 'Overall planning for fisheries in Tam Giang Lagoon. Inception research reports', unpublished.

Vietnam,Socialist Republic of (2003) *The Comprehensive Poverty Reduction and Growth Strategy (CPRGS)*, Government Office, Hanoi, Vietnam.

Vietnam, Statistics Office of Thua Thien Hue Province (2003) *Statistic Year Book 2002*, Hue City, Vietnam (in Vietnamese).

Watkins, K. and Fowler, P. (2003) 'Rigged rules and double standards, trade, globalization and the fight against poverty', Oxfam Campaign Reports, available online at: http://publications.oxfam.org.uk/oxfam/display.asp?isbn=0855985259 (accessed 31 January 2005).

Wells, M. and Hannah, K. (1992) 'People and parks: linking protected areas management with local communities', World Bank, WWF-USA and USAID, Washington, DC.

Wildavsky, A.B. (1979) *Speaking Truth to Power: The art and craft of policy analysis*, Little, Brown, Boston, MA.

World Bank (2001) *World Development Report 2000/2001: Attacking poverty*, Oxford University Press for the World Bank, Oxford.

World Bank (2003) 'Reaching the rural poor: a renewed strategy for rural development', World Bank, Washington, DC.

World Bank (2004) 'World development report 2006. Equity and development', discussion paper, mimeo.

Wrangham, R. (2002) 'Changing policy discourses and traditional communities, 1960–1999', in C.J. Pierce Colfer and I.A.P. Resosudarmo, eds, *Which Way Forward? People, forests, and policymaking in Indonesia*, pp. 20–35, Resources for the Future, Washington, DC.

Ykhanbai, H. (2004) 'Sustainable management of common natural resource in Mongolia, research project: final technical report of Phase II', Ministry of Nature and the Environment, Ulaanbaatar, Mongolia.

Ykhanbai, H., Odgerel, T., Naranchimeg, B. and SUMCNR team (2003) 'Sustainable management of common natural resources in Mongolia', SA/GA case report presented at the SA/GA in NRM 2nd International Learning Studies/Stories Workshop, Ulaanbaatar, Mongolia (6–10 October).

Yuan Juanwen and project team (2004) 'Promotion of sustainable rural development by scaling up CBNRM in Guizhou Province', unpublished Narrative Report, December 2002–December 2003, GAAS and Integrated Rural Development Centre, Guiyang.

Zhou Pidong, Chen Deshou, Pan Jiawen, Sun Qiu and Xia Yuan (1998) 'Community-based natural management in mountainous areas of Guizhou province', GAAS, Guiyang.

Zwarteveen, M. and Meinzen-Dick, R. (2001) 'Gender and property rights in the commons: examples of water rights in South Asia', *Agriculture and Human Values*, **18** (1), pp. 11–25.

Index

The suffix ' *fig*' after a page number denotes figure; '*ph*' denotes a photograph.

www.ingramcontent.com/pod-product-compliance
Lightning Source LLC
Chambersburg PA
CBHW060018030426

42334CB00019B/2092